Praise for Fergus M. Bordewich's
KLAN WAR

"[*Klan War*] joins the shelf of Bordewich's political histories, which have made him one of the outstanding independent scholars of American history. But *Klan War* outdoes them all, in terms of both the depth of its research and the passionate pace of its vivid story-telling. . . . Bordewich's Grant is determined, idealistic, and generous, and on those terms, it would not be too much to describe him as the first civil rights president." —*Washington Monthly*

"Bordewich brings to life in painstaking detail the reign of terror that the Klan wrought. . . . A sobering reminder that rights gained can be easily taken away." —*The Civil War Monitor*

"[A] compelling chronicle [detailing] the astonishing brutality of the Klan." —*The Wall Street Journal*

"Bordewich's book should serve as a cautionary tale to keep us alert to the modern incarnation of the KKK, which has traded its bed sheets and hoods for coats and ties." —*New York Journal of Books*

"Gripping. . . . Bordewich, drawing from a vast array of sources, recounts the Klan's activities in appalling detail [and] brings to life a number of forgotten civil rights figures. . . . In the latest experts' poll, conducted in February 2024 by the American Political Science Association, Grant ranked seventeenth out of forty-five presidents, just below Ronald Reagan. Readers of Bordewich's outstanding *Klan War* will agree that he may well be headed even higher in the future." —*The New York Review of Books*

Fergus M. Bordewich

KLAN WAR

Fergus M. Bordewich is the author of eight previous nonfiction books, including *Congress at War: How Republican Reformers Fought the Civil War, Defied Lincoln, Ended Slavery, and Remade America; The First Congress: How James Madison, George Washington, and a Group of Extraordinary Men Invented the Government* (winner of the 2019 D. B. Hardeman Prize in American History); *America's Great Debate: Henry Clay, Stephen A. Douglas, and the Compromise That Preserved the Union* (named best history book of 2012 by the *Los Angeles Times*), and *Bound for Canaan: The Underground Railroad and the War for the Soul of America.* He lives in Washington, D.C., with his wife, Jean Parvin Bordewich, a writer and playwright.

KLAN WAR

ULYSSES S. GRANT
AND THE
BATTLE TO SAVE
RECONSTRUCTION

Fergus M. Bordewich

Vintage Books
A Division of Penguin Random House LLC
New York

Published by Vintage Books, a division of Penguin Random House LLC, 1745 Broadway, New York, NY 10019. Originally published in hardcover in the United States by Alfred A. Knopf, a division of Penguin Random House LLC, New York, in 2023.

Vintage and colophon are registered trademarks of Penguin Random House LLC.

All art images are courtesy of the Library of Congress.

The Library of Congress has cataloged the Knopf edition as follows:
Names: Bordewich, Fergus M., author.
Title: Klan war: Ulysses S. Grant and the battle to save
Reconstruction / Fergus M. Bordewich.
Description: First United States edition. | New York: Alfred A. Knopf, 2023. |
Includes bibliographical references and index.
Identifiers: LCCN 2022058874 (print) | LCCN 2022058875 (ebook)
Subjects: LCSH: Grant, Ulysses S. (Ulysses Simpson), 1822–1885. | Ku Klux Klan
(19th century) | Reconstruction (U.S. history, 1865–1877) | Domestic terrorism—
United States—History—19th century. | United States—
Race relations—History—19th century.
Classification: LCC E668.B677 2023 (print) | LCC E668 (ebook) |
DDC 973.8/2—dc23
LC record available at https://lccn.loc.gov/2022058874
LC ebook record available at https://lccn.loc.gov/2022058875

Vintage Books Trade Paperback ISBN: 978-0-593-31082-3
eBook ISBN: 978-0-593-31782-2

Author photograph © David Altschul
Book design by Anna B. Knighton

penguinrandomhouse.com | vintagebooks.com

Printed in the United States of America
10 9 8 7 6 5 4 3 2 1

The authorized representative in the EU for product safety and compliance is
Penguin Random House Ireland, Morrison Chambers, 32 Nassau Street,
Dublin D02 YH68, Ireland, https://eu-contact.penguin.ie.

In memory of my friend

Nathaniel Lee Hawthorne,

the bravest man I ever knew, who faced down the
Ku Klux Klan in Lunenburg County, Virginia

What does it all mean? I cannot understand
it at all. This Ku Klux—what is it anyway?
Is it a *real,* or an *imaginary* thing?

—Louise Sinclair to a friend, November 1871

To persons who had not the strongest evidence of the
facts, a history of the Ku Klux would be incredible.

—former Attorney General Amos T. Akerman, 1874

CONTENTS

PART FOUR: RECESSIONAL

A Note on Language

The meaning of words evolves over time, in politics as in every other sphere of culture. Most significantly, although the words used by political groups to describe themselves in the 1860s and 1870s will be familiar, their meanings are quite different, and their alignment, to at least some readers, may be surprising.

The Republican Party, though increasingly the party of established power, generally supported remarkably forward-looking policies with respect to race and civil rights, and favored stronger, activist central government. The Republican Radicals, who figure prominently, had nothing to do with socialism, but rather were those who pressed the hardest for policies of racial fairness and for vigorous federal action in the South. The Liberal Republicans, who would deeply affect Reconstruction policy, were not liberals in modern terms, but rather favored laissez faire economics, prioritized bureaucratic reform over civil rights, and urged conciliation with the South.

The Democratic Party, in contrast, was the less "progressive" on most issues. It was wedded to traditional states' rights philosophy, hostile to Reconstruction, and unabashedly Negrophobic in its rhetoric. The party's northern wing harbored the former "Copperheads" who had opposed the Civil War, while its southern wing welcomed former Confederates and often acted in concert with the Ku Klux Klan.

Both parties included men who described themselves as "conservatives." But its meaning depended on context. While some Republican conservatives opposed parts of Reconstruction, others supported it if less vigorously than did the party's Radicals. In the South, "conservative" was often synonymous with "reactionary," and referred to those who sought to roll back the results of the Union victory in the war.

In some states, as in South Carolina, the discredited Democrats temporarily renamed their party the Conservatives in hope of competing more effectively in elections.

Some readers may feel that this book's occasional references to "white supremacy" are anachronistic. They are not. The term was in common use in the post–Civil War era, along with variants such as "white man's rule," in speechmaking, newspaper articles, and popular discourse. Among Democrats it was generally embraced, and by Radical Republicans, in particular, condemned.

The same might be thought of my use of the terms "terrorist" and "terrorism." But both words were sometimes applied to the Ku Klux Klan in precisely the way in which they are understood today. More commonly, however, Americans referred to the Klan's horrific criminal acts—homicidal raids, torture, mutilation, and rape—as "outrages," a word which today lacks the frightening impact that it universally had then.

Some other terms may also be disturbing. Certain words that are rightly repellent today were not only commonplace but ubiquitous then, and not only in the former Confederate South. Southerners and northerners alike casually used crude racial slurs in published writing, court testimony, newspapers, and ordinary speech. I believe that in order to fully understand the thinking and actions of Americans of a century and a half ago we must hear them as they spoke and wrote, whether on the floor of Congress, on street corners, or in the dusty and, for Black Americans, extremely dangerous hamlets of the South.

The most polite term for Black Americans in the Reconstruction Era was "colored," the norm for virtually all Blacks and their white allies. "Negro" was also widely used and regarded as respectful and inoffensive. "Black" was somewhat less common and often, but not always, carried a slightly disdainful connotation.

Today, we know the organization that lies at the center of this story as the "Ku Klux Klan," or simply "the Klan." Americans of the 1860s and 1870s wrote of it in a myriad ways, for example, "Kuklux," "Ku-Klux," "Kluxers," "Cuclucks," and other variants. Except where I am quoting contemporary writers and speakers, I have generally hewed for simplicity's sake to present-day usage.

PREFACE

About 11 p.m. on February 26, 1870, the nighttime silence was broken by wild hallooing and the pounding of horses moving fast through the drizzly mist. Their riders wore white gowns and masks and they surrounded the small frame house where Wyatt Outlaw lived with his small children and elderly mother. Twenty men burst into the house. (His family name was an old and familiar one in Alamance County.) "They had great torches lighted," Jemima, Wyatt's mother, later told state officials. "First they came and threw the cover all off of me. Then they said to me, 'Where is Wyatt' One says, 'Say! Say! Say!' There were two who had swords and there were pistols. One said, 'Cut her head off,' and another said, 'Blow her brains out.' They went out of that room and as they passed one says to the other, 'Let us set the house afire,' and as they went around to the room and I heard the little child cry—that is the baby—'Oh, daddy Oh, daddy!' I ran and opened the door, and they were all around him, all around my son. He was putting on his pants, and I run back and got a stick and laid away as hard as I could. They jumped on me, they did, three of them, and stamped me, and I arose three times and they knocked me down. After they stamped they said, 'God damn you, you strike a white man?' And they stamped me three times in my breast and on my head and arms. And then I hollowed for murder, and they went off with him. They hollowed like geese, and they went hard as thunder, riding."

Wyatt Outlaw was about fifty years old that night, a light-skinned man of mixed-race, a "mulatto" in the parlance of the time, with black wavy hair and beard, an earnest manner, and a notably bold, self-confident gaze. He had escaped slavery in 1864, made his way to Union lines and enlisted in the cavalry, and served with it through the end of the Civil War and for a while after. When he came home, he opened a woodworking shop where he repaired wagons and made coffins, and managed a sort of informal tavern where white and Black working-men gathered. He was counted among Graham's small Black middle class and quickly gained a reputation among freed people as a man who knew things, who could speak with confidence, who could persuade, a natural leader. In 1866, he had represented Alamance County at a statewide freedmen's convention. He was the local leader of the Union League, the organizing arm of the Republican Party, a founder of Graham's first AME church, an elected town commissioner, and helped form an armed patrol of Blacks and whites to protect against the rising threat of Ku Klux Klan violence. When others called for retaliation, he counseled restraint, urging Blacks to "be as industrious as possible, give no cause for complaint, and trust in the law."

Outlaw's captors dragged, pushed, and beat him, half-dressed and barefoot, a half-mile down Main Street to the courthouse at the center of town. They strung him up with a bed-cord from the branch of an elm tree that reached toward the Italianate courthouse from which, for the past year, the Republicans had governed Graham. If Outlaw had any final words, no one recorded them. One of the Klansmen slashed his mouth with a knife, a last bit of pointed savagery toward a man who had too often spoken out for the rights that Black men had been told by the national government, and by North Carolina's embattled Republican governor, were now theirs. His body dangled in front of the courthouse until the middle of the next day, when it was finally cut down by the sheriff, a former member of the Klan. The coroner ruled that Outlaw had died at the hands "of persons unknown." Not long afterward, a Black man named Puryear claimed to know who the murderers were. A few days later he was found floating dead in a pond. In the months that followed, without Outlaw's leadership, the Union League fell apart and frightened Republicans fled town.

Wyatt Outlaw was but one victim, a grimly typical one, of a movement that was sweeping the former Confederacy. Its targets were freed people and their white allies, who by their words or actions, however tacit, sought to transform the South from a region where power had been organized to protect the economic engine of slavery and now the debasement of former slaves, into a democracy where Black and white, rich and poor had a place in the dynamic arena of politics. With the

Confederacy's defeat in 1865, there was reason for hope. The South seemed poised for a racial revolution that would transform former slaves into free actors in national life, and overthrow the white oligarchies that had ruled the slave states since the founding of the republic.

Triumphant Republicans believed that the Reconstruction was irreversible and that southerners would acquiesce peacefully, if reluctantly, in the new reality. As one white South Carolina Republican put it, slavery was dead and those who hoped for its resurrection and "chained themselves to the corpse of a dead policy were like the stubborn man who refused to pay for a ferry across the Mississippi River until the river ran by." What many failed to realize was that for ex-Confederates the war had not ended but was about to enter a new and dangerous phase: not a war of vast armies and grand maneuvers, this time, but a systematic war of terror on the part of men determined to protect white supremacy at all costs. "The negroes are no more free than they were four years ago, and if anyone goes about the country telling them that they are, shoot him," a former—nominally Unionist—Tennessee congressman scathingly declared in 1865.

No consensus existed on what the South's future would be. How radical would Reconstruction be? Who would rule—whites, Blacks, the army, the federal government? Would Black Americans be permitted to live as citizens in fact, not just in name? Would they be permitted to vote? To hold office? To enjoy social equality? Would former Confederates be willing to cooperate with them to rebuild the South, and on what terms? Could the races live together harmoniously and prosperously? How long would white northerners support military rule to protect the civil rights of southern Blacks? "We have nothing in the way of historical precedent to guide us," the *New York Times* worried in May 1866. "In no country have the white and black races existed under circumstances at all analogous to those that now obtain in the South." Race relations were simple under slavery, where peace between them was secured by brutality on one side and fear on the other. It was no longer simple at all. "Neither [race] knows exactly how to do, or act toward the other," James Atkins, a federal tax collector born in Georgia told visiting congressmen. "The white man feels a little unkind towards the Negro, and the Negro has something of a corresponding feeling toward the white man. It operates in our church relations, our social relations, in fact, in all the relations of our life." Even the most optimistic knew that the answers would not be found without titanic social conflict. Few were prepared for the hurricane of violence that came.

Almost as soon as the war ended, a determined reaction set in across the South, at first scattered and impulsive, later brutally systematic, determined to negate and gut every measure that was intended to equalize the races. Resistance groups called themselves by various names: "Regulators," "White Caps," "Pale Faces," "Knights of the White Camellia," and other equally exotic sobriquets. Nearly all of them became subsumed into, or loosely linked to, the paramilitary movement known as the Ku Klux Klan, the first organized terrorist movement in American history. It first stirred as a sort of veterans' fraternity, more men's club than political movement. The Klan's bizarre mumbo jumbo and calculated mystifications left many Americans, including even some who lived in peaceful parts of the South, wondering whether it was anything serious. "What does it all mean?" a young Virginia woman wrote to a friend in South Carolina in November 1871. "I cannot understand it at all. This Ku Klux—what is it anyway? Is it a *real,* or an *imaginary* thing?"

The Klan was, most certainly, real. By 1868, it had spread across the South to serve in many areas as the de facto military wing of the Democratic Party's most reactionary elements. It grew with astonishing speed and quickly turned to violence. Racist foolery became floggings and beatings, and then lynchings and shootings, often of savage cruelty, accompanied by systematic torture, burnings, castrations, and sexual humiliation. Despite later efforts to sanitize the Klan, notably in such films as *The Birth of a Nation* (1915) and *Gone with the Wind* (1939), terror was not a side effect of Klan movement: it was at the movement's core, to scare Blacks and white Republicans away from the ballot box. As a former Union soldier from Alabama wrote to President Ulysses S. Grant, one of countless freedmen's letters that reached his desk, "They go to our churches on the Sabbath and disturb o[u]r Sivil courts and they whip or Kill someone every Saturday and oft times from five to ten in one night. [W]e are all poore men have to work hard alday and be on guard all night for fear of the Ku Klux. [T]he rebs tell us we cant get help."

Although the Klan's apologists justified its atrocities as self-defense against supposedly corrupt Reconstruction governments and imaginary Black crime waves, its most frequent victims were the most able, best educated, and most assertive Blacks, men such as Wyatt Outlaw. At the Klan's peak, tens of thousands belonged to its loose networks. The total is unknowable, but contemporary estimates ran as high as 300,000. It was not a fringe movement of a few socially marginal individuals. Some, of course, were hoodlums and roughnecks. But everywhere the Klan existed it included leading men in their communities—doctors, lawyers, journalists, and churchmen. Where the Klan rode, a beleaguered white Republican wrote, "One would wake in the morning to see ten feet of new manila rope dangling from a limb in your front yard with a pine box coffin at the root of the tree inscribed 'Get out.' It was something to think about. Every time one's dog barked you listened for a battering ram at your front door. Our houses were veritable arsenals, and every time we answered the doorbell at night we carried with us a cocked revolver." In countless communities, as far as Republicans were concerned, the law was a dead letter; jurors would not convict, trials were a farce, witnesses refused to testify, and jailed Klansmen were broken free as a matter of course.

Racial violence had been ubiquitous in the antebellum South. But it was usually privately administered by enslavers against their human property in accordance with—however cruel—established laws and social conventions. Whites armed with military weaponry did not disguise themselves to systematically murder their neighbors. While there was sometimes an element of frightening randomness to Klan terror, its overall strategy was unambiguous: to subvert trust in government, prevent freedmen and white Republicans from voting, reverse the Union victory in the Civil War as thoroughly as possible, and cripple the great social experiment that was born from that victory. The Klan's goal, in short, was a counterrevolution.

During Andrew Johnson's presidency, the Klan thrived amidst inconsistent and haphazard resistance from cowed local officials—many of whom were members of the Klan or its enablers—and federal troops hobbled by lack of will on the part of the president, whose commitment to Black Americans began and ended with the passage of the Thirteenth Amendment and whose political future depended on the restoration of southern Democrats to power. Only with the inauguration of Ulysses Grant did the federal government begin to act. When it did, it acted decisively, undertaking what was in essence a guerrilla war across the former Confederacy, involving the United States Army, prosecutors, judges, and ordinary citizens who took their lives in their hands to sit juries that were willing to judge Klansmen who had shown little mercy to public officers of any type.

The story that this book tells will range from the farmlands and crossroads hamlets of the former Confederate States to the White House and the marble corridors of Congress, where the war against the Klan was fought out as contentiously as it was in the plantation country and piney woods of the South. On Capitol Hill, Republican Radicals struggled against war weariness, cynicism, and pervasive Negrophobia to craft legislation that made it possible for President Grant to send the U.S. Army and federal prosecutors into the deepest hotbeds of Klan activity, enacting a raft of laws that for the first time brought the power of the federal government to bear within the states to protect the safety of individual citizens and their civil rights.

The Klan's rise was swift, and its fall almost as fast, thanks to Grant's decisiveness. By 1872, the organized Klan was in retreat. What federal officers had accomplished in the field, however, was eventually undone by the politics of Republicans in Washington who preferred conciliation of the South to a prolonged and costly investment in the rights of Black Americans. The victory over the Klan was real, but incomplete, leaving local networks of unreconstructed southerners sufficiently intact that they could later regroup and seek to achieve their ends by (mostly) less savage means. However, the Ku Klux Klan that took shape in the twentieth century—notably following the spectacular success of *Birth of a Nation*—had only a tenuous connection to the original Klan, mostly in the form of a few old Klansmen hauled from nursing homes to lend an artificial link to what was actually a dynamic new nativist movement with aspirations to national power. Since its heyday in the 1920s, when this "second Klan" spread over most of the United States, including the North, the movement has waxed and in recent decades mostly waned, after a resurgence in the 1950s and 1960s in reaction to the modern civil rights movement. It is a dark testament to the Klan's effectiveness that later generations would choose to emulate the most anti-American movement ever generated on American soil.

The real history of the original Klan has been largely overshadowed by both the gilded aura of Hollywood's romance with the "Old South" and by the more immediate savagery of the Klan in the twentieth century. Klansmen of the 1860s and 1870s liked to think of themselves as soldiers, even crusaders, in a noble cause, a fantasy that was long abetted by the defenders of the South's "Lost Cause." In fact, much like terrorists the world over, they relied on shock, cruelty, and hit-and-run tactics rather than anything even close to battlefield bravery. Their victims were typically caught helpless, alone, and unarmed in isolated rural cabins, usually in the middle of the night. Their elaborate disguises ensured a degree of anonymity among themselves, which in turn fostered the sadism that was often a hallmark of their attacks. Even other participants in a Klan raid may not always have been sure of who was perpetrating the most heinous crimes. The Klan bequeathed to later generations a model for secretive nativism, racial triumphalism, and belief in the efficacy of terror as an instrument of political control. It was, in effect, a laboratory in which racial ideologues invented the ruthless enforcement machinery of white supremacy.

This book is the story of how the federal government under Ulysses Grant fought and beat the Klan. It sheds a stark light on the most violent period in American history, on the murderous potential of unrestrained racism, and on the courageous determination of public officials and ordinary citizens, newly enfranchised African Americans in particular, to protect the freedoms enshrined in the Thirteenth, Fourteenth, and Fifteenth Amendments. What happened then still matters. The urgency of containing domestic terrorism and racial zeal-otry have not gone away. Nor has the need to protect basic civil rights, including the right to vote. This is a work of history, not a prescription for meeting the nation's present-day challenges. But the story it tells shows that forceful political action can prevail over violent extremism. It also shows that when political courage succumbs to partisan self-interest the darker impulses that are always present in America inherit a fertile ground in which to thrive.

PART ONE

THE TERROR

AN EXPERIMENT IN GOOD FAITH

The work does not end with the
abolition of slavery, but only begins.
—FREDERICK DOUGLASS

On November 27, 1865, Ulysses S. Grant, war hero, paramount commander of the nation's armies, and the most admired man in the triumphant Union, left Washington to assess postwar conditions in the South. He would see only a small part of the former Confederate States, and that mostly from the windows of a moving train. Dressed in black civilian broadcloth, brown-haired and stoop-shouldered, modest in demeanor, a cigar forever between his fingers or plugged into his lips, at forty-three he was the sort of man who might easily have passed unnoticed but for his entourage. He returned to the capital on December 11. He had been away all of sixteen days.

Grant's brief report was an upbeat one. "I am satisfied that the mass of the thinking men of the South accept the present situation of affairs in good faith," and regard the divisive questions of slavery and states' rights "as having been settled forever," he told President Andrew Johnson. He was pleased to say that every town he visited displayed such "universal acceptance of federal authority that the mere sight of soldiers, regardless of their numbers, would be enough to maintain order." He cautioned that wherever possible the garrisons ought all be *white:* the presence of Blacks with guns might "demoralize" recently emancipated freedmen by encouraging them to challenge their employers and provoke violent reactions from whites who still believed that their former human property belonged to them. Grant had met few Blacks, apart from the formalities of a torchlight parade in his honor at Richmond and a review of "colored" troops at Hilton Head. What little he had to say about Blacks seemed to echo what he may have been told in interviews with elite whites, who repeated the common prejudice that without white men to drive them they were chronically lazy and dependent. Of Blacks, Grant wrote, "I am sorry to say, the freedman's mind does not seem to be disabused of the idea that a freedman has the right to live without care or provision for the future." The result was widespread "idleness," a deplorable situation that would surely lead to widespread "vice" and disease, which in turn would "tend toward their extermination, or great reduction of the colored race." In other words, he implied, freedom might prove fatal. Still, since southern ideas about slavery and race that had hardened over years couldn't be expected to change overnight, the freedmen would need the "fostering care" of white Americans a while longer.

GRANT'S HISTORY WITH Black Americans was complicated. In his late-life memoirs he called slavery "an institution abhorrent to all civilized people not brought up under it, and one which degraded labor, kept it in ignorance, and enervated the governing class." But that was a truth that it took him years to fully realize. Although he was raised by an outspokenly antislavery father, he disdained abolitionists as troublemakers and voted Democratic in the years before the Civil War. He was sufficiently tolerant of slavery that he accepted the use of three enslaved house servants when he married into the Dent family of Missouri, and he briefly owned a young slave in his own name but then emancipated him even though he could have sold him for $1,000, money that he sorely needed at the time. "I have no hobby of my own with regard to the negro, either to affect his freedom or to continue his bondage," he wrote to his father in the summer of 1862.

Like most northerners, he found slavery personally distasteful, but was willing to leave it alone in the South as long as it didn't seek to aggrandize its power at the expense of the rest of the country. When he volunteered for military service in 1861, he assumed that once the rebellion was suppressed the Union would be restored to its prewar status. Yet he warned his pro-southern father-in-law, "In all this I can but see the doom of slavery. The North do not want, nor will they want, to interfere with the institution. But they will refuse for all time to give it protection unless the South shall return soon to their allegiance." Soon the flood of freedom-seeking slaves who fled to federal camps forced him to decide what he really believed. He at first allowed southern masters to reclaim their human chattels, but began to resist them when he realized that every slave he sent back helped sustain the Confederate economy and its war effort. By 1863, he had put thousands of former slaves to work for the Union Army and welcomed their recruitment as soldiers, a position more in line with the antislavery Radicals in Congress than with most of the army's conservative officer class. "By arming the negro we have added a powerful ally," he wrote to President Lincoln. "They will make good soldiers and taking them from the enemy weaken him in the same proportion as they strengthen us." And to his friend and political patron Rep. Elihu B. Washburne of Illinois, he wrote, "As anxious as I am to see peace reestablished I would not therefore be willing to see any settlement until this question [of slavery] is forever settled." Grant had, in spite of himself, become an abolitionist.

Grant sought no partisan role for himself in postwar politics. His primary and all-consuming job was to manage the reduction of the army from more than one million men to just 80,000, which Congress would insist be further shrunk to 53,000, including all branches of the service, a prodigious task that involved both redistributing men to the western frontier and manning a multitude of garrisons across the occupied South. Still, he could not escape politics entirely as long as the army remained responsible for the controversial feeding, clothing, housing, and protection of hundreds of thousands of destitute freed people through the quasi-military Freedmen's Bureau, which was staffed mainly with serving officers and men. He was further torn between what would prove irreconcilable imperatives: determination to prevent the Union's battlefield triumph from being squandered by shortsighted politicians, and his hope that compassion toward the defeated would encourage southerners to collaborate willingly on the rebuilding of the country. In this, he was entirely in tune with the president.

Grant's report on the South allowed President Johnson to claim that the seceded states were stable, and that the former Confederates were embracing reunion—in short, that his conciliatory policies were working. At fifty-seven, Johnson's black hair was tinged with gray, but his black eyes still glowed with sometimes disconcerting intensity. Temperamentally, he remained as confrontational as ever. Though rough-cut, he was a skilled political infighter and, as Grant phrased it, "one of the ablest of the poor white class." Born dirt-poor, never schooled, he began his working life as a boy indentured to a tailor in whose shop he learned proper English by memorizing the speeches of William Pitt, Edmund Burke, and other orators that a customer liked to read aloud. A lifelong Democrat, he was elected his town's alderman at the age of twenty-one, mayor at twenty-six, and congressman at thirty-five, by which time he was the owner of several slaves, the cynosure of success in the Tennessee of the day. The idea of racial "amalgamation" viscerally disgusted him and before the war he had always defended slavery as Blacks' natural condition. He was also, however, a passionate Unionist like most of the inhabitants of East Tennessee. When his state seceded only Johnson, among all the South's senators, chose to remain in Congress. During the war, he served effectively as the Union's state governor. In 1864, he was rewarded with the vice presidential nomination, with Abraham Lincoln, as the candidates of the Republican-dominated National Union Party, a wartime artifice designed to win the votes of War Democrats who might resist voting for a Republican. More from political expediency than conviction, he freed his own slaves and in 1864, astonishingly, declared to a rally of Black Tennesseans, "I will be your Moses and lead you through the Red Sea of war and bondage."

The nation was haunted by Lincoln's decision to accept the Tennessean as his running mate. Lincoln's first vice president, Hannibal Hamlin, was a highly respected abolitionist from Maine who had served creditably for years in the Senate. Had he become president instead of Johnson, he would undoubtedly have encouraged the evolution of a biracial society and punished whites who defied federal law. Johnson hadn't even voted for Lincoln in 1860. His wartime support for antislavery legislation was tactical at best, but most Republicans took his professed commitment to racial justice at face value. Sen. Charles Sumner of Massachusetts, for one, reassured his abolitionist friends in 1865, "In the question of colored suffrage the President is with us." Although Johnson accepted the Thirteenth Amendment as a fait accompli, his continuing belief in states' rights and his unapologetic commitment to white supremacy had more in common with reactionary Democrats than with most Republicans. His racism was crude, and shocking even then. Of the intellectual and perfectly mannered Frederick Douglass, he coarsely remarked, "He's just like any nigger, & would sooner cut a white man's throat than not."

In the field, Reconstruction was a work in progress, without uniform policy or leadership, and with only equivocal political support from Washington. Its driving engine, the Freedmen's Bureau (officially the Bureau of Refugees, Freedmen, and Abandoned Lands), was established in March 1865 under the leadership of the evangelical, West Point–trained, and passionately antislavery Gen. Oliver O. Howard, who had risen in the course of the war to command a wing of William Tecumseh Sherman's triumphant army, and would later give his name to Howard University. Congress initially allowed the bureau only the optimistic lifespan of a single year, during which it coordinated emergency relief for freed people and white loyalist refugees, promoted the establishment of schools, oversaw work contracts between former slaves and employers, and, as best it could, defended its charges against vengeful whites. The bureau functioned under the aegis of the War Department and suffered from chronic understaffing. Most of its agents, only about nine hundred of whom were on duty at any given time, were serving officers often on short time and with widely varying degrees of commitment to the newly free. Isolated and overworked, they were often the only federal presence among hostile ex-Confederates, and the only people to whom former slaves could appeal for a fair hearing on their needs. Although many performed their duty to the point of physical collapse, some at the cost of their lives, others regarded their job mainly as a problem of labor management and fraternized openly with local planters.

Politically, Reconstruction was a battlefield. Northern Radicals wanted to permanently break up the plantation economy, strip the South's traditional ruling class of power, and fully integrate the freedmen into the body politic. Working-class southern Unionists, who had always been shut out of government by the wealthy and had suffered under Confederate rule, expected to be rewarded with political power and appointments. Both groups squared off against President Johnson, who made clear almost from the start that he intended to foster white supremacy and reinstate the prewar elite. "I despair of the Presdt," Sumner sadly reflected. "He is no Moses but a Pharaoh to the colored race."

With Johnson's tacit approval, southern states' prewar Black Codes were renewed, binding freed people to remain where they had been enslaved, empowering sheriffs to seize children and place them in servitude until they came of age, and rent out adult Blacks who failed to pay fines; they also barred Blacks from carrying knives or guns without written permission, as well as from preaching, gathering in numbers, and sometimes even from hunting, fishing, and owning houses. Local magistrates received blizzards of complaints from plantation owners who charged that workers had left their property without permission to attend "meetings of negroes." Charles Howard, the editor of a southern agricultural magazine, expressed astonishment that Black women declined to do heavy field labor as they had during slavery days: "They have the idea that, since their emancipation, they should live very much like ladies, and consequently they will merely take care of their own households and do but little or no work out of doors." Blacks must be forced to work for whites by any means necessary, declared the *Edgefield Advertiser,* in upcountry South Carolina, "They must then labor or starve." Workers who attempted to advocate for themselves were often punished. In one particularly hideous case, a field hand reported to the Freedmen's Bureau that when he demanded better pay "he was seized and had the sinews of his legs cut and part of his toes cut off."

Nearly all the governors Johnson appointed were wealthy prewar Unionist Whigs who were acceptable to ex-Confederates and declared their support for "white man's governments." They in turn reappointed thousands of Confederate officeholders to their former jobs as local officials of all sorts, and reassured whites that emancipation would lead to neither Black suffrage nor social equality. Although certain Confederates were initially barred from office, Johnson issued pardons wholesale, often by the hundreds in a single day. He then ordered 850,000 acres of confiscated lands returned to pardoned whites, forcing the freedmen living there to leave farms they believed had been allotted to them. Former Confederates felt increasingly confident that they would be allowed to steer the South's postwar transition and emboldened to disregard the representations of the beleaguered agents of the Freedmen's Bureau. "The President was very anxious to be rid of every prominent officer who was reported to have been long the freedmen's friend," General Howard later wrote. "Any agent who took the part of the freedmen against a Southern planter, especially one who had the hardihood to arrest a white man for misusing a negro, was traduced and often his discharge was brought about."

In his first State of the Union address that December—in keeping with the custom of the time, it was read to the House and Senate by the clerks of the respective houses—Johnson proclaimed the virtues of his "healing policy" toward the South to an increasingly skeptical Congress in which Republicans enjoyed immense majorities: 42 to 10 in the Senate and 149 to 42 in the House. Prolonging military rule, Johnson said, would only divide the people "into the vanquishers and the vanquished" and feed sectional hatred. Rather, what the country needed was a speedy restoration of "affection" to reunite the whites of the alienated sections. Johnson was well aware that the Republicans in Congress were talking about extending the vote to freedmen. Judiciously picking his words, he did not quite say that he opposed it, but rather pointed out that it had always been up to the states alone to set their qualifications for voting. Moreover, he pointedly added, bestowing the franchise on the freedmen by government fiat would have extended it to *all* colored men, in the northern and western states, as well as the southern—something that had repeatedly been rejected by whites in all but a few Yankee states. If freedmen showed "patience and manly virtues" perhaps they might someday be allowed to vote, but in the meantime no "hasty assumptions" ought to be made about the ability of the races to live side by side "in a state of mutual benefit and good will." Industry ought to be opened to them, but their success would depend entirely on themselves. They might "fail, and so perish away," but the nation, he intimated, would be none the worse for it.

Grant's report wasn't the only one on conditions in the South. On December 18, the same day that it was released to the Senate, another appeared, penned by former Union general Carl Schurz. Grant had spent a total of fifteen days in the South; Schurz three months. Schurz, too, had been dispatched by Johnson. But, in him, the president got more than he was prepared for. Schurz was a man of outspokenly independent views, as well as a professional journalist with a national following, especially among the country's large, politically active German population. A swashbuckling activist for republicanism in his native Germany, he fled to the United States after the collapse of the 1848 revolution there and readily embraced abolitionism and the Union cause, rising during the war to the command of a division in the Army of the Potomac. For Johnson, Schurz's report was a disaster.

Schurz described with sometimes chilling acuteness what Grant hadn't noticed and what Johnson doubtless knew but calculatedly ignored. Schurz traveled slowly across South Carolina and Georgia, then through Alabama to New Orleans, back to Alabama, and finally northward up the Mississippi River. He saw almost everywhere a human landscape of poverty, instability, and seething anger toward both Blacks and Yankees. At Charleston, his first stop, signs of wartime devastation were everywhere in the deserted warehouses, shell-damaged mansions, and the "vast graveyard" of the city center. In the countryside, once thriving plantations were crushed by debt, returning soldiers' families were living hand-to-mouth, and the effects of runaway inflation impoverished everyone.

With an ever-inquisitive eye—to pay his way, Schurz also arranged to write a series of articles for the *Boston Daily Advertiser*—he talked to people of all kinds, Unionists and "incorrigibles," soldiers and civil officials, planters, merchants, and former slaves. Unlike Grant, he saw multitudes of hopeful freed men and women banding together to demand pay for their work, organize schools, build churches, and learn their new rights. He saw that Johnson's conciliatory policy was already failing. "The loyalty of the masses, and most of the leaders of the southern people, consists in submission to necessity," he wrote in his forty-six-page report, which was accompanied by many more pages of supporting documents, mainly from military officers serving in the occupation army. "There is, except in individual instances, an entire absence of that national spirit which forms the basis of true loyalty and patriotism. The emancipation of the slaves is submitted to only in so far as chattel slavery in the old form could not be kept up." Southerners, he wrote with some astonishment, "honestly maintained and believed not only that as a people they were highly civilized, but that their civilization was the highest that could be attained, and ought to serve as a model to other nations the world over." They were "so wrapt up in self-admiration as to be inaccessible to the voice even of the best-intentioned criticism. Hence the delusion they indulged in as to the absolute superiority of their race."

Ex-rebels complained relentlessly about having to deal with freed people and demanded federal compensation for the value of their lost slaves and for wartime damage by the Union armies. The only aspect of emancipation that former masters welcomed was that they were no longer obliged to feed or shelter the people who worked for them and were free to leave the weak and infirm to fend for themselves. A plantation owner in north Georgia complained to a Union officer about his former slaves: "When I tell them to go to their quarters and they do not do it, we cannot put up with it." The former slaves were still forced to work "under the lash" wherever their employers could get away with it. Many whites, not just planters, wished they could rid themselves entirely of the Black population. (Whites sometimes tried simply to wish Blacks gone through magical thinking: an Alabama newspaper editorialized that as a result of their alleged "ignorance, carelessness, improvidence, filth and immorality," Blacks were "likely to pass away as the poor Indians have done, and ultimately to become extinct.")

Schurz wrote to his wife, "The prevailing sentiment seems to be that if they cannot have the negro as a slave, they do not want to have him at all." He reported that loyal Blacks and whites alike suffered constant harassment. At Selma alone, the military documented twelve murders of Blacks who were simply "trying to come to town," while near Mobile white patrols posted on the rivers "hang, shoot, or drown" former slaves found trying to escape from plantations on boats. Opposition to the education of Blacks was intense. "Hundreds of times," Schurz wrote, he heard the assertion that "learning will spoil the nigger for work."

The consequences of all this were dire, he warned. "The distrust between the whites and blacks is so great, and the ill-will with which the negro is looked upon by the whites so apparent, that it absolutely requires the presence of the troops to prevent explosions." Military protection for freed people and loyalists was just the merest minimum. Nor was simple tinkering with the political machinery of the states and their constitutional relationship to Washington a solution. The "whole organism of southern society" had to be reconstructed to bring it in harmony with the rest of American society, Schurz wrote. Long-term stability demanded the extension of the vote to Blacks, who stood at the center of every problem in the region, and whose voices had to be included in the search for solutions. Nothing else could help more "to obliterate old antagonisms." Men with political power were far less likely to be victimized than those who were completely subject to the will of others. "A voter is a man of influence." Otherwise there would be little chance of escape from "violent reaction and civil disorder." The many embittered and furious ex-Confederates he encountered "will deal largely in tar and feathers," he predicted, and "practice private vengeance whenever they can do it with impunity." In short, unless the government changed course soon it faced an epidemic of terrorism.

Johnson treated Schurz's report as a personal affront and suppressed it until Grant's whitewash was available. Conservatives tried to dismiss Schurz as a "featherweight" who merely wanted to "blacken the Southern whites and to whiten the Southern blacks." However, the Senate Radicals immediately published the report and distributed 100,000 copies of it nationwide, where it did much to build public support for forceful Reconstruction policies. When Grant read it he was embarrassed at how much he had missed. To his credit, he had the character to tell Schurz so. In December, Schurz wrote to his wife, Margarethe, that Grant confessed to him that he had been wrong in his optimistic assessment of the situation in the South, and that Schurz had been correct. Grant also acted: he ordered his subordinates in the South to report directly to him the kinds of atrocities that he had failed to see. Nevertheless, Reconstruction's fate still lay in the hard fist of the president.

In the months that followed, the political war over Reconstruction accelerated as Congress forcefully asserted itself against Johnson's expansive claims of executive authority. While one kind of struggle played out across the landscape of the South, another was being fought out in the nation's capital, in the late 1860s a half-built city that was still in the making. "There is a fairy-tale sense of instability," wrote a journalist. "The city looks as if a whirlwind had picked up some great town, mixed the big houses up with the little ones, then cast the whole together in one big miscellaneous mass." The worst of the downtown's famously boggy streets were being paved and beautified with trees and lights, but palatial homes still jostled alongside hovels, well-upholstered politicians gathered in grand hotels such as the Willard, and disintegrating wartime fortifications still dotted the suburbs, where families of impoverished freed people by the thousands populated sprawling shantytowns and scrambled to find work. The locus of power, the city's great gladiatorial arena, was of course the floor of Congress, where, ultimately, the fate of states and of millions of Black Americans would be determined.

Capitol Hill, then as now, was the spiritual heart of the nation's secular religion. The atmosphere was less solemn than seething. Lobbyists and sharpers of all sorts freely roamed the halls. Souvenir hunters chipped off pieces of furniture, chunks of marble from statues, and snipped swatches from curtains and draperies. Snack vendors hawked their wares in the Rotunda. Pickpockets plucked purses from the unwary. Fake guides hustled the multitude of tourists. On the floor of Congress, rhetoric ranged from the erudite oratory of a Sumner, who lavishly quoted Classical authors, to the colorful lingo of a Tennessean who declared that a deceased colleague had "gone down to his last grave, wrapped in the peaceful soliloquy of his blood." Decorum was pompous in principle, rather less so in practice. While debaters loudly called for "a pint [*sic*] of order," members could be seen reading newspapers with their muddy feet on their desks, eating sandwiches, puffing cigars, chewing tobacco and shooting it in the direction of spittoons, and stretched out on sofas at the rear of the chambers, sound asleep and, in the words of a reporter, "sweating like a bull's nose in winter." Especially during late-night sessions, after a hearty, wine-soaked dinner, it wasn't unusual to see a member too drunk to stand up straight, struggling incoherently to deliver a speech. In summer, members complained that the sweltering House Chamber, in particular, was like "the Black Hole of Calcutta, where we are likely to be killed by breathing foul air," as one New Yorker put it.

In Johnson's most egregious affront to Congress, he maintained that he alone possessed the authority to set the terms for the southern states' readmission to the Union. "Our worthy president fancies himself a sovereign power," sneered Pennsylvania congressman Thaddeus Stevens, the staunchest of abolitionists in the House and co-chairman with Maine Senator William Pitt Fessenden of the potent new Joint Committee on Reconstruction, which was established at Stevens's prompting in 1865. An egalitarian to his bones, he believed that no distinction ought to be tolerated among citizens "but what arose from merit and conduct." Earlier than most, Stevens had correctly surmised that Johnson wanted to kill Reconstruction in its cradle. At seventy-three, Stevens, though suffering from ill health and hobbled since infancy by a clubfoot, remained a ferocious debater and one of the chamber's most skilled legislators, as well as its most indefatigable advocate for racial equality. He had never trusted Johnson, and he now set out to politically destroy him. Radicals, Stevens among them, believed that the seceded states had destroyed their prior relationship with the Union and that Congress ought to treat them as territories under military rule until a complete revolution in southern society scrubbed out the last vestiges of the prewar slaveholding society.

Stevens argued that the prewar southern states in fact no longer existed: by making war, the secessionists had "torn their constitutional states into atoms." Dead states, he asserted, cannot restore their own existence. "We have conquered them, and as a conquered enemy we can give them laws, abolish all their municipal institutions and form new ones," Stevens told a Republican rally in his hometown of Lancaster, Pennsylvania. "If we do not make those institutions fit to last through generations of freemen, a heavy curse will be on us." The millions of acres of land confiscated from leading rebels should be distributed among the freedmen, he urged, and whatever was left over sold off and the profits applied to veterans' pensions, paying down the war debt, and reimbursing loyal southern men for the damages they had suffered in the rebellion. But the greater revolution that must be undertaken must be more than economic, and overthrow forever the principles and feelings that underpinned racism. "This may startle weak minds and shake weak nerves," he declared. "So do all great improvements in the political and moral world."

The legislation that emerged from the Republicans in January 1866 was less radical than Stevens hoped for, but it seized the initiative from Johnson. First, on January 19, Sen. Lyman Trumbull of Illinois, the author of the Thirteenth Amendment, called for prolonging the mandate of the Freedmen's Bureau for another two years. Despite its ongoing shortcomings, the bureau was continuing to perform a function that no one else did, particularly in its attempts to investigate crimes against freed people, its efforts to defend their rights against encroachment, and in what may have been its most significant achievement, the establishment of some 4,300 schools with a total of almost a quarter-million students, plus the recruitment of thousands of northern teachers to serve in them.

More far-reaching was the second measure, the Civil Rights bill, which at a stroke transformed relations between whites and Blacks and between the national government and the states. Before the war, none but the most extreme abolitionists could imagine "white men's" rights ever being extended to Blacks. The bill's language was blunt and bracing. It proclaimed that all persons "of every race and color" born in the United States except nontaxpaying Indians were citizens and guaranteed all the basic rights that until now belonged only to whites: to enjoy the full protection of the law, inherit property, give evidence in court, lodge lawsuits, make and enforce contracts, and more. (The bill also implicitly invalidated many discriminatory laws in the North.) In trying abuses committed under the act, federal courts were for the first time made paramount to state courts. Significantly, the bill also empowered the president to order federal troops to enforce civil rights.

Taken together, the bills sought to lift the freed people from dependency to self-sufficiency and to help them defend themselves in federal courts. Republicans supported both bills with near unanimity and assumed that Johnson would sign them. Instead, Johnson shocked everyone by vetoing both bills, a rare and dramatic event in that era, dismissing the Freedman's Bureau as a sewer of patronage, and declaring that the very idea of civil rights for Negroes, compounded by such an overbearing assertion of federal power, violated "all our experience as a people." He clearly expected the country to rally around him. Although he was well attuned to the prejudices of white southerners, he was tone-deaf to popular sentiment in the North, where most citizens saw the measures as reasonable extensions of the winning of the war. The vetoes fatally shredded his already frayed relations with Congress. By March, few Republicans were willing to give him the benefit of the doubt any longer. Wrote Rep. Elihu Washburne of Illinois despairingly to his wife, "The president has gone over to the enemy." Johnson remained defiant. Standing in front of the White House on George Washington's birthday, he denounced the two most prominent Radicals, Stevens and Sumner, as "traitors" out to destroy the Constitution. Soon after, both houses of Congress overwhelmingly overrode Johnson's vetoes to enact both the Freedmen's Bureau and Civil Rights bills.

On the last day of April, what Carl Schurz feared came horrifically to pass in Memphis. A brawl between demobilized Black soldiers and local policemen quickly escalated into a three-day massacre of defenseless Black civilians by white mobs. Virtually every Black school and church was burned to the ground, Black women were raped in their homes, and scores of Blacks were murdered by roving bands of thugs that included city policemen. News reports were stark: "Four Negroes were locked in a house and the house set on fire. . . . A colored boy on Main Street had his brains beaten out. . . . A man appearing to be a policeman took twenty-nine dollars from Rob't Jones (colored) and, as he turned to leave, thrust a knife into his back. . . . A negro was shot in the knee near the corner of Howard's Row for the sake of amusement. . . . Sixteen-year-old Rachel Hatcher was trapped in a burning house and then shot to death when she tried to flee. . . . A crippled woman was raped by seven men, two of them policemen." Crowed the city's leading Democratic paper, the *Avalanche,* "Thank heaven the white race are once more rulers of Memphis." Garbled early reports suggested that Blacks had instigated the riots. But Elihu Washburne, who went to Memphis to investigate, grimly reported to Thaddeus Stevens, "It was no 'negro riot,' for the negroes had nothing to do with it but to be butchered. The rebel spirit here is rampant, defiant, intolerant." In all, forty-six Blacks were killed, seventy-six injured, and eighty-four homes burned to the ground. The mayor promised unpersuasively that no guilty person would go unpunished. Washburne declared in his official report that the riots were "only a specimen of what would take place throughout the entire South, should the government fail to afford adequate military protection."

Ulysses Grant was deeply affected by the events in Memphis. It was now thoroughly clear to him that the former Confederates were bent on reclaiming power by any means necessary and that without the will to stop them the freed people were helpless before them. "A year ago, they were willing to do anything; now they regard themselves as masters of the situation," he told a reporter for the *New York Times*. They "had somehow got the idea that treason, after all, was not very bad, and that the 'Southern cause' as they phrase it, will yet triumph, not in war but in politics." He deployed more troops to Memphis and ordered the arrest of the massacre's ringleaders: "I think it ought to be done with a strong hand to show that where the civil authorities fail to notice crime of this sort there is a power that will do so." His decisiveness was immediately thwarted by the president, however, who through his attorney general, James Speed, a conservative Republican, declared that the Memphis atrocities did not constitute *federal* crimes: since civil courts were now operating in Tennessee that was where victims ought to seek redress. A general on the scene reported to Grant that although the ringleaders had been identified, the local grand jury "failed to take any notice whatever of the offenders or the riot."

Meanwhile, white violence churned across the South. The Freedmen's Bureau recorded scores of Blacks murdered by whites in Tennessee, Arkansas, the Carolinas, and Kentucky, some on isolated farms, more clubbed and flogged to death under the eyes of witnesses, others hanged by mobs. In Texas, a bureau official reported, Blacks "are shot down like wild beasts, without any provocation." From Arkansas, an unnerved white Republican wrote to Thaddeus Stevens, "the rebs" had some kind of dispute with some Freedmen near Pine Bluff. That night the sky was lit up by flame. "The next morning I went to the spot, when I Saw a sight that apald Me 24 Negro Men Woman and Children weare hanging to trees all around the Cabbins. Sir, there Must be something done or else I think the Rebbels are going to rise again." Then, in July, a white mob in New Orleans led by city policemen, most of them Confederate veterans and encouraged by the mayor, attacked a march by Black veterans and a racially mixed convention that was discussing the prospect of Black voting rights. The rioters attacked the delegates, firing their revolvers into the convention hall and murdering those who tried to escape as they jumped from the windows. At least thirty-four Blacks and several white Republicans died, perhaps many more, and 184 were wounded, including a former white Unionist governor of the state, who was crippled for life. "It was an absolute massacre by the police," Gen. Philip Sheridan reported to Grant. Widespread as such incidents were, the violence was still localized and often impulsive, without any guiding hand beyond a fevered desire among embittered southerners to stave off the advancement of their former slaves.

On Capitol Hill, congressional support was steadily coalescing around what would become the Fourteenth Amendment. Its first section declared Blacks to be citizens, empowered the federal courts to overturn discriminatory state laws, and barred states from depriving any person of basic freedoms—free speech and assembly, trial by jury, the bearing of arms, protection against cruel and unusual punishment, and freedom from unreasonable search and seizure—none of which enslaved people, and even many free Blacks, had ever enjoyed, and which were being violated across the South even as Congress debated. Another section barred from state and federal public office anyone who had taken an oath to support the Constitution and then broken it to join the rebellion, excluding thousands of men from former U.S. senators and congressmen down to local tax collectors and postmasters, including numerous Johnson appointees, until 1870. To those who protested that such an exclusion was unduly harsh, Stevens exclaimed, "Too strong? It is too lenient for my hard heart. Not only to 1870 but to [the year] 18,070 every rebel who shed the blood of loyal men should be prevented from exercising any power in the government. Let not these friends of secession sing to me their siren song of peace and good will until they can stop my ears to the screams and groans of the dying victims at Memphis."

The proposed amendment also significantly increased the power of the federal government by giving Congress the authority to enforce the provisions. (Separate legislation required the southern states to ratify the amendment before being readmitted to the Union.) Some Republicans protested that the amendment was unneeded because virtually identical provisions had been articulated in the Civil Rights Act. But as Stevens pointed out, a mere *statute* could be repealed anytime by a new Congress with a simple majority. Only a constitutional amendment could permanently safeguard freedmen's rights.

One thing the amendment did not do was guarantee Black suffrage. "If you deny them the elective franchise, I know not how they are to be protected," Massachusetts Radical George Boutwell, a Stevens ally, had argued. "Otherwise, you furnish the protection which is given to the lamb when he is commended to the wolf." Presciently, he predicted, "If you leave these four million of people to the care and custody of the men who have inaugurated and carried on this rebellion, then you treasure up for untold years the elements of social and civil war." But the Republicans faced a conundrum. Before the war, slaveholding states were permitted by the Constitution to count three-fifths of their enslaved population toward their congressional representation, giving them an extra bonus of votes. With slavery abolished and all Blacks now counted, southern states could collectively enjoy as many as forty more votes in the House and the Electoral College. Thus, if whites could prevent Blacks from voting, they would have even more power than they had enjoyed before the war. But if Blacks voted freely, most likely for Republicans, they would counterbalance the anti-Reconstruction white vote, and in some they would even overtop it.

The most obvious solution was to extend the franchise to Blacks. But even the loyal states were not yet ready for such a radical measure. Probably only a dozen members of the House and even fewer senators supported extending the vote, which was still denied to Blacks even in most *northern* states, while support among southern whites was faint indeed. (When later that year a convention of southern Unionists voted against Black suffrage, Frederick Douglass furiously demanded: "In your resolutions you talk about equal justice. In God's name, what do you mean by it? What do you mean, while denying equal rights to men of my color?") Some Radicals also feared that Black suffrage would actually work *against* the Republicans' interests because, they imagined, freedmen would tend to vote as their former masters told them to. In the end, the amendment attempted to solve the conundrum with a clever formula: while congressional representation would be based on the total number of persons in each state, it would be reduced in proportion to the number of male inhabitants over twenty-one who were denied the right to vote in state and local elections. This created an incentive for southern states to enfranchise Blacks on their own, or else lose representatives in Congress.

Stevens was deeply disappointed, but finally conceded that the country wasn't yet prepared to take the leap. A realist as always, he told his fellow congressmen, "It falls far short of my wishes, but it fulfills my hopes. I believe it is all that can be obtained in the present state of public opinion. I will take all I can get in the cause of humanity and leave it to be perfected by better men in better times. It may be that time will not come while I am here to enjoy the glorious triumph; but that it will come is as certain as there is a just God." On June 13, with unified support from both Radicals and moderate Republicans, the amendment easily won approval by large margins in both houses over Johnson's spluttering attacks against his enemies on Capitol Hill, whom he assailed as "a body called, or which assumes [itself] to be the Congress of the United States," while virtually its every action "fostered *dis*union."

Johnson and the Republicans alike regarded the November congressional elections as a potential turning point. The president knew that his only hope for regaining the political initiative lay in crafting an alliance between the Democrats and conservative Republicans who still had reservations about Reconstruction. What was left of the National Union Party had gathered in May in a failed attempt to build a lasting organization from the ruins of the Democrats, who were still compromised by the remnants of its prewar secessionist wing, and a rump of disgruntled Republicans. The Democrats warned hysterically that, unless Johnson's men were elected, "negro governors, negro mayors of cities, and negro occupants of every grade of office State and municipal" would take over government. In an effort to inspire the electorate, Johnson embarked on a whistlestop tour on behalf of conservative candidates that took him from Philadelphia and New York across the Midwest to St. Louis, and back again, dubbed the "swing around the circle." To lend glamour to his stump speeches, he dragooned Adm. David Farragut, the hero of the battle of Mobile Bay, the swaggering young cavalry commander George Armstrong Custer, and an unenthusiastic Ulysses Grant to travel along with him. The trip was a disaster. In an ongoing display of ill-temper and self-pity, Johnson proposed that God had removed Lincoln so that he could become president, compared himself to Christ for his pardoning of Confederate "sinners," blamed Radicals for the New Orleans massacre, and suggested that Thaddeus Stevens ought to be lynched. Disgusted Republican mayors and governors snubbed him. Crowds repeatedly begged for Grant to speak instead. Adding to the sense of snowballing failure, at Johnstown, Pennsylvania, a platform holding spectators collapsed killing thirteen people as Johnson's train raced away toward his next rally. Grant maintained a dignified public silence as long as he could. In private, he wrote to his wife, Julia, "I have never been so tired of anything before as I have been with the political stump speeches of Mr. Johnson. I look upon them as a national disgrace." In November, the voters decisively repudiated the president and rewarded the Republicans with overwhelming, veto-proof majorities of 57 to 9 in the Senate and 173 to 47 in the House.

The Memphis massacre, Johnson's grossly inept campaign, and continuing confirmation of Carl Schurz's warnings all nudged Grant toward an embrace of the Radical agenda. For more than a year, he had watched the fruits of the Union's victory slipping away. The would-be conciliator of 1865 was gone, replaced by a man who believed in freedmen's rights and was willing to contemplate mobilizing federal power to protect them. When Johnson hinted to him that he might declare the new incoming Congress invalid because it didn't have enough southerners and conservatives in it, Grant bluntly told him that if he tried that, "The army will support the Congress as it is now and disperse the other." Grant preemptively instructed that federal weaponry be removed from southern arsenals and shipped north, and ordered Gen. Philip Sheridan, his proconsul in restive Louisiana and Texas, to take care that "if a crisis does come, that no armed headway can be made against the

Union." On his own initiative, he issued orders protecting soldiers, freedmen, and Unionist civilians from frivolous criminal charges in southern courts, and he staunchly resisted appeals from southern officials for the withdrawal of federal troops. When southern newspapers launched vicious attacks against the occupation, he temporarily shut down the worst of them. When Johnson tried to sideline him by sending him off on a mission to Mexico, Grant refused to go. He was learning that his stubbornness was a match for that of the president. It would be further tested in the months to come.

2

APPARITIONS IN TENNESSEE

Call you this liberty?

—Rep. Thaddeus Stevens

On March 27, 1867, a terse item in the *Citizen,* published in Pulaski, Tennessee, announced teasingly that "The Kuklux Klan will assemble at their usual place of rendezvous, 'The Den,'" on Tuesday "exactly at the hour of midnight in costume and bearing the arms of the Klan." It was signed "Grand Cyclops." The announcement was accompanied by a seemingly perplexed editorial comment: "What does it mean? What is a 'Kuklux Klan,' and who is this 'Grand Cyclops'? Can anyone give us a little light on this subject?" From then on, the *Citizen* typically ran a KuKlux item almost every week. One reported that the "Grand Turk of the Kuklux Klan" had visited the newsroom, noting dryly that he was no more than eight feet tall and wore "a flashy suit of scarlet velvet roundabout and knee-breeches," portentously intoned the word "nix-cum-a-r-o-u-s-c-h!" then disappeared "as noiselessly as a graveyard," leaving behind a message from the Grand Cyclops announcing that the order would assemble for a business meeting Saturday night "in the forest." Another story reported that numbers of the Klan had been observed "walking quietly and boldly about the streets, dressed in the gorgeous array of the Klan, seemingly bent upon the accomplishment of some great object." Another that the Grand Cyclops had recently entered a local hotel and politely inquired for accommodation for sixty-five ghostly men, who having traveled 175 miles by foot since morning were "a little fatigued." All this generated considerable local curiosity and talk. But it was an elaborate in-joke. The articles were almost certainly penned by the paper's erudite and playful young news editor, Frank McCord, a founder and leading member of the spooky new organization.

Pulaski, prosperous as a market town before the war and home to two colleges and several churches, was a mere husk of the bustling place that it had once been. Nestled in the hills seventy-five miles south of Memphis, it had repeatedly been occupied and reoccupied by both armies. Among ex-Confederates, the atmosphere of defeat still stung like bitter smoke in the air. Fire had left half the downtown charred. Roughnecks brawled in the streets. The exuberant boldness of once docile former slaves who made up almost 40 percent of the population shocked whites who had been bred to believe that servitude was sacred and eternal; years after the war, the local sheriff still listed his ex-slaves as property for tax purposes. Young whites idled gloomily without jobs or direction. McCord, who had served in a Confederate infantry regiment, pressed his restless friends to come up with some kind of entertainment to enliven things, something theatrical perhaps, to help young veterans like themselves escape despair and dissipation. A half-dozen of them—all well educated and most of them professionals—first formed a guitar-and-fiddle group they called the "Midnight Rangers." Then, sometime in mid-1866, they came up with something more original. They redubbed themselves the "Ku-Klux," a deliberately enigmatic coinage which echoed the name of a popular college fraternity, the "Kyklos Adelphon," or "Circle of Brothers." (Oddly named college groups were common in the era—the "Sons of Confucius," the "Guiasticutus," and others.) Later they added the word "Klan," which vaguely evoked the Scottish Highland novels of Sir Walter Scott, which had been fantastically popular in the antebellum South. "Had they called themselves the 'Jolly Jokers' or the 'Adelphi,' or by some similar appellation," wrote an early historian of the Klan, they would probably have soon been forgotten, but "there was a weird potency in the very name Ku Klux Klan."

In its early days, the Klan mainly practiced a sort of comic street theater. They would turn up suddenly at picnics and dances disguised preposterously in star-spangled funnel-shaped hats, red, white, or blue lace-trimmed gowns, fake beards, masks made of squirrel skin or painted with eyes and teeth, and sometimes adorned with horns or mules' ears. Among themselves, they communicated by means of complicated hand signals, passwords, and codes, and invented a panoply of baroque titles vaguely inspired by the Masons and other harmless secret societies, dubbing their chief officer the "Grand Cyclops," his assistant the "Grand Magi," and other officers "Grand Turk," "Lictor," and so on. Their elaborate initiation rites, which took place at secluded spots in the woods, typically barraged blindfolded candidates with cryptic questions, compelled them to swear an oath of absolute secrecy, undergo a symbolic "journey" over physical obstacles, and agree to a catechism they called their "Prescript." In its original form, this consisted of eight pages of dense mumbo jumbo with excerpts from Shakespeare, the poetry of Robert Burns, and a flotsam of puzzling Latin quotations: *"Damnant quod non intellegunt"* ("They condemn what they do not understand") . . . *"Cessante cause, cessat effectus"* ("The cause ceasing, the effect must cease") . . . *"Hic manent vestigial morientis libertatis"* ("Here lie the remains of dying liberties") . . . *"Nemo nos impune lacessit"* ("No one attacks us with impunity") and more.

Although the Klan had no evident political agenda, its antics gradually took on a racial coloration. Oft-repeated Klan lore held that credulous Blacks were always terrified by "humorous" claims that they were the ghosts of the Confederate dead, and by such crude gimmicks as "drinking" buckets of water that were actually poured into hidden sacks, and extending skeletal hands from beneath their robes. A Klan parade through Pulaski on July 4, 1867, reportedly sent Blacks running. And even if the Klan was not yet a political force, the *Pulaski Citizen* was. Perhaps not coincidentally, as early as April of that year, next to a tongue-in-cheek "report" on a visit from a robed apparition there appeared an editorial advising "the colored population" of Pulaski to vote for the local conservatives— essentially Democrats under another name—against the Radicals, Republicans in all but name, who the paper perversely alleged were the real heirs of the prewar "slave owners" and "slave haters." In May, McCord publicly and without disguise flogged a Black male schoolteacher who had dared to whip a white boy even though it was at the request of the boy's mother. Gradually, wrote an early member, J. C. Lester, in a history of the Klan, disguised riders began to act as "regulators" to "preserve peace and order" by frightening "insolent" Blacks who suffered from "the delusion that liberty meant license," and white Unionists "who, like scum, had been thrown to the surface" by the upheaval of Reconstruction.

Then something changed. In late May, or possibly early June, about fifteen Klansmen from Middle Tennessee, Alabama, Arkansas, and perhaps North Carolina met at Nashville's Maxwell House hotel. The hotel, later to become famous as the city's poshest, had served variously as a federal barracks and prison during the war, and was still unfinished and commercially struggling. There is no record of what took place at the meeting. But the Klan that emerged from it was no longer a private club: it was a movement with a clear purpose, a hierarchy, and a semi-military structure that would enable it to expand with astonishing speed in the months to come, alter the course of Reconstruction, and ultimately cast its long shadow over relations between the races down to the present day. The gathered Klansmen designated the organization they were creating the "Invisible Empire," a term that would from now on be synonymous with "Ku-Klux." They also unveiled a new, less ornate Prescript that was meant to be distributed to all new "dens." Its author was probably George W. Gordon, one of the youngest generals in the former Confederate army, and perhaps the central figure in this stage of the Klan's development, though as with many other aspects of the early Klan his precise role remains unclear. The Prescript created, in theory at least, a bureaucracy of "Realms" that matched the various southern states and were in turn divided into "Dominions" that corresponded to congressional districts, and "Provinces," that were coterminous with counties, a structure that in outline seemed to define the Klan's budding political ambitions. Each "Realm" would be headed by a "Grand Dragon" assisted by eight "Hydras," and each "Dominion" led by a "Grand Titan" assisted by six "Furies," and furnished with a judicial council of "Yahoos" and "Centaurs," and so on. The Prescript further stipulated that each "den" must produce quarterly reports, collect membership dues, keep track of disbursements, and obey the dictates of the Grand Wizard, who "shall instruct his Grand Exchequer as to the appropriation and disbursement of the revenue." Each Grand Titan would "transmit through the Grand Giants to the subordinates of his Dominion all information or intelligence conveyed to him by the Grand Dragon for that purpose," while the Grand Turk, the executive officer of the Grand Cyclops, was charged with notifying "the ghouls of the Den" of any informal meetings. In effect, the Prescript created an entire, if partly aspirational, underground bureaucracy that even if it never functioned as fully as envisioned nonetheless reveals its grandiose ambitions.

After Nashville, the Klan became more visible, courting publicity, staging public demonstrations, and issuing pronouncements to be published in friendly newspapers. It also turned decisively toward political harassment. The *Citizen* might still scoff that "squads" of four or five "harmless" Klansmen might be seen in Pulaski's streets from time to time, and sneeringly advised anyone who felt bothered by them to "take a dose of quinine, you old granny, calm your fears about the Ku-Klux and go to bed." (The new organization's name would continue to be written in a variety of ways, sometimes with a hyphen, sometimes without, sometimes as a single word, and only rarely in the early years as the now familiar "Ku Klux Klan.") Before the year was out a Republican paper in Nashville would report that the very mention of the Klan was provoking widespread fear among Radicals and Blacks, and in the first mention of the Klan in the federal records, an officer of the Freedmen's Bureau in Tennessee would report that its main purpose was "to annoy and intimidate the colored people." From now on, "Ku Klux" would begin to pass inexorably into the nation's vocabulary as a synonym for terrorist violence.

While Frank McCord and his friends were spooking the citizens of Pulaski, Thaddeus Stevens was embarking on one of the last crusades of his rapidly ebbing life. Now seventy-five, drained by long and debilitating illness, he summoned his last reserves of strength to assert, albeit with more passion than precision, that the continuing mayhem in the South was "daily putting into secret graves not only hundreds but thousands of the colored people." Nearly every day brought more news of armed whites breaking up Black prayer meetings and mixed-race gatherings, confiscating freedmen's guns, flogging workers who demanded fair wages, ambushing Black soldiers, and murdering ordinary Black citizens who failed to show the expected degree of slavish deference to what whites liked to call "the superior race." The Freedmen's Bureau reported that at least 440 freed people had been murdered in cold blood by whites over the previous year; the true number was undoubtedly greater since so many killings took place in areas unmonitored by the army or the bureau. By failing to protect them, the government was cruelly betraying the most loyal Southern friends it had, Stevens caustically told the House. "We have unchained them from the stake so as to allow them the power of locomotion, provided they do not walk in paths which are trod by white men. We have imposed upon them the privilege of fighting our battles, of dying in defense of freedom, but where have we given them the privilege of ever participating in the formation of the laws? By what civil weapon have we enabled them to defend themselves against oppression and injustice? Call you this liberty?"

Stevens was addressing not just the mayhem in the South, but implicitly a recent Supreme Court decision that had all but crippled the army's ability to deal with it. In December 1866, the Court had ruled that military commissions could not constitutionally exert judicial power anywhere that civilian courts were in operation. The case, *Ex parte Milligan,* overturned the wartime death sentence of an Indiana Copperhead who had been convicted of conspiracy by such a commission. Stevens and the Radicals immediately recognized that *Milligan* would paralyze the pursuit of southern criminals by handing them over to sympathetic local courts. Their fears were well founded: when President Johnson ordered the Freedmen's Bureau to stop sending such cases to the army, prosecutions plummeted.

Following Stevens's lead, in 1867, Congress reacted to the crisis in the South with a spate of new laws that went further than the previous year's Civil Rights Act. These measures wrenched power away from southern state governments and Reconstruction policy from the president. Rep. James G. Blaine of Maine, then a young Radical and a pillar of the Republican establishment for decades to come, called these Reconstruction Acts "the most vigorous and determined action ever taken by Congress in time of peace." In essence, they asserted that the army derived its authority directly from Congress, not the president. The first, enacted on March 2, 1867, divided the former Confederacy into five military districts, each commanded by a general who was empowered to supersede civil courts, and charged with suppressing violence, punishing criminals, and protecting the rights and safety of all persons regardless of "race, color, or previous condition." This was a blunt declaration that Congress intended to stand by the freed people and was prepared to use force on their behalf. The act further required each state to ratify the Fourteenth Amendment, thereby recognizing the freed people as citizens, and to call a constitutional convention whose delegates must be elected by all male voters including Blacks, but excluding certain categories of former rebels. The new constitutions that emerged from the conventions must then explicitly extend the franchise to Black men, who as an unstated corollary would become powerful political forces in all the southern states and majorities in three of them. Only once that was done would the states become eligible to again participate in the United States Congress. Until then, the existing civil governments in the former rebel states were to be treated as merely "provisional," and subject to federal authority to "abolish, modify, control, or supersede" them at any time. During the debate, the scholarly Rep. James A. Garfield, the future president, forcefully declared that the time for political conciliation was past: "We must compel obedience to the Union, and demand protection for its humblest citizen wherever the flag floats. The time has come when we must lay the heavy hand of the military authority upon these rebel communities, and hold them in its grasp till their madness is past."

Subsequent legislation required voters to swear under "ironclad" oath that they had neither held Confederate office nor given aid or comfort to the insurrection; it also gave military commanders the explicit authority to remove civilian officials, and made them responsible for registering voters and overseeing the elections to ensure that they were free of "restraint, fear, or the influence of fraud." This significantly strengthened the federal government's judicial hand in the South and reempowered the army to maintain law and order. Legislation was one thing, however; political will was another. Furious Democrats charged the Republicans with creating a military despotism in an effort to "Africanize" the South, a potent accusation in a country that reflexively feared both military rule and Black political power. Johnson denounced the measures as he had earlier ones, declaring that they were unconstitutional and vetoed all of them. Congress then repassed them over his veto by commanding majorities.

Also on that watershed day of March 2, Congress firmly cemented the power of Ulysses Grant with the passage of an act that required all presidential orders to the army to go through its commander—that is, Grant—whom the president could now neither fire nor reassign outside Washington without Senate permission. Still another measure enacted that day would soon have seismic ramifications, the highly controversial Tenure of Office Act, whose deceptively dry language declared that members of the cabinet could not be removed without the consent of the Senate, a provision specifically tailored to protect Secretary of War Edwin Stanton, Grant's ally and the only Radical left in the cabinet. Although superficially not a piece of Reconstruction legislation, it was a core part of Congress's struggle for power with the president, impeding his ability to thwart the army's implementation of Reconstruction. Put simply, Congress trusted Stanton and Grant to carry out its political will, and Johnson not at all. As expected, Johnson immediately vetoed these acts, too, but before the day was out he was overridden by both houses.

By seizing control of Reconstruction, Congress had resoundingly embraced Black suffrage and officeholding, both unimaginable before the war, and until now by no means foreordained. Although the Reconstruction Acts applied only to the South, it was clear that it would be only a matter of time before the northern states that still held back would have to enfranchise Blacks as well, a prospect that threatened white prerogatives everywhere, as well as the deepest fibers of the South's social fabric. Stevens and the rest of the Radical vanguard did not get everything they wanted, however. Congress declined to strengthen Blacks' freedom by guaranteeing them homesteads and free universal education through federal law, yielding to the seductively libertarian belief that once they had the vote they ought to be able to take responsibility for themselves without ongoing federal support. As Radical senator Richard Yates declared, "The ballot is the freedman's Moses."

Nor did Congress see fit to expand the occupation force in the South. The military now had to do much more with a lot less. Nearly four million freed people, not to mention hundreds of thousands of white Unionists, depended on the army to protect them, their property, and their vulnerable schools and churches. The army continued to hold a nominal monopoly of force in the South, but its power to wield that force inexorably diminished as volunteer units were mustered out of service. From more than one million men posted across the South in May 1865 the occupation force dropped to 87,000 by January 1866, more than half of whom were posted on the Mexican border and in the Far West, and to just over seventeen thousand by December. Only fifteen military posts remained in South Carolina, ten in North Carolina, six in Mississippi, and eight each in Georgia and Louisiana, with similar numbers in the other occupied states. Barely eight hundred soldiers attempted to police all of Alabama, and even fewer in Mississippi, down from almost eight thousand and more than nine thousand respectively a year earlier. The troops that remained were based around cities and railroad junctions, leaving loyalists in the hinterland largely unprotected. Significantly, the dispatch of virtually all the army's cavalry to the West further hobbled its ability to respond quickly to attacks, since mounted terrorists could always outrun infantry. As historian Gregory P. Downs has put it, "A patchwork occupation produced patchwork rights."

Grant was determined to do the best he could with what he had. When a reporter from the *New York Times* expressed the view that the rebel states ought to be speedily restored to the Union, Grant gruffly retorted that there was still much work to do in the South. The war was only over on the battlefield: politically, victory was not yet assured. The South, he said, "will have to take the [Fourteenth] Amendment, and manhood suffrage besides." The will of Congress, he had come to believe, now embodied the true spirit of the nation for which he and many hundreds of thousands of northern men had fought. Scorning the president, he named trusted generals to head the newly created departments in the South and gave them considerable latitude to enforce the law. Although their degree of personal commitment to the freed people varied, they removed disloyal local officials, ignored Black Codes, banned whipping, prosecuted crimes against Blacks, and jailed lawbreakers in army brigs. Philip Sheridan, the most radical of Grant's top lieutenants, acted with exceptional vigor in New Orleans, where he ousted officials who had failed to stop the 1866 massacre or to prosecute its perpetrators, including the mayor, a local judge, twenty-two aldermen, the city's attorney, its financial officers, and treasurer, and a judge who refused to let Blacks testify in court. He also desegregated the city's streetcars by fiat, warning their operators that if they discriminated against Black passengers they would be barred from the streets. "It is just the thing," Grant wrote approvingly. When Sheridan came under political attack for his boldness Grant praised him. "He shows himself the same fearless, true man that he did in the field," Grant told Washburne. Piecemeal though the army's efforts were, they helped to cement the loyalty of freed people by demonstrating that in a landscape of deepening menace the federal government offered their only hope of safety and opportunity.

Emboldened by the passage of protective legislation, grassroots activism among Southern Blacks surged. Before the war, no political voices could be heard in the slave states except those of slavery's advocates. Even in the North, only the words of Frederick Douglass and a handful of other Black abolitionists reached the ears of white Americans, most of whom greeted them with apathy or disdain. Now the voices of the once enslaved and the free-but-ignored multiplied, filling the air and the newspapers with their personal and political hopes, their demands for fair treatment, education, and safety. They exploded in a cacophony of Black rights conventions, mutual aid societies, benevolent associations, Masonic clubs, newspaper-reading circles, and educational organizations. The illiterate flocked to schools, and the newly literate instructed others. Petitioners called for the repeal of the Black Codes and the enfranchisement of freedmen. Cotton pickers agitated against abusive overseers, longshoremen struck in southern ports, workers demanded fair wages. Protesters defied the segregation of railroads, streetcars, and steamships. Black soldiers paraded, Black newspapers were founded, Black entrepreneurs founded businesses.

Everywhere natural leaders emerged from Black churches, from Freedmen's Bureau's schools, from long-submerged Black communities where leadership had never been permitted before. Some had always been free, others free for only a few months. Many had acquired a degree of literacy before the war, often surreptitiously, by puzzling out discarded newspapers or white children's books. Others were unlettered, which was hardly a barrier to public life in a nation that had produced unschooled autodidacts such as Abraham Lincoln and Andrew Johnson. They organized churches and schools, Union Leagues, Republican clubs, militia companies, and lobbying groups, and in time, by the hundreds and eventually the thousands, stepped into the political arena as constables, magistrates, election officials, county clerks, state legislators, and national officials. "The best of us are ignorant, but some know more about things than the others," Thomas Allen, a Baptist minister, who organized for the Republican Party in Georgia, told members of Congress. "In my county the colored people came to me for instructions, and I gave them the best instructions I could. I took the New York Tribune and other papers, and in that way I found out a great deal, and I told them whatever I thought was right. I said to them that I thought they had been freed by the Yankees and Union men, and I thought they ought to vote with them."

These new men were remarkably diverse in their origins. Benjamin Turner, a former slave, ran a stable and an omnibus line in Selma, Alabama, and would eventually be elected to Congress. Shandy Jones, an entrepreneurial barber and one of the few prewar free blacks in Tuscaloosa, would be elected to the state House of Representatives. Robert Smalls, an enslaved Charleston harbor pilot who during the war had seized a Confederate ship and turned it over to the U.S. Navy, founded the first Republican club in South Carolina. In Georgia, it was said, virtually every AME churchman was engaged in political organizing, while at one point tobacco factories in Richmond, Virginia, had to close because so many Black workers were attending a Republican convention. Remarked one disconcerted white conservative, freed people seemed virtually possessed by a "speech-making mania." Most dramatic was Blacks' universal rush to register and vote. Within the space of just a few months, as elections neared for the states' mandated constitutional conventions, more than 600,000 Black men registered across the South. In South Carolina alone, more than eighty thousand men registered—94 percent of those eligible—surpassing the total of white voters by about eighteen thousand. In Alabama, Black voters outnumbered whites 89,000 to 74,000. In all, possibly as much as 96 percent of Black men throughout the South registered.

Emerging new voters coalesced with three other groups to form the rudimentary foundations of the Republican Party: transplanted northern blacks, native white Radicals, and newly arrived northern whites, many of them war veterans who had decided to make new lives in the South. These, too, were remarkably varied groups whose members did not always fit neatly into conventional categories. In South Carolina alone, the erudite, British-accented Robert Brown Elliott came from Boston to edit the *South Carolina Leader,* one of the first newspapers in the South to be published by Blacks; Robert C. De Large and Martin Delany came as agents of the Freedmen's Bureau; and F. L. Cardozo, a graduate of the University of Glasgow, came as a representative of the American Missionary Association to found one of the largest Black schools in the state.

Native white Republicans, known rudely but universally as "scalawags," were derided by conservatives as "white trash." The pro-Klan *Atlanta Constitution* crudely defined the "scalawag" as "a low, worthless fellow; a scape-grace. It is particularly expressive in these degenerate days, when the scum of society is drifting to the top." In fact, they came from every layer of southern society. Some indeed were poor men who before the war had been excluded from politics by the planter elite, others were opportunists, while still others saw the Republican Party as the engine of long overdue economic change that could transform the South's ruined economy by developing manufacturing on the northern model. They ranged from Simeon Corley of South Carolina, a tailor who had advocated for abolition even before the war and declared that the freedman was "worth a thousand times more as the State's voter and defender" than he ever was as a slave; to Jefferson Allgood, a former Mississippi slave trader, now a Republican, who declared that "the Negroes" were "a much better people than they have credit for; I have bought and sold hundreds of them"; to the hardscrabble John Stephens of North Carolina, who had served in the Confederate army and after it became a fiercely combative organizer for the Union League; to James L. Alcorn, the owner of the largest plantation in the Yazoo

Delta region of Mississippi; and Gen. James Longstreet, a corps commander under Robert E. Lee during the war and afterward the Republican police chief of New Orleans. More typical of working-class "scalawags" was a white Louisiana woman who wrote to President Grant's wife, Julia, that she had clung to the Confederacy to the end but had since come to feel the result of the war had been God's will and that it was now her duty to "harmonize" with it: "I am glad that the Federal arms were triumphant, that the black was freed, and more than all, that the poor white has been liberated from a bondage which he hardly knew shackled him." In a similar vein, the *Knoxville Whig* urged whites to see Black men as their natural political allies, predicting, "The slaves, since they have been allowed to vote will vote with our honest, poor white laboring men to put down the old slave aristocracy."

Not all southern white Republicans advocated for Black equality, but most pragmatically accommodated themselves to it, recognizing that their own route to political power, indeed their political survival, depended on a biracial alliance. Longstreet told the *New Orleans Times,* in June 1867, "I shall be happy to work in any harness that promises relief to our distressed people and harmony to the nation. It matters not whether I bear the mantle of Mr. Davis or the mantle of Mr. Sumner." Many, sometimes to their own surprise, overcame generations of ingrained prejudice as they learned to work together with the former slaves. Of the former slaves, one white Georgia Republican wrote to Thaddeus Stevens, "Being elevated as they have been to a position almost equal to their former masters one might suppose that it is not fully appreciated by them, but I tell you in all candor, there is a self-respect and a disposition exhibited on their part to do good which seems almost incredible under the circumstances." (Blacks also struggled with racial mistrust: when one Black speaker at a political rally in South Carolina declared that he wanted no white man on the platform, he was chided by others, "If dere skins IS white dey may have principle.")

Although the enemies of Reconstruction saved much of their harshest opprobrium for the northern men they derided as "carpetbaggers"—"vampires" and "burlesque upon humanity," in the words of one southern politician—comparatively few of them fit the stereotype of predatory opportunists out to squeeze fortunes from the ruined and helpless South. One particularly nasty piece of doggerel heard in Louisiana ran like this:

> *I am a carpet-bagger—*
> *I've a brother scalawag—*
> *Come South to boast and swagger*
> *With an empty carpetbag,*
> *To rob the whites of Green-backs*
> *And with the blacks go bunk*
> *And change my empty satchel*
> *For a full sole-leather trunk.*
> *I'm some on constitution,*
> *For a late rebellious state,*
> *And I'm some on persecution,*
> *Of disloyal men I hate;*
> *I'm some at nigger meetings*
> *When white folks ain't about,*
> *And I'm some among the nigger gals*
> *When their marms don't know they're out.*

Many newly arrived northerners were young war veterans who had fought in the South, others were lawyers and doctors, churchmen who represented missionary organizations, and others idealistic teachers—the majority of them women—who went south to serve in the new freedmen's schools, often at great personal risk. Laura Towne, a medical student from Pittsburgh, Pennsylvania, devoted thirty-eight years of her life to teaching Black children on St. Helena Island, South Carolina, sometimes paying fellow teachers from her own pocket when salaries did not arrive on time. Marshall Twitchell, a veteran from Vermont, became a dynamic Republican organizer and eventually state senator in Louisiana's Red River Valley. Arad Lakin, the former chaplain for an Indiana regiment and an evangelical pastor hardened by work in New York's Five Points slums, helped build the Methodist Episcopal Church in northern Alabama and endured savage political attacks as president of the state university in Tuscaloosa. Albion W. Tourgée, a wounded war veteran and lawyer from Ohio, moved to North Carolina to start a business but, appalled by the violence visited upon the freed people, threw himself into the cause of equal rights and eventually became one of the most aggressive judges in the South during campaigns against the Ku Klux Klan.

Men, and a few women, from all these groups coalesced in the militant Union League. The league was founded in the North during the war and by 1867 it had taken on a dynamic role among the Southern poor, serving both as an agent of civic education and as an armature for the molding of the Republican Party in states where it had never previously existed. Although the league was nominally integrated, most branches were tacitly segregated, while overall membership was heavily Black, typically reaching 80 or 90 percent in most localities, a disproportion that tended to grow over time. At weekly league meetings held in churches, schools, and homes, or in the open countryside, members learned parliamentary procedure, and discussed everything from lawmaking, taxes, workers' rights, contracts, and literacy to presidential impeachment, and raised money for the building of schools and other benevolent causes. Where Leaguers felt endangered, membership was secret, but elsewhere they wore uniforms and marched boldly in parades with flags and fife and drum corps. By July 1867, the league had enrolled an estimated 300,000 members in thousands of branches across the South, and it continued to grow. One Alabama organizer claimed that he was recruiting Talladega Blacks into the league at a rate of about one hundred per week, and another that he had organized eleven branches in three weeks, averaging fifty members in each. The league represented precisely what conservatives most feared: a dynamic Black political movement allied with Radical whites and determined to revolutionize government in the South. Klan night riders repeatedly cited its very existence as a rationale for their campaigns of terror. As J. C. Lester put it in his account of the order's origins, the league was a "desperate" organization composed of "the disorderly element" of the Black population and controlled by the worst sort of unprincipled white man, race traitors who "literally breathed out slaughter."

Meanwhile, in Washington, a perilous *pas de trois* was being enacted as Johnson, Grant, and Secretary of War Stanton maneuvered around each other in Washington's steambath summer heat. Johnson had long made clear that he considered Stanton an obstacle that he wanted to remove from the path of southern conciliation. Grant, for his part, reminded the president that the Tenure of Office Act prevented him from firing Stanton, and warned that "common sense, and the mass of loyal people" wanted Stanton to remain in place. Johnson ignored him. On August 5, he ordered Stanton to resign. Stanton refused to vacate his office. Grant saw his job in soldier's terms, as a matter of duty to the nation and to Congress. "I feel the same obligation to stand at my post that I did whilst there were rebel armies in the field to contend with," he told Elihu Washburne. Johnson next decided to co-opt Grant. On August 11, he cleverly told Grant that he would only *suspend* Stanton, not fire him, thereby evading the strictures of the Tenure of Office Act, and asked Grant to step in as "interim" secretary of war. Johnson was gambling that Grant could be tamed by pulling him into the executive branch. Grant, for his own part, reluctantly agreed to enter the cabinet, surmising that if he didn't do so Johnson would appoint a malleable Democrat instead, but he insisted on retaining his office as commander of the army, the first time that a person held both jobs simultaneously. When Grant was in place, Johnson ordered him to fire Sheridan, who had infuriated Louisiana's conservatives, and replace him with Gen. Winfield S. Hancock, another popular war hero but a conservative congenial to the president's views. Grant protested that Sheridan's removal would encourage "the unreconstructed element" in the South and spur them to further defiance. He knew that as a member of the cabinet, he was subject to Johnson's will. But in a smoldering letter he repeated his confidence in Sheridan, adding, "I would not venture to write as I do if I did not see great danger to the quiet and prosperity of the country in the course being pursued." He made his point by ordering Hancock not to reappoint the men Sheridan had fired. However, Hancock succeeded in weakening the freed people's fragile safety net by shifting troops from Texas's populated east to the Indian frontier.

Never a natural politician, Grant found this dance morally exhausting and emotionally depressing. To Gen. William T. Sherman, he confessed in September, "All the romance of feeling that men in high places are above personal considerations and act only from motives of pure patriotism, and for the general good of the public has been destroyed. An inside view proves too truly very much the reverse." Yet, in spite of himself, Grant was learning to fuse his instinct for command with the subtler arts of the bureaucratic battlefield. He ordered his field commanders to protect Black voters and to ensure that no disqualified ex-Confederates were allowed to cast ballots. Orders from Washington did not guarantee peace, however. Just in North Carolina, troops had to be dispatched to Fayetteville to keep order; whites assaulted freedmen in Sampson County; a Republican candidate in Elizabeth City was severely caned; in Kinston there were reports of a shadowy new organization calling itself the "Ku-Klux" posting menacing images meant to scare Black voters; and in Caswell County the Radical white candidate for the state Senate felt so threatened that he asked for an army escort while he campaigned. Similar reports flowed into Grant's office from every former Confederate state. In the face of intimidation, however, Blacks almost universally spurned the condescending appeals of their former masters: where they could vote, they voted solidly for Republicans.

The elections were seismic. For the first time in history Black Americans were elected wholesale to public office. Between November 1867 and the following June every southern state convened a convention to rewrite its constitution to conform to the new order and, collectively, elected Black men to more than one-quarter of the seats. Over the coming months, conventions reinvented the South. Despite sometimes bitter floor debates over questions of social equality between the races, most of the conventions adopted extraordinarily progressive new constitutions establishing the South's first public schools, sanitariums, orphan asylums, and systems of relief for the indigent poor. Flogging as punishment was banned, property qualifications for voting, officeholding, and jury service were jettisoned, and in most states the Declaration of Independence's language of human equality was written into law. Florida even set aside two seats in its state legislature for Seminole Indians.

Sneered at by Conservatives as the "Congo convention," South Carolina's convention—one of two in which the majority of delegates were Black, the other being Louisiana's—banned imprisonment for debt, made discrimination in public accommodations illegal, and for the first time legalized divorce and gave married

women control over their own property. North Carolina's constitution, largely crafted by the former Ohioan Albion Tourgée, for
the first time apportioned state Senate seats according to population
rather than wealth, required that state Supreme Court justices face
the voters every eight years, and embraced a new penal code that
emphasized rehabilitation over punishment. Tourgée, like other
idealists, saw the moment as a revolutionary one that would transform the known political world. "Shall the new state have an Oligarchy or a Republic? An Aristocracy or a Democracy?" he asked
the voters. "Muscle is no longer bought and sold, nor is brain made
the subject of barter. Wealth is no longer the great I Am, nor manhood a political cipher."

Southern elections were an almost unbroken panorama of victories for Radical Republicans, as Black turnout ranged from 70 percent to as much as 85 percent in the states of the old Confederacy.
Although native whites and northern transplants dominated Republican Party lists, Black law officers, school board officials, and state
legislators were elected in a stunning demonstration of the new balance of power. The year's northern state elections seemed to take
place in a different universe. There the Republicans lost support
in almost all the twenty states that cast votes between March and
November. Voters in Ohio, Minnesota, and Kansas turned back
attempts to legalize Black suffrage, and in Ohio and New Jersey
newly elected legislatures even tried to rescind the earlier approval
of the Fourteenth Amendment. Fears grew among Republicans that
the Union's soldiers might have won the war on the battlefield but
were now about to lose it at the ballot box.

In an extraordinarily violent State of the Union message on
December 3, Johnson attacked the mere concept of Black enfranchisement in language that echoed the utterances of the most hostile former Confederates. He demanded the repeal of legislation
that placed southern states under "the domination of military
masters," claiming that congressional "usurpation" had bound the
states "hand and foot in absolute slavery" under "a strange and hostile power more unlimited and more likely to be abused than any
other now known among civilized men." African Americans, he
charged, were neither morally nor mentally fitted for the vote. In all
the world's nations, he said, "Negroes have shown less capacity for

government than any other race." On the contrary, "wherever they have been left to their own devices they have shown a constant tendency to relapse into barbarism." To save the Union as the Founders intended it to be, the southern states must speedily be restored to their rightful place in it. The alternative, he warned, was the dread specter of "Negro supremacy." Southern reactionaries couldn't have asked for more encouragement.

The Republicans in Washington, not to mention those struggling to thrive in the southern states, knew that if Reconstruction was to succeed in the face of such defiance, or even just *proceed*, it was imperative to secure the White House in next year's elections. They bruited various names as their prospective candidate for the presidency: Supreme Court chief justice Salmon P. Chase, or perhaps the outspoken Radical senator Benjamin F. Wade of Ohio. But there was only one man who commanded the confidence of the nation: Ulysses S. Grant. Carl Schurz, soon to be a candidate for the Senate in Missouri, pronounced his nomination a certainty, while *New York Times* editor Henry J. Raymond, a stalwart of the party's conservative wing, could hardly contain his enthusiasm, telling Grant that he already had the nomination in the bag. "The people want a MAN," Raymond declared. "They dare not and cannot nominate anybody else. All you have to do is *stand still*."

3

A MONSTER TERRIBLE BEYOND QUESTION

Wisely and humanely, or roughly
and cruelly, the work was done.

—JOHN MORTON, KLANSMAN

On April 12, 1864, a Confederate cavalry force commanded by Nathan Bedford Forrest surprised the federal garrison of Fort Pillow, Tennessee, overlooking the Mississippi River north of Memphis. The fort's garrison included fewer than six hundred men from two Black artillery units and the 13th Tennessee Cavalry, a white Unionist regiment. Oriented toward the river, the fort was hard to defend from the landward side, which faced broken land that gave cover to the attackers. Under a white flag, the Confederates, between 1,500 and 2,000 in number, filtered through the ravines and gulches until they were just below the fort's gun emplacements. Then, crying, "No quarter!" they sprang over the earthen defenses. Soldiers who tried to surrender were shot, hacked with sabers, and beaten to death with rifle butts. Wounded men were murdered where they lay. Several were burned to death in huts. A Confederate trooper, Achilles Clark, wrote to his sisters, "The poor deluded negroes would run up to our men, fall upon their knees with uplifted hands scream for mercy but they were ordered to their feet and then shot down. Blood, human blood stood about in pools and brains could have been gathered up in any quantity." Of the fort's 585 defenders, at least 277 were killed, an overall death rate of 48 percent, astronomically higher than any other battle in the war. But of the 269 Black soldiers, 195 were killed, a rate of 72 percent. The "battle" was in fact a white massacre of disarmed Black men, the worst wartime atrocity ever committed on American soil, apart from the Indian wars. Forrest boasted to his superiors, "It is hoped that these facts will demonstrate to the Northern people that the Negro soldier cannot cope with Southerners." Challenged after Robert E. Lee's surrender to defend what he had done, he replied, "When I went into the war, I meant to fight. Fighting means killing." Anyway, he added, the fort was full of "niggers and deserters from our army." Three years later he was recruited to become the first Grand Wizard of the Ku Klux Klan.

Forrest was a master of surprise and deception, of the quick strike, the "Wizard of the Saddle," as he was sometimes called. He was in many respects the opposite of a disciplined West Pointer. Although he was intolerant of insubordination among his own men, he ignored conventional tactics, disdained drill, and focused instead on charging and fighting, and the clever deployment of his often modest numbers so that they had the greatest impact where his enemies least expected it. He was an offensive fighter who never failed, when he had the choice, to take the initiative and deliver the first blow. "He struck as lightning strikes, and his tactics were as incalculable as those of the electric fluid and as mysterious to the enemy," an admirer wrote. He went into the war a private and came out of it a lieutenant general.

In private life he was by instinct a brawler who pretended to a degree of social polish that he never possessed. Lee Meriwether, the son of one of his closest associates, remembered him as a bully who menaced even friends who crossed him. Like many southerners of his type, he was hypersensitive about matters of personal honor and "never content unless he was whipping somebody." Raised poor on the Tennessee frontier, unschooled, and indeed semiliterate to judge by his scanty writings, he nonetheless possessed an entrepreneurial instinct that made him a rich man before he was out of his thirties, as well as a modestly prominent public figure in prewar Memphis. He traded in cattle, horses, and real estate, but his forte was human beings, slaves, whom he bought cheap in the hinterland and sold high to planters. In the late 1850s, his net income from slave trading alone was between $50,000 and $96,000, enough to make him one of the wealthiest men in Memphis.

After the war, with slavery dead and his fortune gone, Forrest shifted from one shaky business venture to another. Engulfed in debt, he auctioned off his plantations piecemeal and by 1866 he was sharecropping land he had once owned. He tried operating a sawmill, wholesaling commodities, selling other men's cotton. He tried forming a fire insurance company, but it failed. Then he tried promoting a railroad from Memphis to Little Rock, for which he hired a thousand Black laborers from the Freedmen's Bureau. In the summer of 1867, he was trying to sell paving bonds for the city of Memphis. But he still put up a bold front. At forty-six, he remained a commanding figure, muscular and tall, decisive, and endowed with dark gray eyes that emanated a penetrating gaze from beneath bushy black brows.

Sometime toward the end of 1867 Forrest's life suddenly took on new purpose. He had certainly heard rumors of the Ku-Klux as it spread across Middle Tennessee. The Klan had already outgrown its jokey origin and it needed a charismatic and seasoned commander who fit its hardening political ambitions and its growing taste for violence. The precise sequence of events that led Forrest to the Klan remains vague. He may possibly have been recruited in Memphis by former general George Gordon, one of the Pulaski men. It seems certain that he traveled to Nashville where he was aware that a gathering of Klan leaders was under way. There he made contact with John Morton, his wartime artillery chief. According to Morton, he said, "John, I hear this Kuklux Klan is organized in Nashville, and I know you are in it. I want to join." Morton drove Forrest to a secluded spot outside town, administered a preliminary oath, and told him to go to a room at the Klan's favored hostelry, the Maxwell House, where more would be revealed. By that night, Morton says, Forrest was "a full-fledged clansman," and was soon elected "Grand Wizard of the Invisible Empire." An eyewitness to a meeting at the Memphis home of Minor Meriwether, a wartime aide to Forrest and the Klan's "Supreme Counsellor," recalled seeing Forrest, former Confederate Tennessee governor Isham Harris, and former Confederate general John Gordon, now the Grand Dragon of Georgia, agreeing that the only way to save the South was by terrifying "carpetbaggers" and Blacks, and killing them if necessary, to prevent them from voting. Interrogated by a congressional committee in 1871, Forrest freely admitted to having been the Klan's commander, though he muddied his answers to nearly everything else the congressmen asked.

Forrest's name had a martial potency that electrified angry war veterans and declassed slaveowners who dreamed of recapturing political power from the ashes of defeat. In years to come such "Redeemers," as they called themselves, would view their ambition as a quasi-religious mission of "Redemption." The South was awash in fear, Blacks' fear of white violence, of course, as well as their fear that vengeful Democrats would somehow reinstitute slavery; but also whites' pervasive fear of Blacks, fear of the uncertain future, fear of change, fear of impoverishment. Recalled one North Carolinian, "Law was not enforced, crime was common, neither life nor property was secure, desperadoes and ruffians paraded the streets day and night with a Colt's revolver in one pocket and a bottle of mean whiskey in the other, carousals and broils were the result of every public gathering." It was a climate in which the Klan flourished like a jungle growth. Yet, as late as the spring of 1868, mentions of the Klan were still rare in the press. In April, the *New York Tribune* could still describe it vaguely as "a secret organization whose purposes are unknown" made up of obscure men who threaten Union men, and speculate that "The name Kuk-klux is said to be derived from the noise of the cocking of a rifle."

Just how much of the Klan's spectacular expansion in the coming months can be credited to Forrest is unknowable, however. It's possible that he served less as a field commander than as the Klan's paramount organizer, renewing old wartime contacts, cultivating new ones provided by the well-connected John Gordon and others, like a sort of reactionary Johnny Appleseed planting the germs of new dens wherever he went. As a cover for his work, he was appointed the "General Traveling Agent" for the Memphis-based Southern Life Insurance Company, which also employed John Gordon to head its Atlanta division, later hired the highly political former general Wade Hampton of South Carolina as one of its chief officers, and named the Confederacy's chief executive Jefferson Davis its titular president. Wherever Forrest went, the Klan seemed magically to appear. When he visited Atlanta, a friendly local news-paper reported that the "Mystic Order of the Ku Klux Klan" was prospering, and advised its members to be "wise, cool, calm, cautious, wary, and brave." Within days of Forrest's arrival in Columbus, Georgia, in March 1868, strange signs and drawings of skulls, coffins, and skeletons appeared scrawled on the homes of Union men, and the local tax assessor, a Republican, found a bag of bones attached to his door with a warning to "prepare for sudden death." An editorial in the *Columbus Sun* named several prominent Union men and declared, "The Kuk-Klux-Klan has arrived, and *woe to the desperate.* . . . Something terrible floats on the breeze."

The imminent prospect of freedmen voting loomed ogrelike in the feverish imaginations of white southerners. And the words of egalitarians such as Thaddeus Stevens chilled them: "Let him who is the most worthy, who climbs the highest upon the ladder of merit, of science, of intellect, of morality—let him be the ruler, according to law, of all his sluggard neighbors, no matter what may be their color, no matter who they are, whether they be men of nobility or whether they be of common rank." Putting an even finer point on what lay in store, Philip Sheridan, Grant's outspoken viceroy in Louisiana, told an Ohio newspaper: "It is too late to go backward. The negro has been admitted to the ballot box. All the power on earth cannot keep it from him now. He has not only been taught to *read,* but to *vote* also. He can unlearn neither the one nor the other." With so many whites disenfranchised, registrars enrolled an astonishing 703,000 new Black southern voters in 1867, making them a majority in Alabama, Florida, Louisiana, Mississippi, and South Carolina, and a significant minority in every other former rebel state.

Their numbers told at the ballot box, as voters approved constitutions that opened government to the masses. Rarely if ever had any Americans demonstrated such soaring hope as African Americans now did that democracy would redeem the suffering of generations. "In defiance of fatigue, hardship, hunger, and threats of employers," Blacks flocked en masse to the polls, an Ohio newspaperman wrote on Election Day. Not one in fifty wore an "unpatched garment," few possessed a pair of shoes, yet for hours they stood in line in a "pitiless storm." Why? "The hunger to have the same chances as the white men." In North Carolina and other states, Republicans swept virtually all the statewide offices, winning majorities in the state legislature as well as ratification of the new constitutions. Conservatives were in shock. In Montgomery, Alabama, a meeting of leading white citizens from around the state announced a day of fasting and prayer "to Almighty God to deliver the people of Alabama from the horrors of negro domination."

During the ensuing months, with Forrest, Gordon, and a clutch of other former Confederate officers at its helm, the Klan expanded rapidly from its epicenter in Tennessee. On March 5, a member of that state's legislature reported in trepidation that "an organized body of men, who, without provocation, in violation of the law— seemingly desperate in purpose—are scouring the country by night, carrying dismay and terror to all." Public sentiment, by its silence, not only was encouraging them, "but in many forms affords direct sympathy." The Klan seemed to be everywhere. Menacing notices appeared tacked onto city halls, post offices, Unionists' homes, the doors of isolated cabins. Night-riding, threats, floggings, and the intimidation of Black voters spread over West Tennessee. In Maury County and Marshall County, in Rutherford and Cannon counties, in Humphreys County west of Nashville, there were sudden spikes in violence. In Pulaski, Klansmen who didn't even bother to disguise themselves killed one of the town's few outspoken Black leaders, Orange Jones; four days later, they seized five men from a home, flogged them, and threatened to kill them for voting the Radical ticket. The pro-Klan *Nashville Union* blithely declared on its front page that a Black Union Leaguer who had led an unarmed march through the town of Gallatin "deserves to be killed." A Union veteran named Graham was driven out of Mount Pleasant, where he was mobbed by Klansmen led by the town constable and given five minutes to leave under threat of immediate execution. At Waverly, another Unionist who had fled at the start of the war and returned to reclaim his farm was tied with a rope around his neck, kicked, beaten, dragged up and down a rocky streambed, and left comatose. At Memphis, Klansmen in full regalia openly rode up to police headquarters and challenged the police to arrest them, while the pro-Klan *Memphis Avalanche* welcomed the Klan to town.

The Klan was no longer a phenomenon confined to Tennessee.

In Augusta, Georgia, a public rally of Klansmen cheered for Jeff Davis and booed "The Star-Spangled Banner." A Republican meeting at Valdosta was broken up by a Klan mob, who had placed powder under the building where a Republican congressional candidate was to speak. In Tuscaloosa, Alabama, a Black voting registrar was taken away by robed Klansmen who, it was reported, "outraged his person in an infamous manner." In the *Tuskaloosa Monitor*, Alabama Klansman and editor Ryland Randolph announced with undisguised relish that "three notably offensive negro men were dragged out of their beds, escorted to the old bone-yard and thrashed in the regular ante-bellum style until their unnatural nigger pride had a tumble and humbleness to the white man reigned supreme." Wrote Forrest's close ally John Morton, "The news of the good effects flew from community to community, and everywhere the law-abiding element saw the means of substituting order and peace for the injustice and indignities so long borne." By the "law-abiding element" Morton of course meant the Ku Klux Klan.

Morton viewed Klansmen almost mystically as "the silent representatives of the white man's will." The mere knowledge that the Klan was present in a town was sometimes enough to scare people into silence. Their appearance was all the more intimidating because it was unpredictable. Raiders might strike suddenly at a single home, or spread out through an entire isolated Black community, dragging out every known Radical to be flogged in the public highway. Or they might appear in ghostly crowds on the roads, seemingly everywhere all at once, in thundering bands of a hundred or more. Wrote Morton, "Those who advocated and practiced social equality of the races, and incited hostilities of the blacks against the whites, were given a single notice to depart in haste. Wisely and humanely, or roughly and cruelly, the work was done," wrote Morton.

Despite later denials, the Klan's intentions were always made crystal clear. Asked why he had joined, recruit Thomas Willeford replied, "They told me it was to damage the Republican Party as much as they could—burning, stealing, whipping niggers, and such things as that." Sometime in 1868, a new Prescript added a number of "interrogatories" for prospective members: "Are you now or have you ever been a member of the Radical Republican party?"; "Are you opposed to the principles and policy of the Radical party?";

"Did you belong to the federal army during the late war, and fight against the South?"; "Are you opposed to negro equality, both social and political?"; "Are you in favor of a white man's government in this country?"; "Are you in favor of the re-enfranchisement and emancipation of the white men of the South, and the restitution of the Southern people to all their rights, alike proprietary, civil, and political?" Inductees were also warned that any member who dared reveal or betray the order's secrets "shall suffer the extreme penalty of the law"—in other words, death. Initiation could be very elaborate. When James Boyd, a North Carolina lawyer, joined, members stood in a wide circle around him then at a signal "rushed upon him with curious noises, and rubbed him with their horns," then fell back while the chief administered the oath. Boyd further pledged "never to vote for any man for office who was in favor of the civil or political advancement of the Negro race, and to resist by force the civil or political advancement of the Negro."

Meanwhile, in Washington, the first impeachment of a president in American history had at last come to pass after months of jockeying at both ends of Pennsylvania Avenue. Andrew Johnson had defied the Tenure of Office Act in August by firing Secretary of War Stanton and replacing the military commanders in the South with men loyal to himself. On January 10, the Senate's Military Affairs Committee ordered Johnson to restore Stanton to his former office. Four days later, Ulysses Grant told the president that he could not and would not continue as interim secretary of war against the Senate's wishes and vacated the office to make way for Stanton's return. Two days after that, Stanton took over once again with his customary imperious flourish.

Then, on February 21, Johnson suspended Stanton *again* and appointed a pliable replacement, Gen. Lorenzo Thomas. The Senate immediately passed a resolution denying that Johnson had the power to do what he had done. In the House, Stevens roared to his colleagues, "Didn't I tell you so? If you don't kill the beast it will kill you." Johnson, meanwhile, tried without success to persuade William T. Sherman to take *Grant's* job as commander of the army. Although Sherman was unfriendly to Reconstruction, he was profoundly loyal to Grant, who had rescued him from oblivion early in the Civil War and repeatedly promoted him to higher command. Grant's anger fairly boiled from the pages of a long letter he addressed to the president on January 28, essentially calling Johnson a manipulative shyster, caustically declaring, "I can but regard this whole matter, from the beginning to the end, as an attempt to involve me in the resistance of law." (Stevens was impressed: Grant "is a bolder man than I thought him," he reflected.) Two days later, the Senate voted not to sustain Stanton's suspension and the Joint Committee on Reconstruction reported out an impeachment resolution, accusing Johnson of "high crimes and misdemeanors."

The Tenure of Office Act was essentially a legal trip wire. Stevens believed that impeachment existed to punish an official not only for crimes that would be actionable in a court but for political malfeasance that included the president's unilateral Reconstruction policy, his high-handed pardoning of rebel leaders, and his disregard for the rights of the freed people. "Andrew Johnson has succeeded to the bad eminence once occupied by Jefferson Davis," fulminated the *New York Tribune,* the primary mouthpiece for Radical opinion. "One was the apostle of secession. The other is the chief adversary of Reconstruction. One was the advocate of war. The other is the promoter of an anarchy which is worse than war, the fomenter of hostility more bitter and dangerous than that which animates soldiers in the open field."

Stevens was dying. Tortured by chronic rheumatism and suffering from a painful edema, his body was giving way. Unable to haul himself up the Capitol's steps, he had to be carried in a chair by a pair of muscular young men. (He was heard to jokingly ask them one day, "Who will be so good to me and take me up in their strong arms when you two mighty men are gone?") On February 24, calling Johnson "a detestable tyrant," he asserted that the president had shown "open evidence of his wicked determination to subvert the laws of his country." Beyond the legal mechanics of impeachment, however, soared Stevens's vision of a nation freed from racial bigotry, which he believed must rise from the wreckage of the old— essentially a second American revolution, one that could only be carried forward after Johnson had been removed. "We are not now merely expounding a government; we are building one," he told the House. "We are making a nation."

That vision was precisely the one that the Klan sought to prevent from ever coming to fruition. In March, the Klan made clear to Stevens that it was paying close attention to what was happening on Capitol Hill. He received two bizarre hand-printed letters filled with the Klan's trademark mystification and menace. (The language of the first of these, oddly enough, hinted that the writer had somehow encountered the Thai language, of all things):

16   To the veiled Brother hood of Sub Div   16
Kala Sokkaraja ++++
Somdetch Phra Paramender
Maha Mongkut
          Phra Kodom−−−−+.
The warning has been served thrice
No more shall we delay.
Blood Blood, Blood Thrice.
     By ord.   G.C.C.   KKK
16   Dark Moo moon   16
          Bloody month Silent hour.
     Thrice have we called.
                    Grave Mound.
                    No 391
+++   K.K.K.   +++!!!!
X *! *** !!   12 East
The dark and bloody moon is fast approaching
     L.H.I.S.
By command Great Grand Cyclops.
     K.K.K.
Your doom is sealed!!!!!
Prepare thy soul for its swift fight. The bony finger has
Touched your pillow, nothing can change its decree.
     H.K.3.0.7.,
Sub R.T. and Bearer of Diadem

A second message, a few weeks later, was less cryptic:

Thaddeus Stevens
Thou hast eaten the bread of wickedness, and drunk the wine of violence. Thou hast sown to the wind, thou shalt reap the

whirlwind in the moon's last quarter. Thy end is nigh, the last
warning

By order of the RHP of the
Ku Klux Klan

Stevens shrugged the letters off. He was not easily frightened.
And now, with death imminent, there was nothing the Klan could
do to him that his own body was not likely to do first. Under his
direction, eleven charges were drawn up accusing Johnson of having
violated the Tenure of Office Act and the Constitution, conspired
to prevent Stanton from holding his office, and ignored the will of
Congress. Johnson, for his part, maintained that nothing he had
done rose to the level of misbehavior that justified impeachment.
His allies, nearly all Democrats by this point, further contended
that when Johnson attacked Congress he was merely exercising his
freedom of speech. They argued—an assertion that would crucially
influence some Republican senators—that if a president could be
impeached for violating the Tenure of Office Act then Congress
could pass any kind of unconstitutional law and that a president
could be impeached simply for testing its constitutionality.

To an admiring journalist Stevens looked "strong enough to live
as long as a hemlock which never dies until its sap is dead." But his
once robust voice failed him. Although Stevens had hoped to deliver
the opening argument, he barely achieved a whisper. He handed
over the prosecution to his fellow Radical Benjamin F. Butler of
Massachusetts, who in the words of one observer was "impossible to
embarrass, bold to any length in attack, [and] wily to an extreme."
A former Democrat, Butler had nominated Jefferson Davis for
president at their party's 1860 convention, but later embraced the
cause of emancipation and civil rights, declaring, "We spurn the
dogma that this is a white man's government." Always a populist,
he was also an early and ardent advocate for the eight-hour workday
and for women's rights. Johnson's defense was led by the statuesque
Henry Stanbery, who had resigned as attorney general on March 12
to defend the president. Although Stanbery was a Republican, he
was the kind that ex-Confederates could happily live with, having
successfully argued *Milligan,* in 1866, which held that military tribunals were illegal where civil courts were in operation. He had

followed that with two more recent suits—*Mississippi v. Johnson* and *Georgia v. Stanton*—which further inhibited federal courts from enforcing Reconstruction measures. Like Johnson, he regarded the Reconstruction Acts as an unconstitutional infringement on states' rights. Within a few years, he would emerge as a leading courtroom defender of the Klan's terrorists.

On March 30 began what the *New York Tribune* breathlessly deemed "the greatest constitutional state trial of modern or ancient history." Chief Justice Salmon P. Chase and fifty-three senators formed the court and jury. From the galleries, 195 representatives, the foreign diplomatic corps, most of Washington's fashionable women, and almost a thousand citizens looked tensely on. At 1 p.m., the prosecutors entered the chamber—Butler with the sober and straitlaced John Bingham of Ohio, the abolitionist George Boutwell of Massachusetts with the former harness-maker James Wilson of Iowa, wartime general John Logan of Illinois with the elderly Thomas Williams of Pennsylvania—each pair arm-in-arm. Stevens entered by a different door, clasping a huge walking stick in hands so skeletal that they seemed transparent. For the next three hours, Butler laid out the articles of impeachment, disappointing listeners in the gallery who expected a slashing attack, until the end when he scathingly declared of Johnson, who gained power only by virtue of John Wilkes Booth's bullet, "By murder most foul did he succeed to the presidency and is the elect of an assassin to that high office, and not of the people."

That same day, 750 miles to the south, in the war-battered Chattahoochee River mill town of Columbus, Georgia, a quite different audience had gathered at Temperance Hall, this one mostly Black, many dressed in the ragged and patched clothes of farmhands and laborers, interspersed with a handful of whites, many of them, too, in workmen's rough garb, all Republicans and eager to learn what the revolutionary promises of Reconstruction had to offer them. They had come to hear two men. The first was the freeborn, silver-tongued Rev. Henry McNeal Turner, who though only thirty-four years old was already the most famous Black man in Georgia, the first African American to serve as a chaplain in the U.S. Army, and a rising star in the AME Church. (His fiery style was later evident when he replied to a congressman who asked him if he had ever heard of anyone who had been harmed by the Ku Klux Klan: "I have seen scores of them. I have seen men who had their backs lacerated. I have seen other men who had bullets in them. I have seen others who had their arms shot off. I have seen others with their legs shot off.")

The other speaker that day was the less polished but two-fisted egalitarian white politician George W. Ashburn, then fifty-three years old, a "scalawag," a turncoat, in the eyes of ex-Confederates, who despised him. Turner probably regaled the crowd, as he had a different gathering the day before, with the news that the local Republican tax assessor had received what was obviously meant to be a frightening warning from the Klan—a bag of bones that turned out to be those of a mere turtle. Ashburn's remarks went unrecorded. But he, too, likely excoriated the local Democrats, scoffed at the Klan, and pumped up enthusiasm for the upcoming vote on the state's new constitution, which he and Turner had had a hand in crafting. Both men were also candidates for the state senate and were expected to win handily given the huge new Black vote.

Before the war, Ashburn had farmed, taught school, traded cotton, and operated a hotel in Macon. A minister who knew him then remembered him as "clever and kind," enthusiastic and earnest, and in politics a man of "very stern and unflinching Union proclivities." Early in the war he had fled with his family to Union-occupied Tennessee, where he recruited troops for the federal army, rose to the rank of colonel, and disposed of confiscated cotton for the military. A soldier friend who was with him on "many a hard-fought field" described him as a man of inflexible will who "seemed to have but one aim in life, and that was to restore the government of the old flag to Georgia." Since his return, he had advocated forcefully for Black civil rights and the desegregation of schools and public accommodations and opposed allowing former Confederates back into political life. He was not afraid of making enemies, and he had made many.

After the rally, Turner left town for his next speaking engagement. Ashburn went home to the rented room he shared with Alexander Bennett, a fellow Republican, in Hannah Fluornoy's boardinghouse on Oglethorpe Street. Conservative white opinion was so hostile to Ashburn that no respectable hotel would allow him a room. Fluornoy was a Black woman, a fact that lent itself to predictably nasty innuendo. She also let a room to a young white prostitute, Amanda Patterson, which was sufficient in the minds of the city's respectable class to describe her boardinghouse, with considerable exaggeration, as a "brothel."

Ashburn was in his nightshirt and in bed when the masked men came, sometime after midnight. There were at least twenty of them, perhaps as many as thirty. They all wore black clothes and pasteboard masks and pounded on the front door demanding to see "Mandy"—Amanda Patterson. Fluornoy refused to open the door, so they broke it down and pushed their way along the hall to the third room on the left. When it was opened, one of them yelled, "There's the damned shit!" From the doorway, half a dozen men drew revolvers and blasted away at Ashburn standing in the flickering candlelight. One shot hit him in the thigh, another in the mouth, a third between the eyes.

Four policemen were close enough to the boardinghouse to hear the cocking of pistols. They walked away without raising an alarm. That evening, it was later reported, the city's deputy marshal and chief of police were seen at a downtown hotel with several policemen, all wearing "masquerade clothing." The next morning, the county physician Elisha Kirkscey arrived with two other men to perform the inquest, followed by the mayor and several policemen. Kirkscey determined that Ashburn had been killed instantly. Fluornoy, who was in the hall when the murderers pushed past, said she didn't recognize anyone. Neither did Ashburn's roommate Alexander Bennett, who was hiding behind a door. Mandy Patterson first told the inquest that she saw one attacker's mask fall off and then quickly said she hadn't seen that at all. Ashburn, the inquest determined, had been killed "by persons unknown."

Conservatives suggested that Ashburn had been killed by federal soldiers, or by Negroes, or by a Radical "clique" that wanted to eliminate him, or that the killers had gone to Fluornoy's boardinghouse with innocent intention but that Ashburn had fired at them and they were merely defending themselves. The *Louisville Courier,* anticipating rumors already in the air, huffed that Ashburn was so far beneath contempt "that respectable white men should as a body plan murder was incredible and unworthy of credence for a second."

The pro-Klan *Memphis Appeal* mordantly asserted that "Ku-Klux" was an ancient Hebrew term that meant "straws show which way the wind blows," that is, in the direction of unforgiving violence.

News of Ashburn's murder raced across the country, jolting public opinion. What lingering sense there was that the Klan was merely a passing curiosity evaporated. For months, there had been murky reports that it had killed Black men in the southern hinterland. But now they had killed a *white* man, and a public figure at that, a man on the cusp of election to the Senate of his state, and in the middle of a *city*. If such a man, in such a place, could be murdered in cold blood, the menacing hands of the Klan could reach anywhere. The *New York Tribune* cited Ashburn's murder as evidence of the dangers of the president's views toward Reconstruction, and proof of the urgency of his impeachment, declaring on April 9 that "Andrew Johnson is the very man who, more than all others has incited and inflamed the fiendish spirit which impelled to this murder. The animus of that infernal document"—Johnson's violent State of the Union address in December—"is identical with that evinced in the butchery of Ashburn."

Perhaps the outcome of Johnson's trial would have been different had Thaddeus Stevens been able to steer the prosecution forward more vigorously. But his legendary rapier of sarcasm was rarely brandished anymore. Despite his aversion to alcohol, he sustained himself as best he could with occasional sips of wine and brandy. When he managed to make it to the House floor, he often seemed shadowed by a morbid pallor, "like an unearthly apparition." One morning he failed even to recognize his own attendant.

The prosecution relied almost entirely on Johnson's violation of the Tenure of Office Act, which was of dubious constitutionality and hard to justify no matter how many times the Republicans tried to explain it. The managers mostly repeated the same charges, often in abstruse legal language that drove all but the most addicted spectators out of the galleries. One memorably embarrassing exception was prosecutor George Boutwell's bizarre assertion that he wanted to transport Johnson to a "hole in the sky," which supposedly existed above the Southern Hemisphere, "that dreary, cold, dark region of space, there forever to exist in a solitude eternal." Boutwell's extravagance was widely mocked and materially undermined the prosecution's case. The country, the *Boston Post* declared, had "stopped its ears."

That Johnson had thwarted the will of Congress and sped the empowerment of ex-Confederates was beyond doubt. Certainly he had morally betrayed the party that had elected him. He had been added to the Union ticket in 1864 in hope of winning border state votes, replacing Lincoln's first-term vice president, Hannibal Hamlin, an abolitionist, whose elevation to the presidency instead of Johnson would have utterly changed the course of Reconstruction. But it was hard to persuade many members of the Senate, not to mention the public, that Johnson was guilty of anything more than a political disagreement, no matter how great its ramifications on the lives of southern freed people.

Stevens said little, though on April 27 he tried. He struggled to read his speech from the secretary's desk, then begged to sit, then finally gave up and handed the speech to Butler to finish. The president, "this offspring of secession," Stevens said, via Butler's nasal Yankee voice, had no legal right to interfere with the sovereign power of Congress. Instead, he had "directed the defunct states to come forth and live by his breathing into their nostrils the breath of life." If Johnson was unwilling to execute the laws passed by Congress, then he ought to resign "and retire to his village obscurity."

The trial climaxed on May 16. The visitors' galleries were again full, ablaze with female spectators flourishing "a great deal of showy silk, a fluttering of crystal and gold bedecked fans." Every senator who was ambulatory, and some who weren't, was somehow gotten into the chamber, Jacob Howard of Michigan leaning on the arms of friends, James Grimes of Iowa carried in an invalid's chair. Thousands of ordinary citizens waited expectantly in the Capitol's corridors and on the grounds outside. A reporter later remembered the strange, sweet odor of newly mown grass wafting eerily over everything. Thirty-six votes were necessary for conviction. The final tally was 35 to 19 against the president. The verdict came down to a single vote, that of Sen. Edmund G. Ross of Kansas, who had once been counted reliably among the Radicals. The *New York Times* punned, "Conviction had him to dinner last night; but Acquittal slept with him overnight." (There were rumors, likely true, that Ross had been bribed by Johnson's friends.)

Had the Republicans voted as a bloc Johnson's fate would have been sealed. But the bloc fractured. Some of the defectors dreaded the ascent to the presidency of the flamboyantly outspoken Radical Ben Wade of Ohio, the president pro tem of the Senate, who in line with the laws of the time would replace Johnson, since there was no sitting vice president. (His fellow Ohio Republican, Rep. James A. Garfield, disdained Wade as "a man of violent passions . . . and a grossly profane coarse nature.") Others were concerned that Johnson's ouster would irreparably upset the balance of power between the executive and legislative branches. Most, however, simply didn't believe that Johnson had done enough to justify impeachment. Of William Pitt Fessenden of Maine, the most eminent of the Republican defectors, an observer remarked, "He preferred the individuality of conscientious conviction to the questionable subservience of party policy."

Johnson's acquittal pitched Stevens into a fury. As his attendants carried him off the Senate floor, he barked to the stunned crowd in the marble hall outside the chamber, "The country is going to the devil!" Later, resting in Wade's office at the Capitol, he moaned, "It is the meanest case, before the meanest tribunal, and on the meanest subject in human history." Conservatives were jubilant. The pro-Johnson *New York Herald* crowed, "The great Radical party has been thrown completely on its beam ends." The *Memphis Appeal* mocked the entire impeachment process as a "harlequinade"— a clown show—and sneered at the disappointed Republicans as "a ring of speculators and swindlers, meaner than the meanest of the issue from obscene Afric's dusky loins." Yet, the impeachment had achieved one thing: it left Johnson humiliated, isolated, and politically neutered. Wrote French correspondent (and later president of France) Georges Clemenceau, "Mr. Johnson, like Medea, stands absolutely alone. He is his sole remaining friend. Unhappily he does not suffice."

In failing so spectacularly to evict the president the Radicals had revealed the limits of their power. Only Grant, who had made no public statements, remained unwounded. The *New York Times* had urged him during the trial to keep his opinions to himself, since any hint that he favored impeachment would, in the public eye, be seen as tantamount to marching troops into the Capitol. Grant didn't need such advice. Silence was his norm. "Grant's chance for the White House is worth tenfold that of any other man," the New York diarist George Templeton Strong acutely reflected. "This is due partly to the general faith in his honesty and capacity, and partly to his genius for silence." If strategy it was, it was a winning one. Public support for him steadily grew.

On May 21, the Republican National Convention in Chicago unanimously nominated Grant for president on the first vote and selected House Speaker Schuyler Colfax of Indiana for vice president. Grant's brief letter of acceptance—nominees did not typically appear in person at party conventions—was concise, pragmatic, and judiciously vague, declaring that the unstable, fast-changing nature of the times precluded the presentation of a rigid agenda. His concluding sentence was the only one that everyone would remember. It would later be thrown back at him by the Ku Klux Klan: "Let us have peace."

4

AN ALARM BELL IN THE NIGHT

There is not a Radical leader in this
town but is a marked man.

—NATHAN BEDFORD FORREST

George Ashburn's murder, carried out boldly in front of witnesses in a city occupied by federal troops, was a deliberate public statement. It was, in a sense, the Klan's debut on the national stage. It announced that no public figure was beyond the Klan's reach. Ashburn was not an obscure freedman dragged from a backwoods cabin or a town jail. He was one of Georgia's leading Republicans, a political power immensely popular with the freed people, who marched in great number at his funeral. His murder proclaimed that no Republican was safe, that those who dared to align themselves with Blacks would not be spared, and that the Klan had no fear of retribution.

The Klan may in part have been testing the federal government to see how it would react to such blatant terrorism. The answer was mixed. The trial of the accused murderers revealed much about how the Klan operated, what kind of men joined and led it, and how thoroughly politicized it had become. It also made clear that the Klan had won over the city's Democratic politicians and police, infiltrated the army's occupation force, and gained leverage on at least some local Radicals. It further demonstrated that the Klan was neither as mysterious nor as impenetrable as it pretended, and that when the army acted decisively the terrorists could be exposed and prosecuted, lessons that would later inform Ulysses Grant's war against them. The trial's ultimate outcome, however, would also demonstrate that despite a prosecution bolstered by thorough investigation, local courts could not be trusted and that without a political revolution in Washington even military justice could still be summarily thwarted.

Just days before the murder, Gen. George G. Meade, the Louisville-based commander for the region that included Georgia, had in a letter to Grant expressed skepticism that the Klan even existed. (Meade was a capable soldier who had won the battle of Gettysburg for the Union, but a conservative Democrat in politics who was disinclined to provoke what he regarded as needless conflict in the South.) Grant had no such doubts. On April 2, he directed Meade to immediately undertake an investigation and to ensure that "justice be meted out promptly by Military Commission, if the civil courts cannot be relied on." Meade thereupon suddenly discovered, he informed Grant, that "within the last ten days a spirit of disorder and violence has manifested itself in both this state and Alabama." Given his marching orders, Meade removed the city's mayor, the Board of Aldermen, the marshal and his deputy, and appointed an army captain to govern Columbus. "Good citizens," Meade reported to Grant, had certainly taken part in the outrage, and the city government showed no interest in pursuing the truth on its own. Probably working from evidence provided by local Blacks, the army arrested twenty-two people, some as suspects and others as witnesses. Nine men were finally accused. One was none other than Elisha Kirkscey, the same county physician who had overseen the inquest. The others included William Chipley, the chairman of the Democratic Party's executive committee; Robert Wood, a deputy city marshal; Alva Roper and James Wiggins, both policemen; James Barber, a Democratic candidate for county clerk; and three others, Columbus Bedell, William Duke, and Robert Hudson, all of them most likely Democratic Party activists.

Meade set out to assemble an airtight case. He summoned one of the best detectives of the day, Hiram C. Whitley, a goateed native of Maine who during the war had infiltrated rebel spy rings in New Orleans and more recently gathered evidence to be used against Andrew Johnson in his impeachment trial. Whitley dropped what he was doing—he was in Kansas investigating tax-dodging bootleggers—and immediately entrained for Georgia. He quickly took the Ashburn case in hand. He moved the prisoners away from their families and friends in Columbus to isolation at Fort Pulaski on the Atlantic Coast, where he successfully pressured two of the more vulnerable men to confess and turn state's evidence, persuading them that the leaders were well-connected "men of property" who would just as soon let them hang. He urged them, "Save your neck by coming out with the truth." Whitley then put one of his new informers into a cell with a particularly uncooperative prisoner who, the turncoat reported, sneered that a "God damned sight of fuss was made about killing that son-of-a-bitch, Ashburn, and by God there would [soon] be more of the same stripe missing." Other hostile whites were assigned to pungent sweat-box cells near the prison latrines. Whitley also turned two reluctant Black eyewitnesses into jailhouse informants, reporting to Meade, "I know the negro character well, and I know that he has been subjected to intimidations all his life, and is naturally more easily frightened than white men."

The trial of the accused murderers was organized with remarkable speed. Meade correctly surmised that the defense would play for time in anticipation of the state legislature's imminent approval of the Fourteenth Amendment, which would cause the case to revert to the civil courts. The trial began on June 29 and continued for almost a month. The prisoners all pleaded not guilty. The well-funded defense hired a dozen of the best lawyers in Georgia led by Alexander H. Stephens, the former vice president of the Confederacy, and the former attorney general Henry Stanbery. The prosecution offered its own star, the former Confederate governor of Georgia, Joseph Brown, now a Republican, whom the government paid the astronomical sum of $5,000 for his services. On both sides, the caliber of the attorneys was testament to the significance that the government and its enemies alike attributed to the case. Meanwhile, the murderers' apologists did their best to smear Ashburn's character, alleging variously that he was a corrupt opportunist, that before the war he had been a notoriously cruel overseer of slaves, that he had spied for the Yankees, and that after the war he had abandoned his white wife to live with a Black prostitute. The only part that was true was his wartime service to the Union.

As the trial unfolded, it was clear that the plot's main organizer was Dr. Kirkscey, and that Chipley, whom the others referred to as the "captain," led the assault team. The government's first witness was a New Jersey Yankee, twenty-seven-year-old Sgt. Charles Marshall of the 16th Infantry, a partisan Democrat. As the senior sergeant in his company, he had free run of the city, where he spent his off-duty time in gin mills fraternizing with local Democrats. In early March, Kirkscey invited him to help kill Ashburn. The day of the murder, a Black man brought Marshall a package containing a pasteboard mask and a message directing him to meet the rest of the party at midnight in a vacant lot near Ashburn's boardinghouse. There he found twenty or thirty masked men, one of whom gave him a gray coat to conceal his clothing.

Marshall seemed nervous, as he well might, since he was probably facing his fellow conspirators for the first time since their imprisonment. "What induced you to take part in the killing?" Marshall was asked. He replied, "Various inducements. The various associations I had. Different people. The influence was so great over me. I suppose, I could not resist it—I didn't resist it, anyhow." He testified that he was given a gold watch worth $300 or $400, which was "handed to me by a clerk in a jeweler's store," as well as a $100 "loan" from the city's then-mayor, who had earlier testified to the supposedly good character of all the accused.

Until his arrest, even though he was on active duty, Marshall had campaigned against the state's new constitution with other defendants and with several of his fellow soldiers, for whom he kept sets of civilian clothes. On Election Day, he said, he was assigned to escort Black voters to the polls and he had tried to persuade them to vote for the Democrats.

The prosecution's second witness, George Betts, a sometime police officer, testified that Kirkscey had promised him "fifty or a hundred dollars" to join the plot. Asked what reason Kirkscey had given him for killing Ashburn, Betts replied, "To get him out of the way in election times. I thought he was a tyrant to the place and ought to be out of the way."

The next witness for the government was Alexander Bennett,

a Republican and Ashburn's roommate, who said he was hiding behind women's clothes hanging on a door in the hall when Ashburn was shot. The story Bennett told was a murky one. He was a regular customer of the prostitute Amanda Patterson, who lived at the boardinghouse. He also seemed to be on friendly terms with the town's leading Democrats, who had advised him to break with Ashburn because "something was going to happen." Asked why he had not said as much at the coroner's inquest, he replied, "Because I would have been cutting my own throat. The Ku Klux Klan would have put an end to me, as they threaten to do anyway."

Bennett was, or had been, an active member of the Union League, although he was plainly a disgruntled one, having been jailed some weeks before the murder for ordering a shipment of whiskey for the league but then taking it for himself. Through his jailer, Bennett had offered to give the Democrats "certain papers and letters," including one by Ashburn, and to report to them the names of the Union League's white members, if the Democrats would pay his fine. In short, he agreed to become an informer for the Democrats and, at least indirectly, for the Klan. Bennett also promised to help Chipley in the elections. Chipley told him, he said, that "I need not be afraid of the Ku Kluxes if I helped them politically, or something of that sort, that there would be no danger for me."

It was unclear what exactly Bennett's motives were the night of the murder. He claimed that he had gone to the boardinghouse to collect $67 that Ashburn owed him, and to see Patterson. Had he perhaps actually gone there to ensure that Ashburn was present when the assassins came? The court seems not to have asked him. Bennett admitted to asking for Ashburn's revolver, claiming that he wanted to defend them. But perhaps his job was to see that Ashburn was defenseless when he was attacked. In the event, Ashburn kept his gun, but failed to get off a shot. Later, Bennett asked one of the accused men why he hadn't been killed with Ashburn. "Because you turned Democrat," he was told.

The Democrats had also promised Bennett money if he spirited Amanda Patterson out of town. But Whitley arrested him before they could flee. Whitley told Bennett that he would keep him in jail "till I rotted," unless he confessed what he knew. Once he had, Bennett said, he "volunteered" to join the Klansman George Betts in his cell to see if he could induce him to give state's evidence. Meanwhile, a steady stream of Democrats who had not yet been charged visited Bennett in jail. Kirkscey and Chipley wanted to know if there was any evidence against them other than the testimony of Blacks, which they evidently believed could be easily discredited. Two other men, a cotton merchant and a banker, also visited and asked Bennett if he knew what evidence Mandy Patterson might have, telling him, "If she would go away there would be plenty of money furnished."

Patterson herself was the next witness. She was seventeen years old and without resources except for her body. She knew all the men on trial, several of them powerful figures in Columbus, and had had sex with several of them. She admitted that she had lied at the inquest because "I knew they would have me killed if I had told anything on them." But she was also frightened of Whitley, who had threatened to keep her in prison unless she revealed what she knew. The killers apparently had thought nothing of discussing their plans in front of someone they regarded as insignificant as Patterson. A week before the murder she had heard Jim Barber say to Bedell, another of her clients, "We are going to kill old Ashburn." Later, Chipley had warned her to keep her mouth shut or they would kill her. Now, in front of the Yankee military tribunal and plainly terrified, she identified Chipley, Kirkscey, Hudson, Bedell, Barber, Betts, Duke, and another man named Daniels.

After Patterson, a young harness-maker named Wade Stephens, a white man, testified that three weeks before the murder Kirkscey had offered him $50 to join a party that intended to "put an end" to Ashburn. Stephens was afraid of what he might be getting into, and declined. He, too, had lied at the inquest for fear of being murdered. He was particularly afraid to cross someone of Kirkscey's stature. He said by way of explanation, "Dr. Kirkscey is a rich man, sir, and I am a poor man."

Another witness, Sally Bedell, apparently a Black servant and probably a former slave of the Bedell family, testified that the Klansman Columbus Bedell told her to lie and say that he was at home the night of the murder. She also testified that Wiggins, one of the city constables, had a stash of what she called "masquerade costumes," apparently masks and robes. Abraham Johnson, a former Confederate soldier, then testified that he heard Kirkscey say to Bedell that if the Yankee commander General Meade came to Columbus "*we* Ku Kluxes" would "fix him" the way they had Ashburn. Next, Burrill Davis, an elderly wagoner, testified that the day of the murder he had driven the half-drunk James Barber, who told him, "We Ku Kluxes, they will do what they say they will do, in spite of men and hell," and then, "Mr. Ashburn will be a dead man shorter than any of you have knowledge of."

Witnesses for the defense, including the deposed mayor F. G. Wilkins, testified to the accused men's "unimpeachable" character. Kirkscey's family claimed that he had been at home the night of the murder, and Duke's that he had been forty miles away. A friend of Chipley swore that he was a homebody who rarely went out at night except occasionally to a chess club. Bedell's "body servant," a Black man, testified that his pistol hadn't been fired or moved from its usual place on the night table.

But evidence for the defendants' guilt was overwhelming. Their conviction seemed inevitable. Then, on July 21, suddenly everything changed. The Georgia state legislature approved the Fourteenth Amendment and thereby pushed the state over the political threshold for readmission to the Union and the reestablishment of civilian government. (Under the Supreme Court's *Milligan* ruling, trial by military commission was barred wherever civil courts were functioning.) Three days later, the military tribunal abruptly aborted the trial and handed the case over to the civil courts. Marshall and Betts, the government's key witnesses, were escorted to the railroad station under military protection and sent to New York for their own safety. The prisoners were freed on bond and returned to Columbus where they were welcomed as martyrs and heroes. They published a statement claiming that they had been tortured by being confined in small, smelly cells and barred from receiving the delicacies that friends tried to give them in jail. The *Atlanta Constitution* celebrated them as "innocent and outraged young men." Investigation into Ashburn's murder was never resumed.

For Radicals, the Ashburn trial's collapse was a political alarm bell in the night. The murderers of a public official had gotten off scot-free despite the government's impressive prosecution. From now on, it would prove an even greater challenge to bring Klansmen to trial and to persuade witnesses to testify against them. If the Klan wanted to grab national attention, it had succeeded triumphantly. But pressure would also build to come to grips with an organization that clearly posed a mortal danger to the rule of law, the survival of the Republican Party in the South, and the congressional plan for Reconstruction. The *New York Tribune* admitted that it had been slow to credit rumors about the Klan, but that it was now convinced that "there is solid reality under the stuff and nonsense": Ashburn's murder proved that the Klan, after all, was "a powerful organization" that meant "dangerous mischief."

Yankees might now quake with fear, but conservatives rejoiced. In the Klan, they had found a ruthless champion. "It proposes to bring into the field for the defense of our lives, liberty and property hundreds of thousands of those heroic men who have been tried and indurated by the perils, dangers, and sufferings of military service," the *Richmond Examiner* expostulated. "Under its cap and bells [the Klan] hides a purpose as resolute, noble and heroic as that which Brutus concealed beneath the mask of well-dissembled idiocy. It is rapidly organizing wherever the insolent negro, the malignant white traitor to his race, and the infamous squatter are planning to make the South utterly unfit for the residence of the decent white man."

Although Ashburn's murder cannot be traced directly to Nathan Bedford Forrest, there is some evidence that he may have been in Columbus the night of the murder. It hardly seems coincidental that the Klan's savage debut there took place just weeks after the Grand Wizard's organization of the city's first dens. If Forrest sanctioned the murder, or even instigated it, it may have been regarded as a personal triumph, as well as proof that his policy of terror worked. Meanwhile, in Memphis, Forrest was busy building what he evidently hoped would evolve into a conventional political career. (Although many high-ranking Confederates had been pardoned of their crimes, they were still barred from seeking political office, though not excluded from party politics.) In June, the local Democrats selected him as a delegate to the party's national convention in New York, where a candidate would be chosen to challenge Ulysses Grant for the presidency. Hoping to reassure moderates that he was no longer the barbaric "butcher of Fort Pillow," as Radicals continued to call him, he blandly emphasized support for the Constitution and admitted that slavery was finished, although—in tune with Democratic Party orthodoxy—he reiterated that the Negro was "totally unfit to exercise the full prerogatives of citizenship" and spurned the idea of allowing freedmen to vote as a "political crime." The *Memphis Appeal,* a pro-Klan sheet, fulsomely praised him for his profoundly "patriotic feeling."

Even as Forrest talked of moderation, night riders continued terrorizing Tennessee freedmen, teachers, and officeholders. Governor William Brownlow received a death threat from a "Grand Cyclops" who styled himself *"Stella Mortem,"* Latin for "Death Star," which declared, "We intend to keep the law in our own hands, and administer justice by—Lash, Hanging and Shooting. By saying the word, I could have you sent into the bottomless pits of hell." Brownlow, a combative wartime Unionist and rival of Andrew Johnson, promised to become a formidable foe of the Klan as it spread through the state. North of Nashville, pistol-waving Klansmen brandishing a noose invaded a train hoping to seize, without success, Radical U.S. Rep. Samuel M. Arnell. Another gang attacked Judge Fielding Hurst while he was holding court in West Tennessee. Such daring demonstrations were further proof that the Klan was now bent on carrying its war beyond isolated hamlets and hollows to the leadership of the Republican Party. "If a war of races is to be inaugurated, *the White People of the state will not shirk* from the responsibility of the contest," the pro-Klan Knoxville *Press and Herald* threatened.

Forrest, meanwhile, was hobnobbing with national Democrats at Tammany Hall, the headquarters of New York City's powerful Democratic Party, which with its coffered ceiling, gilded ornamentation, and other lavish appointments resembled a sort of populist Versailles-on-the-Hudson. Among the southern delegates were many former rebels, at least several other leading Klansmen, and wartime Copperhead sympathizers with the Confederacy. Democrats knew that their only plausible path to victory lay through the thickets of white supremacy. Indeed, the convention's tone was established from the start with the adoption of its official slogan: "This is a white man's country. Let a white man rule." Speaker after speaker hammered at the same theme. The committee on war veterans declared that the Republicans were forcing helpless southern states to submit to laws "framed by ignorant negroes," and that it could not be surprising if suffering white men—an elliptical reference to the Klan—were "unwilling to be ruled by their recently emancipated slaves." Former Confederate vice president Alexander Stephens asserted in a message to the delegates that Black suffrage could only be granted by the states, not the federal government. Another letter, this one from women's rights advocates Elizabeth Cady Stanton and Susan B. Anthony, charged that the Republican Party had disgraced itself by having with one hand lifted up Black men "and crowned them with the honor and dignity of citizenship, [while] with the other they have dethroned fifteen million white women, and cast them under the heel of the lowest order of mankind."

Struggling to satisfy both its northern and southern wings, the party's platform asserted that since the problems of slavery and secession had been "settled for all time," the southern states deserved to be immediately restored to their place in the Union and that all laws "designed to secure negro supremacy" and the "usurpations" of Congress must be immediately reversed. Significantly, despite the florid abundance of racist rhetoric that characterized the convention, the party's platform did not contest the principle of Black suffrage, which the great majority of Democrats, including even Forrest, now considered a fait accompli. Many were still certain that compliant freedmen could be persuaded by their former masters to vote Democratic. Failing that, once control of the franchise was restored to the states, it would be easy to exclude Blacks from the polls if that proved necessary. Editorialized the *Atlanta Constitution,* even as it predicted a heavy Black vote for the Democrats, "By the enfranchisement of the lowest class in our midst without distinction, and the wholehearted disenfranchisement of our best citizens, we have certainly taken a retrograde movement not at all in consonance with the progressive spirit of the age." In this sort of topsy-turvy logic, racial discrimination was thus a cynosure of progress, and freedom a surrender to backwardness and reaction.

Fourteen men were placed in nomination for president, all but one of them conservatives, among them Andrew Johnson and Gen. Winfield Scott Hancock. The only exception was Salmon P. Chase, the chief justice of the Supreme Court, whose roots lay in the antislavery movement. His advocates argued, ineffectually as it turned out, that his nomination alone could demonstrate that the party had cut loose from "the old pro-slavery slag." After twenty-two ballots, the nomination finally went to former governor Horatio Seymour of New York and, for vice president, Francis P. "Frank" Blair Jr. of Missouri. Seymour was best remembered for ineffectually trying to mollify the draft rioters who ravaged New York City and lynched Blacks for three days in 1863. Blair, a onetime Republican who had fought capably as one of Sherman's generals, just days before the convention authored a notorious and widely reprinted letter which demanded, "How can Reconstruction be overthrown?" The only answer, he wrote, was election of a president who would declare the Reconstruction Acts void, oust the "carpetbag" regimes, and help southern whites regain control of their states.

On his return to Memphis, Forrest and his cohorts formed a Democratic "club," apparently as an auxiliary to the regular Democratic Party organization. Its president was former Confederate general Albert Pike and its corresponding secretary Minor Meriwether, both leading Klan officers. Soon similar "clubs" burgeoned elsewhere. In many if not most instances, they overlapped with membership in the Klan. The clubs seem to have focused on collecting information on voters, which likely helped terrorists to identify and target Republicans. Around the same time, the Klan made a grandiose public demonstration in Memphis, with a dramatic parade of robed and masked men who processed in eerie silence through the city on horses with their hooves muffled in burlap. On July 17, the *Nashville Banner* published a Klan directive ordering Blacks in several nearby counties to disband their self-defense companies, adding disingenuously, "We are not the enemy of the blacks, as long as they behave themselves." As outrages spiked, Brownlow called for the enlistment of a racially mixed loyalist militia—a prospect that repelled even many Republicans, who feared that it would trigger full-scale race war. He then appealed for federal troops, but the region's commander, Gen. George Thomas, refused, reminding him that since Tennessee had been restored to the Union it was no longer subject to federal martial law and must cope with internal disorders on its own.

In an effort to checkmate Brownlow, Forrest led a "peace mission" of a dozen other ex-generals to Nashville to lobby for the full restoration of political rights to disenfranchised ex-Confederates. At least three members of the delegation, including Forrest, and perhaps all of them, were high-ranking Klansmen. Implicitly speaking on behalf of the Klan, they coyly told the state legislature's Joint Military Committee, which oversaw the militia, that "that class" of men who "seemed hostile" to the administration—that is, the Klan—didn't want to overthrow the government at all. Indeed, they said, no such subversive society even *existed* in Tennessee, "public or secret." But they added, meaningfully, that restoring former rebels' voting rights—and abolishing the Union League, by the way—would "remove all irritating causes now disturbing society." In other words, they would guarantee that the supposedly nonexistent Klan would stand down if its members were guaranteed a route to political power.

The committee was not to be bullied, however, and issued a devastating seventy-six-page report that detailed Klan outrages in the state. Both Black and white witnesses, mainly from Giles and the surrounding counties in Middle Tennessee, recounted nighttime invasions of their homes, murderous threats, floggings, beatings, trashed property, and terrified flights for safety. John Dunlap, an Ohioan working as the principal of a Black school in Shelbyville, reported that fifty robed men wearing "pyramid-shaped" hats and false faces cheered for Andrew Johnson as they dragged him out of his home into the public road, flogged him, and ordered him and his Black teachers to get out of town, warning: "If not, we will take you out, tie you to a stake, and then burn you to death." State senator William Wyatt, a sixty-six-year-old farmer in Lincoln County, testified that between fifty and sixty masked men smashed in his front door, dragged him out of bed, and pistol-whipped him amid the family's shrieking womenfolk. Pink Harris, a farmer, reported that a band of Klansmen broke into his home, stripped and whipped him "for having been in the U.S. Army," and swore that they would hang him if they came again. Benjamin Martze, a twenty-eight-year-old carpenter, hid beneath the floorboards of his house while Klansmen savagely beat his wife on the floor above and swore that they would kill every member of the Union League "from fifteen years [of age] upwards." Twenty-one-year-old Washington Davis, a blacksmith, reported that when Klansmen invaded his house they also had "under arrest" two naked and barefoot Black men, but he didn't know what happened to them. Lewis Powell, a Union Leaguer who had fled to the woods, watched in horror as Klansmen shot his wife to death in front of their house. Charles Bellefont, eighteen, testified that masked attackers "gave me about two hundred lashes. They said I was a damned nigger and had been a Yankee soldier, and they were going to kill all that had been in the Yankee Army, or that had belonged to the Union League."

When a squad of Klansmen failed to capture Violet Wallace's husband, a neighbor testified, the night riders beat her with a bridle rein, then with a pistol, and then stomped on her when she collapsed. Then one of them pulled down his pants and sat on her face. She knew some of them but wouldn't divulge their names for fear that they would do the same thing again. After digesting this and more of the same, the state legislature enacted a muscular law prescribing five years in prison and a $500 fine for membership in any secret terrorist organization. Brownlow again tried to raise a loyalist militia, without success, but this time his desperate efforts did manage to convince the army to dispatch a regiment of federal troops to Tennessee.

In response, Forrest abandoned the sugarcoating: his message to supporters in Memphis was as blunt as could be. He charged, in mid-August, that the "alleged" acts of violence that Radicals had reported were mere "fabrication," fake news as it were, that was simply intended to inflame northern public opinion against the South. Unless the disenfranchised got their way, he threatened, "there will be civil war." He didn't want that war, he said, "nor do I want to see negroes armed to shoot down white men. If they bring this war upon us, there is one thing I will tell you: that I will not shoot any negroes as long as I can see a white Radical to shoot. But if they send the Black men to hunt those Confederate soldiers whom they call kuklux, then I say to you, 'Go out and shoot the Radicals.' If they do want to inaugurate civil war, the sooner it comes the better, that we may know what to do."

The Klan now "spread over the South like the dew," as a South Carolina newspaper put it. With or without formal authorization from Tennessee, new dens sprang up seemingly overnight, in cities and towns, and in the rural hinterland—seven within just a few weeks in a single county in North Carolina. In many areas, already existing groups of freelance "regulators" transformed themselves wholesale into "Klan." The Klan also absorbed veterans of the old prewar slave patrols that had monitored the movements of slaves and free blacks, and hunted down freedom-seeking runaways, punishing offenders under the Black Codes of the time. "They perpetuate the same outrages in the same manner and upon the same persons," a U.S. attorney in Kentucky reported. "Since the war and the freeing of the colored men, these same men do the same thing and are equally endorsed by the public sentiment." There was a significant difference, however. Slaves were private property and had market value; freed people had none. Patrollers, who were paid by local slaveowners, had nothing to gain if they damaged the men and women they hunted down. Klansmen had no such restraints at all.

How much of the Klan's spread can be credited solely to Forrest personally is hard to say. At first, the Pulaski founders claimed the sole right to authorize new "dens" or "klans." The early historian and member of the Klan, J. C. Lester, wrote, "A stranger from West Tennessee, Mississippi, Alabama, or Texas, visiting a neighborhood where the order prevailed, would be initiated, and on his departure carry with him [permission] to establish a den at home." Another early member, R. J. Brunson of Pulaski, wrote that in July 1868 former general George Gordon had personally directed him to "take some of our rituals" to South Carolina and organize the dens there. Brunson, who claimed to have been the Klan's first organizer in that state, stayed three months and organized several dens. Forrest's far-flung connections exponentially widened the Klan's reach, although little but circumstantial evidence remains to tie him and other Klan agents to long-distance recruitment. One tantalizing anecdotal report, left by Vergil Stewart Lusk, a prominent North Carolina Republican, asserted that the Klan was formed in his area, at Asheville, in the winter of 1868 by a one-armed ex-Confederate soldier from Memphis named Sanders. A seeming "gentleman of leisure," Sanders brought with him a "cadaverous-looking individual" named Miller, a pretty woman claiming to be Sanders's wife, and an immense St. Bernard dog. Miller claimed to be planning to start a commercial stable, though he never acquired horses, carriages, or gear, while Sanders, who had no visible business of his own, Lusk said, turned out to be a professional organizer for the Klan.

A rare Klan charter from June 1868 is preserved in the papers of Iredell Jones, a law student, who helped form a den at Rock Hill, South Carolina. It makes no reference to Forrest, Brunson, or Pulaski, but it seems to be based on the founders' model, even to its niggling bureaucratic tone.

By virtue of the authority in me invested by the Chief of first Division C.C.C. [J. K. Chambers] I do hereby authorize and empower Iredell Jones and Thomas May members of the 6th Division C.C.C. [Chester Conservative Clan], to organize a Division in the vicinity of Rock Hill, to be known as Division No 13 and to consist of a chief, 1st asst. chief, 2nd asst. chief, 3rd asst. chief, and not less than 20 nor more than 50 members. Said officers to be elected by the members and hold office during good behavior. The chief shall appoint a secretary whose duty will be similar to that of an orderly sergeant. Immediately after organizing the chief shall cause the secretary to forward to Hd Qrs of the 1st Division a list of the names of the officers and members. Division No 13 may after organizing adopt such rules and regulations not inconsistent with the purposes had in view by its organization as it may deem proper & necessary for its government & etc. Every member shall take and subscribe the following oath.

The document went on to incorporate the usual oath of secrecy and a promise to "counteract the evil influences" of the Union League.

As dens proliferated, oaths and rituals tended to become simpler, even perfunctory. Initiation often involved little more than swearing to the group's oath, which sometimes was performed at the start of a "raid," the Klan's standard euphemism for a spree of flogging, torture, and murder. The Klan's emphasis on secrecy, if anything, deepened as its terrorism metastasized. Crude warnings were still issued: vicious letters were sent to public officials, dead cats dropped into Radicals' wells, obscene filth scrawled on the walls of freedmen's schools, Klan notices pasted on the backs of hogs and cows set loose in the streets. The death toll steadily mounted. In

Pulaski, Tennessee, a hundred or more Klansmen broke into the jail, lynched a Black man accused of attempted rape, and left his shot-up body on the street. The *Mississippi Sentinel* reported that scores of masked horsemen had swarmed into Coffeeville, placed pickets at all important points—"everything was done so quick that no one was aware of it"—then surrounded the jail, overwhelmed the jailers, seized two Black men who had been accused of killing a white man, and spirited them out of town: "Nothing more was seen next morning but the bodies of the two prisoners found dangling in the air from a sweet gum tree." In some areas, the Freedmen's Bureau stopped holding meetings of any kind, knowing that Blacks who attended would instantly become victims.

The Klan embodied an ugly paradox. Although sadistic terror was its trade, the terrorists, or at least its leaders, were usually drawn from members of the prewar elite whose stake in power was great and whose wealth suffered most from the emancipation of their slaves. The Klan's Pulaski founders were all college-educated. Forrest, John Gordon, and their closest associates were all businessmen and professionals. George Ashburn's murderers included the county physician and the chairman of the Democratic Party. Iredell Jones was married to the daughter of a former South Carolina governor. Ryland Randolph served simultaneously as chief of the local Klan, a Democratic state legislator, and editor of a pro-Klan newspaper, the *Tuskaloosa Monitor,* a spelling favored by Democrats. Its slogan was "White Man—Right or Wrong—Still the White Man," and regularly printed broadsides from the Klan, for instance, announcing a meeting at "the den of the snakes—the Giants' jungle—the hole of Hell!" and threatening "Shears and lash! Tar and feathers! Hell and fury! The hour is at hand!"

While many rank-and-file Klansmen were middle-class professionals and small businessmen, most were dirt farmers who had never owned slaves but before the war had aspirationally embraced the hope of slaveowning as the southern version of the American dream. Others were attracted at least partly by the Klan's colorful mystifications. "I have always had curiosity enough to join almost any secret organization that came up, if I had an opportunity to do so," B. F. Briggs, a state assemblyman in South Carolina, remarked. "I have been a Mason, an Odd Fellow, a Son of Malta, a Loyal

Leaguer, and everything else that there is," adding, however, that he had no objection to the Klan's aims, since "the negroes were turbulent and rather troublesome in character." Where the Klan enlisted the majority of a community's white men, as it did in many areas, it became ever harder to stand aloof.

In countless communities, Klan terrorism simply became an accepted part of life. Reuben Reynolds, a Mississippi lawyer who defended many Klansmen, blithely told visiting members of a congressional committee, "If any man has committed a crime which, in the opinion of others, should render him subject to lynch-law, it is not only reasonable, but probable, that those men who favored lynching him, should assemble together simply for the purpose of taking his life. I think it most reasonable, if I and my neighbors determined to correct a private wrong in our neighborhood, that we ourselves should do it; but if we desired to evade the law to get someone else to do it. One neighbor can go and have the combination formed elsewhere and get it done that way."

The Klan's defenders claimed that it was simply reacting to violence perpetrated by Blacks and Radicals, and that no victim was punished except after "a full and ample investigation" in which "all the facts were found out and thoughtfully weighed." Such deliberations sometimes did take place. Jasper Wood's den in Alamance County, North Carolina, debated how to punish "an old negro man" who had allegedly burned a house down for spite. The den's leader initially argued that hanging was "too good" for him, while others argued against lynching. Finally a vote was taken and it was decided that the man be given fifty lashes. When such "deliberations" took place at all, however, they were in secret and usually based on some combination of hearsay, personal malice, political prejudice, and Negrophobia. Threats and punishments often differed by race. The Klan's elaborate written threats were always directed at literate whites, while Blacks, who were presumed to be hopelessly superstitious, were menaced with crazy tales of swamp-dwelling, Negro-eating monsters and grotesque performances by the supposedly risen Confederate dead. Blacks rarely received any mercy beyond a first warning, if that, and were often tortured hideously before they were killed. Whites were more likely to suffer some form of less lethal humiliation. Since, for security, punishment was often though not always meted out by Klansmen from a district different from the one in which a victim's home was located, the perpetrators might know nothing at all about the men and women they abused and killed. Wyatt Outlaw's murder, for instance, was ordered by an Alamance County den, but carried out by a different one from the county's hinterland. When particularly monstrous killings occurred, the Klan habitually blamed the "excesses" on a few "reckless and cruel" men or undisciplined "poor white trash" who had overstepped the Klan's standards of "honor" and "justice."

At the end of August, Nathaniel Bedford Forrest gave a sensational interview to a reporter from the *Cincinnati Commercial,* a leading regional newspaper. In a remarkably loquacious discourse, he oscillated between tepid reassurance, exaggeration, and calculated menace. He claimed that despite the oppression of white Tennesseans that was "growing worse hourly," he had always advised his "supporters" to obey the state's laws even though they were "unconstitutional" and had been enacted by a regime whose very legal existence he denied. When the reporter ventured that the Klan might exist only in the "frightened imaginations of a few politicians," Forrest quickly sought to disabuse him. "Well, sir, there is such an organization, not only in Tennessee but all over the South, and its numbers have not been exaggerated." He asserted that in Tennessee alone there were over forty thousand members, and in all the southern states about 550,000. These numbers, in fact, were typical Klan propaganda, the verbal equivalent of its morbid emblems and bizarre costumes. Forrest knew that such shocking claims would draw national attention even if he later denied them, as he would. He went on to describe the Klan, accurately enough, as a "political, military" organization that gave its support, "of course, to the Democratic party." Asked directly if he was a member of the Klan, however, Forrest denied it, saying primly that he was "in sympathy" with them and would "cooperate with them." Surprisingly, however, he then went on to explain the Klan's structure, apparently in its guise as a political "club." In each voting precinct, he said, there was a captain who, in addition to his "other duties," was required to make out a list of all the voters in the precinct, "giving all the radicals and all the Democrats who are positively known, and showing also the doubtful on both sides and of both colors." This list, he said, was then forwarded to the grand commander of the state, "who is thus enabled to know who are our friends and who are not."

Pressed to discuss Black suffrage, Forrest declared that he opposed it under all circumstances, but added that he was not the Negro's enemy, boasting that of the forty-seven enslaved "boys" he had taken to the war to drive teams for his troops, all but two had remained with him. "We want him here among us; he is the only laboring class we have." Asked what he thought would happen if the state militia tried to hunt down the Klan, Forrest snapped out of his conciliatory mode and promised open war: "I intend to kill the Radicals. There is not a Radical leader in this town but is a marked man; and if a trouble should break out, not one of them would be left alive. Their houses are picketed, and when the fight comes not one of them would ever get out alive."

When the interview appeared in print, Forrest realized that he had said too much. He quickly backpedaled in an attempt to disclaim his most shocking statements, asserting that he only "believed" there were forty thousand Klansmen in Tennessee and that the order was "stronger" in other states. He also asserted—against all evidence—that the Klan would obey all laws, "so I have been informed." But the interview had served its purpose. It was widely reprinted, especially in the North. Along with the summer's spate of savagery, it helped to shape Americans' idea of the Klan as a huge and ruthless terrorist army. Fear of what it might do seemed more warranted by the month as the nation approached the presidential election.

5

FIELD OF BLOOD

A revolution gave us the right to vote, and it will
take a revolution to get it away from us.

—Anonymous Black Georgian

On July 6, white South Carolinians awoke to a nightmare come
true. Eleven days earlier, Congress had pronounced the state qualified for readmission to the Union, joining all but three of the former Confederate states—Texas, Mississippi, and Virginia—in their
return to civilian government. The new state legislature met that
day in a borrowed hall at the state university, in Columbia, a few
blocks from the once magnificent capitol, still a roofless ruin burned
in the last days of the war. To the horror of conservatives, Black
Republicans comprised one-third of the members of the state Senate and nearly two-thirds of the House of Representatives. "Military rule has done its work thoroughly, and we shudder to think
of the government for which it is now to be exchanged," lamented
the *Charleston Mercury*. The Republicans, Black and white, overwhelmed the diminished rump of Democrats who had ruled the
state longer than anyone could remember. When whites expressed
fear of "negro rule," this was what they had in mind: former slaves
debating the future of the state, enacting laws, and presiding over
the political future of their onetime masters. "No true South Carolinian could visit their place of meeting without feeling the humiliation of the hour," groaned the *Charleston Daily Courier*. "The places

once filled by the wisdom, the substance, and the honor of the state, we found usurped by a motley crowd of negro men, and whites for the most part aliens to the state."

In his opening remarks, newly elected Republican governor Robert Scott, a Union Army veteran from Pennsylvania, extended an olive branch to distressed whites. He spoke of conciliation and called for patience. "Let us recognize facts as they are," he said hopefully, "and rely upon time, and the elevating influence of popular education to dispel any unjust prejudices that may exist among the two races of our fellow citizens." When he concluded with the solemn words "God save the State of South Carolina," Black lawmakers echoed him with an exuberant cheer, clapping, stamping feet, and waving their hats in sheer joy at this climax of long-suppressed hope and confidence in the future that was opening before them as citizens and political players.

No fewer than six members of that assembly would eventually be among the first Blacks to serve in the United States Congress. For now, they threw themselves into a rivalrous contest to elect one of their number Speaker of the House. Whites and some Blacks supported Franklin Moses, a native white Republican. Others supported Robert B. Elliott, a type of Black man who was never seen in South Carolina before the war: polished, self-confident, ambitious, and utterly uncowed by privileged whites. His origins were vague. Some said that he was Boston-born and had come south with the all-Black 54th Massachusetts Infantry during the war, others that he had been educated in England and had served in the federal navy. He was put into nomination by his law partner William Whipper, another Black northerner, who declared that Blacks, with power finally in their hands, must learn to use it and step forward to claim their full share of public offices. Elliott's bid for the speakership failed, but even unfriendly whites acknowledged that a revolution had occurred. The *Mercury,* once the trumpet of secession, reflected, "This harangue, emanating from so influential and so thoughtful a colored man, and the feeling excited by it are indications of that aspiring spirit among the Blacks, which may render them less pliable as the tools of designing men."

Once it had organized itself, the legislature's first substantive order of business was momentous: ratification of the Fourteenth

Amendment. With that decisive action, South Carolina—the cradle of secession—became the twenty-seventh state to do so, thereby achieving the three-quarters of the states required to turn the amendment's revolutionary cargo of transformative rights into law as part of the U.S. Constitution. Former slaves were now citizens, nullifying the Supreme Court's prewar *Dred Scott* decision; state and local governments were for the first time prohibited from depriving persons of life, liberty, and property without due process; and all were promised equal protection under the law.

Although no man could claim to have given birth to the Fourteenth Amendment single-handedly, none did more to shape it than Thaddeus Stevens, who, long before most of his congressional colleagues, had argued for the extension of rights to Black Americans as a matter of both moral and political urgency. One day earlier, Stevens, sick and enfeebled, speaking from his chair because he was too weak to rise, delivered what proved to be his last speech in Congress. "My sands are nearly run, and I can only see with the eye of faith," he said. "I am fast descending the downhill of life, at the foot of which stands an open grave. If you and your compeers can fling away ambition and realize that every human being, however lowly or degraded by fortune, is your equal, that every inalienable right which belongs to you belongs also to him, truth and righteousness will spread over the land, and you will look down from the top of the Rocky Mountains upon an empire of one hundred millions of happy people." It was his political epitaph, the final breath of one of the most formidable gladiators ever to tread the halls of Congress. "If it were not for the fire smoldering in the depths of his piercing eyes, one might imagine life had already fled from that inert body, but it still nurses the wrath of a Robespierre," the French journalist Georges Clemenceau wrote.

On August 11, in the middle of the night, at his home in Washington, Stevens roused himself to ask for some ice, and then died. The nominal cause was advanced rheumatism. He was seventy-six years old, and perhaps the only American still in public office who had been born during the presidency of George Washington. Over forty years in public service, he had done more than any other white American to politically advance the cause of civil rights. Of Stevens, declared Frederick Douglass, "There was in him the power of conviction, the power of will, the power of knowledge, and the power of conscious ability [which] at last made him more potent in Congress and in the country than even the president and the cabinet combined." Life had never rubbed off the sharp edges of Stevens's youthful radicalism. If anything, the trench warfare of politics had fortified his conviction that government was a moral endeavor and that men must be pushed as well as led toward fulfillment of the Founding Fathers' ideals. Charles Sumner, in his eulogy on the Senate floor, said of Stevens, "Speech with him was at times a cat-o'-nine-tails, and woe to the victim on whom the terrible lash descended. [But] he saw clearly that there could be no true peace except by founding the new governments on the equal rights of all." In his will Stevens stipulated that he was to be buried in the only cemetery in his hometown of Lancaster, Pennsylvania, that was not racially segregated. He would be sorely missed in the political battles to come.

The urgency of those battles was crudely illustrated in the September issue of the *Tuskaloosa Monitor,* which prominently displayed a deliberately disturbing woodcut. It showed two dead bodies hanging from an oak tree, with a horse marked "K.K.K." trotting away. It was titled: "A Suggestive Scene in the City of Oaks"—Tuscaloosa's nickname—"4th of March 1869." The bodies were readily identifiable as those of Rev. Arad Lakin, a Methodist missionary from Ohio who was serving as president of the University of Alabama, and Alabama-born "scalawag" Dr. N. B. Cloud, the state superintendent of education. The attached text, penned by the paper's editor, Ryland Randolph, declared: "It requires no seer to foretell the inevitable events that are to result from the coming Fall election throughout the southern states. It will be seen that there is room left on the limb for the suspension of any bad Grant negro who may be found at this propitious moment." As the presidential campaign gathered momentum the image was widely reprinted as a warning to Radicals about what they should expect if the Democrats won the election. The image represented a salvo in the Klan's two-pronged strategy: to collaborate with the established Democratic Party and to spill as much blood as necessary to win the coming election.

The Democrats were confident of victory. Party leaders were

convinced that a solid majority of white voters, North as well as South, shared their hostility to Reconstruction in general, to Black equality in particular, and to what they alleged was Republican "tyranny." Presidential candidate Horatio Seymour called for a policy of "fraternal affection" toward the South, code for the empowerment of former Confederates, but he was generally restrained in his public statements. His running mate, Frank Blair, however, loudly denounced Radicals as "revolutionists," and proclaimed that he would "risk my soul's salvation to preserve the freedom of the whites." The *New York World,* the country's most popular Democratic paper, railed against the Republicans for embracing an alleged "African supremacy platform" and subjecting the southern states to "the political control of the brutalized and ignorant negro population." The *World* smugly predicted, "The doom of radicalism is sealed."

No one considered Ulysses Grant a Radical, including himself. He kept his political views close to his vest, at least in public. For Republicans, Grant remained a blank canvas upon which they could paint almost any image they wanted. Radicals saw in him their quiet champion impatient to be unshackled from Andrew Johnson; conservatives saw a brake to keep the Radicals in check. For many others, he simply represented order. Grant himself remained silent. His modesty was genuine. He saw himself as a political outsider, and to a great extent he was. His very ordinariness accentuated his soldierly charisma. He was fundamentally shy, often awkward in the presence of men with greater book learning and knowledge of the law. He already missed the army. (So did his wife, Julia, who told him, "A soldier has always been my ideal," and pointed out, doubtless unnecessarily, what a hard time the politicians had given Andrew Johnson.) A month after the Republican convention, he confided to William T. Sherman that he had been pushed into the nomination in spite of himself: "I could not back down without, as it seems to me, leaving the contest for power for the next four years between mere trading politicians," who might squander what had been achieved by the war. In keeping with prewar custom, he didn't campaign and instead took off on an inspection tour of forts in distant Colorado and Wyoming with Sherman, Phil Sheridan, and his own sixteen-year-old namesake son, known as "Buck." Typically for western travelers at the time, they enjoyed blasting away at wild game from their train car as they rolled along. They also stopped near St. Louis, where Grant took legal possession of a farm that had belonged to his once slaveowning in-laws, and in a personal strike against an institution he hated he ordered the former bondsmen's cabins torn down.

In the time left to him, Johnson, now a de facto Democrat, continued to do all he could to thwart Reconstruction, pardoning former Confederates wholesale, firing federal officers who advocated too vigorously for the freedmen, and directing them to obey civil laws administered by unreconstructed ex-rebels. The steady drain of occupation troops from the South also continued, leaving an ever wider swath of the South with scant military presence. The Democrats' hopes were less well founded than they imagined, however. Many white southerners were simply exhausted and sick of political appeals. Wrote one disillusioned South Carolinian, "Everybody seems to think and speak of politics again. I never have believed in them, and think less of them now as to principle & more especially as to policy than I ever did." Many northern voters who shared the Democrats' racial animus still regarded the party's southern leaders as the unforgivable engineers of secession and war. Walt Whitman, a former Democrat himself, scoffed at Seymour and Blair as "a regular old Copperhead Democratic ticket, of the rankest kind—probably pleases the old Democratic bummers around New York and Brooklyn—but everywhere else they take it like a bad dose of medicine." Georges Clemenceau acutely remarked, "The Democrats simply will not understand that the revolution which has been carried out in spite of them is not of the kind that can be undone, and that there is no use reacting against it," adding, "They are behaving like the savage, who, wielding his tomahawk and shouting his war cry, dashes at an approaching steam engine with the hope of stopping it." Many voters also saw the election through the caustic lens of the cartoonist Thomas Nast, who in a *Harper's Weekly* sketch portrayed the Democrats as a demonic trinity—an Irish hooligan, the Democratic financier August Belmont, and a knife-wielding Nathan Bedford Forrest—all with their boots atop the sprawled body of a Black Union soldier clutching the American flag. Just beyond the soldier's reach, a toppled hourglass suggested that time was running out for both Reconstruction and Black rights.

With respect to newly enfranchised Black voters, the Democrats were delusional, imagining, as one editorialist put it, that the "more intelligent and reflecting of the race, those who are disposed to take counsel of reason and common sense," would follow the dictates of their old slave masters. The *Macon Telegraph* confidently predicted in July that between 80 and 90 percent of Georgia's Black voters would support the party in November. Conservative newspapers abounded with coerced announcements by Blacks that they had abandoned the Republicans for the Democratic ticket. In a typical one, which appeared in the *Tuskaloosa Monitor,* a Black minister named W. E. Foster wrote, "Having seen and felt the evil effects of Radical misrule for the past two years, I hereby renounce all connection with that party. We cannot disguise the fact, if we would, that the whites possess the wealth and the intelligence." This was of course just what ex-rebels wanted to hear. The same issue of the *Monitor* also carried another perhaps more meaningful announcement: "Five notoriously bad negroes were found swinging by the neck in the woods of Colbert Court a few days since. They had been guilty of making threats against the whites."

In the North, the campaign charged along with the customary hoopla and brio—with rallies, pig-roasts, torchlight parades, marching bands, and orators haranguing the party faithful and excoriating the opposition from stumps, wagon beds, and music halls, not infrequently accompanied by brawls, riots, and bloodshed. In Philadelphia, 55,000 Republicans marched for Grant, with wagonloads of veterans who had survived the Confederate death camp at Andersonville, Georgia. In the Democratic stronghold of New York City, an equally huge procession included "a powerfully-built Irish girl" dressed as the Goddess of Liberty, brandishing a pike in one hand and in the other a broken chain, symbolizing the party's desire to "liberate" the southern states from federal rule. Republicans brandished banners promising that Grant—a onetime tanner—would "tan" Seymour and Blair; Democrats sported buttons stamped with the party slogan, "This is a white man's government."

The campaign's most chilling feature was a wave of ever more daring attacks on Republican candidates, state officials, and federal officers. "Political murders seem to be the order of the day throughout the entire South," the *New York Times* declared in October. Democrats—when they admitted that any violence had occurred—usually blamed it on defiant Blacks who allegedly shot first, or claimed that whites were forestalling a (nonexistent) Black insurrection. Clemenceau reported cuttingly, "In all events of the kind, the remarkable feature is that according to telegraphic reports there is always a band of heavily armed negroes attacking a handful of harmless whites. Then when it comes to counting the dead, a few negroes are always down, but of the white men, not a trace." A deputy sheriff in Arkansas serving a subpoena was seized by Klansmen, tied to a Negro, and both of them shot to death. In Calhoun County, Georgia, a Black Republican named Walker was dragged from his house and murdered for organizing a Grant club. In Huntsville, Alabama, a white Republican judge and two Blacks were gunned down. In Texas, a former federal army captain, George Smith, was murdered with several Black companions after leaving the state constitutional convention at Austin. Hardly a day seemed to pass without a similar report appearing in the newspapers.

South Carolina had been spared organized Klan terror until that spring, but it now spread rapidly. In September, Governor Scott reported that Negroes were being shot and killed almost daily, some simply for admitting that they were Republicans. Gun-toting whites were accosting Black men in their fields and ordering them to sign pledges to vote Democratic. Four Black politicians were murdered in the state's Third Congressional District. In Newberry County, an estimated forty Radicals were killed, including the president of the Union League. In Abbeville County, two Blacks were murdered, "their throats cut from ear to ear," as were two members of the state legislature, one white and one Black, the latter, B. F. Randolph, shot in broad daylight on a train platform. One of Randolph's murderers, William Tolbert, later confessed to being a member of the Klan, and that they were determined to "kill out the leaders of the Republican party."

The season's most notorious racial bloodletting occurred at Camilla, Georgia, in mid-September, where Black Republicans attempting to hold a political rally were attacked by whites led by the town sheriff. Widely reported in the North, the Camilla massacre fulfilled the fears of Republicans who had warned of what would happen if the former Confederate states were readmitted prematurely. The massacre climaxed a tumultuous political drama that had been playing out since July, when the state legislature expelled its thirty-two Black members, whom it deemed "ineligible on account of color," in raw defiance of the just ratified Fourteenth Amendment. Conservative Republicans joined the Democrats in claiming that because the eligibility of Blacks for office was not explicitly affirmed in the state's constitution they had no right to serve. General Meade, who interpreted his responsibilities as narrowly as possible, refused to deploy federal troops to prevent what was, in essence, a legislative coup. "I did not see that in the case of a parliamentary body that I was called on to decide in the qualifications of the members," he informed the War Department.

The Georgia legislature's Black members were understandably shaken and bitter, not least by their blatant betrayal by so many of their erstwhile white Republican allies. Henry McNeal Turner, who had strongly advocated for the seating of the former Confederates who now ousted him, spoke for all his unseated colleagues, in an erudite riposte that cited the writings of Jefferson, Madison, the Protestant Reformation, and ancient Greek and Roman law. "Am I a man?" he demanded. "If I am such, I claim the rights of a man. Am I not a man, because I happen to be of a darker hue than honorable gentlemen around me?" He added, "No man has been more deceived by that [Anglo-Saxon] race than I have." Georgia's helpless Republican governor, Rufus Bullock, could do no more than weakly object to the legislature's high-handed action.

Shortly before the massacre at Camilla, five cases of new repeating rifles had been delivered to the local Democratic "club" in nearby Albany. This "club," as in Memphis and elsewhere, was likely the local Klan by another name. Its secretary, James Armstrong, an agent of the Southwestern Railroad Company, visited Camilla just before the massacre. He later claimed that he was there exclusively on railroad business. Camilla was then effectively cut off. Letters from the Freedmen's Bureau in Albany were monitored, and the telegraph office there refused to accept any dispatches addressed to the bureau unless they were prepaid. Republicans had planned a conventional political rally, replete with a brass band. About three hundred Black men, women, and children from the farms around Camilla paraded into town accompanied by the band and several Republican politicians, including Philip Joiner, a former slave, one of the Blacks ousted from the state legislature. They walked into a trap. One hundred or more white gunmen had positioned themselves around the town square. Others concealed themselves in stores. When the Republicans reached the square the whites opened fire, catching them in a crossfire. The few Blacks who had guns fired back, but quickly ran out of ammunition. In panic, they fled to the woods outside town and tried to hide in creek beds and underbrush, but mounted whites shot down any Blacks they saw and finished off the wounded where they lay on the ground. In all, at least twenty Blacks were killed and perhaps forty wounded. Meade, once again, seemed oblivious to what was at stake. After dispatching a single officer to investigate the events at Camilla he concluded that, while the local white authorities were mainly at fault, the Black Republicans were also to blame "by their want of judgment and their insistence on abstract rights."

The bloodiest episode of the entire campaign season took place at Opelousas, west of Baton Rouge. Tensions were already high when the fiery young editor of the Radical *St. Landry Progress,* an Ohioan named Emerson Bentley, received a message illustrated with a dagger dripping with blood and the words "E.B. Beware! K.K.K." He defiantly pinned it to his chest and strode down Main Street "with a feeling of pride," he later wrote. On September 28, three men led by a local judge thrashed Bentley in front of the young Black children he taught at a freedmen's school. Rumors spread that Bentley had been murdered, although he had actually fled town. When freed people gathered to protest, armed whites took over the town, invaded the *Progress* office, where they smashed the press, assassinated Bentley's coeditor, C. E. Durand, and brandished his bloody body outside a drugstore. For two weeks, white gunmen swept the countryside, running down and killing as many Blacks as they could catch. At least one hundred and probably as many as two hundred freed people died. Of this slaughter, a New Orleans paper blandly reported, "The plantations were visited and the negroes made to understand that unless they surrendered their arms, they would be taken out and shot."

Louisiana was something of an anomaly in the history of Reconstruction Era white supremacist violence. Killings were endemic in the back country, while political mob violence and race riots repeatedly scarred the then-capital of New Orleans. But only a limited proportion of all this turbulence can be traced directly to the Ku Klux Klan. The Klan was but one of a bewildering, fragmented, and overlapping patchwork of organizations, nearly all of them unique to Louisiana: the Knights of the White Camellia, the Swamp Fox Rangers, the Seymour Knights, the Hancock Guards, the misnamed "Innocents," White Leagues, and assorted freelance terrorist gangs. The Klan itself, which waxed and waned in strength, was mostly active in the state's northern counties, along the Arkansas state line. Some organizations practiced rituals similar to the Klan's, others not at all. A few wore disguises on their raids, but most did not. Indeed, the largest group of all, the Knights of the White Camellia, which claimed fifteen thousand members in New Orleans alone, predated the founding of the Klan, publicized its meetings in newspapers, and enjoyed a reputation, likely undeserved, for shunning the worst kinds of violence in favor of a policy of quiet intimidation.

Federal officials reported a steady drumbeat of killings that autumn. Fifteen Republicans were reported killed in a "fray" at Shreveport. Dozens of bodies were counted floating down the Red River. A Republican judge and the county sheriff, a Union veteran, were assassinated in St. Mary Parish. At Gretna, three Blacks were murdered. An unarmed Black man was shot dead by Democrats parading through St. Bernard Parish, where some 150 armed white "roughs" also seized the county police station and killed three Black policemen. Forty-two Blacks were murdered in Caddo Parish, 162 in Bossier Parish. Scores were killed by white rioters in New Orleans, including a city policeman during an altercation at a parade, after which all the city's Black policemen were fired and replaced by whites. The federal commander on the scene, the conservative Gen. Lovell Rousseau—Andrew Johnson's approved replacement for the Radical Philip Sheridan, and a onetime slaveowner—did little to stem the bloodshed, reporting to Grant after a spate of murders, "I do not think the matter serious." So dangerous had the state become by Election Day that the Republican leadership urged Blacks in many communities not to vote at all.

Across the Mississippi in Tennessee, Nathan Bedford Forrest continued his march toward respectability. His political prospects surged with his deepening friendship with Democratic vice presidential candidate Frank Blair, who was rapidly shifting rightward in his politics and investing in a Mississippi cotton plantation, apparently with Forrest's guidance. On September 21, the two men strode with conspicuously linked arms into a Memphis hall, where Forrest delivered a fulsome introduction for his new friend, the Democratic vice presidential candidate. The next day, Blair wrote to his influential brother, Montgomery, a former member of Lincoln's cabinet, asking him to try to procure a full pardon for Forrest, despite his responsibility for the Fort Pillow massacre and his involvement with the Klan. If the Democrats won in November, his ambitions would be unbounded.

When not fawning over the powerful, Forrest continued to cultivate the company of the government's enemies. In October, he may personally have led one of the Klan's boldest operations ever, essentially an act of piracy on the Mississippi River. A steamer carrying four thousand rifles and ammunition for the embattled Republican-led state militia in Arkansas was boarded by a gang of sixty or more masked Klansmen who had been alerted to the shipment by disloyal telegraph agents in Memphis. Using a commandeered tugboat, they overtook the steamboat, drove off the crew, threw the weapons into the river, and were picked up by a coordinated flotilla of small boats and returned to Memphis. There, several of the raiders who were apparently well known to Memphis society could be seen later that evening parading with be-gowned ladies at a grand soiree.

Although he tried, Forrest was unable to fully escape the weight of either his wartime actions or his unsavory present associations. The facts of the Fort Pillow massacre were well documented. When challenged, however, Forrest denied that there had even been a massacre, or, alternatively, claimed baselessly that Black soldiers from Fort Pillow had pillaged the countryside and "committed the most brutal outrages upon highly respectable women." Since many of his men were relatives of these alleged "victims," who begged him to attack the fort, Forrest said, he "had no alternative" but to do so. Preposterously, he further asserted that if any wounded federal soldiers *had* been burned to death in the fort's hospital, then the *defenders* must have done it. Referring to him sarcastically as "a shining light of the Democratic Party," the *New York Times* also reported a lesser-known wartime incident in which Forrest had allegedly shot to death a free, Pennsylvania-born Black civilian who was captured at the battle of Murfreesboro. Nor could Forrest easily shed his involvement with the Klan since he had openly boasted of it. The *New York Tribune* reported that former South Carolina governor Benjamin Perry had heard Forrest brag at the Democratic convention that at any moment he could call out sixty thousand gunmen in Tennessee alone.

Despite Forrest's transparent lies, it appears that he urged the Klan, or at least that part of it he influenced, to be "cautious, discreet and moderate" in the run-up to the election. This was mainly strategic, since Tennessee's legislature had enacted a raft of laws that authorized imprisonment for anyone prowling the roads in disguise, disqualifying jurors who had Klan ties, punishing anyone who threatened voters, and mandating public officials to swear that they had never been members of the Klan "or any other disguised body of men." Forrest and his group were also astute enough to recognize that unbridled violence had a negative impact on potential Democratic voters in the North. Thus a "General Order" issued by "Headquarters" to the dens of Middle Tennessee complained that "imposters" were flogging Negroes, and ordered that den leaders be properly elected and new members inducted only in accordance with "prescribed forms." In at least one instance, Forrest was reported to have dispatched his loyalists to rein in freelance raiding in Madison County. The state leadership wasn't rejecting physical violence as such, which after all it had pioneered, but rather straining to assert control over a movement that was rapidly spreading beyond its reach as independent Klan cells increasingly acted on their own. If there was violence to be done, the Tennesseans at least wanted to be in charge of it. In any case, their caution went only so far. Claiming that the prospective recruitment of Blacks into the state militia meant that they were organizing to "exterminate" the Klan, the "General Order" warned, "We are not the enemy of the Blacks as long as they behave themselves. But if they make war upon us, they abide the awful retribution that will follow."

For most white voters, at least in the North, the election blended the three-ring entertainment of a carnival and the gravity of a drama, in which anyone could play a role. As Clemenceau described the campaign,

> Untrammeled freedom of speech and the press is here, freedom to jeer, to insult and deride and bear false witness, to arouse hatred and scorn of anything and everybody. Some are fired with enthusiasm for an idea, others with admiration or hatred for a man; everyone finds something to excite his good or bad nature, and gives it free play. Pools are made up as if at a horse race. All this time meetings go on, over and over again, with the necessary accompaniment of billboards, fireworks, music, parades, transparencies, torchlight processions, floats, masquerades, illuminations, cannon shots. Each man can flatter himself that he is a fine public speaker, and can have the pleasure of haranguing men of his own opinions, who for the asking will wind up by carrying him off on their shoulders, as he will carry them the next day. Orator can vociferate against orator. If the temper of their audience is calm and serious, they hold a debate. But at times, angered by the constant interruptions of an unsympathetic audience, they lose their tempers, hurl insults at each other, and perhaps end by using the pedestals they stood on to break each other's heads.

American newspapers, Clemenceau continued, were bursting with "outrageous attacks, libels, and calumnies, and the caricatures they publish strike at the private lives of the candidates, and which respect nothing whatever." Grant, meanwhile, "remained at his home in Galena [Illinois], saying nothing about the political questions of the moment, while Seymour retired to his farm in New York and focused, it was put about, on restocking his herd. Blair, whose ferocity had alienated voters, was sent off to the West to get him out of the way, while Colfax, also campaigning in the West, was almost captured by Indians."

For embattled Republicans elsewhere in the South, however, the Klan's putative restraint was more honored in the breach than the observance. In many areas, the Freedmen's Bureau advised Blacks not to even risk holding campaign rallies. Fearful Republican governors continued to beg for more troops, usually with little effect. In Arkansas, the Republican governor and many of the state officials camped out for days in the statehouse surrounded by federal troops, for fear of assassination. From his headquarters in Atlanta, General Meade wrote to army chief of staff John Rawlins, "I have no doubt that any effort will be & is being made within what is considered the strict letter of the law, to paralyze and render impotent the several State Governments." Of South Carolina in particular, Meade wrote, "there is practically *no Government*," and such that did exist outside the main cities was subverted by officials who felt no loyalty to the Republican governor and by the fears of "those who though in full sympathy with the party in power *are afraid* to act." Wrote one desperate Georgian to Grant, echoing many other correspondents, "We Republicans in Savannah are in *Enemys Country*. We await with anxiety news from the loyal North, to determine by *your election* that as American Citizens we have rights in Georgia."

By the last days of the campaign, attacks on both candidates were savage. Republican cartoonist Thomas Nast caricatured Seymour with his hair twisted up into devil's horns, a murdered Black infant at his feet and a lynching victim nearby, reminding voters of the Democrat's support from Klansmen like Forrest. Democrats, for their part, relentlessly smeared Grant as a "nigger lover," a hopeless drunk, and a gauche dolt. Though it was not publicized at the time, he also received death threats which his aides took seriously. Republicans attacked the Democrats as the party of disloyalty and treason, and hammered Seymour as a wartime defeatist, whose "rebel friends," such as Forrest, were the instigators of the Klan's "quasirebellion" ravaging the South. They also accused him, not without reason, of planning to shrink the army to the point where it could no longer protect loyal southern citizens. "Camilla," "Fort Pillow," and "Opelousas" all became potent Republican rallying cries against southern efforts to undo Reconstruction. By late October, the Democrats' early cockiness had evaporated. Trounced in state elections in Pennsylvania, Ohio, and Indiana, spooked party leaders instigated a fumbling last-minute movement to dump Seymour and Blair for candidates more palatable to conservative Republicans—

perhaps Supreme Court chief justice Salmon P. Chase, or the party's 1864 candidate, George B. McClellan, the popular general Winfield Scott Hancock, or, a desperate prospect indeed, Andrew Johnson.

On Election Day, Democrats mobilized with their armed auxiliaries to suppress the Black vote wherever they could. Republicans were ruthlessly harassed. The homes of election officials were stoned or fired into. Registrars were threatened while they were making out certificates or bribed not to do their jobs. Black voters were paid to vote Democratic, reportedly as much as $600 in one notorious Charleston case. White poll workers pocketed ballots and "lost" others. In Gaston County, the Klan threatened to shoot any Republican who dared to publicly campaign. In Newberry County, South Carolina, when Klan chief William Tolbert was asked how Republican speakers were to be treated if they attempted to campaign in the county, he replied, "Shoot them, kill them, stop it." In rural Louisiana, Blacks were herded to polls by armed men and forced to vote Democratic. In some places, Blacks who voted for conservatives were provided on the spot with certificates of "good conduct," while those who cast Republican ballots were told that they would be fired from their jobs. In one Tennessee town, mobs yelled "colored" every time a white man voted the Republican ticket; in another, Democrats seized a white Republican and pretended to auction him off as a "white negro." In at least two South Carolina counties, gangs of Klansmen seized all the Republican ballots. In many districts Republican constables were too afraid to guard the polls. In others, white mobs physically pushed Blacks away from the ballot boxes. Elsewhere, clerks claimed that they could not find the names of Republican voters on their registration lists, or summarily ordered would-be Black voters away. In New Hanover County, North Carolina, "colored" voters were forced into the headquarters of the Democratic Party and made to swear under threat that they would vote for Seymour and Blair. In Savannah, Georgia, when an altercation occurred between Blacks and whites, local police shot and killed several of the Blacks, and drove the rest from the polls.

Grant sat out election night in Galena with his wife, Julia, in a handsome new hilltop house that the citizens of the city had donated to him for his service in the war. At about 10 p.m., he and his advisors met at the home of Rep. Elihu Washburne, Grant's friend and longtime ally. Outside, the local Lead Mine Band played patriotic airs. Newspaper reporters, out-of-town politicians, and ordinary citizens crowded into the library, where a cozy hickory fire burned on the hearth. A telegraph terminal set up in the house ticked madly as the returns trickled in. Grant, equipped with his habitual cigar, chatted amiably with everyone until the early hours, seemingly unconcerned at the election's outcome.

Despite the Democrats' efforts to suppress Republican voting, Grant nonetheless won 214 electoral votes to Seymour's 80, and carried twenty-six states including six newly reconstructed ones in the South, among them South Carolina, where Grant overcame Seymour by a margin of 63,000 to about 45,000. In Galena, Grant's victory was celebrated by bonfires and a massive torchlight procession, including a contingent of the Galena tanners, representing the profession at which Grant had once unhappily worked. Among the states of the old Confederacy, Grant lost only Georgia and Louisiana, which were in political chaos. (Unreconstructed Virginia, Mississippi, and Texas didn't vote.) He tallied 53 percent of the popular vote, a solid but hardly overwhelming victory. The Republicans also retained overwhelming control of both houses of Congress. In the new Senate, fifty-seven Republicans would overpower the eleven Democrats; in the House, where the Democrats gained twenty seats, the Republicans still wound up with 143 seats to the Democrats' 72, falling one vote short of a two-thirds majority. Black suffrage was also on the ballot in several northern states, but the results were mixed: although it passed in Minnesota and Nevada, it was soundly defeated in both Michigan and Missouri, underscoring the irony that as Reconstruction expanded Black voting rights in the former Confederacy, they were still rejected by white voters in significant swaths of the North.

The Republicans could count the election a triumph. But there were worrying signs. The willingness of Democrats to resort to violence demonstrated clearly that the fragile new Republican governments in the South were barely able to defend themselves, especially where federal troops were spread thin and the Union League had been damaged by Klan attacks. Many frightened Blacks had stayed home on Election Day. In the most Klan-infested counties, the Democratic ticket won heavily even where Blacks had a majority of voters. In Lincoln County, Tennessee, for instance, 780 votes had been cast in 1867 for Radical governor William Brownlow, but in 1868, only four were cast for Grant. In Newberry County, South Carolina, where there were four times as many registered Blacks as whites, only two Blacks tried to vote and both were told to "go somewhere else." In Camilla, Georgia, only two Republican voters dared to show up at the polls, and in St. Mary Parish, Louisiana, not one vote was cast for Grant out of a total of 4,787, just seven months after the parish had delivered more than 2,500 votes for the Republican candidate for governor. Reported the parish's Republican registrar, "No man on that day could have voted any other than the Democratic ticket and not been killed inside of twenty-four hours."

On Election Day, James Martin, a Black Republican in Edgefield County, South Carolina, was told by a white neighbor, "We intend to kill everyone who starts [for the polls], for no d____d nigger shall vote in this county." Martin, who was fired from his job when he said he intended to vote, set out anyway, and en route met two friends who had tried to vote and been shot. Undaunted, he arrived at the polls to find that no voting was taking place. Although terrorism had depleted Black turnout in many areas, massive numbers of freedmen had defiantly braved intimidation in order to cast their first vote. This did not happen by magic.

Grant's victory was a triumph for the embattled Union Leagues, the harvest of many months of intense labor by the leagues and organizers such as Wyatt Outlaw, the Graham, North Carolina, carpenter, and thousands of Republicans like him, both Black and white, in every southern state. They mobilized freedmen in rural hamlets, towns, and city neighborhoods alike, training them in the principles of government, hunting up candidates, promoting their campaigns, and often arming enough of them to protect voters on Election Day. In many areas, Leaguers mustered the night before, and then in the morning marched to the polls en masse for safety, to reach the polls ahead of their enemies, encouraged along the way by their wives and daughters. As one Black Georgian put it, "We's a poor, humble, degraded people, but we know our friends. We'd walk fifteen miles in war time to find out about the battle; we can walk fifteen miles and more to find out how to vote."

Had it not been for the 400,000 newly enfranchised Blacks who voted for Grant in spite of the challenges, he would have lost the election and Reconstruction would have come to an abrupt halt. The South's infant Republican Party had survived its first great test, and it had mostly prevailed. Its future, Republicans and Democrats could both see, depended on the courage of Black Americans to keep casting votes. With Johnson gone, Grant in the White House, Republican governments controlling almost every southern state, and lopsided Republican majorities in both houses of Congress, Reconstruction could go forward with new vigor. The election had indeed wrought a racial revolution: Black men had been elected to serve in hundreds of local and state offices, where they would govern whites, legislate for them, and be able to hold them to account. A whole new generation of assertive, talented, mostly young Black leaders was emerging on the political scene. They were determined never again to submit to the racial degradation that had been Black Americans' unwilling way of life for as long as any could remember. As an unidentified Black orator declared in Savannah, "A revolution gave us the right to vote, and it will take a revolution to get it away from us. We will be peaceful citizens if you so wish, but fighters if you force us to it."

Part Two

GRANT TAKES COMMAND

6

THE SPHINX

God Knows I am done my Husbands blood calls upon
his country for vengeance upon his murderers.

—SALLIE ADKINS, Georgia widow

The 4th of March 1869 dawned in Washington to a rain-soaked sky
and mist so thick that the Capitol could barely be seen from the
White House. At 10:50, Ulysses Grant emerged from army headquarters at 17th and F Streets and climbed into an open carriage
alongside his closest aide, Gen. John Rawlins. Andrew Johnson, bitter in defeat, refused to join Grant for the ceremonial ride to the
Capitol. (Later, Johnson called it his "Emancipation Day," sarcastically declaring that for the last four years he had been "the greatest slave on earth," shackled to the nagging demands of Negroes
and Radicals.) A seventy-man cavalry escort immediately formed
around Grant's carriage, and as it turned into Pennsylvania Avenue, the rest of the inaugural parade swung into step behind him:
regiments of infantry, militia units from as far away as California,
batteries of artillery, contingents of Zouaves gaily dressed in bil-
lowing red trousers and tasseled red caps, drum corps, cornet bands,
grizzled veterans of the War of 1812 and the Mexican War, fire companies tugging exotically decorated engines, strutting members of
both white and Black Republican clubs each with its own banners
and badges, a miniature replica of the USS *Constitution* fully rigged
in man-o'-war style and towed by six magnificent horses, and fifty

carriages filled with the members of the Supreme Court, senators, congressmen, diplomats, territorial officials, and local politicians. Boys clung like monkeys to trees, awning posts, and overhead signs, while every window and balcony the length of the avenue sported the national colors and packed knots of onlookers. Grant waved his hat to the assembled multitudes who cheered him as he passed.

At 11:55, Grant's carriage arrived at the Capitol's East Front amid a clatter of hoofs, a cacophony of dueling brass bands, roaring Union veterans, and a tumult of waving flags, many of them scarred by the shot and shell of the war's battlefields. Grant went directly to the Senate Chamber where, in accordance with custom, Schuyler Colfax was first sworn in as vice president and accepted the handover of power from the old abolitionist gladiator Ben Wade, the Senate's president pro tem. Flanked by members of Congress, Grant then stepped outside onto a broad wooden platform, which to one mordant observer suggested a scaffold where Andrew Johnson would symbolically "take his final drop." Glancing to the right and left, nodding amiably to friends, Grant's face was as unreadable as always, whether concealing happiness or anxiety no one could tell—"the Sphinx to the last," remarked the *New York Times*'s reporter. The oath of office was then administered to him by Supreme Court chief justice Salmon P. Chase, who probably chafed at swearing in a man he considered his intellectual and political inferior. Just then, the sun cracked through the lowering clouds, like the smiling promise of a new era that Republicans, the Radicals most of all, prayed had arrived at long last, after the four grindingly disappointing years of the Johnson era. Twenty-one guns thundered a mighty salute. Declared the *Times*'s correspondent, "The reign of Grant and loyalty, and truth and patriotism has begun."

Eventually, Grant took a sheaf of foolscap from his pocket, adjusted his glasses, and began reading in a conversational tone. Soon afterward, his young daughter, Nellie, alarmed by the clamor and crowds, ran to his side and grabbed his hand until a chair was found for her and she sat, seemingly assured that she was safe by her father's side. His short speech was, like the man, devoid of affectation. "The office has come to me unsought," he said. "I commence its duties untrammeled." By this he meant that he had no compromising political debts. He made clear that he didn't share Andrew Johnson's disdain for Congress. "All laws will be faithfully executed," he promised, "whether they meet my approval or not. I shall on all subjects have a policy to recommend, but none to enforce against the will of the people. Laws are to govern all alike—those opposed as well as those who favor them." He then noted the obvious, that difficult questions bequeathed by the war still remained painfully unresolved, but he intended to face them without rancor. He spoke bluntly to the South: any solution of those questions "requires security of person, property, and free religious and political opinion, in every part of our common country, without regard to local prejudice." Grant was not yet contemplating outright war against the Klan, but he was making abundantly clear that he meant to enforce the law whether white southerners liked it or not. He went on to acknowledge the immense financial burden inherited from the war; he reassured the country that the war debt would be paid in full and the national credit restored, and that reliance on specie would soon be reinstituted, thanks to the vast resource of precious metals that were being exploited in the West, "as if providence had bestowed upon us a strongbox which we are now forging the key to unlock." He also promised "practical retrenchment in expenditure"; that is, major cuts in federal spending. Although he failed to mention the implications of this for Reconstruction, in practical terms it would inevitably mean further reductions in the federal occupation force in the South. He then called for "patient forbearance one towards another throughout the land," a hope, surely, more than it was an expectation. He then promised his support for one of the most revolutionary measures that had ever been put before the American people: ratification of the Fifteenth Amendment. "The question of suffrage is one which is likely to agitate the public so long as a portion of the citizens of the nation are excluded from its privileges in any state," he declared. It was time to settle the question.

Republicans universally believed that the vote was both the ultimate expression of full American citizenship and the most powerful defensive weapon in the armory of democracy. Enfranchising the freedmen, proclaimed the *New York Tribune,* "can no more be left to the former ruling element in the South to decide than we could submit to the same element the question of Union or Secession. The voice of the nation at large must guarantee union, freedom, and equal political rights." The vote would not only pave southern Blacks' path to political power, it would also significantly enlarge the pool of Republicans in the border states and the North. Although Black populations there were comparatively small, they could still mean the margin of difference between victory and defeat. Their hopes were poignantly expressed by a freedman named Stephen Walker who wrote to the new president from North Carolina: "We beleav here in this destressed place it the lord hav place you in a place for as a father for We poor colred people."

Influential Blacks urged Grant to appoint "trustworthy colored men" to federal patronage positions and to public roles in the Republican Party. "We desire that the political experience of Northern colored men and the political power enjoyed by Southern colored men may blend so completely as to cause the entire people to forget color or section in the recognition of patriotism," the wealthy Black New Yorker George Downing wrote hopefully to Grant. The most politically sophisticated among them, such as the Black Ohioan John Mercer Langston, acknowledged however that "removing the rubbish, the accretions of the now dead slaveholding oligarchy" would not be an easy task, or quickly accomplished.

Langston also knew that not all the obstacles to progress were to be found in the South. Northerners, increasingly, seemed more interested in sectional healing than in further moral crusades. Despite news of continuing Klan attacks, few believed that southern reactionaries would pursue a reign of terror so savage and sustained that it could ever effectively turn the Reconstruction Amendments into dead letters. Most were idealistically confident that the power of the vote would be sufficient for the freedmen to protect themselves. The *New York Tribune* rosily asserted, "On the whole, the South is looking up. There is a fraction of her people who still choose to put on masks and ride about at midnight to assault Unionists white or black, and burn negro schoolhouses. But these are not half so many as they were, and their number is still decreasing. We shall be disappointed if they are not reduced to a few isolated gangs of ten or thirty within the next two years."

"There has been no event since the close of the war in which I have felt so deep an interest as that of the ratification of the Fifteenth Amendment," Grant told Republicans gathered one day outside the

White House. "It looked to me as the realization of the Declaration of Independence." Congress had approved the terse language of the amendment barely a week before the inauguration: "The right of citizens of the United States to vote shall not be denied or abridged by the United States or any State on account of race, color, or previous condition of servitude." Its passage had climaxed years of often bitter controversy, as the principle it proclaimed slowly trickled from the remoter eddies of abolitionism into the political mainstream. Republicans had argued that anything short of a constitutional amendment was inadequate to protect Black voters, since a mere law subject "to all the vicissitudes of politics and changes of opinion" could easily be reversed by future Congresses, as George Boutwell of Massachusetts, who led the floor debate in the House of Representatives, put it. A constitutional amendment would be far more difficult to repeal.

Early in the debate, Henry Wilson of Massachusetts, the measure's strongest advocate in the Senate, predicted optimistically that within four years "we shall become accustomed in all parts of the country to see all classes of our citizens peacefully exercising their rights . . . and the people will wonder why it was that they ever made any opposition to its accomplishment." (Wilson, sometimes known as "the Natick cobbler" because he had been a shoemaker earlier in life, had been born into poverty as the son of an alcoholic day laborer; his empathy with the struggles of African Americans was deep and personal.) Wilson readily admitted that the amendment would cost Republicans votes. A "storm of passion and prejudice," he said, had blown up every time the party enlarged the rights of Black Americans—when it abolished slavery in Washington, when it armed Black men to fight as Union soldiers, when Lincoln issued the Emancipation Proclamation, and when Congress enacted the Thirteenth and Fourteenth Amendments, the Civil Rights Act, and established the Freedmen's Bureau. "But no matter how unpopular [the amendment] is, no matter what it costs, no matter whether it brings victory or defeat, it is our duty to hope on and struggle on and work on until we make the humblest citizen of the United States the peer and equal in rights and privileges of every other citizen of the United States."

There was more than idealism at work. Boutwell estimated that although the amendment might mean the loss of perhaps 10 percent of Republican voters in the North, the party would gain a quarter-million Black votes in the South, and many more new votes in the border and northern states, where—apart from eight states mostly in New England—even free Blacks had never been allowed to vote: 45,000 in Kentucky, he estimated; 35,000 in Maryland; 24,000 in Missouri; 14,000 in Pennsylvania; 10,000 in New York; 7,000 in Ohio; and more across other northern states. "Are we to decline the services of one hundred and fifty thousand men who are ready to do battle for us at the ballot-box?" he demanded.

Legislators like Boutwell and Wilson were in a hurry to achieve as much as they could while it was still possible. They knew that most Republicans regarded the amendment less as the beginning of a new, more enlightened age for civil liberties than as the climax of the long and exhausting campaign to cleanse the country of the sin of slavery. Even many lifelong abolitionists thought so, including many members of the American Anti-Slavery Society, whose president, William Lloyd Garrison, proclaimed that the battle for African Americans had been won, and officially declared the organization defunct. But the amendment wasn't as watertight as it seemed. It left the states free to restrict suffrage in ways that its language failed to anticipate. "The learned and the rich scarcely need the ballot for their protection," argued Sen. Willard Warner of Alabama, a former Union general who had moved south after the war and purchased a plantation near Montgomery. "It is the poor, unlearned man who has nothing but the ballot to whom it is a priceless heritage, a protection and a shield."

While Radicals held that Congress retained the authority to oversee Reconstruction measures in the South whether states had been readmitted to the Union or not, more conservative Republicans believed that federal power was already too great and bridled at the prospect of any further interference in state affairs, no matter what the cause. Many of those who backed the amendment in principle supported neither federal enforcement of its provisions nor the guaranteed enfranchisement of every voter. In reply, Rep. Samuel Shellabarger of Ohio, a Radical, presciently pointed out that the amendment's wording left the "treason-blighted South" quite capable of subverting the amendment's intent. "Let it remain possible, under our amendment to still disenfranchise the body of the colored race in the late rebel states and I tell you it will be done," he grimly predicted, adding, "A mistake here is absolutely fatal."

Several Radicals attempted without success to guarantee Blacks the right to hold office. Wilson, for one, reminded his colleagues that Georgia's legislature had summarily expelled its elected Black members because their right to sit in it wasn't stipulated in the state constitution. Failing to protect Black officeholders, he warned, would only embolden other states to imitate Georgia's example. Others tried to include revised language that would give Congress the clear right to regulate suffrage in the states, but they all failed. Sen. Charles Sumner's proposed version, the strongest, declared: "That the right to vote, to be voted for, and to hold office shall not be denied or abridged anywhere in the United States under any pretense of race or color." Federal courts would have exclusive jurisdiction over all offenses against the act, which included attempting to hinder either a voter from casting his ballot or interfering in the work of a registrar, with both crimes subject to imprisonment and a fine of up to $3,000. Had these provisions been adopted, much of the violent repression that was to come might have been forestalled. But Sumner's proposal was crushed in a vote of 47 to 9.

These more ambitious versions of the amendment fell victim to the desire of some northern Republicans to preserve inequalities among *whites* in their own states. Pennsylvanians, for example, had to prove that they had paid state taxes. Rhode Island required foreign-born citizens to own at least $134 of real estate. Massachusetts and Connecticut insisted on evidence of literacy. Chinese were barred from voting on the West Coast. And nowhere were women permitted to vote. (The failure of the amendment to enfranchise women created a lasting rift between many Black activists and their once close female allies.) The limited version that was hashed out behind closed doors thus opened the gate to poll taxes, literacy tests, and property qualifications for Blacks in the South, all of which would later prove to be potent tools in the hands of racist conservatives.

On February 25, the House passed the amendment by a vote of 144 to 44, and the Senate shortly afterward by 39 to 13. The mistake that Shellabarger warned of was made. Several disheartened Radicals declined to vote at all. Wilson voted unhappily with the majority. The expansive vision that he and his allies had espoused, he said with palpable bitterness, "I am sorry to find, is too broad, too comprehensive, too generous, too liberal for the American people of today." Whether Grant would have preferred a stronger amendment is unclear. Had he advised its rejection, however, or had he been indifferent to its fate, the amendment surely would have failed.

Grant had other things on his mind. Like all new presidents, he was preoccupied with building his administration. "They say he chose mediocre men," Clemenceau wrote, echoing the judgment of some elite Republicans. "Granting this to be true, their mediocrity is probably the very quality for which the president values them. American democracy is a little afraid, and with some reason, of men of genius, of saviors guided by mysterious inspiration, who are charged by Providence to think and act for other men." This was unduly harsh, although Grant did largely bypass the party's establishment. He tapped his chief of staff, Gen. John Rawlins, for secretary of war, the Radical George Boutwell—"twenty years of caucus, wires, and stump," harumphed one critic —for Treasury, former general and conservative Republican Ohio governor Jacob D. Cox as interior secretary, and for attorney general Ebenezer Hoar, a former member of the Massachusetts Supreme Court, and friend of Emerson, Longfellow, and Holmes. To the surprise of many, Grant declined to name the very expectant Senator Sumner as secretary of state, and instead appointed his longtime congressional patron Elihu Washburne; then, when Washburne hit congressional resistance, Grant replaced him with Hamilton Fish, New York's cosmopolitan former governor and senator, who was commonly regarded as the cabinet's most capable member.

Some of Grant's lower-level appointments were potent with symbolism. He named former Confederate general James Longstreet, once Robert E. Lee's highest-ranking subordinate but now a committed Republican, to the important position of federal customs officer in politically volatile New Orleans. Having been dogged by accusations of anti-Semitism, deriving from a wartime incident for which he apologized, Grant appointed numerous Jews to important posts, as consuls, district attorneys, and other offices, including Edward Salomon to take charge of the sprawling Washington Territory, making him the nation's first Jewish governor. Grant also nominated his former military secretary, Ely Parker, a Seneca from western New York, to head the Bureau of Indian Affairs, long a swamp of corruption—the first high-level appointment of a Native American in the government's history. In keeping with his public pledge to reform Indian policy, which tended to oscillate between neglect and spasmodic violence, Grant initiated what he termed a "humane and Christianizing" policy that would eventually guide Indians toward "civilization and ultimate citizenship." Although culturally insensitive by present-day standards, it was a remarkably sympathetic approach for its time, reflecting Grant's deeply held sentiment "that the whole race would be harmless and peaceable if they were not put upon by the whites."

With respect to Black Americans, Grant was not free of at least some of the racial assumptions of his era. In January, he had told a gathering of Black well-wishers, with mingled reassurance and condescension, "I hope sincerely that the colored people of the nation may receive every protection which the laws give them. They shall have my efforts to secure such protection. They should prove by their acts, their advancement, prosperity, and obedience to the laws worthy of all privileges the government has bestowed upon them by their future conduct and prove themselves deserving of all they now claim." But when it came to concrete measures, he didn't equivocate. He appointed so many Black men as postmasters that the unfriendly *New York Herald* complained that he had embraced "an extreme view of the effect of laws to give niggers civil rights." And in April he met with the first Black public official ever to dine at the White House, Lt. Gov. Oscar J. Dunn of Louisiana. He tapped the energetic John Eaton, a Presbyterian minister and former army colonel who had commanded Black troops during the war, to head the anemic Bureau of Education, which had been ignored by Andrew Johnson, declaring, "With millions of ex-slaves upon our hands to be educated, this is not the time to suppress an office for facilitating education." Acknowledging the courts' frequently lackadaisical attitude toward Black rights, he also named liberal-minded men to nine new federal judgeships, several of whom would figure significantly in the looming war against the Ku Klux Klan.

The government, like the country, had changed dramatically

since Abraham Lincoln's arrival at the White House in 1861. Before the war, the national government had barely touched ordinary Americans, apart from the delivery of their mail. Now it had conscripted them into the army, taxed their income, built them a railroad that spanned the continent, thrown open the western prairie to their homesteads, borrowed from them prodigiously to pay for the war, and paid them in new national greenback currency. Webs of railroads and telegraph lines helped energize an economy that for the first time was becoming truly national as the decentralized business landscape of prewar times burgeoned into an industrial behemoth. Power had centralized to a degree once unimaginable: before the war, Americans commonly spoke of the United States in the plural, now they did so in the singular, as one irrevocably welded together nation. Management of the ballooned war debt, demobilization, the disposition of vast land grants, and the swollen trough of lucrative federal contracts fed new government bureaus that proliferated in Washington like tropical vegetation. Sophisticates mocked Grant's ignorance of the ways of the capital. But he was not really the political ingenue that he seemed in caricature. Although he lacked the conventional seasoning of career politicians, he had commanded the largest and most modern army ever fielded in the Western Hemisphere, worked skillfully with Congress and two presidents, and had succeeded in avoiding the political pitfalls that had prematurely ended the careers of other generals.

He acted with efficiency and dispatch to restore the government's credit: the first legislation he signed provided for paying off in gold the holders of $2.5 billion in outstanding bonds and redeeming hundreds of millions more in paper money as quickly as possible. In foreign policy, he faced knotty negotiations with England over compensation for the depredations of British-built Confederate raiders that had ravaged northern shipping during the war. The press and public were clamoring for intervention on behalf of Cuban insurgents who promised to free the Spanish-owned island's half-million slaves. And expansionists were urging him to acquire the Dominican Republic, usually known then as Santo Domingo, which shared the island of Hispaniola with Haiti. The most ardent annexationists were driven by both the desire to exploit Santo Domingo's natural resources and to use it as a naval base to counter British designs in the region, but Grant also saw it as a possible home for numbers of the South's suffering freed people.

Absent from Grant's agenda was a comprehensive plan for pacification of the South. Public sentiment in the North strongly supported the readmittance of all the former Confederate states, three of which still remained under army rule: Virginia, Mississippi, and Texas. Grant understood that the completion of Reconstruction depended on the Republicans retaining power, but framing a policy posed enormous difficulties. Although he was committed to preserving the fruits of Union victory and sympathized deeply with the plight of southern Republicans, he was shackled to the government's commitment to hand authority back to the restored state governments. On April 7, he told Congress, "The authority of the [government] must undoubtedly be asserted for the absolute protection of all its citizens in the full enjoyment of the freedom and security which is the object of a republican government . . . but whenever the people of a rebellious state are ready to enter in good faith upon the accomplishment of this object" in conformity with the authority of Congress, "it is certainly desirable that all causes of irritation should be removed as promptly as possible." For this, the *New York Herald,* which was often critical of Republicans, praised Grant as "a practical statesman" who sought to "temper justice with kindness and conciliation."

Conditions in the South varied widely and in complex ways. Biracial governments were at work in several states, while almost everywhere reactionaries were jockeying to regain control, with varying degrees of success. Blacks wielded considerable political power in South Carolina, Mississippi, and Louisiana, where they formed the majority; in other states, they were potent minorities, and in still others, such as Arkansas and Kentucky—which though it had remained with the Union during the war was increasingly aligning politically with the former Confederate South—Black populations were comparatively modest. Quite apart from Negrophobia and racism, other issues also separated the races, the competition for patronage, for example, and support for free public education, which Blacks intensely desired but tax-averse whites often opposed. Georgia was in near chaos, with widespread lawlessness and the Republican governor at loggerheads with the now all-white conservative legislature. Conservatives were also on the brink of regaining power in Tennessee. Although Republicans nominally controlled most of the other states, the reach of official power was shaky. Protecting freed people, white Republicans, and public institutions from the gathering assault by the Ku Klux Klan remained a continuing, worsening problem. As federal troops were withdrawn from central Alabama one frightened Republican was heard to say, "The U.S. forces might as well be located in Maine."

Meanwhile, the Klan was about to embark on its most explosive growth yet. In nearly every southern state, the Klan was thriving, with increasingly aggressive local chiefs and dens which exhibited little evidence of loyalty to leaders outside their own region, or even just their county or town. Still feeling his way into the presidency, Grant genuinely hoped that the South's frail Republican state governments would manage to keep the surging violence in check. But he was soon disabused. He would certainly have read about the attack on the home of Daniel Blue, who had dared to serve as a witness against Klansmen in Moore County, North Carolina: the night riders first shot to death Blue's pregnant wife and one daughter, then set fire to his house, and burned four more of his children to death. He had read the report from Georgia where, one of his generals wrote, many parts of the state were without law and order because civil officials were afraid to do their duty and "numerous insurrectionary organizations" were free to commit crimes with impunity. Letter after letter from beleaguered Republicans flooded his desk, piling one plaintive plea atop another with their harrowing tales of cruelty, until the entire South must sometimes have seemed to be erupting in one vast cry of pain. "How long, O Lord, *how long,* are the true Union men of Georgia to be thus hunted down and mercilessly shot?" Edward Hulbert wrote from Atlanta. G. W. Barber, "a poor farmer," wrote from Jacksonville, Florida, begging Grant to "send a lot of troops here immediately and Breakup these clans of miserable robers" and their "secrete meatings." A man named Woodruff wrote from Tuscaloosa that there had been twenty-six murders in the space of a few months, with no arrests made: "Kansas people are protected against Indian massacres—Why cannot we be protected against these enemies of the U. States ('Ku Klux Out Laws')?" Another correspondent, "A. Bridgewater," wrote from a hiding place in the woods where he had taken refuge with other loyal men that he was "living in a den of those midnight murders that has caused so much distress in Kentucky," and that "last week they made a charge on our neighborhood and shot a man 40 times for saying that he had stood gard before your tent at Vicksburg." Charles Arnold, a Republican-appointed postmaster in Georgia, begged for protection from the Klan, "which infest this state," writing, "Should I be murdered hereafter, I ask of your Excellency the arrest and punishment of those men." He added, "This is confidential, as if it were known that I had written such a letter, I would be murdered Instantaneously."

Another distraught Georgian, Sallie Adkins of Warren County, wrote to Grant to report that her husband, an advocate of emancipation who had been jailed by the Confederates for his Unionism during the war, had just been murdered on a public road. He was the second member of the state constitutional convention and the fourth member of the legislature to have been slaughtered within twenty miles of her home, "and the number of negroes thus dispatched is legion." No inquest into his murder was held, no move made to arrest his assailants. "His murderarrs are now at large openly, no body moves, no body cares," she wrote, while her neighbors were "still shunning & scorning us even in our agony," and laughing at her when she met them on the road. "It may be that Republics have no remdy for such state of things,—If so Republics are bad *things*," she wrote. "God Knows I am done my Husbands blood calls upon his country for vengeance upon his murderers—I have no hope of redress from the effete, helpless over powered thing called the Government of Georgia—It is a sham, a mockery, a mere modification of the Confedercy—The Ku Klux control it. I demand that you *President Grant* Keep the pledge you made the *nation*—make it safe for any man to utter boldly an openly his devotion to the United States & his confidence in you."

If such voices did not infest Grant's dreams, they certainly must have haunted his waking hours. He had been hearing them in a rising crescendo for the past four years, from Carl Schurz back in 1865, from private informants, from his officers across the South, from Republican officeholders, and from ordinary men and women both white and Black. For a soldier, he was a man of exceptional sensitivity, who, though he had ordered thousands of men into battle and to their deaths during the war, seemed to feel the pain of the vulnerable deep in his bones. He well knew that the Republican experiment and the promise of active citizenship for freed Blacks could not long be sustained against an enemy whose ruthlessness was more evident by the month.

There was a troubling irony to the election victories that had placed most of the southern states under Republican-dominated governments: while this ousted the old white elites and inspired hope in Blacks, it also eliminated Republicans' best shield, the federal military. Grant quickly reshuffled military commanders by appointing men who more closely reflected his views. He named Gen. Joseph A. "Fighting Joe" Mower, a reliable Vermonter who had served under Sherman, to volatile Louisiana; handed Mississippi to the politically ambitious young abolitionist Gen. Adelbert Ames; and replaced the conservative Meade with Gen. Alfred H. Terry, a Yale-educated lawyer with long wartime experience in South Carolina to oversee the vast Department of the South, which comprised all the seaboard states from North Carolina to Alabama. However, as each state returned to the Union, the army was obliged to shut down its military commissions, turn over its prisoners to the civil courts, and yield to state court orders. It was such a recalibration that had already led, in 1868, to the abrupt abandonment of the prosecution of George Ashburn's murderers. Whites felt that they didn't need to submit to any laws passed by what they contemptuously called "negro government," by which they generally meant *any* government that included Blacks. The *Edgefield Advertiser,* based in what was soon to become a hotbed of Klan activity in upcountry South Carolina, ominously editorialized that "the continued denial of our Gd-given privileges and rights justify the resort to extraordinary means for their recovery and perpetuation!" That moment, the editorial added, "is approaching in the history of our downtrodden people."

Whites and Blacks alike were reluctantly beginning to come to grips with the fact that the gains of Reconstruction probably could not be sustained without a willingness on the part of the government to use force. As Sen. William Pitt Fessenden of Maine, a conservative Republican but a staunch supporter of Reconstruction, told his colleagues, "The great difficulty has arisen from the fact that we diminished the army far below what was necessary and what will be necessary for some years to come, without providing an adequate military force in the States. [A] military power of some kind is necessary in most of these states, if not all of them." Now, when local officials begged for help from the army, they rarely got it, and when commanders did respond, they had fewer and fewer troops to offer. Only a skeleton force of about twelve thousand soldiers now remained in the former Confederate states, outside Texas. Under continuing pressure to reduce the federal budget and the war debt, Grant was expected to continue shrinking the army's southern footprint. However, many northerners, including Republicans, agreed with Andrew Johnson's complaint, in his final message to Congress, that "one hundred millions annually are expended for the military force, a large portion of which is employed in the execution of laws both unnecessary and unconstitutional."

There was an alternative to the army: state militia. Up to now, southern states had been explicitly barred from raising militias, for fear of rearming former rebels. In December, South Carolina senator Fredrick A. Sawyer, a Massachusetts-born Republican, had pleaded for legislation that would permit his state government to protect itself. "We are not in a condition of society in the South where we can appeal to men's Christianity or civilization to protect us. We"—that is, Republicans—"are in the peculiar position of being apparently the dominant power in the state, while in fact we have not one single firearm where those who are opposed to us have ten."

In December, Congress had repealed the militia ban in the South. But another set of fraught problems arose. Could Blacks be enrolled and armed without provoking even more violence from the Klan, and if they were not enrolled could all-white militias—if they could be recruited at all—be trusted to protect African Americans? In Arkansas, where two state senators had recently been murdered, Republican governor Powell Clayton, a former federal cavalry commander, fielded an eight-hundred-man militia, a quarter of it Black, ordered the execution of assassins, and imposed martial law across most of the state. But Clayton was exceptional. In most areas, Blacks begged to serve, but the prospect of them with arms in their hands terrified whites. Typically, the *Charleston Mercury* warned that if the state armed Blacks they would turn into "swaggering buck niggers" who would immediately attack white women. The Georgia legislature forbade the governor to organize any militia, Black or white, and instructed the federal troops who remained in the state to disarm Blacks and disperse their political gatherings. And in South Carolina, the captain of a white militia company, challenged on his willingness to fairly enforce the law, stated, "In case of difficulty, I will go with my race."

The limitations faced by even the most forceful Republican governors were highlighted by a sequence of events that unfolded in Tennessee. At the start of the year, Tennessee seemed prepared to go to war with the Klan. Governor Brownlow hired a Union veteran from Ohio, Seymour Barmore, "a shrewd, sharp sort of man," to infiltrate the order and expose its leadership. On his first attempt, Barmore was captured by the Klan and warned that he would be executed if he tried again. Undeterred, he obtained a set of regalia, disguised himself, and managed to penetrate the Klan's Pulaski "mother den." He was en route back to Nashville when, at 3 a.m., some twenty-five Klansmen dressed in scarlet boarded his train and seized him. "No one interfered in his behalf," the *Knoxville Whig* reported. They had been tipped off by a local telegrapher who served the Klan and were likely assisted by members of the train's crew. Weeks later, Barmore's horribly decomposed body was found floating in the Duck River, with a rope around his neck, his arms tied behind him, and a bullet hole in his head.

Barmore's murder prompted Brownlow to declare martial law in nine counties and to muster eighteen hundred State Guardsmen from the staunchly loyal eastern counties. He made it clear that he was prepared to enroll Blacks as well as whites, if he had to. Open war seemed imminent. Then, suddenly, the entire political landscape changed. Brownlow abruptly left the governor's office to enter the U.S. Senate, to be replaced by his lieutenant governor, Dewitt Senter. It was assumed that Senter would continue Brownlow's forceful policy toward the Klan. Instead, he softened martial law, moved Klan trials to civil courts, and by May discharged the militia. He then won conservative support, and at least tacitly that of the Klan, when he announced his intention to repeal all legislation that limited the political activity of former Confederates. The result was the election of an overwhelming conservative majority to the state General Assembly, and the effective end of Reconstruction in Tennessee.

With the uncompromising Brownlow gone and the compliant Senter in his place, the Klan's nominally "official" leadership liquidated itself. In March, the "Grand Wizard of the Invisible Empire"—that is, Nathaniel Bedford Forrest—issued a "General Order" for the destruction of masks and costumes, and the cessation of all "demonstrations" unless they were authorized by a "Grand Titan," the chief of a congressional district, or a higher authority. It is possible that all this was theater, a feint to forestall the crackdown that seemed imminent after Barmore's murder. But the Pulaski den did cease its activities, at least to all appearances, and the several Nashville dens, three hundred strong, ostentatiously paraded in full regalia through the streets of the state capital in what they claimed was the finale to the Klan's flamboyant career.

When Forrest was summoned to testify before a joint committee of Congress investigating the Klan, in 1871, he claimed virtually total ignorance of the organization. He first asserted that, as best he knew, the Klan had "dispersed" in the "spring of 1868." Or it might have been in the early summer, "I cannot say." Or maybe later. Or perhaps when Senter was elected governor, in the autumn of 1869. Forrest figuratively shrugged: "I do not recollect, I have never paid attention to the elections." Nothing that Forrest said could be taken at face value, of course, since he obfuscated without compunction about every aspect of his association with the Klan. Asked why exactly it had been disbanded, Forrest replied, because there was no need for it anymore, because "the country was safe." If there had been any assaults since then by men *calling* themselves Klansmen, then those were just "wild young men and bad men" who had no organization at all. He claimed to know nothing about such people.

By this time, Forrest liked to present himself as the very model of a reformed rebel, opposed to violence, earnestly engaged in business—"Railroads had no politics," he told his interrogators—and entirely comfortable with the new status quo. No one in the South, he asserted with faux naïveté, believed that killing a Negro was any less of an offense than killing a white man. He boasted that he had freed the forty-five slaves on his plantation in 1863, two years before the war's end, and said that he not only supported the Fourteenth and Fifteenth Amendments but had advocated for them to "our people," because "they were inevitable and should be accepted."

It is just barely possible that Forrest was sincere, despite the mass of lies he told about his affiliation with the Klan. At bottom, he was an opportunist. In business, as a would-be politician, and as a soldier, he was a man who seized the advantage when he was certain to prevail, slipped away when the odds were decisively against him, and never undertook a battle that he didn't need to fight. He had come to the conclusion that he had no future in politics, for which he was temperamentally unsuited. Now he was dependent on attracting northern investment for his railroad schemes, and he also needed willing Black labor to work for him: the "butcher of Fort Pillow" and the "Grand Wizard" were roles that no longer played to his advantage. (In the years to come, as he struggled to recoup his fortunes, he pioneered the exploitation of prison labor as a business, one which differed very little from his use of slaves on his plantations in prewar times.)

No matter what Forrest said, or may actually have meant, in his edict of 1869, it seems to have applied only in Tennessee, and it was not universally obeyed even there. The dissolution of the Pulaski den meant little. It had long since ceased to serve as more than a symbolic touchstone for a movement that had grown far beyond anything that the founders had imagined. Forrest was no longer needed: he had given the Klan his best, and then neatly extricated himself before he was targeted by the federal government. Although his full role is hard to define with precision, he lent more than his charisma to the Klan's development. He pioneered the organized application of terror: the exploitation of his wartime style of warfare for political ends, the lightning strike, the rapid concentration of overwhelming force—now against unarmed civilians rather than Yankee soldiers. He and the commanders he recruited and encouraged had shown that Forrest's quintessential tactics could work anywhere in a region where the Klan's enemies were vulnerable, isolated, and defenseless. He had, in short, taught the Klan how to wage guerrilla war.

7

THE FACE OF REVOLUTION

There exists in this state a secret, oath-bound, armed
organization which is hostile to the state government
and to the government of the United States.

—Gov. William H. Holden

In November of 1868, North Carolina's aggressive populist Republican governor William W. Holden had boasted after the Republicans' triumph in the recent elections, "The Ku Klux—nobody is afraid of them now. The truth is, we were never afraid of them here in North Carolina—the Ku Klux have failed." Holden's self-confident and sadly baseless optimism heartened Republicans everywhere, who hoped that Grant's election would finally bring peace to the tortured South. Holden apparently believed what he said. But it was tragically premature. For the next three years, North Carolina was destined to be a bloody cockpit of surging Klan activity, and indeed to become a sort of political petri dish in which the seesawing struggle to stamp out terrorism played out earlier and more dramatically than almost anywhere else in the South. In this, North Carolina both epitomized the challenges that Republican state governments faced in confronting the Klan and foreshadowed the federal crackdown to come. Washington would be closely watching what happened there.

Republicans were probably never in a better position to cripple the Klan than in the months after Grant's election. It was a time of rising hope for supporters of the new order in every southern state,

North Carolina prominent among them. Although the Republicans had lost ground locally in some counties, Grant had nonetheless carried the state decisively, and the party had won six of its seven congressional seats. Had more federal troops been available, politicians might have been more willing to confront the Klan's leadership. But only three hundred were left to patrol the entire state. Keeping the peace thus rested in the hands of beleaguered and compromised civil officials. Agents of the Freedmen's Bureau were also helpless, or worse. When Klan violence surged in Caswell County, hard by the Virginia state line, the bureau's nearest officer, a man named Dawes, cavalierly dismissed the threat. Republican state senator John W. Stephens, an exceptionally outspoken white Radical popular with the freed people, complained to Holden, "Lieut Daws thinks that trupes is not kneeded and also advises that it will be best not to organize the militia at all as the Rebles ar so mutch opposed to it they Sware that they will not submit to Negros being armed as I came through the village [of Yanceyville] the K.K.K.'s raised sutch a yell of oustrasism after me that they was hurd over a mile from the village." The fearless Stephens was an exception. Most Republican politicians, concerned for their own safety, hesitated to criticize the Klan too forcefully. There were of course Democrats who despised the Klan's methods, but they rarely if ever protested, since the Klan's ultimate goal, along with the destruction of Black leadership, was to restore them to power.

What Stephens may not have known was that the Klan's county leader, John Lea, had already been courting the pliable Lieutenant Dawes, about whom little is otherwise known. In an interview years later, Lea recalled that he took Dawes hunting with him and "we had beautiful chase." On Election Day, Dawes companionably told Lea that he was supposed to carry the county election for the Republicans, and confided to him where he would find the unguarded ballot box. A few months earlier, in the gubernatorial election, Caswell County had delivered the Republican Party a decisive 2,800-vote Republican majority for Holden. This time, Lea chuckled, "we elected a Democratic ticket by 27 votes."

Among southern Republicans, Holden was a formidable opponent. Native-born, tough-minded, combative, and opportunistic, he was the state's only experienced politician who had thrown in his lot with the Republican Party. Raised in poverty, he was apprenticed in childhood to a printer, then worked as a typesetter, and eventually became the editor of one of the leading newspapers in Raleigh. Although he owned six slaves before the war, he retained a yeoman's ingrained dislike for the aristocratic planter class. He had initially supported secession, but soon became a harsh critic of the Confederate government and began urging peace with the North as early as 1863. Appointed the state's provisional governor by Andrew Johnson, he at first paternalistically advised Blacks to be "temperate" and industrious and told them that they shouldn't be expected to understand such things as constitutions and laws. Realizing that his most viable political future lay with the Radicals, however, in 1867 he announced his support for Black suffrage, and declared himself as an acolyte of Thaddeus Stevens, proclaiming, "The two races together will govern!" On July 4, 1868, in his inaugural address, he declared himself in favor of "liberty for the whole people, of whatever origin, color, or former condition," and asserted that there was no longer any power that could deprive Black citizens of their rights. This was likely just a rhetorical turn, but it was nonetheless inspiring to the newly enfranchised freedmen. He went beyond talk. He acted decisively to replace county and town officials with Republicans, including Blacks, and called for equal justice in law enforcement and for free public schools, both high priorities for Blacks. Conservatives, who had distrusted him during the war, loathed him with smoldering intensity. Reported one Gates County man, among his neighbors the Republicans "are looked upon as the filth of Creation," and Holden as "a Damned Negrofied son of a bitch."

The Klan emerged later in North Carolina than it had west of the Appalachians, but once there it spread fast and virulently. As late as April 1868, David Schenck, a conservative Lincolnton lawyer, had barely heard of it. "Its movements and designs are still so mysterious that no one has [a clear] idea of its designs; but by cabalistic signs, methods and advertisements they strike terror into the hearts of the blacks," he wrote in his diary. Within months, he would establish the first den in his county. Interestingly, Nathan Bedford Forrest's name was almost never mentioned by North Carolina Klansmen—suggesting that his leadership, such as it was, had faded or never played a significant role in the state. Many recruits took it for granted that the Klan's real founder had been former president Andrew Johnson, whose name was by now a cynosure of white supremacy. (This myth was not unique to North Carolina; Johnson, whatever his shortcomings, and they were many, was no friend to the Klan.)

By that summer, reports of Klan attacks came at Holden from every direction. One Warrington County Republican reported, "Sir a great deal of shooting by those who are [with] the ku-klan-kluck . . . the rebbles have said that they endend [intend] to destroy every loyal man." From Caswell County, another pleaded, "Execpt we have some forest [force] of the union Army we Can not stay hear." Silas Curtis wrote from Granville County, "it is getting to be a genrel thing, on Saturday Night last the KuKulx wer raging in [the towns of] oxford and tally ho Thursday night last they went to a Colored mans house and got him out and Beet him Cruly beet his wife and cut her dress open and tied her to a tree. They then went to another ones house and commence tarring [tearing] the top of his house off."

The true size of the Klan in North Carolina is unclear. However, Klansmen themselves believed that the three affiliated orders active in the state collectively mustered between forty and fifty thousand men among them. By some estimates, as many as half the white men in some areas, or even more, belonged to the Klan during its peak; of one county, a member later testified, "Pretty much all the men belonged to it." The Klan's three local incarnations—the White Brotherhood, the Constitutional Union Guard, and the Invisible Empire—all purported to be independent organizations. However, all three were known both to the wider public and for the most part to their own members as the "Ku Klux Klan." Their memberships overlapped; they acted cooperatively in the same areas, carried out raids on each other's behalf, swore the same oaths, wore the same sort of disguises, and perpetrated identical attacks on similar victims. To some extent, the organizations may have reflected differing local loyalties. More important, their several names provided plausible deniability when members were forced by the authorities to answer questions about what they had done and at whose orders they had done it.

James Boyd, a candidate for the House of Representatives, belonged to at least two and perhaps all three Klan organizations, joining the White Brotherhood in November 1868, in the town of Graham, at the office of another lawyer, Jacob Long, the White Brotherhood's Alamance County chief. Later, during the winter session of the state legislature, Boyd visited state senator Dr. John Moore, another prominent Klansman, in Raleigh. Under questioning, Boyd later testified, "He told me they were getting up an organization to supersede the KuKlux. He hadn't yet got the oath, but he did have the handshake, holding your forefinger in a certain way against the palm." Moore also told him that "nearly all the Conservative members of the legislature were members." Asked if he had joined the Ku Klux Klan, Boyd could say, with a distorted sort of honesty, "No, sir. I joined what was called the White Brotherhood." Then, asked by the investigating judge if he knew why the organization called itself the White Brotherhood, Boyd said, "I understood it to be so that if a man was called upon to say he was a member of the KuKlux, he could say he didn't know anything about them."

"Would you suppose a respectable member, if asked if there was any such thing as KuKlux, would say he didn't know?" Boyd was then asked. He replied, "Yes, sir."

"And think to escape punishment in that way?"

"He couldn't do otherwise without violating the oath he took as a member."

In North Carolina, as in the rest of the South, the Klan was most aggressive where the two races were evenly matched and whites were weakened by disenfranchisement. It was least active or even nonexistent in areas that had heavy white or Black majorities and Conservative Party control was either assured or impossible. (As they did in several southern states, Democrats in North Carolina temporarily dubbed themselves Conservatives in the hope of winning support from disaffected Republicans and politically orphaned prewar Whigs who had shunned direct association with the official Democratic Party.) Although the Klan rooted its appeal in what it asserted was the naturally shared interest of all white people, it was highly class conscious. As elsewhere, its leaders were usually drawn from among the local pool of lawyers, doctors, large landowners, and former Confederate officers, and its rank and file from among the often marginally successful farmers and workmen who had served as foot soldiers during the war, along with boys too young to have fought but who were instilled with the racial vengefulness of their parents. David Schenck, the Lincolnton attorney who professed to disdain violence, blamed the Klan's worst "excesses" on members whom he condescendingly described as "in the lower orders of life." Observed another North Carolinian, the Klan's chieftains tended to be the same men who had promoted secession and were now "pushing the poor men, the laboring men, forward to commit these deeds, and that when the day of trial came their secession leaders would step behind the curtain and say, 'I had nothing to do with it,' and leave the poor boys to suffer."

Although the lowly might perhaps be persuaded to commit heinous deeds by men they had been taught to think of as their "betters," they understood the Klan's aims perfectly well. John W. Long, a voluble bricklayer who rode with the Klan in Alamance County, testified: "It was to prevent the colored man from elevating himself with the whites, and to overthrow the Republican party." Asked how far the obligation to aid a fellow Klansman in difficulty extended, Long said, "To carry away men, and hanging around the jury and the sheriff and getting in as jurymen." When members were selected for a jury it was always their duty to deliver a verdict in favor of a fellow Klansman, regardless of the facts of the case. "We regard our oath as binding, and we shall swear for members at all hazards, and prove them at home"—that is, to swear that they were in their own house—"if they are arrested at any occasion." If an order came from another "camp" to carry out a raid on its behalf, they were bound to execute it without any questions. Long cited as an example the burning of a school for Black children, in which he had participated. He had "just followed orders" from his camp's chief, he said. "I was just as much under that chief as a soldier is under his officer."

The interrogating judge then asked Long what he would do if his chief ordered him to shoot a man or burn down a house.

Replied Long, "I would have done it."

"Didn't you know it was wrong?"

"I didn't think it right," Long said, but, "I took an oath not to expose them. I didn't screw my heart up at all. I didn't think it very right nor very wrong. I was afraid I would be killed if I told of it, and am a little afraid yet."

The Klan's political strategy generally targeted local officeholders and community leaders like Wyatt Outlaw: schoolteachers, independent craftsmen, former Union soldiers, churchmen, and the organizers of self-defense units as well as their white allies, such as state senator John Stephens, who were willing to speak out against terrorism. Few victims, however, were prominent enough to draw official retaliation, or even much notice, thereby encouraging northerners tired of the South's problems to shrug off the pleas of the terrorized as exaggerations. Although, as Boyd testified, the "outrages" were commonly committed on request by dens from neighboring counties, perpetrators and victims were just as frequently neighbors. As one Republican, William Howle, told congressional investigators in 1871, "Your strongest friends in the day-time are your enemies at night; they will drink toddy with you in the day-time, and Ku-Klux you at night."

In fact, Klan atrocities often took place in front of witnesses. Most, perhaps the vast majority, were too afraid to testify, a perennial problem even where there were local officials who were willing to prosecute; others were complacent, or even complicit. From his own doorway, state senator John Moore calmly observed the highly public kidnapping of Alonzo Corliss, a crippled white teacher of Black children, at the town of Company Shops (now Burlington). Hearing "a terrible noise," he later told a court, he went to his door and watched the Klansmen carry their victim off. "I only saw a white object," he claimed. "I didn't know anything about what was done until the next morning."

"Didn't you halloo?" Moore was asked.

"No, sir," he replied. "There were half a dozen other men by. There wasn't one of them that would go."

"Well, what does that mean? There were five or six men, and you saw them carry off and whip this man, and you let them?"

"Yes, sir."

"And you made no outcry?"

"No, sir."

Corliss survived the flogging, but it was made clear to him that he would not be given a second chance. He fled north to save his life.

The Klan's depredations continued to spread. In January 1869, five prisoners, four of them Black, were abducted from a jail in Kinston, shot, and dumped into a river. In May, terrorists assassinated Jones County sheriff Orson Colgrove, a New York–born soldier who had stayed on after the war, and killed a white county commissioner and two Black men who worked with him. In June, Col. M. L. Shepherd, who had organized a Black self-defense group, wrote to Governor Holden, "When I am killed (doing my duty) and in defeince of the Law then my Friends will have to take my place": two months later, he was murdered with his workers at the sawmill he owned. In August, a Black Republican in Orange County was found with his throat cut and his tongue torn out. Then, in February 1870, came Wyatt Outlaw's lynching at Graham. One of the participants, in sworn testimony later that year, said, "Outlaw was hung because he was a politician. He had been a leader of the negroes and had been elected once. There was no other crime alleged." (Later, when Graham's conservatives realized that federal troops might descend on the town to investigate Outlaw's murder, a petition was quickly circulated to denounce the lynching as an "outrage"; James Boyd, a lawyer who was party to the killing, later testified, "Most of the members signed it. I signed it myself.")

In a shocking number of instances, Klan outrages took on a sadistically grotesque character that went far beyond simple physical violence. When a Black man was murdered for supposedly raping a white girl in Chatham County, the local newspaper reported, "They skinned him." An Alamance County man named Nathan Trollinger, who was alleged to have "grossly insulted" a white woman, was flogged with hickory switches, then made to "take out his penis and stab it with a knife," a Klansman later testified. (Trollinger fled west, where he died from his wounds.) In Rockingham County, a Black man was forced to go through the motions of sex with a Black girl while Klansmen whipped him and forced her mortified father to look on. And in Chatham County, a white woman named Frances Gilmore, probably a prostitute, who was found with two Black men in her house, was stripped and whipped by Klan raiders who burned her pubic hair off with a hot knife, "and made her cut off herself the part that they did not burn."

Such behavior occurred almost everywhere the Klan operated. In

Wilkinson County, Georgia, a Black Republican organizer named Henry Lowther was captured by Klansmen who asked whether he would "give up his stones" in return for his life; when he agreed, they castrated him on the spot. In Claiborne Parish, Louisiana, a freedwoman was first raped and then nearly beaten to death by four disguised men who, it was reported, were stopping at all cabins in their route committing violence and maltreating women. In Arkansas, Klansmen murdered a deputy sheriff, then killed an innocent Black man, tied the two of them together as if they were kissing and embracing, and left the two bodies in the road as a public spectacle. Dennis Rice testified to congressional investigators that his brother, a local evangelist, had been murdered and savagely mutilated after the Ku-Klux had warned him to stop preaching. "A colored man is not to preach in this township," they told him. He preached a little that day, "but the congregation wouldn't stay to hear him; they were afraid." That night he was abducted by masked Ku-Klux. His body, when it was found, was "stabbed—cut open. His private parts were cut off, and his body was dragged along the road and stabbed—cut all about with stabs in the body." Near Spartanburg, South Carolina, Klansmen took Republican activist Clem Bowden, a middle-aged freedman, and his wife from their home, stripped and flogged them, and then forced them to participate in a disgusting ritual involving William Champion, a white man who taught a Sunday school for Blacks. Champion later told congressional investigators that he had also been stripped, and then, "They made me kiss the negro man's posterior, and held it open and made me kiss it, and as well as I remember a negro woman's too"—presumably Mrs. Bowden's—"and also her private parts, and then told me to have sexual connection with her. I told them, they knew, of course, that I could not do that. They asked me how I liked that for nigger equality."

The Klan's predilection for sexual perversity always implicitly and sometimes quite explicitly had a political dimension: it was designed to shatter the self-confidence of newly freed men and women, and to cripple the revolutionary self-assertion that had begun to take place in Blacks' personal relations with whites. Needless to say, the humiliation of whites like Champion was also meant to scare away those who risked allying themselves with aspiring Blacks. The rape of Black women by Klansmen is impossible to quantify, but it clearly was common. Southern whites' warped belief that Black men were inherently sexual predators, with vile designs on white womenfolk, inverted the truth that while rape had been universal in the antebellum South it was committed by white men upon enslaved Black women—and not infrequently against free Black women—who had little or no recourse to the law in order to protect themselves. Put in the starkest terms, Black bodies, male and female, were always fair game for white men long accustomed to owning the flesh of the people they had enslaved.

In December 1869, in his first annual address to Congress, and by implication to the nation, President Grant made no mention of the increasingly horrific violence that was being perpetrated by the Ku Klux Klan. His words were studiously hopeful and reassuring: "Happily," he said, "harmony is rapidly being restored within our borders." He spoke approvingly of the improving national credit, decreasing federal debt, his desire to restore the country's finances to a hard-currency basis, warming relations with Latin America, treaty negotiations with the various European powers, the urgency of establishing a humane policy toward the native tribes of the fast-opening West. Of the South, he observed only that seven former Confederate states had now been fully restored to the Union and that Virginia, Texas, and Mississippi either had just approved or were about to vote on new constitutions that would make their readmittance possible. Only Georgia, he regretted, had had to be remanded to federal oversight, until its political instability was brought to an end. His single mention of Black Americans was to note that the freedmen were reportedly "making rapid progress in learning, and no complaints are heard of lack of industry on their part where they receive fair remuneration for their labor."

Grant's glaring failure to mention the pervasive instability in the South seems inexplicable, especially since his personal desire to elevate the public stature of Blacks had, if anything, continued to grow. He appointed the first Black diplomat in the nation's history, Ebenezer Bassett, the grandson of a slave, as minister to Haiti. (He would later name another African American as minister to Liberia.) And in November, he had accepted the credentials of a Haitian ambassador, Alexander Tate, the first ever Black credentialed as a diplomat to the United States. "If any proof were wanting of the unfounded character of the prejudice which, until recently, pervaded at least parts of this country against the race from which you are sprung," Grant declared, the ambassador's polished eloquence had provided it. "Like all similar prejudices," Grant said, "no matter how deeply implanted, [it] must sooner or later yield to the force of truth." Politically, Grant's support for the Fourteenth Amendment was unyielding. At the same time, however, he was hoping that the restored southern states would now be able to manage on their own, without federal interference.

Grant was still trying to find his footing as president. A friendly but reticent man, he was besieged by office-seekers—a perennial nuisance in the nineteenth century—and annoyed by the incessant clamor of tourists invading the White House, strolling through what Americans regarded as a public building, peeping into the kitchens, gawking at the furniture and housekeeping arrangements, poking around the basement where they might see servants ironing the president's nightshirts. Politically, too, the first months had been more difficult than he had bargained for. In the words of his biographer Ron Chernow, he sometimes seemed like "a onetime warrior ambushed by a sudden outbreak of peace." After the years he spent as commander of the army, civilian politics demanded skills that didn't come naturally. "Having acquired a military point of view, he clung to it tenaciously in a political environment," the historian Allan Nevins observed. "His subordinates he regarded as so many staff officers or field commanders; his policies were to be executed like campaigns." Before becoming president, he disdained what he considered "mere trading politicians," but he was quickly coming to realize that his new office lacked the absolute authority to which he had been accustomed in the army. Much of his labor in those early months went into repairing the executive's relations with Congress after the violent ruptures of the Johnson years.

Gradually, as the months passed, he built alliances on Capitol Hill, notably with Rep. Benjamin Butler of Massachusetts, an incompetent and troublesome field commander when he served under Grant in the war, but now emerging as a Radical leader destined to play a pivotal legislative role in the president's campaign against the Klan. Redheaded and confrontational, Butler descended from a family of swashbucklers whose line went back to 1637, but who were hardly the stereotype of stiff-necked, Bible-stroking Puritans. His grandfather fought at Bunker Hill and his father sailed as a privateer during the War of 1812, dying of yellow fever in the West Indies. Originally pushed toward the ministry by his widowed mother, he regularly paid a fine in order to skip sermons. During the Civil War, as the military governor of New Orleans, he was accused of pilfering silverware from confiscated Confederate estates and pilloried by the city's elite for ordering respectable women to be treated as "women of the town" if they insulted the national flag. With his appetite for notoriety, he was the near opposite of the phlegmatic Grant.

Admirers of Grant found him frank and direct, and averse to pretension. Rep. Elihu Washburne praised him for his "remarkable executive ability—quick, ready, comprehensive," in his efficient "dispatch of public business." The historian Allan Nevins, who was not fond of Grant, conceded that "like Lincoln, he was essentially democratic; he treated everyone, great or small, with courtesy." Shy and thin-skinned, Grant was notably uncomfortable with personal conflict and seemed unprepared for the often intense personal attacks that would continue to beset him as president. Harsh criticism was to be expected from the Democrats. But he was also the target of increasingly vicious assaults by elite Republicans such as Sen. Charles Sumner and the journalist, later historian, Henry Adams, the grandson and great-grandson of presidents, who savaged Grant with astonishing cruelty: "For stretches of time, his mind seemed torpid." Even members of his cabinet, Adams claimed, "could never measure his character or be sure when he would act. They could never follow a mental process in his thought. They were not sure that he did think."

By now, North Carolina governor Holden's early optimism had faded to the vanishing point. The Klan, he had to admit, was far from dead. He agonized, correctly enough, that northerners failed to grasp "our real situation," and he was growing desperate. He knew that he would have to take some kind of action, but he feared that a show of force would provoke a general rebellion among the Klan's supporters, and possibly an all-out race war. As he temporized, the situation in some parts of the state was slipping beyond his already tenuous control. He learned that military weapons, including repeating rifles, were being imported into the state and distributed in several counties with intent to "subvert the government." He warned militant whites that while the government had spared the lives and property of those who had engaged in rebellion, magnanimity would not be extended any further: if there was any attempt to intimidate voters, "force will be met with force." In a somewhat quixotic attempt to cripple the Klan, he enlisted a team of detectives that included native-born whites, former Confederate soldiers turned Republicans, Union Army veterans, one or two Blacks—one of the latter, Alexander Bryant, was described as "a collard man and is remarkably *sly* and sharp"—and at least two turncoat Klansmen to investigate terrorism in Jones and Lenoir counties, in the southeast part of the state, but it bore little lasting fruit. Then, in mid-April 1869, he urged the state's General Assembly to pass legislation criminalizing mask-wearing and disguise "with intent to terrify," declaring, "The humblest and the poorest are entitled to this protection equally with the wealthiest and most exalted."

As he contemplated the deteriorating security situation, Holden had before him the example of neighboring South Carolina, which was enrolling Black militiamen to counterbalance the Klan. Further afield, the aggressive Republican governor of Arkansas, Powell Clayton, had fought the Klan to a standstill after a campaign of terror that took the lives of at least two hundred freedmen, lawmen, army officers, county voting registrars, and a Republican member of Congress, James Hinds, who was blasted with a double-barreled shotgun on a public highway. Sleeping in the statehouse under round-the-clock guard for fear of assassination, Clayton declared martial law in the insurrectionary counties, ordered companies of both Black and white militia into the field, and effectively crushed the Klan in the course of a four-month campaign. Clayton had demonstrated that the Klan could be beaten, but Holden hesitated to follow his example. He deemed too few whites trustworthy enough to arm, while the prospect of a virtually all-Black militia, he feared, would likely have an incendiary effect on the white population.

In the early months of 1870, Holden's frustration came to a head as spiking terrorism roiled Alamance County, in the Piedmont just northwest of Raleigh. The crusading anti-Klan Judge Albion Tourgée pronounced it "decidedly the worst county in the district," with the juries "all Ku Klux," and "nothing done by white conservatives considered as a crime." Defectors from the Klan later testified that the county hosted no fewer than ten loosely independent "camps" of the White Brotherhood, mustering between five and eight hundred men, including church elders and ministers, the county sheriff and eleven of his deputies, not to mention state senator John Moore; the Brotherhood's county chief, John Long, was clerk of the county court. (About one hundred more Alamance Klansmen belonged to the Constitutional Union Guard.) Alamance, perhaps uniquely, also employed the services of a professional flogger, a man named Foust, who "whipped for all the adjoining Klans." Although many of the county officials were members of the Klan, Alamance was also distinguished by a significant Quaker minority who had facilitated the prewar Underground Railroad and opposed secession, and now, although they resisted social equality with Blacks and shied from violent confrontation, could be counted on to turn out a dependable vote for the Republican Party. Their support had helped to elect state senator T. M. Shoffner, a blacksmith and stolid wartime Unionist, who undertook to sponsor the most forceful political assault on the Klan this far.

The Shoffner Act, which became law at the end of January, strengthened the governor's authority to raise militia, if he chose to do so, and empowered him to declare a county in insurrection if the local officials were unable to enforce the law. The Klan regarded the act as a declaration of war and immediately began plotting to kidnap and kill Shoffner, and possibly Holden himself. Eli Euliss, a schoolteacher, testified that his camp of the Constitutional Union Guard had received a coded message from another Klan unit in nearby Orange County, requesting it to send assassins to hang Shoffner. John Moore, the state senator and a member of the White Brotherhood, claimed that Shoffner's life was saved only by his opportune intervention. In Graham to see a sick child, Moore later told state investigators, James Boyd casually remarked to him that Shoffner was to be killed that night, saying, "They are going to suspend Shoffner's writ of *habeas corpus*." Moore, more alert than other Klansmen to the potential political consequences of killing a state senator, claimed that he replied, "This will not do. It is going to bring ruin on Alamance County." (It is also possible that rivalry between the White Brotherhood and the Constitutional Union Guard played a role in Moore's reaction.) Learning where he could find the assassins, he told them that he was an elected representative and "begged" them to desist, saying then that Shoffner had in fact gone to Greensboro and that no one was at his home but his sick wife.

In court, Moore took the same transparently evasive tack that he had when questioned about the kidnapping of the crippled white teacher Alonzo Corliss. Asked by the investigating judge if the would-be murderers were "members of the order," Moore rather preposterously asserted that he had no way of knowing. The judge, clearly irritated, then sarcastically asked, "Can you tell me their complexion?" Replied Moore, "I know they were all white men."

"What size were they?" the judge demanded.

Replied Moore, "Some of them small and some large."

"How did it happen that you didn't ask them who they were?"

"Simply because I didn't want to know."

Shoffner knew that he would not get a second reprieve. He fled to Indiana and never returned.

Holden finally decided to act. He declared Alamance County in a state of insurrection. Then he wrote to President Grant, "There exists in this state a secret, oath-bound, armed organization which is hostile to the state government and to the government of the United States. Bands of armed men ride at night through various neighborhoods, whipping and maltreating peaceable citizens, hanging some, burning churches, and breaking up schools which have been established for the colored people." To defeat them, he emphasized that white militiamen "of the proper character" couldn't be found in sufficient numbers, "and it would but aggravate the evil to employ colored militia." He asked the president to suspend the writ of habeas corpus in Alamance and other counties so that the perpetrators could be tried before military tribunals and shot, as he curtly put it. "The remedy would be a sharp and bloody one, but it is indispensable."

On the afternoon of February 25, 1870, the day after the lynching of Wyatt Outlaw, a different kind of drama unfolded three hundred miles to the north of Graham, on the floor of the United States Senate. Henry Wilson of Massachusetts left his desk and stepped to the lounge at the back of the chamber, where a large-bodied man in black broadcloth rose to meet him. Together they strode in silence to the dais where Vice President Schuyler Colfax, the presiding officer, waited as the men and women who packed the visitors' gallery stood in a single motion to witness what had never before taken place in either house of the United States Congress. Reported the *New York Times,* with its customary restraint, "Mr. [Hiram Rhodes] Revels, the colored Senator from Mississippi, was sworn in and admitted to his seat." It was a political retort to the savagery of the Klan and a symbolic moment of seismic proportions, the nation's first Black senator taking the place of Jefferson Davis, who had vacated the same seat nine years earlier when he defected to the Confederacy and became its president.

Revels's admittance to the august body had been preceded by three days of racially charged debate. One Democrat, Garrett Davis of Kentucky, went so far as to appeal to the prewar *Dred Scott* decision—which had effectively been nullified by the Fourteenth Amendment—to argue that Blacks were noncitizens who could not constitutionally hold office. Another charged that only the federal army's "bayonet rule" in Mississippi had enabled Revels to win election by the state's legislature. The outnumbered Democrats forced a vote on his credentials but were crushingly defeated, 48 to 8. Declared the *Philadelphia Inquirer,* sneering at the Democrats' panic, "We have not had an earthquake, our free institutions have not been shaken to their foundations, nor have the streets of our large cities been converted to blood."

So little known was Revels in the nation's capital that his name was variously reported in the press as "W.H. Revel," "Ravel," and even "Kevalls." Some newspapers described him as "a dark mulatto," others as "light-skinned" with "grizzled" hair, a brownish beard, and a "decided Caucasian nose." Born free in North Carolina forty-two years earlier, Revels had served primarily as a missionary for the AME Church, which dispatched him to Mississippi after the war. He entered politics only in 1868, as a town alderman in Natchez, and then the following year was tapped as a compromise candidate for the state Senate. In January 1869, he had opened the Senate session with an invocation that so moved his colleagues that they elected him to the remaining one-year term in the U.S. Senate.

To Radicals, Revels was the very face of revolution, living proof that a better, more enlightened South was really taking shape. Mississippi representative George C. McKee crowed that although loyal men continued to struggle against "the aristocracy," Republicans white and Black "are fast obtaining possession of the various offices," and would soon consolidate power. Thirty-one of the eighty-three members of Mississippi's heavily Republican House of Representatives and five of twenty-six members of its state Senate were Black. Although the proportion of the races varied, a comparable upheaval was visibly taking place in Montgomery, Little Rock, Austin, Tallahassee, New Orleans, Atlanta, and Raleigh. The racial breakdown in other states was dwarfed by South Carolina, where 75 of the 124 seats in the House of Representatives and ten of the thirty-one members of the Senate were represented by Black Republicans. Blacks were also superintendents of education, commissioners of agriculture, members of state land commissions, cabinet members, judges, and appointed officials of all kinds, not to mention a host of new town and county officeholders ranging from magistrates, tax assessors, and voting registrars to sheriffs and militia captains, all of them the political foot soldiers of the nascent Republican Party. Whites and Blacks alike were awed by what was happening. Sen. Simon Cameron of Pennsylvania declared that the very sight of Revels sitting among his fellow senators "somewhat shocks my old prejudices [that] one of the despised race should come here to be my equal; but I look upon it as the act of God."

8

A MEPHISTOPHELES IN GLASSES

And yet the government sleeps.

—JUDGE ALBION W. TOURGÉE

The veteran Washington reporter Ben Perley Poore described the look of newly minted Sen. Carl Schurz of Missouri as "very like that of Mephistopheles, except that Schurz wore glasses." Tall and graceful, strikingly blue-eyed, blond-haired, and courtly of manner, he was intellectual to a degree rare in American politics. Having arrived in the United States in 1852 as a fugitive from his native Germany, Schurz was already famous for his daring exploits during the failed democratic revolution of 1848. Trapped in a fortress captured by the royalists and in danger of execution, he escaped through a sewage tunnel, then sneaked back in to rescue his favorite professor, one of the revolution's leaders. In America, Schurz soon earned a reputation as what a later age would call a "public intellectual," publishing and lecturing widely on political and cultural topics of the day including the struggle against slavery, which he saw as an apocalyptic one "between advancing civilization and retreating barbarism; between the human conscience and a burning wrong."

Schurz campaigned vigorously for Abraham Lincoln during the 1860 presidential campaign, and was a popular guest at the White House, where he often played the piano for the president, impressing Lincoln's secretary John Hay with his "vigor and animal arrogance."

Lincoln rewarded him for his political loyalty with appointment as ambassador to Spain. Impatient to play a more active role in the war, he lobbied incessantly for a field commission. Lincoln eventually agreed in 1862, and despite Schurz's paucity of battlefield experience, appointed him the commander of a division of mainly German-speaking troops, which he led with more self-confidence than skill through several battles. After the war, Schurz had hoped to establish an intimate relationship with Andrew Johnson, who trusted him sufficiently to send him on the fact-finding tour of the South, in 1865. However, Schurz's scathing report on the violence across the region infuriated the president by contradicting his assurances that former Confederates would prove cooperative. Spurned by Johnson, Schurz retreated to St. Louis to become the editor of a German-language newspaper, which in turn launched him into a meteoric ascent in Missouri politics, and back onto the national stage as the de facto leader of the nation's large, politically potent German minority. In 1868 the Republican Party selected him as both the chairman of the presidential nominating convention and its keynote speaker. During that year's campaign, he barnstormed for Grant, who he allowed himself to believe was as committed as he was to replacing political patronage with a merit-based civil service, a reform which Schurz increasingly felt was the most urgent political cause of the postwar era. When one of Missouri's Senate seats became available in 1868, he was the Republican Party's obvious choice to fill it.

Three years earlier, Schurz had been among the most clear-eyed of Radicals. His report on the South had accurately described the widespread white resistance and bloody reprisals against the freed people that foreshadowed the Ku Klux Klan. Although Schurz still believed in racial justice, he also now wholeheartedly embraced, to the dismay of his Radical friends, the restoration of voting privileges to former Confederates, insisting that it was necessary in order to heal the nation's lingering sectional wounds. Beneath this principled position lay a substratum of flinty Missouri politics, however. Schurz owed his election to not just the German vote but also to the calculating support of conservative Republicans and Democrats, who hoped to exploit him as a counterweight to the state's other senator, an unequivocal Radical. Schurz didn't hesitate, on occasion, to denounce the hypocrisy of Democrats who encouraged violent resistance to the law, "themselves fanning the flame, [while] they on the other hand deny the necessity of quenching it." But he also expressed his gratitude to former rebels who came to his rallies as he campaigned around the state. When they professed loyalty to the national government and willingness to accept their former slaves as citizens, he naively took them at their word. He confidently asserted, "They do not want to beat the war drum longer than it is called for." He assured himself that new, enlightened majorities would both preserve Blacks' civil rights and purge the body politic of the corruption and favoritism that he believed fatally tainted Radical rule. Optimism and faith in the basic decency of human beings were his greatest strengths and, perhaps, equally great weaknesses. He failed to appreciate that white reactionaries were engaged in cynical political theater. They professed willingness to swallow Radical prescriptions on paper in order to escape military rule, but they had no intention of allowing their society to be revolutionized along Yankee lines.

Schurz's distrust of strong central government blinded him to the conservatives' barely concealed determination to crush the life out of the Republican Party wherever they were strong enough to do it. He was by no means the only Republican whose commitment to Reconstruction was softening. But no other broke so dramatically with his recent Radical past or swallowed the ideology of reconciliation with more credulous enthusiasm. In this, he would decisively shape the still inchoate shift in public opinion away from support for full-throttle Reconstruction in ways that increasingly set him in opposition to Ulysses Grant. Schurz's sea change revealed itself in a series of debates that took place in late winter and early spring, first over the readmission of Virginia—which had met the conditions imposed by Congress, but elected a conservative state government opposed to Reconstruction—and then over the even more fraught situation in Georgia.

In December, Grant had remanded Georgia to military rule, swayed by pleas from embattled Radicals and heart-wrenching letters from terrified citizens such as Louis Foy, a farmer, who wrote, "I have tried in every way as a poor colored man to get justice of the Courts of my [su]it. I was badly beaten and shot in my [o]wn house by some white Rebels. Went over to a Justice of the Peace who the second night after I was there being present allowed the Ku Klux to come and take me down to a bridge at night Two miles off, and shoot me *through* and *through* and when I fall off into the creek 15 feet below in the dark I drift off a mile they still shooting at me and I crawl to a frinds who cares for me and I am able to slip off." Grant had said little about the South in his annual address, but he stood by his inaugural pledge to protect the freed people. At his urging, Congress retracted Georgia's readmission to the Union, ordered the reseating of the ousted Black legislators, required members of the legislature to swear an ironclad loyalty oath—almost two dozen failed to and were expelled—and demanded ratification of the Fifteenth Amendment before Georgia could again be reinstated in the Union. The issue was not whether Georgia would be readmitted, since virtually everyone agreed that it should, but whether the restored state legislature should be sustained in power.

The congressional Radicals also wanted to extend the Georgia state legislature's life for two more years, to enable the Republicans to consolidate power, while conservatives demanded that new state elections be held that autumn. The debate was often technical and legalistic, but the stakes were high. Coupled with conservatives' recapture of Tennessee's state government, events in Georgia and Virginia demonstrated just how precarious Reconstruction's future might be if former Confederates were allowed to slip back into power. Whatever policy was set for Georgia would likely set a precedent for neighboring states. As Sen. Jacob Howard, a Michigan Radical, put it, unless Blacks' right to vote was guaranteed for the next century, "we are destined at no very distant day to see a repetition of the war through which we have just passed." The debates were essentially tests for whether a state could obey the letter but violate the spirit of the Reconstruction laws. As they unfolded through the late winter and spring they exposed the widening fissures between Radicals, who were willing to guarantee civil rights with the army's bayonets, if necessary, and those, like Schurz, who feared federal power more than they worried about the survival of Black freedom.

In his first speech on Reconstruction, on January 14, Schurz fulsomely praised Virginians for "cast[ing] out of their minds their old animosities," and joining in the march toward "equal rights, universal liberty, peace and good will for all the children of the American Republic." He called upon his colleagues to trust the former rebels to do the right thing: they needed compassion, not condemnation. "We want to treat you like gentlemen, as we want to be treated like gentlemen by you," he urged. Astonishingly, he shrugged off as mere "hearsay" the reports of southern election fraud and violence—precisely what he had warned of in 1865. Echoing Democrats, he disparaged his own party in the reconstructed states as grossly guilty of factionalism and "mismanagement." There were security problems in the South, he admitted, but further restrictions on whites would only cripple "healthy" political development. It was inevitable that the former rebels would regain political strength in the South. Republicans simply ought to accept it. With that in view, he asked, why rekindle ill-feeling among conservatives who were now on the brink of abandoning their Confederate past and ready to embrace the new order of things?

On March 18, Schurz again attacked the proposal to extend the life of Georgia's legislature. Nothing, he said, could do more damage to "republicanism"—that is, the principle of popular representative government—than legislators claiming the arbitrary power to continue themselves in office "at their own pleasure." The restored state government still had eight months to do whatever legislating it wanted. "Are we reduced to that pitiable extremity of declaring that we can protect the citizens of the United States in their rights only by a violation of the Constitution and the laws?" he asked. "Have senators considered the consequences of imposing a set of usurpers"—that is, Schurz's own fellow Republicans—"upon the neck of an unruly people under circumstances like these? Have they considered that the very performance of such an act will be like a bugle-blast for the Kuklux Klan in the South, and will call recruits for the work of evil out of every neighborhood there?"

Then, shifting to the kind of lofty intellectual terrain that most impressed his admirers, he added, "Every rebellion from the beginning of history to the present day has had its epilogue, and those epilogues have certain characteristic features which are almost invariably the same. When a rebellion is defeated some of those who took part in it will inevitably be seduced by vague illusions and false hopes." Schurz was of course thinking about the failed German revolution of 1848, imposing the template of its comparatively civilized aftermath on the barbarism of the Ku Klux Klan. Eventually, he opined, troublemakers would simply learn that it was impossible to overturn the new order of things, the more reasonable of them would join the law-and-order party, and they would suppress the reckless ones who persisted in committing "excesses." It was a predictable process of "fermentation," he said, which could not be prevented either by laws or draconian executive orders. It would work itself out, "just like fevers, which have to pass through a crisis before they can be finally cured."

On April 19, Schurz returned once again to Reconstruction, further refining what would soon become the national platform of the party's defectors, who were beginning to call themselves "Liberal Republicans." Even more bluntly than before, he declared that it was time for the federal government to cut its losses and disengage from the South. Military "interference" could not continue indefinitely. He declared, "It seems to me we have accustomed the loyal people of the South a little too much to look to Congress for all they believe themselves to stand in need of. We cannot always act as their guardians in every emergency."

Schurz was echoed by Sen. Lyman Trumbull of Illinois, the longtime chairman of the Judiciary Committee and primary author of the Thirteenth Amendment, whose political trajectory was following a similar arc. A onetime Democrat, Trumbull was basically a conservative constitutionalist who embraced antislavery and the early Reconstruction measures from a sense of duty to beleaguered southern Unionists. But he had become increasingly disenchanted with the Radicals, whom he regarded as unrealistic and overzealous. More specifically, he believed that the Georgia legislature was within its constitutional rights to expel its Black members. He believed that Reconstruction was doomed to fail if for no other reason than it was opposed by the majority of a state's white population. Like Schurz, Trumbull also disparaged the reports of Klan atrocities. He alleged bizarrely that the vast majority of murders there were probably committed by Blacks against others of their race, and claimed, gratuitously, that he had heard of "two or three" murders of white men by Blacks, and of "several rapes upon tender infants by colored men." Whether he actually believed such southern propaganda or was merely manipulating it for the sake of his argument is unclear. In fact, assaults and political assassinations of Republicans were reported in most of Georgia's counties, with dozens of Blacks shot just for voting Republican, and even state officials and U.S. marshals "chased and hunted like foxes." (Henry McNeal Turner, the Black Republican leader and AME bishop, privately reported to Sumner that "if I had not secreted myself in houses at times, in the woods at other times, in a hollow log at another time, I would have been assassinated.")

In any case, Trumbull continued, "Whose fault is it that the peace is not preserved in that state? It is the duty of the states to preserve the peace within their own borders, not when some man is murdered in a county, not when a sheriff is shot down, to fly to Washington and ask the president for troops, martial law, and the suspension of *habeas corpus*." He said, "Let the law-abiding people of the South learn to rely on themselves." Finally, after advising Blacks to "beware how you usurp unauthorized power . . . now, in the first hour of your emancipation," he concluded, "I think that too much attention is being given by the colored people of the South to this right of suffrage and political questions." He added in exasperation, on January 13, "When is this question of Reconstruction to end?"

Such views were finding a ready audience in the North. "The people here are very apathetic about affairs down in Tophet"— a biblical site associated with cruelty, death, and child sacrifice— "and I don't see any prospect of stirring them up till you are all killed off," a discouraged friend wrote to the North Carolina Radical Albion Tourgée. Of like mind, *The Nation,* one of the most influential journals in the North, which generally espoused a conservative Republican line, disgustedly snarled on April 28, "The South ought now to be dropped by Congress. All that paper and words can do for it has been done."

The Radicals replied with ferocity. Schurz's Missouri rival, Charles Drake, read aloud a letter from North Carolina governor Holden begging for military tribunals and the suspension of habeas corpus. Drake then declared, "I will die in my seat before I vote for anything whatever that shall tie the hands of the loyal men of Georgia or give aid to their diabolical enemies." Sumner, though close to Schurz and at odds with Grant, scoffed at southern states' conversion as political fakery and accused Trumbull of being willing to hand Georgia over to the Ku Klux Klan. And Sen. Oliver P. Morton of Indiana warned that truncating the legislature's term would "carry exultation to every unrepentant rebel in the South."

Hiram Revels in his maiden speech, the most memorable of his short stint in the Senate, touched a deeper chord. The speech was an extraordinary event, the first by a Black man on the floor of the Senate. A huge and unprecedented biracial crowd gathered in the visitors' gallery to witness this human embodiment of the Fifteenth Amendment. "Not since the birth of the republic has such an audience been assembled under one single roof," recalled a witness. Revels began hesitantly, then quickly gained momentum. He called for a renewed commitment to "my downtrodden people," declaring, in his sonorous, pulpit-trained voice, "I stand today on this floor to appeal for protection from the strong arm of the Government for her loyal children, irrespective of color and race." Americans who opposed the empowerment of Blacks warned incessantly that it would unleash Negroes' supposed inherent savagery and lead to bloody race war, he said. Such fears should be groundless since, he reminded his fellow senators, during the war slaves had protected their mistresses and their property even when they could have walked away. Even now, as freed people, they bore "no revengeful thoughts, no hatreds" toward their former masters. Northerners, too, were under a deep obligation to "the colored race." When the federal armies were "thinned by death and disaster" Black volunteers had stepped in to save the Union. If the thousands of Black soldiers who had sacrificed their lives on the battlefield could still speak, he intoned, "what a mighty voice, like to the rushing of a mighty wind, would come up from those sepulchral homes!" Surely they would beg senators not to undermine the restored legislature and its Black members. "Could we resist the eloquent pleadings of their appeal?"

The most passionate Radical speech was delivered by the youngest, and one of the most flamboyant, members of the Senate, moonfaced, goateed George Eliphaz Spencer of Alabama. Just thirty-three years old, Spencer was born in New York, had studied law, panned for gold in Colorado, and led the only regiment of Alabama cavalry to serve in the Union Army, during Sherman's march through Georgia and the Carolinas. He was a political brawler: "When driven fairly to the wall, I am bound to show fight, and I will make it war to the knife and the knife to the hilt," he once wrote. He ardently supported the confiscation of land that had belonged to rebel leaders, argued for continuing military rule, and fully recognized that the Klan was an existential challenge. Unreconstructed rebels were already boasting that they would soon take control of Alabama, as they effectively had Tennessee, he warned. "From almost every corner of Alabama the blood of Union men, assassinated for their patriotism, calls from the ground, I will not say for vengeance," but "[it] calls on Congress to pause ere it puts more power into the hands of those political thugs." He then read into the record an editorial by Ryland Randolph, the Klan leader and editor of the *Tuskaloosa Monitor:* "The sooner the negro is made to sink into his low sphere the better for all concerned. A little blood spilt promptly and judiciously may save torrents of the red fluid that procrastination will render necessary should be poured out." None of this, however, neither Spencer's warning nor Revels's heartfelt plea, was sufficient to sway the Senate. The legalists won the battle. Their colleagues voted to readmit Georgia without extending the life of its Republican-controlled legislature.

John W. Stephens was the kind of embattled southern Republican that Spencer, Morton, and Sumner were talking about. By the exacting standards of North Carolina's planter elite, he was a no-account white not much above the Blacks in tobacco-growing Caswell County. A thirty-five-year-old sometime harness-maker and small-time tobacco trader before the war, he had been raised on a scrap of a farm, and only scantily educated. He had served the Confederacy reluctantly, buying horses for its cavalry, then after the war went to work for the Freedmen's Bureau. He was tutored in the law by Albion Tourgée, the idealistic Union veteran who had largely authored the state's new constitution. With the support of a strong Black vote Stephens was elected justice of the peace in Yanceyville, the seat of Caswell County, just below the Virginia state line, and was then elected to the state Senate, where he championed public education and the rights of the former slaves.

By the spring of 1870, Stephens was marked as a race-traitor in conservatives' eyes. The Klan informed him that he was targeted for assassination and ordered him to resign from the Republican Party or leave the state. He shrugged off such threats, telling a friend that thousands of "poor, ignorant colored Republican voters" had stood by him and elected him at the risk of persecution and starvation, and that he had no intention of abandoning them to the desperadoes of "the Ku-Klux." But he fortified his house, bought life insurance, and began carrying a horse pistol and two derringers with him wherever he went. He corresponded regularly with Governor Holden, who relied on him as a key informant in Caswell County. On May 16, he wrote to urge Holden to send troops if he could, reporting that "the leading Republicans has bin driven off, [and] the K.K. will have everything their own way. . . . I am Satesfyed that I am no safer than [a black Republican colleague] exsept I am better fortified against their assalt."

On May 21, Stephens settled onto a bench in the second-floor meeting room in Yanceyville's handsome courthouse, where the county's Democrats were gathered in convention. His presence there of course offended men who hated his politics, but party events were open to anyone; rowdy Democrats commonly showed up at Republican rallies to hoot at speakers. Outside on the street, a half-dozen armed Black men loyal to Stephens stood near the courthouse door, an excessive degree of insurance, Stephens believed, since the Klan was unlikely to attack him in the daylight. Slouched on his bench, scribbling notes, he was tapped on the shoulder by the county sheriff, Frank. A. Wiley, a Democrat, but a man Stephens hoped to persuade to stand for reelection on the Republican ticket. Wiley told him that there was a problem with Republican voter registrations, and he was needed downstairs. Stephens followed Wiley down the curved "white men's" staircase—Blacks were required to use the unadorned stairs at the other end of the room—and through a crowd of farmers, both Black and white, in town to pay their taxes or on business in one or another of the county offices.

Then Stephens disappeared.

When he failed to come home for dinner his wife, Fannie, began to panic. "I was flustrated, having spasms," she later testified. She sent Merret Corbett, "a colored lady," to look for him, then a man named Fred Graves. A general search was mounted, and Stephens's steps retraced until, apparently, they were lost in the ebb and flow of men in the courthouse's corridors. His two brothers and his friends questioned everyone who might have seen him. Several people saw him in the corridor. Sheriff Wiley thought he had left the courthouse by the back door. Someone else said he saw him in the town square two hours after the Democratic convention ended. Another said he saw him at the town pump. Another thought he'd seen him on the road a few miles outside town. Still another said he saw him just before sunset, heading toward a "colored" meeting at the schoolhouse. Every room in the courthouse was searched repeatedly except the former Freedmen's Bureau office where lumber was stored, for which the key had been lost. Through the night, Republicans milled outside the courthouse hoping for news.

A little after dawn, a Black man named George Bowe climbed onto a box to peer in the window of the lumber room. He saw what Stephens's friends dreaded. His body lay slumped, half-concealed in a hollow in the woodpile. A man was boosted through the window and unlocked the door from the inside. The scene was enough to make grown men gag. Dr. N. M. Roan, who was among the first to enter the room, testified at the inquest that a rope had been drawn so tightly around Stephens's neck that the flesh bulged around it, and that he had been stabbed in the heart and in the neck, severing the windpipe. There was blood on the walls. He had apparently been killed on the table: alongside it, a bucket had been carefully placed so that his blood would pour into it and not flood beneath the door into the busy corridor.

Republicans theorized that Stephens might have been decoyed into the lumber room by someone he trusted, and was then murdered. Meanwhile, there were more attacks: a white Republican farmer named Butts was flogged by "disguised assailants," and a family named McLeod murdered in cold blood. Then, in neighboring Alamance County, a Black man who it was believed had overheard Wyatt Outlaw's murderers discussing their deed suddenly disappeared. A few days later he was found drowned in a mill pond bound hand and foot, with a large stone tied to his neck. Names had surfaced of men who had been noticed near the lumber room after Stephens's disappearance, some of them prominent men, including Dr. Roan's son. At the inquest it was determined only that

Stephens had died "at the hands of persons unknown." In the hope of forestalling a crackdown by the army, local Democrats crafted a platform condemning violence and secret organizations. Among its authors were members of the Ku Klux Klan and at least two of the men who were later implicated in Stephens's murder.

Locally, the murder was a political catastrophe. "Another brave, honest Republican citizen has met his fate at the hands of these fiends," Stephens's friend and mentor Judge Albion Tourgée wrote to U.S. senator Joseph Abbott on hearing the news. "Warned of his danger, and fully cognizant of the terrible risk which surrounded him, he still manfully refused to quit the field," reiterating that Black voters "had stood by him and elected him, at the risk of persecution and starvation, and that he had no idea of abandoning them to the Ku Klux Klan." Tourgée added ominously, "Nearly six months ago, I declared my belief that before the election in August next the Ku-Klux would have killed more men in the state than there would be members to be elected to the legislature. A good beginning has been made toward the fulfillment of this prophecy." Once again, Republican leadership had been decapitated, as it had been in Alamance County with Wyatt Outlaw's killing, in Columbus, Georgia, with George Ashburn's assassination, and in scores of other communities across the South. Wilson Carey, Caswell County's leading Black politician, fled for his life, while the pro-Klan *Raleigh Sentinel* smeared Stephens's memory, alleging that he was a chicken thief and suggesting that he had murdered his own mother. In the state elections that August, Black voters shied away from the polls and the county's Republican vote shriveled. But his death was not wholly in vain. News of it quickly reached the state capital in Raleigh, where Governor Holden set in motion a concerted campaign to combat and crush the Klan in North Carolina, one that would also serve as a model for a broader and decisive federal campaign in the months to come. It also directly influenced the speedy passage of the first of three federal enforcement bills designed to give the national government new power to bring to bear against Klan terrorists who almost everywhere disregarded local law enforcement with virtual impunity.

After months of temporizing, Holden prepared for war. The

barbarous Stevens assassination coming on top of the slaughter of Wyatt Outlaw—both close allies of the governor—pushed him over the edge. Until now, he had hesitated to mobilize the state militia for fear that Klansmen would infiltrate white units and that the deployment of Black ones would exacerbate racial friction. He now decided that he had to act regardless of consequences. Having determined that the Klan was growing in at least twenty-five counties, he grimly wrote to the chief justice of the state Supreme Court, Richmond Pearson, "To the majority of the people of these sections the approach of night is like the entrance into the valley of the shadow of death. The men dare not sleep beneath their roofs at night, but abandoning their wives and little ones [they] wander in the woods until day. Thus civil government is crumbling around me." Holden moved with decision. He declared martial law and indicated that in Klan cases he would ignore writs of habeas corpus brought on behalf of alleged terrorists.

He appointed two war-hardened officers, William Clarke, a former Confederate colonel, to command a mixed regiment of Black and white troops, and George Washington Kirk, a swashbuckling, deceptively baby-faced wartime loyalist, who recruited four hundred tough white Union veterans from the mountains of Eastern Tennessee and western North Carolina. Clark was made responsible for the central Piedmont, including the capital, and Kirk for the most violent Klan-infested counties, Alamance and Caswell. Sweeping first through Alamance, Kirk marched into Yanceyville, where he immediately arrested two dozen men, most of them notorious members of the Klan, including a former congressman and a onetime Freedmen's Bureau agent. Kirk's men, many of whom had fought a guerrilla war against the Confederacy, were not gentle. In one heavily reported and widely condemned incident, his second-in-command, Lt. Col. George Bergen, had thrown a rope around the neck of one prisoner to encourage him to confess, while ex-sheriff Wiley—the last man to have been seen with Stephens—was seized in his tobacco field, tied to a horse and, Wiley alleged, whipped all the way into town, where he was threatened with immediate execution if he didn't tell all he knew about Stephens's murder.

They also arrested the combative Raleigh newsman Josiah

Turner, a former member of the Confederate Congress and now editor of the *Weekly Sentinel,* who was supposed by Republicans and even some Klansmen to be the order's state commander. He was not that, but he did serve as the Klan's de facto press officer, publishing a stream of articles damning Holden as "the devil incarnate," glorifying the night riders, blaming their worst atrocities on Radicals, and asserting if the Klan *had* committed any outrages they were entirely justified in order to stop a "negro crime wave." With mordant irony, Kirk's men incarcerated him in the room where Stephens was murdered. Although Turner was soon released, conservatives celebrated him as a martyr, a role that the editor played to the hilt, groaning about his incarceration in "Holden's Bastille."

In all, about one hundred men were arrested in Alamance and Caswell counties. False tales of supposed "atrocities" perpetrated against them ricocheted around the conservative press—one Greensboro newspaper declared the militia campaign to be "the last desperate act of [Holden's] insanity"—and even reached the ill-informed North, where the *New York Times* denounced Kirk's actions as a cruel and "odious" reign of terror manifesting "unbridled partisanship." Conservatives smeared Kirk's men as an illiterate "gang of cutthroats," although they in fact killed no one, much less by throat-slitting. The frothing *Asheville Citizen* urged "the uprising of an indignant people to slay the monster of Radicalism," and the *Weekly Sentinel* called for a popular uprising to drive the Republican-controlled General Assembly from the Capitol.

In the wake of the arrests, scores of panicky Klansmen signed confessions in hope of receiving amnesty. Others fled: the Alamance County Klan chief Jacob Long was rumored to have gone west, having told friends that "he was going where hemp didn't grow"—in other words, where he would not be hanged for his crimes. The prisoners had little to fear, however. Few witnesses were willing to come forward either because they sympathized with the Klan or, with reason, feared retribution. In Caswell County, local Blacks— "worthy darkies," in the contemptuous words of a Klansman—were taken to a local graveyard and given a scare, to discourage them from revealing anything to the courts. The Klan's grip on at least some judges further insulated the accused. Judge James Boyd arranged for one of the men implicated in Stevens's murder, John Lea, the scion of a prominent local family and a Confederate veteran, to be released from his cell and invited him to walk to his house, where the two men relaxed together on the porch. Lea recalled years later that over dinner Boyd said, "Lea, I was a Ku Klux. I have disgraced myself and my little wife." Asked how he had done that, the judge replied, "I turned state's evidence." Why had he done that? "Moral cowardice. [They] came to me and put the rope around my neck and I wilted." (The judge was speaking figuratively.) Boyd and his wife both burst into tears. Boyd then said, "Lea, I will never expose you. I know you are the county commander in Caswell."

Although Holden lost no tears over the treatment meted out to Kirk's less well-connected prisoners, he was astute enough to know that he couldn't afford the political blowback that resulted from it. He warned Kirk to keep his men in check: "All prisoners, no matter how guilty they may be supposed to be, should be treated humanely." On July 20, fearing open war with the Klan, he asked Grant to send more federal troops to North Carolina, warning, "The defeat of state and federal troops in any conflict, at this crisis, would be exceedingly disastrous." He also reiterated the shopworn charge that ex-President Johnson was the real head of the Klan. This Grant wisely disregarded, but he did create a temporary military district for the state under Col. Henry J. Hunt, his trusted wartime artillery commander, and ordered a contingent of seven hundred fresh soldiers to be distributed at potential flashpoints around the Piedmont. It was the president's first step toward war.

Holden's most controversial action, a politically fatal one as it proved, was his refusal to honor writs of habeas corpus, that is the right to due process. This was particularly risky for the governor because as a newspaper editor during the war he had stridently challenged the state's Confederate governor for failing to honor such writs; after the war, Holden had also championed the new liberal state constitution, which had enshrined habeas corpus as a basic right of citizens. In the face of howls from conservatives, and some Republicans, he telegraphed Grant on August 7 to tell him that he intended to keep the prisoners unless the army demanded their release with the president's explicit approval. Holden conspicuously ignored several writs issued by Judge Pearson, a fellow Republican, on behalf of prisoners assigned to his court. Pearson ruled that Holden had the right to declare counties in a state of insurrection and to hold all suspects detained there. Attorneys then petitioned Federal District Judge George Brooks, who ruled that in accordance with the due process clause of the Fourteenth Amendment— which was intended to protect freedmen from arbitrary arrest but was now being exploited on behalf of accused terrorists—that Kirk must immediately release his prisoners to the courts, among them the gloating editor Josiah Turner.

Holden was confident that the president would back him up. But on August 8 he was shocked to learn that Grant's new attorney general, Amos T. Akerman, had ruled against him and directed him to yield to the federal judiciary. Holden reluctantly directed Kirk to deliver the prisoners to Pearson and Brooks, and to parole all the accused "in whose honor he can confide." (He told Kirk to leave a hundred picked men at Yanceyville, "*taking special care* that his prisoners are not maltreated.") Brooks immediately released all the prisoners who were turned over to him. Pearson held fifty-nine of them for trial by local courts. None would ever be convicted.

Even the once irrepressible Albion Tourgée felt discouraged, after his five frustrating and increasingly dangerous years in North Carolina. For him, the war against the Klan was a personal crusade. Two of his closest associates had been savagely murdered, Wyatt Outlaw and John Stephens. Reports of new brutalities came to him daily—two hundred Klan attacks in Alamance County, another two hundred in Chatham County, a seventy-four-year-old woman who had been beaten with a plank, a Black man clamped through his body to a log with an iron staple, a young Black woman gang-raped then forced into bed with a man, bound face-to-face with him, and burning embers piled on them by Klansmen who rode off laughing. Death threats against him never ceased. "My steps have been dogged for months, and only a good opportunity has been wanting to secure to me the fate which Stephens has just met," he confided to Senator Abbott. The Klan, he knew, had sentenced him to death and informed him with "notices of the time appointed, a coffin placed at my door, a paper pinned to the gate with a knife stating that I had been doomed. I still live but really do consider the tenure very precarious."

Tourgée's frightened wife, Emma, a fiercely principled woman who shared his belief in equal rights and had borne social ostracism and sneering insults from her white neighbors for years, was close to a nervous breakdown. Northern friends begged him to leave. "Let some of the natives fight the K.K.'s, for a while," one friend urged. Wrote another, "I wished I had hold of your collar, I would have jerked you out of that infernal hole quick as lightning could scorch feathers." The conservative press relentlessly, and baselessly, smeared Tourgée as a legal ignoramus, a wartime "bummer" and convicted criminal who kept a young Black girl as a concubine, and a troublemaker who "annoyed the farmers" by persuading "the darkies" to sue them over wages. (He in fact held two degrees from Rochester University as well as a law degree, and was a muchwounded veteran, as well as a devoted husband.) His real crime was his willingness to try white criminals and an unbending commitment to Blacks' rights.

"And yet the government sleeps," Tourgée wrote in near despair to his ally Sen. Joseph Abbott.

The poor disarmed nurses of the Republican party—those men by whose ballots the Republican party holds power—who took their lives in their hands when they cast their ballots for U.S. Grant and other officials—all of us must be sacrificed, murdered, scourged, mangled. . . . I could stand it well to fight for "Uncle Sam" on the battlefield, but this lying down, tied hand and foot with the shackles of the law, to be killed by the very dregs of the rebellion, the scum of the earth, and not allowed either the consolation of fighting or the satisfaction that our "fall" will be noted by the government, and protection given to others thereby, is somewhat too hard. I am ashamed of the nation that will let its citizens be slain by scores, and scourged by thousands, and offer no remedy or protection. I am ashamed of a state which has not sufficient strength to protect its own officers in the discharge of their duties, nor guarantee the safety of any man's domicile throughout its length and breadth. I am ashamed of a party which, with the reins of power in its hands, has not nerve or decision enough to arm its own adherents, or to protect them from assassination at the hands of their opponents. Unless these evils are speedily remedied, the Republican party has signed its death warrant.

He added, "any member of Congress who, especially if from the South, does not support, advocate, and urge immediate, active, and thorough measures to put an end to these outrages deserves to be damned."

9

THE FIRST ENFORCEMENT ACT

We must by steady, patient and persevering
work get hold of the state government.

—WADE HAMPTON

On March 30, 1870, Ulysses Grant put his signature to a document
that changed America. It was, in one sense, a simple thing, if long-
delayed: the bill restoring Texas statehood. Its real significance was
much more far-reaching than that, making it one of the most consequential acts in American history, completing the ratification of
the Fifteenth Amendment, and ensuring the right to vote for four
million Black Americans. Its text was brief and blunt. Section 1
declared, "The right of citizens of the United States to vote shall
not be denied or abridged by the United States or by any State on
account of race, color, or previous condition of servitude." Its second section was even shorter, and it gave teeth: "The Congress shall
have power to enforce this article by appropriate legislation."

Sixteen states had ratified the amendment during Grant's first
four months in office, beginning with Nevada in March 1869. Then
the process stalled. (New York even *rescinded* its ratification, but
later restored it.) Grant, who cared deeply about the amendment,
felt more anxiety over its passage than any other piece of legislation that faced the country since he had become president. Ratification was not a foregone conclusion, and its achievement was a
personal triumph for the president. For months, he had exerted his

powers of persuasion to nudge, cajole, and occasionally bully the process forward, pleading as recently as February with the governor of Nebraska to convene a special session of the state legislature to ratify the amendment. With one more state needed, Grant put pressure first on the Republicans who still, if tenuously, governed Texas, and then on Congress to approve the state's speedy readmission. Lincoln's Emancipation Proclamation and the congressional Radicals' passage of the Thirteenth and Fourteenth Amendments had, of course, led to this moment, but no previous president had ever invested as much of his office's moral force and political capital on behalf of such a dramatic enlargement of civil rights. Only a few years earlier no more than a handful of Americans thought the enfranchisement of Blacks possible, and as long as Andrew Johnson was president it was politically unimaginable.

In a proclamation to the nation, Grant declared the amendment, without exaggeration, "a measure of grander importance than any other one act of the kind from the foundation of our free government to the present day." Its adoption, he said, "completes the greatest civil change and constitutes the most important event that has occurred since the nation came to life." What he said next was far-sighted beyond its time. Convinced, like Thomas Jefferson, that an enlightened population was essential to make American democracy work as it should, he called upon Congress to "take all the means within their constitutional powers to promote and encourage popular education throughout the country, and upon the people everywhere to see to it that all who possess and exercise political rights shall have the opportunity to acquire the knowledge which will make their share in the government a blessing and not a danger." Finally, in a plea that went beyond policy prescription to address the poison of racism itself, he urged white Americans—"the race more favored heretofore by our laws"—to "withhold no legal privilege of advancement to the new citizen."

Black communities erupted in jubilation. In Washington, five thousand marched in a torchlight parade to the White House, ringing bells, spontaneously dancing, waving banners praising God and Grant, and shouting "Glory, hallelujah!" Wagonloads of Negro girls dressed in white waved flags. Black policemen and firemen strode proudly in crisp uniforms. More wagons—an extraordinary sight—carried mixed parties of Blacks, whites, Indians, and even Chinese, "representatives of the breaking down of the old wall of partition and the general progress of events," a clearly astonished observer reported. Speaking from the portico of the White House, Grant told the gathered multitude, "There has been no event since the close of the war in which I have felt so deep an interest as the fifteenth amendment. It looked to me as the realization of the Declaration of Independence."

There was an unstated corollary to Grant's public declaration: he had intended to issue a second proclamation simultaneously. It would have declared a general amnesty for the thousands of still disenfranchised former rebels. Grant felt initially that such a generous measure would promote "good feeling and harmony throughout the South," but the unrelenting tide of panicky letters he received from the frightened southern Republicans caused him to stay his hand. In one Alabama county, the probate judge had been threatened and driven from office; in another, all the Republican officials fled for their lives; in a third, robed Klansmen paraded nightly and forced the sheriff to resign; in yet a fourth, night riders shot the Republican solicitor dead in his room. The editor of the *Montgomery Daily Journal* telegraphed Grant, "For Heavens sake don't remove the Troops from our State or City"—without them, it would be impossible to "curb the vicious and encourage the timid." From Kentucky, a beleaguered Republican named George Daniel reported bands of roaming Klansmen "hanging, murdering or whipping" Radicals almost nightly. "We ask in the name of humanity, send a Regiment of Colored Soldiers, and let them hunt down and punish those midnight assassins who are a perfect terror to the Country. In God's name send the soldiers at once." Grant was also influenced by the intense opposition to amnesty from the Radicals on Capitol Hill. As Sen. Jacob Howard of Michigan put it, "I propose to keep this nest of adders, who have given us so much trouble—I mean the ringleaders of the rebellion, those who hissed the loudest and were the most poisonous in their bite—away from my premises." Grant told a reporter for the *New York Herald,* "so long as the state of society in those districts is such as to call for military aid to preserve order it would be useless to recommend to Congress the removal of disabilities."

Grant had hoped for more from white southerners. But he was coming to accept that far more of them were determined to reject the new order of things than he had imagined, and that, if anything, the enfranchisement of the freedmen was likely to exacerbate their resistance. He was also coming to grips with the likelihood that the safety of southern Republicans, the newly won rights of Blacks, and the future of precarious Reconstruction state governments would be unsustainable without federal action on a scale much greater than he had contemplated. He had recently sent a fresh regiment of troops to North Carolina in an effort to help Governor Holden. But the piecemeal shifting around of small companies of soldiers like pawns on the South's Klan-infested southern chessboard was not enough to counter the rising tide of blood-soaked disorder.

Even among themselves, Republicans argued about how much authority the federal government really had to enforce the new amendments in a political landscape where prewar attitudes about the inviolability of state sovereignty were still deeply ingrained. Then, in May 1870, the assassination of John Stephens in Yanceyville, North Carolina, finally pushed them over the edge. Congress gave Grant what he needed. The First Enforcement Act—there would be two more—empowered the president to sustain the provisions of the Fifteenth Amendment by force of arms, if necessary, making it a federal crime to interfere with voting, to discriminate against voters based on their race, or to conspire to prevent citizens from exercising their constitutional rights. It was a dramatic departure: until now, Klan crimes had been treated strictly as state, not federal, offenses despite the fact that southern courts almost everywhere refused to convict Klansmen of anything at all. (As important a step as the act was, it applied only to crimes committed after its enactment, thus excluding federal prosecution for the murders of John Stephens and many other Klan outrages.)

The debate over the Enforcement Act defined the lines of political combat that would be played out on the congressional battlefield for years to come. Proponents argued that the protection of Black voters was not only morally right and politically imperative but also in the highest national interest, since the freedmen's ability to safely cast their ballots was the best guarantee that federal authority would be preserved in the South. Sen. George Spencer of Alabama, a staunch Radical, warned that the fruits of the war were "slipping from our grasp without even the endeavor to clutch them before they pass away," undone by political men who failed to understand that conditions in the South were far different from those in the placid North. Too many of his fellow senators, he said, "in their charity and mistaken philanthropy," didn't want to hear the truth. "There appears to be a species of cowardice coming like a film over the eyes of the body politic. Revolutions do not quiet themselves so quickly as some of my honorable colleagues suppose."

The Democrats knew they lacked the votes to defeat the bill. Nonetheless, they conjured terrifying images of soldiers with fixed bayonets surrounding southern ballot boxes, charging that the law diminished states' constitutional rights, destroyed local government, and would create a vast federal bureaucracy to manage and manipulate elections. Sen. Allen Thurman of Ohio cried that it meant the federal government could now "wipe out the whole state machinery of elections." Sen. Eugene Casserly of California charged, "There is not a precinct in New York or Maine or Oregon where the military may not be summoned by some subordinate." And Sen. William Hamilton of Maryland warned menacingly, "You have made the negro a rival for place, a rival for power; you have made him a rival in legislation; and all that only brings him in the march of events nearer to the fiery energy and consuming ambition of the Anglo-Saxon, and nearer to the dangers of an ultimate fate." What Hamilton meant was racial extermination. It was, he reiterated, "our solemn duty to keep [Negroes] as distinct and separate from the white race as the material interests of the country will justify."

Carl Schurz, who in 1865 was among the first to alert the nation to the wholesale abuse of the newly freed people, now cautiously straddled the political fence. Although in the end he voted for the Enforcement Act, he seemed at best ambivalent about it, expressing his deep unease at the bill's enlargement of federal power. He urged his fellow Republicans to "bridle" their tendency to "thrust the hand of the national government into local affairs on every possible occasion," before they faced a popular reaction to political overreach that they could not overcome. No member of the Senate expressed himself more reflectively. But embedded in his eloquence in the debate were unmistakable signs of a man who was loosening his ideological moorings and drifting toward new and distinctly less Radical political waters.

Meanwhile, in North Carolina, Governor Holden's campaign against the Klan gained ground. The fifty-nine men who had been rounded up by Kirk's militia in Caswell and Alamance counties faced arraignment at the columned Greek Revival Wake County courthouse in Raleigh, for the murder of John Stephens and other crimes. The state's witnesses presented a barrage of powerful evidence. They were, however, with few exceptions Black, a fact that had to be weighed in the balance, given the racial minefield that was a North Carolina courtroom. (The pro-Klan *Weekly Sentinel* openly threatened any Klansmen who might consider turning state's evidence, writing, "The man who would do this to screen himself and implicate others is a cowardly dog, and deserves the execration of mankind.") A Black farmhand named Anderson Graves said that while he was working in Felix Roan's tobacco bed a few days before the murder, he had heard Roan say "that Mr. Stephens would not live but one week." Jim Graves, another farmhand, testified that Roan had said within his hearing that Stephens was "a grand rascal and ought to be killed." Several witnesses said they saw Sheriff Frank Wiley touch Stephens's arm and start downstairs, followed by three of the other accused men, Joseph Fowler, John Kerr, and Thomas Hubbard. Others saw John Lea and J. T. Mitchell talking and laughing with Stephens in the hall outside the lumber room. Joseph Womack, a Black preacher, saw Wiley, Mitchell, Logan Totten, and three other men come out of the lumber room. Wiley, he said, "looked as if he had been exerting himself, for he was sweating." Womack admitted that he had kept silent at the inquest. "I was afraid for my life to say anything about this—I had been Ku Kluxed before." He was so frightened that he had fled to Virginia, but he had come back when the federal troops arrived in Yanceyville. Ruffin Hill also saw Wiley and the others leave the lumber room but, he said, he "was cautioned to keep the matter secret." Judy Robinson, a Black woman, said that she was at Harrelson's store later that afternoon when Wiley came in. He took off his hat and passed his hand over his forehead. Someone asked if he had been running because his face was so red and sweaty. He said, "No, I have not been running, but worse." What the witnesses said ought to have been damning. But the defense's witnesses scoffed at their character: Anderson Graves, they said, was known as a liar and thief when he was a slave before the war, Womack "a loafing, trifling fellow." And so it went.

Wiley's testimony in his own defense was so remarkably detailed and replete with alibis that, to someone so inclined, it must have provoked suspicion. It was *Stephens* who asked *him* to go downstairs, he said, to offer him Republican support in the election, "because he regarded me as a moderate man." Wiley said he then left Stephens in the vestibule, and walked to the town pump where he ran into a friend named Bigelow. "We had a little talk when Mr. John H. Kerr came up." All three then went to Johnston's store where Wiley said he paid Johnston $50. After that, he returned to the courthouse and saw J. C. Wilkerson, a merchant, and had a talk with him about the election. Wiley later saw Stephens at the county assessor's office, and even called Wilkerson's attention to him, he said. Then he and Wilkerson went to get some bitters at Harrelson's store, and came back through the courthouse to the south door, where he saw Dr. Richmond, and Lee Hensley, "a colored boy," whom he had "bound out." Then, sometime between 4 p.m. and 5 p.m. he saw Stephens talking to "a colored man" outside the assessor's office. Wiley then went to Henderson's store for a bucket, walked back to the pump, and had another "colored man" water his horse. "I got in my buggy and started home," he said. "Mr. Wilkerson went seven miles with me, and Mr. Smith went with me to my gate." Wiley said that he had always gotten along with Stephens. "I said to Mr. Watts"—R. B. Watts, the county assessor—"that the people might scorn Mr. Stephens, but I should always respect him." Asked for his opinion about a motive for Stephens's murder, Wiley replied, "I have no way to account for it."

A parade of local white notables testified for the defense. When county assessor Watts was questioned, he denied that there was any ill-feeling against Stephens, adding that no organization called the Ku Klux even existed in Caswell County. George Bigelow testified that Wiley and Stephens had been "on the best of terms." Col. E. B. Withers denied that any Republican, white or Black, had ever been "illegally" whipped in the county. Bryce Harrison denied that anyone "was in the habit of going about in disguise." James Hopkins, who said he was receiving tax payments in the assessor's office all afternoon, saw no one go in or out of the office where Stephens was found and "heard no scuffle or exclamation." J. C. Wilkerson said that back in February he had seen a band of two dozen men in white robes and caps in the town of Leasburg, but they just wanted to buy some tobacco and whiskey. One of the defense's few Black witnesses, Lee Hensley, who lived as a dependent on the property of a white farmer, stated that he "knew nothing about the Ku Klux."

Col. Henry Hunt, the army's commander in North Carolina, who sat in on the arraignments, astonishingly concluded that although the Klan was real, in his opinion its members were no more than local vigilantes who punished thefts and insults to women, and that Stephens's murder had nothing to do with politics. The court's ruling was no less disappointing, if more nuanced. It first acknowledged the obvious, stating that the murder had clearly been premeditated and carried out by a well-organized group of men "to whom the unsuspecting victim was led up for sacrifice." It went on to say that much of the testimony was "unsatisfactory"—a euphemism that essentially meant that the two judges deemed it transparently false. Although there seemed to be probable cause for sending the accused to trial, the court asked, "how much reliance can be put in the testimony of reluctant white witnesses and persons who have been slaves and are now citizens?" What they really meant was that Blacks' testimony could not be entirely trusted. "This is a practical question and the learning of the law does not aid much in its solution." In other words, prosecution was politically impossible. The court then piously stated that it would not be a party to the escape of the guilty and would place no obstacle in the way of bringing criminals to justice. But it had, in fact, done just that.

The prosecution was made even more complicated by the chaotic political atmosphere that surrounded the state's August legislative elections. Although white voters were also inflamed about economic stagnation, taxes, a failed railroad bond issue, and the cost of public education, Holden had been seriously damaged by his suspension of habeas corpus and the fallout from the so-called Kirk-Holden War. The governor's Conservative Party enemies potently accused him of waging "war upon the good people of the state," and claimed that unleashed Blacks were pillaging the countryside, inflating the occasional barn burning into a deliberate arson campaign. The elections were a catastrophe for the Republicans. The Conservatives prevailed over Republican legislative candidates by a two-to-one margin, captured six of the state's seven congressional seats, and elected their candidate for attorney general, the only statewide office on the ballot. Overall, the Republican vote dropped by thirteen thousand from the 1868 presidential election, a measure of the Klan's success at intimidating Black voters, a worryingly large number of whom stayed away from the polls.

The former prisoners returned to Yanceyville to be hailed as martyrs to the cause of white rule. They would never go to trial. Nor would anyone ever be punished for Stephens's murder. A parade was mounted in the martyr's honor; cannons were fired, speeches were made. Recalled John Lea, one of the principal accused, "When I reached home Sherriff Griffith came and summoned me to go with him and we ordered the heads of the Union League to leave the county within 24 hours and they did so without exception."

Sixty-five years later, in 1935, a lengthy item appeared in a Danville, Virginia, newspaper. It revealed the full story of what had happened in the lumber room where Stephens died. It quoted at length from an affidavit signed by John Lea in 1919 and deposited with the North Carolina Historical Commission. It had remained sealed until Lea's recent death at the age of ninety-one. In the affidavit, Lea identified himself as the organizer of the Ku Klux Klan in Caswell County and affirmed that he was the last survivor of the group that had murdered Stephens. He asserted that Stephens had been tried by a Klan "jury" of twelve men, and found guilty for ordering "darkies" to burn down a hotel at Yanceyville and torch the cotton crops of two white landowners. (These actions were supposed at the time to be reprisals against Klan terrorism, but there is no evidence that Stephens had a role in either, or that the hotel-burning was other than an accident.)

"I had ordered all the KKK in the county to meet at Yanceyville that day, with their uniforms under their saddles," Lea's affidavit continued. Sheriff Wiley volunteered to "fool" Stephens into the lumber room, supposedly to talk over Stephens's offer of political support in the upcoming election for sheriff. Mitchell, a former

Confederate captain, James Denny, and a man named Joe Fowler went into the room and Wiley came out. Mitchell took away Stephens's three pistols, then came out and left Denny with a pistol at Stephens's head and told Lea that he couldn't kill him. Wrote Lea, "Wiley came to me and said, 'You must do something. I am exposed unless you do.' Immediately I rushed into the room with eight or ten men and found [Stephens] sitting flat on the floor. He arose and approached me and asked me not to let them kill him. J. Thomas Mitchell then threw a rope around Stephens's neck, then put his feet on Stephens's chest and pulled the rope tight. Another accomplice, Tom Oliver, then stabbed Stephens in the chest and neck. The knife was thrown at his feet and the rope left around his neck. We all came out, closed the door and took the key and threw it into the creek."

The campaign against the Klan that Holden had initiated with such élan, now effectively guttered out. In the mistaken belief that the Klan's predations had effectively ceased, the military District of North Carolina, General Hunt's command, was officially terminated in September. Holden also disbanded the state militia, so hated by anti-Reconstruction whites, and rescinded his proclamation of a state of insurrection in Alamance and Caswell counties. In his last annual message to the General Assembly, he meekly declared that "peace and good order have been restored to all parts of the state." This was far from the truth. But he was desperate to keep his job and to stay out of jail. More gravely, he also faced the prospect of imminent impeachment by the new state legislature dominated by his enemies. Kirk retreated back across the state line into Tennessee with his men, but his deputy, Lt. Col. George Bergen, who remained in North Carolina, was arrested for the alleged abuse of prisoners, and jailed at Raleigh for ninety days.

The Conservative Party's electoral victory in North Carolina was correctly perceived by freed people as a triumph for the whites who sought to "redeem" North Carolina by destroying the Republicans. Rumors of imminent attack raced through Black communities. Freed people as far away as the Klan-infested town of Newberry, South Carolina, even sent a committee to meet with Henry Hunt in Raleigh, begging to know if freed people would now have to carry passes as slaves had before the war. Had public whipping been restored? Were their children now barred again from public schools?

Had their constitutional rights been terminated? Hunt complacently assured the delegation that their fears were unfounded.

The visitors from Newberry went home mollified, but hardly reassured. They were returning to a state that differed from North Carolina in significant ways, but it was obvious to all that a crisis was in the offing. With North Carolina now in the hands of white supremacist "redeemers," South Carolina would soon emerge as the cockpit of Grant's efforts. In some important respects, it offered a promising battleground. There, Blacks formed both an absolute and a voting majority. They also held many jobs in state and local government, comprised a majority in the legislature, and were central participants in the reform of elections, law enforcement, education, and landholding legislation. Before the war, South Carolina was probably the least democratic of all the states in the Union, having excluded even poor whites from the exercise of power. The state's new constitution had vastly expanded political participation. Liberalizing legislation encouraged laborers and tenants to challenge abusive landowners, and promised a fair hearing before officials, often Black, who had been chosen by popular vote or appointed by the Republican governor. Plantation owners, who had barely been taxed before the war, now faced high assessments by the state, counties, and towns, for public education, new hospitals, and other services, all determined by local Republican appointees. Wealthy whites were particularly incensed at the use of taxation to break up large estates, purchase former plantation land, and resell it cheaply in small parcels to the poor, usually freed people. Whatever "technical names" the taxes might be called by, the *Edgefield Advertiser* protested, they were "nothing but measures to steal money from the white people," while freedmen's settlements on newly acquired land were nothing less than "military colonies" intended to terrorize hapless white citizens.

Blacks' political strength in South Carolina also meant that, in contrast to most other southern states, they also formed the rank and file of the state militia. The militia's nominal head was state adjutant general and future governor Franklin Moses, a native-born white Republican from one of Charleston's prominent families. Its driving engine, however, was his ambitious young deputy, Robert Elliott, who had through a dynamic combination of talent, energy, and opportunism rocketed to the top tier of Black state leaders. In contrast to Holden's combination of blundering and hesitancy in North Carolina, Gov. Robert Scott, a tough-minded Union Army veteran, directed Moses and Elliott to recruit every Republican between the ages of eighteen and forty-five, including Blacks. Moses ordered, "Make no exceptions," a directive that was more aspirational than realistic. Elliott also directed federal census takers, most of whom were Black patronage appointees, to act as enlistment officers as well. Although the militia eventually claimed a paper enrollment of 95,000, perhaps as few as 12,000 were ever actually armed, mainly in the upcountry counties where Republicans were most vulnerable to the Klan's threats.

Whites almost universally refused to serve in the militia, but Blacks flocked to the colors, thrilled that for the first time in South Carolina history they would be provided with guns to defend themselves and their families. Along with rifles, Elliott also distributed rations of salt pork and beef, hominy, coffee, molasses, and other commodities. His orders were always crisp and sensible, perhaps reflecting his likely service in the British navy years earlier. (It has been speculated that Elliott was actually British-born and obscured his origins in order to mount his political career in South Carolina.) He advised one militia captain, Prince Rivers, in volatile Edgefield County, "Have your company drilled and ready for action whenever it may become necessary to act," and directed another to strictly refrain from any kind of aggressive behavior, but "be at all times vigilant and prompt to assume the defensive."

While the enrollment of the militia companies inspired Black South Carolinians, it inflamed whites, who, hardly surprisingly, recoiled at the increasingly familiar sight of their former slaves drilling with guns in the streets and squares of towns where, until now, Blacks had been expected to step off the curb in deference to whites. Though they were on the political defensive, whites were far from acquiescent. That spring, they invented a new political organization which they named the Union Reform, or simply "Reform," Party to contest the state elections in October. Like crypto-Democratic parties elsewhere in the South, they hoped to win over conservative Republicans and pliable Blacks to create a new majority, mainly by promising to clean up alleged corruption in the state government.

Less publicly, the "Reformers" served as cover for the vigilantes of the Ku Klux Klan. "We must by steady, patient, and persevering work get hold of the state government," the former Confederate general Wade Hampton, a leading figure in the new party, advised. "This we can do if we determine to accomplish it, and after that all the way is plain and easy." Hampton's relationship with the Klan remains unclear. He may never have been a member and he was sometimes criticized as a conciliator by the most extreme elements. Yet, as time would show, he would eventually become the willing beneficiary of white supremacist terror.

In June, the "Reformers" nominated as a front man for governor an upright, Vermont-born Republican judge named Richard B. Carpenter. The party then choreographed the choice of a candidate for lieutenant governor by having several Black men put in nomination, all of whom declined, according to a prearranged script. A Black delegate—Blacks were paid $2 a day to attend the "Reform" convention—then nominated Matthew Calbraith Butler, a former Confederate general, who was chosen by acclamation. Few Blacks succumbed to such theatrics. Scoffed Robert Elliott, "Today we are welcomed by those who have always declared that we were not fit to occupy a position entrusted to us." Never trust them, he warned. "Our only danger is that they will swallow us entire."

Elliott had already outgrown his position in the adjutant general's office and was about to launch his star into the national firmament. As chairman of the Republican state convention, he presided over the renomination of Robert Scott for a second term as governor and the nomination of the talented Black lawyer A. J. Ransier for lieutenant governor. Three more Black political men were nominated to run for seats in the U.S. Congress. One of them was Elliott himself.

Even as the "Reformers" carried out the political phase of their strategy, paramilitaries prepared for war. In September, the *Yorkville Enquirer* urged the recruitment of armed companies in every township to defend whites against the Black state militia. "With their present instructions (that they are to scare white people), they are liable at any time to commit some act that will throw the county into the horrors of a general strife," claimed the *Enquirer*. The paper advised whites for the time being "to bear patiently anything short of actual dishonor or inexcusable oppression," as hard as that might be, lest an impulsive reaction be exploited by the Republican authorities as a pretext for the imposition of martial law. Only a week later, however, the *Enquirer* edged closer to explicitly advocating white insurrection. "The unarmed race cannot reasonably look upon the arming of the other as anything but an insult; for it must be construed either that the whites are not to be trusted with arms in the cause of law and order, or that the blacks require arms to preserve their rights. Either of these suppositions is an insult to the white people." Armed whites would make clear to the Black militiamen that "the white people are *not scared*." Whites, it added, "must take care of themselves the best way they can." (The *Enquirer* also claimed absurdly that the real reason for arming Blacks was to "prevent colored men from leaving the Republican ranks and voting with the Reform party.")

All-white militias already existed in many towns in the form of supposedly innocent "rifle clubs." The Carolina Rifle Club, for one, in Charleston, purported to be a social club devoted to picnics and target practice, but openly admitted that it had been formed because "the conquerors of our 'Prostrate State' with diabolical spite [had] let loose upon a defenceless community the scum of an inferior race." At Edgefield, whites established a quasi-military "Agricultural and Police Club" led by the county chief of the Reform Party, which required every white man over eighteen to join in his township. Whites who refused to join or obey its rules were subject to the sternest and most unrelenting social proscription. If any white man declined to submit to its regulation of Blacks he was to be treated "as a whole nigger should be treated, pass him and his whole family with silent contempt: let him or any of his household get sick, or even die with none to cheer the lonely hours, or to bury the tainted remains but his nigger associates." The "Club" was, in effect, an aboveground iteration of the Klan by another name. If the "Club" did not get its way, one of its leaders declared, "we have but one other resource left—the Ku-Kluxer's power—the assassin's privilege."

In the run-up to the election, on October 19, Republican politicians and would-be voters were threatened with assassination. Especially in the upcountry counties, candidates hesitated to deliver speeches without protection. In county after county, white gangs seized the weapons from outnumbered Black militia companies—perhaps as many as four thousand rifles in all. At Clinton, in Laurens County, more than a thousand armed whites surrounded the town, cut the railroad, and forcibly disarmed three hundred Black militiamen peacefully assembled there. John Crews, the twenty-year-old son of the white Radical state senator Joe Crews, later testified that he saw "a great many white men were running out of the public square with Winchester rifles and guns, and making threats and yelling," swearing that they would kill both the Crewses when they caught them. With a young probate judge, Volney Powell, an Ohioan, Crews jumped out of the back window of the post office and the two men ran for their lives, dodging shots as they fled through open lots and into the woods. They hoped to make their way to safety in Columbia. They picked up several more men along the way, all Negro. However, they were caught and arrested by a party of whites and taken back to the edge of town, where they were stripped of their money and valuables. Crews recognized some of their horses as belonging to the state constabulary. Several of the men took Crews to the edge of a steep railway cut, where they clearly intended to shoot him. As they raised their guns, he threw himself over the edge and managed to escape into the woods, where he took refuge for two days in the home of a Black family, until federal troops appeared. Crews's father also managed to escape. But Volney Powell, the judge, was murdered in cold blood along with several of the Black men they had fled with.

In spite of such ugly incidents, the elections went off with less mayhem than many had feared. Braving the perceived dangers, Blacks voted in overwhelming numbers, mobilized by the Union League. Rumored invasions by Klansmen from Georgia and North Carolina failed to materialize and the presence of federal troops, however passive, tamped down potential disorders. To the astonishment of many, conservatives and Radicals alike, the "Reformers" were crushed. The Republicans triumphed with a statewide majority of some 35,000 votes out of 135,000 cast. Many Black candidates won office across the state, among them Robert Elliott in his quest for a seat in Congress. Governor Scott wrote to Grant with palpable relief, "We have just passed through an election which for rancor and virulence on the part of the opposition has never been excelled in any civilized community."

In the weeks that followed, the conservatives took stock of their defeat. With their electoral strategy in ruins, and its peace-minded advocates discredited, the initiative passed from politicians like Hampton, to the impatient gunmen of the Ku Klux Klan. Declared the *Charleston Daily News,* "We understand and accept the solid black vote cast against the nominees of the Reform Party as a declaration of war by the negro race against the white race, by ignorance against intelligence, by poverty against actual or potential wealth. Conciliation, argument, persuasion, all have been worse than useless. The white people stand alone. And they must organize themselves, and arm themselves, because the past and present prove that decency, purity, and political freedom, as well as the preservation of society, are identical with the interests of the white people of the state."

Just days after the election, armed whites overwhelmed the local constables at Laurens courthouse, killing several citizens, seizing stored arms belonging to the state, and dragging Black men and women from their homes and flogging them mercilessly. At Spartanburg, whites murdered a Black magistrate and beat up scores of Black men—possibly hundreds—who were known to have voted Republican. "Four peaceable and unoffending citizens of Spartanburg County were at the dead hour of night dragged from their homes and lashed on their bare backs until the flayed flesh hung dripping in shreds, and seams were opening in their mangled bodies large enough to lay my finger in," Governor Scott reported to President Grant. The victims were brought to Scott's office for him to see, "a spectacle that has chilled my blood with horror."

As the outrages mounted, Scott begged the president for immediate help. It was a cry from the heart. He feared a major "outbreak" within days. "It becomes therefore a question with us whether to surrender unconditionally, or fight," he wrote to Grant. The state militiamen were only amateur soldiers and but "imperfectly led." All of them held other jobs, mostly as laborers, while their opponents were Confederate veterans. To go up against them with nothing but inexperienced militia would be folly. "Unless the government gives protection to the loyal people and the authorities in the late rebellious states for some years to come, there can be nothing hoped for except a complete surrender of everything to the old ruling classes, which will be followed by anarchy and destruction of all civil liberties." Not only did control of South Carolina hang in the balance, but implicitly the entire Reconstruction enterprise in the South, and although he didn't say it explicitly, the political fate of all Black Republicans. Scott's language was feverish, but he was not exaggerating. Republicans prayed that finally the national government would act. His appeal did not go unheeded. Disgusted by the Klan's surging violence and with congressional support coalescing behind him, Grant prepared for the battle that he knew must soon come.

PART THREE

WAR

10

SOUTH CAROLINA IN THE BALANCE

Wilst thou Give us Consolation thate We May Singe
Columbia Columbia the home of the Brave lande of the free.

—J. Aaron Moore

Grant's field commander in the coming battle was anything but the
stereotype of a warrior. The new attorney general, forty-nine-year-
old Amos Akerman, was an intellectual-looking, prematurely balding lawyer of modest demeanor whose only military experience
had been a brief and unenthusiastic stint as a supply officer for the
Confederate Army. A native of New Hampshire and a graduate of
Dartmouth, Akerman had been raised poor in a deeply pious family. Like more than a few scholarly young New Englanders with
limited means, he had gone south in the 1840s to make his career as
a teacher. He wound up in Georgia where, in return for tutoring a
judge's children, he was able to study law under the eminent John
Berrien, who had served as Andrew Jackson's attorney general. He
seems to have adapted with little resistance to the South's "peculiar institution," eventually acquiring several slaves and espousing a
conventional southern disdain for abolitionism. "I recoiled from the
horrors that we anticipated as the effect of emancipation," he later
wrote. "I had no conception that slavery could be abolished as easily
and safely as it was actually done."

After the war, moral convictions that had remained quiescent
in Akerman for years erupted with the fervor of a religious con-

version. "The extension of suffrage to colored men was at first an alarming imposition on account of the supposed ignorance of the class to be enfranchised," he wrote. "But on reflection we considered that if ignorance did not disqualify white men it should not disqualify black men." In 1867, he helped ensure that Georgia's new constitution guaranteed the civil rights of former slaves, and the following year he opposed the legislature's high-handed expulsion of its Black members, arguing that the protection of all men's freedoms was the only guarantee of lasting peace. He was rewarded for his party-building work with appointment as the U.S. attorney for Georgia, which empowered him to prosecute violations of the Civil Rights Act. Few Americans outside Georgia had ever heard of Akerman, however. The New York Tribune reported that the Washington establishment responded to his appointment with "profound astonishment."

The circumstances of his selection were purely political. Grant's former attorney general, Ebenezer Hoar, had lost the president's confidence by declining to support his ultimately losing campaign to purchase Santo Domingo as a U.S. territory, an issue that at the time loomed larger in the minds of many congressmen than did the deteriorating situation in the South. With a stubbornness that irritated many, Grant saw the acquisition as both a strategic opportunity to project American power into the Gulf of Mexico and an economic one for American investment in the island's industrial development of coffee, tobacco, and tropical fruits. Grant reflected in a private memo, with palpable astonishment, could anyone "who voted $7,200,000 for the icebergs of Alasca," in 1867, really reject an acquisition that was so valuable in so many ways? Many of the southern Republicans, who were concerned more with civil rights than empire-building, were political allies of Charles Sumner, one of the freed people's leading advocates in Congress, who regarded Grant's plan as naked imperialism and, implausibly, as a veiled assault on Haiti, the hemisphere's only Black republic. (Haiti had intermittently dominated its neighbor and was lending support to rebels seeking to overthrow Santo Domingo's shaky pro-U.S. government.) In return for appointing a southern man—Akerman—to the cabinet, most of the region's Republicans promised Grant their votes for Dominican annexation. But it was not enough to win approval of the treaty. Nevertheless, in Akerman, Grant found precisely the right man for the moment, one who was both perfectly fitted and morally driven to turn the principles of the Enforcement Act into muscular reality.

While the new amendments had made the government stronger, "more national in theory," Akerman wrote in a letter to Sumner, he had observed "even among Republicans, a hesitation to exercise the powers to redress wrongs in the states." He had no such inhibitions. "Unless the people become used to the exercise of these powers now, while the national spirit is still warm from the glow of the last war the 'state rights' spirit may grow troublesome again." He intended not just to act but, with Grant's committed support, to act decisively.

On March 9, 1871, President Grant sent to Congress the message that the Radicals had been longing to hear. He called for Congress to support what he had already decided to do: order the army to take on the Klan. "There is no other subject on which I would recommend legislation during the present session," he declared. For months he had hesitated, lest he be condemned as a military despot. But he could wait no longer. He stated his case forcefully: authority was collapsing in large parts of the South, life and property were at risk wherever the Klan was ascendant, and for public officials even such basic functions as the delivery of mail and the collection of federal revenue were becoming a matter of life or death. "The power to correct these evils is beyond the control of state authorities," Grant said, and his own authority to deal with them was insufficient for the present crisis. "Therefore, I urgently recommend such legislation as in the judgment of Congress shall effectually secure life, liberty, and property, and the enforcement of law, in all parts of the United States."

Grant had now been president for just over two years. He was still a difficult man to read: diffident yet decisive, often sentimental, stubborn, prim, implacable when finally moved to act. "Grant appointed and dismissed men, proposed or opposed legislation with the unconcern of a leader who acts upon intuition rather than prolonged reflection," wrote the historian Allan Nevins, who did not approve of Grant. "He seemed to trust a guiding star, and why not?" The war had rescued him from a slough of failures in the 1850s to the command of the greatest army the nation had ever fielded, and then on to the presidency. Although he remained popular with the public, defection was simmering among conservative Republicans and disappointed reformers. Henry Adams, a cynic unfriendly to Grant, disdainfully remarked, "A great soldier may be a baby politician." Adams compared him to the Italian patriot Giuseppe Garibaldi, a man of "intermittent energy, immensely powerful when awake, but passive and plastic when in repose." Carl Schurz, his radicalism now diminished to the vanishing point, patronizingly grumbled that "having been trained to the military life," Grant was incapable of understanding the give-and-take of civilian government and was crippled by a mind "not supple enough" to function outside a sphere of "undivided power"—an oblique way of saying that he thought the president was a political dolt.

Those who observed Grant more closely were less harsh, even affectionate, recognizing in him a seemingly ordinary man endowed with extraordinary character. He impressed George Boutwell, his treasury secretary, the cabinet's leading Radical, with his clarity of thought, precision of memory, directness, and complete dearth of affectation. The journalist Ben Perley Poore, who had covered several of Grant's predecessors, approvingly described his military regularity. The president rose every morning at seven, read the Washington papers, and breakfasted with his family at eight thirty. He then took a stroll around the neighborhood by himself, always with a cigar in hand. By ten, he was in his office to receive official visitors. In cabinet meetings, held on the second floor of the White House, he listened closely but generally remained silent or noncommittal in his responses. In the afternoon, he visited the White House stables, where he "communed" with his favorite horses, Cincinnatus, St. Louis, and Egypt, and then sauntered along Pennsylvania Avenue, pausing to chat with an old wartime comrade or friend, and always politely lifting his hat when he encountered a female acquaintance. Dinner was served promptly at 5 p.m., and every member of the family was expected to be punctual. Typically the Grants dined plainly on rare roast beef, boiled hominy, and wheat bread, while "Grandpa Dent"—the president's irascible, formerly slaveowning father-in-law—"would sometimes indulge in growls against the progress being made by the black race"—views sharply at odds with Grant's deepening commitment to the advancement of the freed people. Before bed, Grant would light another cigar and smoke while he read the New York papers.

Although Grant was not by nature a crusader, his instinct for racial fairness continued to deepen. The lofty contempt with which Andrew Johnson had dismissed from his presence eminent Blacks such as Frederick Douglass was alien to Grant. On New Year's Day 1870, a White House guard had approached Grant's chief of staff, Orville Babcock, and asked if "the usual custom" of dividing the president's time to receive visitors between Negroes and whites should continue to be observed. Grant first told him without thinking that he supposed he would maintain the segregation, but when he was informed a few moments later that a number of Black guests were already waiting to see him, he ordered that anyone who wanted to come in immediately be admitted. It was an act of courtesy that constituted a social revolution.

The crisis in the South was never far from his mind. Incoming dispatches boiled with a litany of horrors. They came from governors and legislators, ex-soldiers and businessmen, teachers and farmers, the erudite and the barely literate. A Union veteran wrote from Tennessee that loyalists like himself were being "driven from their homes by the very men who fought for four years to destroy the government," citing a message he had received from the Klan's "Den Num 1": "go som where els for we have no earthely use for you nor non of your sort her." In Florida, the last active Republican officeholder west of the Chattahoochie, the clerk of court for Jackson County, had been found dead with thirteen buckshot and one bullet in his body, only a few yards away from the spot where his predecessor had been assassinated. A Yankee who purchased an iron mine in Alabama wrote that disguised men had threatened to hang him if he dared to hire a northern foundryman. The plaintive appeal of Kentuckian J. Aaron Moore still pierces the heart:

Ate this time there is A Clan of Clu clucks or Rebells. They Are treting the rattical party bade they say the raticle party And the Negro has to leave heare Wee do Note Wante to leave oure homes And sacryfise oure propity to plese them if there is Note something done Wee will hafe to leave heare son Wee Wante you to helpe us this oure time of Neede Wee Wante soldiers here Wee Will prove oure loyalty Wilst thou Give us Consolation thate We May Singe Columbia Columbia the home of the Brave lande of the free.

The worst news of all came from South Carolina. There, in the "cradle of secession," potentially the most volatile southern state of all, Klan terror was threatening to overwhelm a great swath of the state. Many state legislators felt like virtual prisoners in the state capital, afraid to return home to their districts, where they feared for their lives. On February 8, the state legislature had declared that "a state of domestic violence, to an alarming extent exists in this State," and admitted that "the civil authorities have failed and are altogether unable" to control it. The wife of a Presbyterian clergyman in Chesterfield wrote to Grant, "There is neither law nor justice in our midst,—our nearest neighbor—a prominent Repub'can now lies dead—murdered, by a disguised Ruffian Band—his wife was also murdered—she was buried yesterday, & a daughter is lying dangerously ill from a shot-wound—we are in constant fear and terror—our nights are sleepless, we are filled with anxiety an dismay.—Ought this to be?—have compassion, & send at once Troops to protect us." For Blacks, as always, the danger was even greater. "The only plan the colored men have of safety in this county near Broad River is to leave their houses at night and get together in crowds of fifteen or more and return to their work in the morning, as if they were living among Indians," the court clerk for Chester County reported to Scott.

When Klansmen couldn't find the men they sought, they often took vengeance on their wives and daughters, some of it utterly unspeakable. Harriet Simril was spat on and almost blinded by raiders who took the food from her cupboard and made her cook them a meal, then dragged her into the road and gang-raped her. In another instance, Klansmen shot Amzi Rainey's small daughter and then gang-raped another girl in front of Rainey's other children. A white woman who was caught hiding two Black men beneath the floorboards of her house during a Klan raid, was forced to lie down in the road and had hot tar poured into her "private parts."

Republican officials were specially targeted. Trial justices were murdered and others forced to resign. York County commissioner H. K. Roberts, having been threatened with assassination, asked the county sheriff for a bodyguard, begging for one who was "not in sympathy with those lawless bands." Increasingly, Black militiamen began to bear the brunt of the Klan's attacks. Just before Christmas, a bootlegger and probable Klansman named Matt Stevens was killed in an altercation with Black militiamen near the town of Union. In retaliation, bands of armed whites seized guns from any armed Black man they found. In an attempt to forestall bloodshed, the local militia captain, Elihu Walker, agreed to surrender himself and his men to the local sheriff, who promised them safety in the county jail. A few nights later, five hundred or more Klansmen in black gowns and masks swarmed into Union, closed off the town, broke into the jail, and demanded the keys to the cells from the jailer, H. T. Hughes, and his deputy. When they resisted, the Klansmen knocked them down, tied them to a stone post in front of the jail, and put a pistol to the head of Mrs. Hughes, threatening to blow out her brains if she didn't tell them where the keys were. In fear, she gave way. The Klansmen then dragged out the eight men associated with Stevens's death, including Walker, and two other Black men with no connection to it. The next morning, eight of the men were found either hanging from a hickory tree or tied to smaller trees with their bodies riddled with bullets. The two others were never heard from again. A note was left at the courthouse, reading in part: "Once again we have been forced by force to use force. Justice was lame and she had to lean upon us. We want and will have justice; but this cannot be till the bleeding fight of freedom is fought; until then, the Moloch of iniquity will have his victims."

Robert Shand, a conservative local lawyer, noted in his diary, "It was a gruesome sight to see the negroes lying dead side by side in the grand jury room of the Court House next morning; but it had a most quieting effect on the negroes." At the next session of the circuit court, the presiding judge submitted the murders to a grand jury, which, according to Shand, was made up mostly of Klansmen. Without investigation, it exonerated all the men supposed to have participated in the raid, and for good measure denounced Governor Scott and the Republican state government. An order from the Klan was found posted on the courthouse door warning every

Republican officeholder in the county to resign immediately under penalty of death. Noted Shand, without comment, "The order was promptly obeyed by every one of them."

Essentially, the Klan ran the entire town. When congressional investigators later visited Yorkville and interviewed Hughes, the jailer—he happened to be the brother-in-law of Matt Stevens, the bootlegger—a senator asked him, "When you were informed that the Ku-Klux had taken these negroes out, it did not strike you that they were going to shoot them?"

Replied Hughes, "I suppose anyone would know they were going to shoot them, if they had any sense at all."

"After you had come with your gun to defend the jail against negroes, you stopped right short, and did not do anything against the Ku-Klux?" the senator then asked.

"What would be the use for me to follow the Ku-Klux?" said Hughes.

The bootlegger's death was just a pretext for a more concerted campaign by the Klan to disarm and destroy the Black militia throughout the upcountry counties. Given that as long as slavery had existed Negroes had been banned from owning arms on pain of death, the sight of Blacks now not only carrying guns but authorized by the authorities to use them deeply unsettled whites as the ultimate embodiment of their world turned upside down. Whites raged that the Republicans had "armed one race with guns bought by money wrung from the other race," and complained of "reckless, dangerous and undisciplined" militiamen beating drums, firing off their guns, scaring ladies, burning the barns of alleged Klansmen, and causing "a feverish feeling of alarm to pervade every community." In mid-February, a party of forty or fifty Ku-Klux surrounded the house of J. R. Faris, a militia captain, eight miles from the town of Yorkville, and forced him to hand over the new Winchester rifles that the state had supplied to him. On the same day, a public meeting in the town of Clay Hill, ostensibly called by local Blacks but actually orchestrated by whites, blamed insecurity in the county on the Union League and declared that the best way to reduce the danger of Ku-Klux raids would be to disband the League. On the 20th, a body of more than fifty "unknown men" invaded the train depot at Rock Hill and seized militia weapons that had been stored there. A few days later, boxes of ammunition that the militia in York had turned over in good faith to the sheriff were seized in the night from the office of the probate judge. An empty box was found the next day on the porch of the local Presbyterian church; on it was tauntingly written, "When do you commence your war?" It was signed "Bushwhacker."

At the beginning of March, a proclamation from the Klan appeared prominently in the *Yorkville Enquirer,* York County's leading newspaper: It "invited" all "well-behaved persons, white and black" to continue quietly at their "appropriate labor" if they wanted to remain safe. "But we *do* intend that the intelligent honest *white* people (the tax-payers) of this county *shall rule it!*" the proclamation then declared. "We can no longer put up with negro rule, black bayonets, and a miserably degraded and thievish set of lawmakers, the scum of the earth, the scrapings of creation. We are pledged to stop it; we are determined to end it, even if we are 'forced by force, to use force.'" The same issue of the *Enquirer* carried a groveling declaration from several Black leaders in the community of Clay Hill that they intended to abandon all connection with the Union League and the Republican Party, "and leave politics to the control of the persons who understand the business better than we do."

When militia units refused to relinquish their weapons, the Klan made clear that it would back up its threats. In early March, in the town of Chester, some three hundred well-organized whites attacked one defiant company of perhaps a hundred men when it mustered to collect its store of ammunition. Reported a local newspaper, with intended humor, "The foresaid colored folks were immediately *advised* to 'git.' After some little 'standing upon the oder [*sic*] of their going,' they agreed to 'go at once.'" They were permitted to leave when they promised to disperse. Instead, "treacherous as by nature they are," they sent off runners in all directions to bring in "reinforcements." This "band of outlaws"—that is, the state militia—"concealed themselves behind rocks and opened fire on the attacking whites." After a "brisk skirmish," they fled in every direction. In fact, the militiamen stood their ground as long as they could and gave way only when they were outflanked and overwhelmed. The number of Blacks killed was uncertain but was probably between eight and ten. Remarked the *Yorkville Enquirer,* "buzzards have been observed circling around and about in a very inquisitive and mysterious manner."

As armed parties of the Klan terrorized the countryside, the order's chieftains, who were largely congruent with "respectable" conservative leadership, staged performative public rallies that purported to call for peace and civic order. At one such gathering in York County, Dr. John Bratton, a large landowner who was later shown to be a prime organizer of Klan raids, piously warned whites away from acts of violence, then ranted against "a negro legislature, negro justices, constables and policemen, monstrous taxation," and the alleged handing out of thirty thousand "black" bayonets to former slaves who were already "armed to the teeth as a military force." He added, "Those who sow to the wind, let them take care lest they reap the whirlwind!"

The conservative press typically denied that any unusual amount of lawlessness existed, sometimes blaming violence on Blacks who had disguised themselves as Klansmen, and sometimes while piously criticizing the cruelest atrocities unblushingly heroized the perpetrators. "They are men of firmness and nerve, who strike because they believe it necessary for the protection of their life, property, and liberty," the *Charleston News* editorialized, in mid-February. And the *Yorkville Enquirer,* writing from the very epicenter of the Klan's worst outrages, praised the "talent, caution, determination, and discipline [which] mark its every act. [M]oving in perfect harmony, almost ubiquitous, and apparently sufficiently numerous to place, in the shortest time, any number of finely mounted and completely equipped men that they may suppose will be required at any given point, it will require something more than force of numbers or indiscreet and coercive legislation to disperse them or drive them from their purpose."

Ill-feeling against Governor Scott grew among Radicals in the state legislature over his failure to curb the violence. Robert Elliott, now a congressman-elect, furiously charged him with "criminal guilt" for hesitating to fully arm the militia, and for ordering those he had armed not to use their weapons, leaving Blacks with little protection. Full of martial ardor, Elliott favored "sweeping things out with the militia." Scott didn't dispute that "a most fearful and alarming situation" existed, but warned that in an all-out war between the Klan and the state's "undisciplined" militia, the militia would likely be slaughtered. Instead, he reiterated his plea for more federal troops. In February, Grant agreed, ordering four companies of the 18th Infantry and four of the Seventh Cavalry into the most "turbulent" districts. These modest reinforcements were meant to be a down payment. Grant also decided to recall both cavalry and infantry from frontier Texas, where, he facetiously remarked to his cabinet, "they are protecting from the Indians a population who annually murder more Union men, merely because they are Union men, than the Indians would kill of them."

The events in South Carolina encapsulated everything that the Radicals in Washington had feared: the total breakdown of law and order, the vulnerability of the militia, the helplessness of the freed people, and the seeming invincibility of the Klan. The price of failing to act earlier was apparent to Grant. He only had to watch the political destruction of North Carolina's now perilously isolated governor, William Holden. In a last-ditch effort to cling to power, Holden abjectly offered to work with the newly elected, Klan-infested legislature. Instead, it crushed him with impeachment, charging him with "high crimes and misdemeanors in office," raising an "illegal" armed force, disregarding writs of habeas corpus, and ordering the arrest of the prominent conservative editor Josiah Turner. The bill's author was Frederick Strudwick, a member of the state legislature whom the Klan had appointed the previous year to assassinate a fellow state senator, T. M. Shoffner, who fled the state. Holden's trial lasted from December until the end of March. (Holden prepared himself by having himself baptized: a member of his congregation caustically remarked to the pastor that he ought to be immersed in lye instead of water.) The defense called 113 witnesses to testify to the ferocity of the crisis ravaging the Piedmont, but Holden's fate was foreordained. His successor, Lieutenant Governor Tod Caldwell, a fellow Republican, was crippled by the legislature, which made clear that he would suffer Holden's fate if he tried to thwart them.

Before his conviction and permanent banishment from state office—the first successful impeachment of a sitting governor in U.S. history—Holden hastened to Washington to warn all who would listen that unless Congress cracked down on the Klan the attacks against Republicans would only grow worse. Holden couldn't save himself. But Grant listened, as he had to South Carolina's overwhelmed governor. In his inaugural speech, Grant had called for "patient forbearance" on the part of all Americans, but he had also promised "the colored people of the nation" that he would defend them. For two years he had struggled to balance the two principles. His patience was now at an end. So was that of the critical mass of Republicans in Congress, who could plainly see that a conservative restoration in the South would have dire consequences for the national party. Shielding Black voters from white vengeance was not only a moral but also a political challenge. The Constitution's three-fifths rule had long ensured that slave states enjoyed additional congressional representation for that proportion of their enslaved population. With the southern states gone from the Union during the war, the Democrats' power had withered. Now the number of representatives allotted to the southern states was surging, so far to the benefit of the Republican Party. But if Black voters were frightened away from the polls, the former Confederate states would wind up with even greater sway in Congress than they had in the antebellum era. Democratic majorities in southern state legislatures would also undoubtedly elect reactionaries to the U.S. Senate, which would in turn threaten to nullify Reconstruction legislation and perhaps even overturn the Fourteenth and Fifteenth Amendments.

Pressure to act had been building in Congress since December, when Senate Republicans formally asked the president to submit a report on politically motivated crimes committed by "organized bodies of disloyal and evil-disposed persons" in the southern states. Grant provided a trove of War Department files, including lists of Klan outrages and victims, trial transcripts, affidavits, and terrorists' confessions, much of it initially supplied to him by Holden. In mid-January, the Senate appointed a Select Committee to investigate the Klan's depredations in North Carolina.

In February 1871, Congress also passed the Second Enforcement Act. This was directed partly at corruption in northern cities, particularly New York, where ongoing federal prosecution of the Tweed Ring was exposing the dark arts of election fraud there. But it also provided another weapon to protect Black voters in the South by explicitly placing the administration of all national elections under federal authority and empowering federal judges and U.S. marshals to oversee local polling places. Neither of the Enforcement Acts was sufficient to stop the Klan's intimidation, but they created a new legal foundation upon which Grant and the congressional Radicals could, and soon would, build even stronger measures.

In keeping with the custom of the time, the Congress that had been elected in November 1870 would not normally have met until December of 1871, but Grant called a special session to deal immediately with Klan terror, beginning on March 4. The makeup of the new Congress, the Forty-second, was less favorable to the Republicans, who had lost thirty-seven seats in the midterm elections. But the Republicans still retained a working majority in the Senate, along with a weakened one in the House. The Radicals' actual strength was less commanding than it seemed, however. A small but significant minority of the Republicans affiliated with the growing Liberal Republican movement led by Carl Schurz and Lyman Trumbull was not only hostile to Grant himself but also far less committed to Reconstruction, Blacks' civil rights, and the hard choices that would have to be made in order to protect them both.

The Liberal Republicans had initially hoped to quietly reform the Republican Party from within. By 1871, however, there was virtually open warfare within the party, with the self-described reformers aligned against administration loyalists. They complained that the party had lost its ethical ballast and turned into a corrupt oligarchy ruled by demagogues, such as Ben Butler and Sen. Roscoe Conkling of New York. Wrote Schurz to E. L. Godkin, the editor of *The Nation,* the Liberal Republicans' flagship organ, in March, "The Republican Party is rapidly going to perdition," and in order to be saved its leadership "must be broken up."

Their complaints were both personal and political. They had little respect for Grant's competence, and they were disgusted by his seeming obliviousness to corruption among his allies, although they did acknowledge the president's own honesty. Their accusations were exaggerated, but they weren't entirely baseless: Vice President Colfax had been tainted by association with a scheme to skim funds from the Union Pacific Railroad; Grant's brother was tangled in an attempt to corner the gold market; and the president's private secretary, Orville Babcock, had been caught taking bribes from whiskey distillers. As an alternative, the Liberal Republicans presented themselves as the advocates for public virtue in government and guardians against creeping tyranny. In practical terms, this meant opposing the spoils system in government appointments and federal "interference" in the southern states, as well as protective tariffs that limited free trade and currency inflation, which they considered a giveaway to debtors.

Their ranks included, along with Schurz and Trumbull, men like Charles Francis Adams, Lincoln's ambassador in England during the war, and his sons Charles Jr. and Henry; Jacob Cox, a former governor of Ohio and Grant's first secretary of the interior; nationally influential journalists such as Godkin, William Cullen Bryant of the *New York Evening Post,* Murat Halstead of the *Cincinnati Commercial,* and Horace White of the *Chicago Tribune,* and others with formerly impeccable Republican credentials. Although Charles Sumner shared their sense of urgency—"There is a *dementia* in the Republican party," he wrote to Schurz, perhaps his closest political friend—and probably loathed Grant more than any of them, he remained at heart a Radical and would show himself to be far more committed to the protection of Black Americans than the others. (Grant returned Sumner's sentiment: having once been told that Sumner didn't believe in the Bible, Grant replied, "No, I suppose not, he didn't write it.")

Schurz, the most dynamic of the movement's leaders, brought intellectual heft, a charismatic personality, and an oratorical force that made him one of the most sought-after public speakers in the country. He had embraced Radical policies during the war as a matter of necessity, including heavy taxes, the suspension of habeas corpus, and military rule over southern territory won in battle. But he felt that the war had produced a "spirit of jobbery and corruption" which now infected the body politic like a disease, all the more dangerously so at a time when federal power seemed to be overreaching in every direction. He tended to see strong government through a European lens as a clone of the monarchical power that he had fought in his youth and as an existential threat to individual liberty. Any assertion of power was thus at least suspect, even when it was exerted to safeguard civil rights. Schurz also feared the festering influence of big business in politics, warning in language that still seems familiar a century and a half later, "The growing political power of moneyed corporations steals upon us with a cat-like step and threatens to make our democratic institutions a mere tool in the hands of despotic monopolies."

A speech by Schurz was regarded as a major event by the men and women who crowded the Senate's visitors' gallery. Although English was his third language, after German and French, his earnest, crisply fashioned, and melodiously delivered orations harked back to the great men of the antebellum era, Clay and Webster, but shorn of their baroque ornamentation. By the early 1870s, he was one of the highest-paid lecturers in America, earning three and four times the rate of most prominent speakers, surpassed only by the essayist Ralph Waldo Emerson. When he rose to speak from the floor, senators stopped scribbling notes, journalists leaned forward cupping their ears, and the society ladies perched on the sofas at the back of the chamber fell silent.

Ambitious for personal political power, Schurz could not of course hope ever to become president since he was foreign-born. But he believed that he could reshape the government of his adopted country, and push it toward an ideal of moral perfection. Envisioning a new Republican Party purified of the "great incubus" of "office-mongers," he was determined to bring about the destruction of the patronage system that for half a century had served as the engine for filling government jobs and as the glue of party loyalty for aspiring job-seekers. To replace it, he and his allies advocated a far-reaching program of civil service reform: defined qualifications for government jobs; competitive examinations for candidates; the publication of all rules and regulations instituted by officeholders; the creation of a nonpartisan oversight board to ensure that appointees really had the required knowledge and skills. In speech after speech, Schurz denounced the "spectacle" of elected officials "taking to pieces the whole machinery of government" with every new administration, and then putting it all back together again from "new materials." What a "wild way" to carry on the affairs of the nation, he exclaimed—poisoning the air so thickly with favor-seeking flattery "that the sound waves of an independent public opinion can no longer penetrate it." If party loyalty no longer served the public good, then jettison it, he urged.

Schurz's growing challenge to the administration on national issues was inextricably tangled in Missouri's feral internecine politics. The state's postwar constitution had barred from power everyone who had collaborated even reluctantly with the Confederates. The imposition of draconian registration rules and test oaths for both voters and officeholders had alienated large numbers of moderate Republicans in a state that had been bitterly and bloodily divided during the war. Schurz cast his lot with those who sought amnesty for the ex-Confederates over the Radicals aligned with the Grant administration, hoping that amnestied voters would throw their weight behind his ideas of good government. In the summer of 1870, the party split when Schurz's faction declined to endorse the Radicals' candidate for governor. During the campaign, Schurz complained that "colored agitators" had been sent all over the state to persuade the freedmen to vote against his candidate and the enfranchising of former Confederates. Meanwhile, Missouri's Democrats sat back to enjoy the spectacle of the Republicans tearing their party apart. They ran no candidate for governor, and welcomed the election of Schurz's insurgents, knowing that the return of the ex-Confederates to political life would soon lead to Democratic control of the state, which it did when, in that year's elections, they won a majority of the state legislature and several congressional seats. Accused of splitting the Republican organization in Missouri, Schurz replied, "So we did." When the Republican cause was subverted by "wire-pullers and spoilsmen," it was better to break the organization in two than to permit the whole to be covered with common disgrace and to be reduced to impotence. In this way we saved the moral power of the Republican cause for the future." Although it seemed that way to the triumphalist Schurz, he had in fact killed the Republican Party in Missouri.

Further complicating the fraught relations between the Liberal Republicans and the White House was the festering problem of Santo Domingo's proposed annexation, which lurched toward unhappy climax in the spring of 1871. In June 1870, despite a last-minute personal appeal by Grant, the proposed treaty was defeated on a vote of 28 to 28, falling far short of the two-thirds it needed to pass. For Grant, it was a stinging defeat. He nevertheless remained unshakable in his certainty that the interests of the United States and Santo Domingo alike justified the annexation. He still had the support of a significant bloc of congressional Republicans and could point to the endorsement of an official fact-finding commission that had returned from the island in February.

The mission's leader, former Senator Ben Wade, a prominent wartime Radical and abolitionist, reported of the Dominicans, "They are so far without exception crazy to be annexed." Wade was seconded by the Black orator and journalist Frederick Douglass, another member of the commission, who further extolled the Dominicans as a "far superior" people to their neighbors the Haitians, and asserted that they would flourish under American rule. (His old ally, William Lloyd Garrison, harshly condemned Douglass's imperialist tendencies and supposed "ambition" and "selfishness," alleging that he was currying favor with Grant in hope of receiving a plum appointment.)

On Capitol Hill, the president's supporters fought a losing rearguard action over Santo Domingo as they mustered their forces for combat over new legislation against the Klan, a battle in which victory for the president was by no means assured. Sumner accused the president, literally, of "Ku Kluxing" the people of Santo Domingo and their Haitian neighbors, crying out with an appalled dramatic flourish, "With what face can we insist upon obedience to law and respect for the African race while we are openly engaged in lawlessness on the coasts of St. Domingo and outrage upon the African race represented by the Black Republic [Haiti]?" He was referring to a threat by Grant to order the U.S. Navy to repel any foreign warships that interfered with U.S. activities on the island. "It is difficult to see how we can condemn with proper, wholehearted reprobation our own domestic Ku Klux while the president puts himself at the head of a powerful and costly Ku Klux operating abroad in defiance of international law and the Constitution of the United States." Even for that era of oratorical brutality, it was a savage performance. After he had finished, Sen. Timothy Howe of Wisconsin likened Sumner to Brutus striking Caesar down with his dagger.

Schurz had rushed to Sumner's assistance with his customary oratorical impetuosity. (On New Year's Day, Schurz had effusively thanked Sumner for the gift of a bottle of wine, writing humorously, "Do you intend to bribe me? Do you think you can induce me to vote with you on Santo Domingo? If such are your designs, you have chosen your means wisely.") Schurz trashed Grant's policy as "the most anti-republican doctrine that was ever broached on the floor of the Senate," making even Andrew Johnson's crimes "pale to insignificance" by comparison. He went on to challenge the whole concept of territorial acquisition, introducing a theme that anti-imperialists would repeatedly raise in the decades to come as American power reached beyond the nation's shores. "Suppose we annex the Dominican Republic; will there be an end to our acquisitions?" he demanded. Where would it stop—Cuba, Puerto Rico, the rest of the West Indian islands, Mexico, Panama? The nation already had enough problems with the South without adding "undesirable" tropical lands filled with "shiftless" people who could never properly assimilate with America's European stock.

Resorting to specious reasoning that was usually the stock-in-trade of the era's "scientific racists," he asserted that man had "always degenerated" in the tropics, and that the people who dwelled there were inherently "turbulent" and "more inclined to appeal to force than to patient argument," and thus virtually incapable of republican self-government. These were of course the same arguments that whites were making all over the South against attempts to empower former slaves through the Reconstruction Acts, although Schurz would never admit that. Schurz's disgust was temperate compared to some of his colleagues, such as Sen. Justin S. Morrill of Vermont, who sneered that a people with such "languid brains and torpid muscles" as the Dominicans, without education, led "by unprincipled and desperate chiefs, destitute of all ambition, reeking in filth and laziness, regardless of marriage and its binding power, who never invented anything, whose virtue is indexed by a priesthood elevated by no scrap of learning and wretchedly debauched in morals," would never be more than a costly financial and moral burden to the United States.

Grant harbored another hope for Santo Domingo that he chose not to articulate publicly. He believed that its acquisition could help solve the American race problem. If his reasoning was impractical, it also revealed something about the personal pain that he felt at the suffering that Black Americans experienced from relentless racism. In a private memo, he reflected that Santo Domingo was large enough and sufficiently underpopulated to support the entire "colored" population of the United States, if it chose to emigrate. "The present difficulty in bringing all parts of the United States to a happy unity and love of country grows out of the prejudice to color," he wrote to himself. "The prejudice is a senseless one, but it exists." Santo Domingo could serve not only as a refuge, but the undoubted success of Black emigrants there would force white Americans to finally appreciate and reward them as productive citizens within the United States.

In the end, despite all Grant's effort, despite the commission's enthusiasm, and despite the support of the Dominican government, Grant could never muster the votes needed to pass the annexation treaty. He finally accepted defeat and retreated from the field with an eloquence of expression that his enemies rarely credited to him. In a message to Congress, he declared, "No man could hope to perform duties so delicate and responsible as pertain to the presidential office without sometimes incurring the hostility of those who deem their opinions and wishes treated with insufficient consideration; and he who undertakes to conduct the affairs of a great government as a faithful public servant, if sustained by the approval of his own conscience, may rely with confidence upon the intelligence and candor of a free people, whose best interests he has striven to subserve, and can bear with patience the censure of disappointed men."

Grant never forgave either Sumner or Schurz, whom he called as much of a rebel as Jefferson Davis. Frustrated beyond measure by Sumner's attacks, he approved his loyalists' ouster of Sumner as chairman of the Foreign Affairs Committee, a post he had held since 1861. Stripped of his committee, never popular among his colleagues, and close to nervous breakdown, the old lion from Massachusetts was written off as hopelessly unstable by his rivals. That diagnosis was premature. But he was a spent force. Schurz on the other hand had made himself a man to be reckoned with. He would soon emerge as the leading Republican critic of Reconstruction and a harbinger of the tectonic shift in both congressional and public opinion that would eventually threaten the president's ability to deal his intended death blow to the Ku Klux Klan.

BEN BUTLER'S APOTHEOSIS

In the name of your again defied and insulted
country, I demand that you give the president
power to strike the conspiracy instantly—dead!

—Rep. Samuel Shellabarger

Benjamin Butler, if judged simply by appearances, was an unlikely
political star. At fifty-three, he was squat, flabby, and wall-eyed,
with a disconcertingly froggy face and a balding pate fringed with
lank, stringy reddish hair. Nor could he claim the kind of wartime
laurels that had catapulted many of his contemporaries, including
Ulysses Grant, from obscurity to fame and power. Before the war,
Butler had been a partisan doughface Democrat who supported
the *Dred Scott* decision and cheerfully put Jefferson Davis's name in
nomination for president at the party's 1860 convention. A canny
Boston lawyer, he had no military experience beyond a ceremonial
post in the Massachusetts state militia. His political clout as a "war
Democrat" earned him a general's commission, although his battlefield performance ranged from merely inept to near catastrophically
incompetent.

Yet, at certain critical moments during the war he had shown
genuine courage, political (if not military) imagination, and unexpected toughness. In 1861, he led the first northern regiments into
virtually defenseless Washington after the firing on Fort Sumter.
Later that year, he invented a brilliant rationale for refusing to
return fugitive slaves to their masters by declaring them "contra-

band of war," a legal device that ensured that many thousands of freedom-seekers would find safety within the Union lines. He also served as the capable, if not entirely scrupulous, military governor of New Orleans after it was captured by federal troops in 1862.

By the war's end he had become a Radical Republican. In this he was hardly alone among ambitious former Democrats with flexible convictions. Elected to Congress in 1866—he declared a seaside tent his home in order to qualify for "residence" in the district in which he ran, to the chagrin of his outsmarted opponent—he soon became a leading advocate for an aggressive program of Reconstruction and the empowerment of former slaves. When Thaddeus Stevens's health worsened, Butler stepped in to lead the congressional team named to impeach Andrew Johnson. He had held a grudge against Grant for sidelining him during the war's last phase, and outrageously slandered him as "a drunkard after fast horses, women and whores," before his nomination for the presidency. (Grant loved fine horses, but had rigidly controlled his alcohol intake for years, and was, if anything, prim in his relations with women.) With his pliant instinct for the dynamics of power, however, Butler had since become one of the president's most reliable defenders on Capitol Hill. The initiative that he lacked on the battlefield he displayed in abundance in Congress. In many ways, he was the opposite of the earnest Carl Schurz, the prophet of political rectitude who was in the process of undermining the greatest moral project of the time, the elevation of Black Americans. Butler was naked in his pursuit of self-interest, but he also impetuously threw himself into the battle on behalf of civil rights as Grant's point man in the legislative phase of the war against the Klan.

The Third Enforcement Act, passed in April 1871, essentially subsumed the two earlier Enforcement measures and became familiarly known as the Ku Klux Klan Act. It was Butler's political apotheosis, the stirring climax of his long and controversial public career. Grant hoped that it would prove the decisive weapon in the struggle against the Klan. It was, in short, as close to a declaration of war as Congress could issue in peacetime. The text that Butler crafted sharply amplified the powers and punishments provided by its two earlier iterations. Where the others outlined a general plan of attack, the third placed the Ku Klux Klan squarely in its crosshairs. As originally conceived, it empowered the president to unilaterally employ whatever federal troops he required to protect the rights guaranteed by the Fourteenth Amendment. It stipulated that anyone found on a public road in any disguise, "armed or unarmed, with intent to do any injury" or "to terrify, frighten, or overawe" would be guilty of a high misdemeanor if the offense was committed in daylight, or of a felony if at night. The bill designated as federal crimes: crossing state lines with the intent to intimidate or terrorize; joining any secret organization that entailed the taking of an oath committing him to perpetrate or conceal an act of terror; counseling or abetting an act of terror; or attempting to rescue someone jailed for such a crime. Punishments were severe. For a "high misdemeanor," fines ranged from $1,000 to $5,000, plus between one and five years in prison; and for a felony from $5,000 to $10,000, and between five and twenty years in prison, or in the case of the worst crimes, execution. The bill also provided for the appointment of federal commissioners in every Klan-ridden county with the power to issue arrest warrants, compel witnesses to appear in court, and to call either directly on the nearest federal troops or on the president himself to enforce the act's provisions. Significantly, the bill also included a draconian and exceptionally controversial provision, permitting the president to suspend the writ of habeas corpus—requiring the government to prove that an arrest was lawful—where he believed that public safety required it.

Although southern lawlessness might once have been explained away as the anarchy that followed war, it was now clearly organized to drive from the South every friend of the administration, Butler said. "Without the power to protect the lives of its citizens a republican government is a failure." Too many in his party had come to naively believe the illusion that the war had settled all fundamental issues between the North and South. But, for those who cared to see the truth, it was obvious that traitors were already creeping back into the political system, helped by well-intentioned conciliation.

Significantly, Butler's bill also called for the empowerment of the Klan's victims to sue for damages from the inhabitants of the county or city where the offense had taken place, making the entire community financially liable for providing redress. "All the inhabitants within a radius of five miles around the place where the wrong is committed shall be responsible," he argued. "The great fact upon which all this stands," he said, is "that no riot can [take] place, that no riotous gathering of men in a community can gain head unless its continuance is winked at or connived at by the leading men of the community. The moment the men of property in the South, the men who have something at stake, understand that they are being injured by Kukluxism, that their taxes are being increased by Kukluxism, that moment they will come forward and put down Kukluxism." Never had such conditions been imposed on an American community. Butler saw it as a sledgehammer: in their own interest, whites would be forced to suppress their local Klans with or without federal intervention.

Despite Grant's clearly stated wishes, there initially seemed little likelihood that the bill would pass. It faced a particularly tough battle in the House of Representatives, where the Republicans had lost seats in the November elections and some Republicans were losing interest in Reconstruction. The mood on Capitol Hill was irritable and abrasive. Democrats wanted no part of any anti-Klan measure and more than a few Republicans, including House Speaker James G. Blaine, usually a reliable administration man, worried that free trade advocates would hijack the session to attempt to force through anti-tariff measures. Some Republican moderates were also uneasy at the bill's enhancement of executive power. Many members, who had been sitting since December, were also simply impatient to go home. Butler complained that his every attempt to get the bill to the floor had been met by motions to delay, motions to adjourn, and attempts to deny the bill even a hearing. Rep. James A. Garfield wrote to an Ohio friend, "Here we are, quarreling among ourselves, mad at each other, and mad at him. I am in great trouble about the whole [thing]." Eventually the Senate passed the bill, but moderates led by Blaine and Garfield broke ranks and joined the Democrats to defeat it in the House.

Even the gala celebration of the long-delayed completion of the paving of Pennsylvania Avenue failed to lighten the mood. While senators and congressmen battled and brooded, just down the hill from the Capitol Washingtonians declared an impromptu two-day holiday at the end of February as the last wooden blocks—a popular paving material at the time—were pounded into what had as long as anyone could remember been a trough, alternately of gritty dust or glutinous mud, depending on the season. Flags and bunting and Chinese lanterns appeared all along the avenue. Horses were raced; goats were raced; wheelbarrows were raced. A grand ball was thrown to raise donations to complete the stumpy Washington Monument. Washington was at last on the cusp, the optimists said, of becoming a modern city.

At the top of the hill, the Enforcement bill remained stuck in legislative limbo. Finally, Grant decided to intervene. The endless reports of whippings, shootings, and mutilations, the assassination of mail agents, the slaughter of federal marshals, the plaintive letters that flooded his mail every day, weighed heavily on his mind. The laconic chief executive now transformed himself once again into the implacable general who had won the war. On the morning of March 23, he marched into the Capitol with members of his cabinet, ensconced himself at a table in the small, ornately frescoed President's Room just off the Senate Chamber, and briskly penned a message to Congress. Rep. George Boutwell, who was in the room, later recalled that Grant remained ambivalent to the last moment, changing his mind several times about the wisdom of urging harsh legislation. Finally, he surrendered to his instinct to make as strong a statement as possible. Grant then wrote "without pause or correction, and as rapidly as his pen could fly over the paper." His words were blunt: "A condition of affairs now exists in some of the States of the Union rendering life and property insecure and the carrying of the mails and the collection of the revenues dangerous. The proof that such a condition of affairs exists in some localities is now before the Senate." However, the president's authority to deal with the emergency under existing law was insufficiently clear. "I urgently recommend such legislation" in order to "secure the life, liberty, and property, and the enforcement of law in all parts of the United States."

The next day, Grant directed Attorney General Akerman to craft a proclamation to justify his dispatch of troops to South Carolina, where Grant had decided that the war on the Klan must begin. It was now beyond the ability of the state to bring the terrorists to heel, he declared. Therefore, "I, Ulysses S. Grant, President of the United States, hereby command the persons comprising the unlawful combinations aforesaid to disperse and retire peaceably to their respective abodes within twenty days." If they failed to do so, they would face the might of the United States Army. Even moderates rejoiced that, at last, the Klan seemed about to get its comeuppance. The *New York Times* praised Grant's determination in the face of "Democratic clamor and Republican lukewarmness," and applauded his decisiveness as the fulfillment of his inaugural promise to stand up for the rights of the newly freed.

The debate that ensued was heated. In the House, newly seated Robert Elliott of South Carolina asserted that six hundred loyal men of both races had already perished at the hands of the Klan in his state—the actual number is uncertain—and demanded to know whether Congress would allow the helpless freedman to be "driven into exile with the pitiless lash or doom him to swift murder" simply because he exercised his constitutional rights. "Those men," he cried, "appeal to you today to do justice to them!" In support, Samuel Shellabarger, an Ohio Radical, admonished members to remember how before the war both Congress and then-president James Buchanan had permitted secessionist treason to thrive. The country could not abide such "imbecility and moral treason" a second time, Shellabarger exclaimed. "In the name of your again defied and insulted country, I demand that you give the president power to strike the conspiracy instantly — dead!" With equal passion, Butler then charged Democrats with knowingly fostering the Klan's war upon the United States. Lawlessness in the South may once have been disorganized "save by its hates," Butler declaimed, but it was now "organized in the service of a political party to crush its opponents and to drive from their borders every friend of the Republican administration." This was an overstatement, but it was no exaggeration to say that in many parts of the South the Klan was virtually congruent with the Democratic Party.

In the Senate, Charles Sumner delivered one of the best speeches of his career. Although he was often at odds with the president, and viciously so over Santo Domingo, he lent his clarion voice to the administration's cause. "What makes us a nation?" he rhetorically asked. "Not armies, not fleets, not fortifications, not commerce reaching every shore abroad, not industry filling every vein at home, not population thronging the highways. The national life of this republic is found in the principle of Unity and in the Equal Rights of all our people." Human rights "being common to all, they must be under the safeguard of all. Equality implies universality, and what is universal must be national." Perhaps, in a theoretical sense, he ventured, the Ku Klux Klan bill proposed a sort of "tyranny," as its enemies disingenuously alleged. But the national government would not enter a state except to safeguard rights that were national in character, "and then only as the sunshine, with beneficent power and, like the sunshine, for the good of all. As well assail the sun because it is central—because it is imperial. Here is a just centralism; here is a just imperialism" that sought only to protect every citizen equally and to make equal rights the supreme law of the land. "Give me the centralism of Liberty. Give me the imperialism of Equal Rights," he cried.

Perhaps the most persuasive case for the bill's passage was made by Mississippi senator Adelbert Ames. What he lacked in oratorical panache he made up for with the gravity of personal experience. Handsome and compact, Ames sported a great bush of a mustache but was otherwise clean-shaven in an era of lavishly bearded men, and at thirty-five was one of the youngest members of the Senate. He was the only member of either house who had actually governed a reconstructed state, as Mississippi's military administrator from 1868 to 1870, when he handed over power to a civilian governor and legislature. Like many professional soldiers, Ames was a man of conservative instincts, but he had been radicalized by the racial injustices he had witnessed. Born the son of a sea captain in Maine in 1835, he graduated from West Point in 1861, just in time to participate in the first battle of Bull Run, where he was severely wounded but refused to leave the field. He was the "beau ideal" of an officer, one of his aides remarked years later, gallant and efficient, and "apparently unmoved by singing rifle-ball, shrieking shot, or bursting shell." Before the war was over he won the Congressional Medal of Honor for bravery on the battlefield.

In the 1869 elections, Mississippi's conservatives had opportunistically nominated for governor President Grant's own brother-in-law Lewis Dent to run as the candidate of the so-called National Union Republican Party. Grant, embarrassed, told Dent squarely, "In public matters, personal feelings will not influence me," and made clear his support for the regular Republican candidate, James Alcorn, a former Democrat and planter who accepted the principle of Black civil rights. In the event, newly enfranchised Black voters easily elected Alcorn and large Republican majorities in the state legislature, including five Blacks in the Senate and thirty-one in the House. The new legislature thereupon elected Ames to the U.S. Senate along with Hiram Revels. "That I should have taken a political office seems almost inexplicable, but then it seemed to me that I had a mission," Ames later wrote. "Because of my course as military governor, the colored men of the state had confidence in me, and I was convinced that I could help to guide them successfully, and the more certainly accomplish what was every patriot's wish— the enfranchisement of the colored men and the pacification of the country." That winter Ames also achieved a spectacular romantic triumph that added fuel to his rapid political ascent: he wooed and won one of the most desirable young women in Washington, the beautiful, superbly educated, and famously charming Blanche Butler, the daughter of one of Ames's former wartime commanders— Rep. Benjamin Butler.

If demographics were sufficient to determine political outcomes, Mississippi should have been one of Reconstruction's success stories. The Black population exceeded the white by some seventy thousand, seemingly ensuring that the freedmen would be the dominant power in the state. Under Ames, Republican government had worked hard to maintain law and order, raised the state's credit from 60 to 95 cents on the dollar, and built thousands of local schools, including many for Black students. Security had seriously deteriorated since the state's return to civilian government, however. Particularly in northern Mississippi, reactionaries were waging an aggressive campaign to regain control of municipal governments, the burning of freedmen's schools was becoming epidemic, and terrorism was on the rise.

Now, in this his maiden speech in the Senate, Ames recalled that only a year earlier Hiram Revels had advocated for the restoration of political rights to ex-Confederates, asking "on behalf of his race" for Congress to "forgive and forget" their treasonous offenses. (Revels's one-year term had ended on March 3, so he took no part in this debate.) Regrettably, that generosity and forbearance had fallen on barren ground, Ames said. The plight of Mississippi's Blacks was now worse than ever. Ku-Kluxers who had been kept in check were reappearing. In some areas it was too dangerous even to speak out as a Republican, and some who did so risked "being hunted like wild beasts," he charged, while "whole counties have become paralyzed."

Ames then told the senators a horror story. He described a massacre that had taken place in the eastern Mississippi city of Meridian the first week in March. For months, bands of Klansmen from Alabama had repeatedly invaded Meridian hunting Black fugitives who had sought safety there and dragged them back across the state line for punishment. Local Black leaders—notable among them a fiery former slave named William Dennis and a teacher named Warren Tyler—urged Republicans to organize in self-defense. After a melee between white Alabamans and Black Republicans on March 6, bench warrants were issued for the arrest of both men and for state representative Aaron Moore, a Black Methodist minister, for allegedly fomenting disorder. Two days later, the three men faced their accusers in court. In the midst of testimony, a pistol shot rang out "like a firebrand in a powder magazine." Everyone in the courtroom leaped to their feet. More shots were fired. In the pandemonium, someone shot the judge, a Republican, who died on the spot. Warren Tyler leaped from a second-story window and was shot in the hip as he swung off, then ran through the streets as best he could pursued by a pack of white men. He finally darted into a shop where he was mowed down, riddled by bullets: "even the boys coming in for their shot." William Dennis, bleeding from several wounds, was thrown out a window to the street into a jeering crowd, where, still alive, someone cut his throat from ear to ear. Then they cut off his ears and placed one over each eye. Whites armed with double-barreled shotguns scoured the streets for more Blacks to attack. They were joined by reinforcements who arrived by train yelling, "Hurrah for Alabama!" Black men were chased into swamps, where they were shot or lynched. Black women were forced to tell where their menfolk were hiding, under threat of death. Others were raped. Aaron Moore, the state representative, covered with blood, was left for dead in the courtroom but managed to slip out of town and fled on foot to the state capital at Jackson, 125 miles away. The city's white Republican mayor was forced onto a northbound train and warned

Ulysses S. Grant. Celebrated for his generalship, underrated as a politician, he sympathized with the aspirations of the former slaves and proved to be a forceful and decisive leader in the federal campaign against the Klan.

Carl Schurz. Crusading journalist and U.S. senator, he was among the first to expose the savagery of white retaliation against the freed people but later turned against Reconstruction.

Andrew Johnson. A staunch Unionist during the war, he fiercely opposed Radical Reconstruction.

Thaddeus Stevens. The leading Radical voice in Congress for Black civil rights, he was the driving force behind the Fourteenth Amendment.

"Andrew Johnson's Reconstruction." Johnson as Iago, offering false assurance to a wounded Black veteran as white violence ravages Black communities.

With most former Confederates disenfranchised, large numbers of African Americans were elected to state office across the South, including South Carolina, where Blacks and white Radicals dominated the legislature.

Granted civil rights for the first time by Radical state constitutions, Black southerners flocked to voter registration offices and debated politics with an enthusiasm that astonished white observers.

"I SHALL DISCHARGE EVERY NIGGER WHO VOTES TO ADOPT THIS RADICAL YANKEE CONSTITUTION."

Where they could, white conservatives often tried to threaten newly enfranchised Black voters and manipulate the results of elections.

"The Shackle Broken—By the Genius of Freedom." Broadsides such as this reminded Americans that Blacks had earned their rights through gallant service in the Union armies.

Robert Brown Elliott of South Carolina. Brilliant, eloquent, and charismatic, he epitomized the generation of ambitious young Black politicians who rapidly rose to prominence during the early years of Radical Reconstruction.

Hiram Rhodes Revels of Mississippi. He was the first Black to sit in the United States Senate.

Nathan Bedford Forrest. A prewar slave trader, he lent his prestige as a flamboyant Confederate cavalry commander to the early Klan and helped to shape its tactics as its first Grand Wizard.

Albion W. Tourgée. An idealistic Union veteran from Ohio, after the war he settled in North Carolina, where he defied the Klan as a crusading judge unflinchingly committed to the protection of civil rights.

"White Man's Government." Republicans portrayed the Democratic campaign of 1868 as an unholy alliance between resurgent Confederates—in the guise of Nathan Bedford Forrest—urban thuggery, and New York capitalists, crushing patriotic Black citizens underfoot.

Klansmen wore a wide variety of outlandish disguises, including bizarre false faces and robes of almost any color. These were captured in Mississippi by federal officers.

"Worse than Slavery." As the Klan spread, organized white terrorism, lynchings, and the destruction of freed people's schools increasingly shaped Americans' image of the South.

"Visit of the Ku Klux." Most Klan terrorism consisted of nighttime attacks on the isolated homes of unarmed Blacks. Although men were the usual targets, women and children were often victims.

"Contemplated Murder of John Campbell."

The Klan issued explicit threats against public officials, such as this one, which appeared in a Tuscaloosa, Alabama, newspaper. Its editor was also the local leader of the Klan; the targets were two prominent educators at the University of Alabama.

"He wants a change too." Ravaged by years of largely unchecked white violence, Black militias were organized for self-defense in many southern states. They were usually outgunned and their members were prime targets for assassination by the Klan.

The Caswell County courthouse, in Yanceyville, North Carolina. In 1870, Republican state senator John Stephens was murdered by Klansmen in one of its rooms while a Democratic Party political meeting took place on the floor above.

Benjamin Butler. A prewar Democrat, he became an outspoken Radical Republican and the driving force in Congress for the Enforcement Acts that enabled President Grant to wage war against the Klan.

Amos T. Akerman. A reluctant Confederate, and postwar Georgia Republican, as Grant's attorney general he led the war against the Klan. His loathing for the Klan and his passion for civil rights stood out in a country that was losing interest in the South's problems.

Horace Greeley. Nationally famous as the outspoken editor of the *New York Tribune,* he challenged Grant for the presidency in 1872, with the support of anti-Reconstruction Democrats and disaffected Republicans. Although defeated by Grant, the campaign marked a watershed in declining public support for Reconstruction.

Maj. Lewis Merrill. Experienced in guerrilla warfare and implacable in his pursuit of the Klan, he led the army's successful campaign to defeat white terrorism in upcountry South Carolina.

"It Is Only a Truce to Regain Power." This 1872 pro-Grant campaign cartoon represents Greeley handing a reluctant Black citizen over to a dagger-wielding white man who wears pieces of a Confederate uniform and a Klansman's mask.

"Murder of Louisiana." Southern propaganda combined an attack on Grant's alleged "tyranny" with a potently sexual allusion to the supposed rape of former Confederate states by Blacks and white Radicals.

Chief Justice Morrison R. Waite embodied the Supreme Court's turn away from federal enforcement of civil rights, writing in 1876 that citizens must now look only to the states for their protection, a hopeless prospect for Black Americans as white supremacists regained political power in the South.

never to return. Estimates of the dead ranged from half a dozen to thirty. Democrats later justified what happened, asserting that "the people had borne the insolence of the 'niggers' long enough," and that "violent measures" were simply the "remedy" to teach them to "keep their place."

Apart from its sheer barbarism, the massacre was an ill omen for the future of Reconstruction far beyond Meridian, underscoring the fragility of isolated Republican governments and their extreme vulnerability to violence. It was also significant that although the Alabamans and their allies in Meridian were universally identified as "Ku Klux" by Republicans, who surely knew what they were talking about, none of the news reports indicated that the terrorists wore disguises or issued the kind of cryptic warnings that the Klan so often employed. While it is possible that some of the white gunmen were not sworn members of the Klan, it seems clear that the vast majority were. They were well armed, prepared to shed blood, and operating according to a prearranged plan, having systematically posted gunmen throughout the city well before the hearing began. As the courthouse emptied out, witnesses reported, the gunmen "fell into line with soldier-like rapidity and precision." The coup, for that's what it was essentially, thus foreshadowed an evolving pattern of terror in places where Klansmen felt sufficiently safe from prosecution or reprisal to put aside their cumbersome disguises and show their faces, and topple legal governments in the bright light of day.

Ames went on to argue that the moral and political challenges now posed by the situation in the South were as urgent now as slavery and rebellion had once been. Senators, he said, had all heard about crimes perpetrated against the freed people, but only a fraction of their suffering had yet been told. Too many whites still refused to face the new reality, that former slaves were now citizens with rights. Too many were still "the blind instruments" of reactionary leaders who had sent them to war and still continued to manipulate them. Unless Congress stood firm against those leaders, he warned, its chambers would soon be refilled by exactly the same men who had led the South into rebellion a decade earlier. Imagine, he said, what must then happen to the freed people if the army's garrisons were removed and southern states restored to the hands of the men who only a few years ago had bought and sold Negroes as "dumb brutes" and still regarded their lives as nothing. Meridian was but an illustration of what lay in store. "Unless the government interferes, hundreds and hundreds of men are yet to be made martyrs. And when this 'white man's party' shall dominate, should it ever, you will see class legislation so harsh and so cruel as to force the colored people into a serfdom worse than slavery."

Congressional Democrats universally opposed Butler's bill. They first claimed that no terror existed in the South, then denied the existence of the Klan, then admitted that it might exist after all but played down the extent of its crimes by blaming them on provocation by Blacks and Republicans, or on the injustice of federal laws that discriminated against former Confederates. Without exception, whatever else they differed on, they asserted that Reconstruction was unconstitutional and that resistance to it was an understandable, "manly" reaction. Alfred Waddell, a Negrophobe from Wilmington, North Carolina, loftily protested that "heroic and gallant" former Confederate soldiers would never stoop to the sorts of crimes they were charged with, and asserted preposterously that "the humblest officer in the state, even though he be a negro constable, so black that charcoal could make a white mark, can go [anywhere] in safety, alone." The patrician Sen. Eli M. Saulsbury of Delaware protested that if there was violence in the South it was no different from anywhere else and would "exist in every part of this habitable globe until the race is elevated far above its present level by the benign influences of Christianity."

Rep. Samuel S. Cox of New York, a Tammany Hall stalwart, raged that the entire debate was "pernicious, pestiferous, in almost every conceivable degree." At worst, he scoffed, the Klan—who he likened to the heroic rebels of the French Revolution and British-occupied Ireland—had done nothing more than "scare the superstitious negroes to stop them roaming about and pilfering." The bill, he charged, was far worse than anything they might have done and would, if passed, soon lead to the wholesale "massacre and murder" of southern whites by stripping white men of their votes and putting their homes, mothers, wives, and children at the mercy of "the inferior race." He rejected the Fourteenth Amendment's obvious intent to extend federal jurisdiction over crimes committed in the states, declaring in the florid style for which he was well known, "If you can thrust in the federal bayonet as an arm of the domestic police without an appeal from the state, you may also make a Draconian code of blood, establish drum-head courts, and erect gibbets in every county."

Rep. Boyd Winchester of Kentucky expressed disgust at Blacks' "unnatural elevation" in the social scale, declaring, "God has divided [the races] by an impassable gulf." He piously asserted that while other peoples might mingle—the Saxon and Celt, the Tartar and the Hun—"it is an inexorable law of nature that the race of Ham"—that is, Africans—"must serve or separate." He blamed Massachusetts in particular for the sinister egalitarianism which he said "has crawled into our schools and colleges, where it points out to youthful ingenuousness the slimy pathway of hypocrisy, cunning, and cant," arraying class against class, and color against color. He further attacked "incendiary adventurers from New England" and "black and mongrel buccaneers" who had seized control of southern states. (Although he didn't mention any name, he was clearly referring to "carpetbaggers" such as Ames and Elliott.) "But let the pirates hearken, for they shall not continue to rule in that fair section, designed by providence to be the dominion of the highest type of the white race. Already we hear the footsteps of approaching revolution."

The oddest Democratic speech of all was delivered by Rep. Robert Barnhill Roosevelt of New York, a wealthy Democrat, the author of several books on fishing, and uncle of the young Theodore Roosevelt, who launched into a startling defense of the slave trade, asking, "Before sentimentality usurped the place of common sense, who was it but the Democracy that sent their ships across three thousand miles of ocean to the realms of barbarous Africa, to import thence a gentleman who, in his native land, had not attained to any great degree of cultivation or happiness, and whose future was worse than precarious?" By way of thanks, Roosevelt bizarrely asserted, the "colored man" had done nothing at all to help the Union during the war. "Did he light a torch or fire a loyal gun?" In fact, he had done all in his power to assist the rebellion, feeding the armies of the South, building their fortifications, and "kept its stomach stout." It was only when the northern armies passed near them "that they scuttled off to liberty and misery as fast as their colored limbs could carry them." (Roosevelt could hardly have been unaware that 170,000 Black men had served in the Union military, many with bravery and distinction.) Butler's bill, he loftily concluded, was the worst Reconstruction measure he had ever seen, but perhaps Democrats should just hold their nose and swallow it, since it would alienate so many Americans and "surely result in wiping out the Republican Party, and anything that will do that must be a great success for the country."

More troubling to Grant and his allies than the Democrats' vicious but predictable resistance was that of dissident Republicans led by Schurz and Trumbull, who pleaded as passionately as any southern conservative for conciliation, regardless of the cost to freed people's rights. Writing privately to the like-minded editor of *The Nation,* E. L. Godkin, Schurz alarmingly described the bill as "insane," saying, "I hope we shall be able to defeat it, if not the whole, at least the worst features of it." (Godkin cavalierly editorialized that southerners ought to be left to their bloody anarchy: "If they are so demoralized that they go on robbing and murdering and 'Ku Kluxing' each other, we cannot interfere effectively, and had better not interfere at all.") Trumbull, on the Senate floor, disparaged the reports of Klan atrocities and predicted that Reconstruction was doomed, declaring, "I am not willing to undertake to enter the states for the purpose of punishing individual offenses against their authority committed by one citizen against another," and warning against federal overreach. "The liberties of the people [and] the rights of the individual," he said, "are safest among the people themselves, and not in a central government extending over a vast region of country."

Schurz, by now wholly estranged from the party's regulars, built on Trumbull's localist reasoning in an extended oration that ventured well beyond the bill itself to place his opposition to it in the context of the larger Liberal Republican program. He presented himself as a hardheaded realist, a problem-solver, in contrast to the fuzzy-minded Radicals and self-interested cynics of the regular Republican Party. He spoke as much as a teacher and a psychologist as he did a politician. He was convinced that he saw political reality and his rivals did not: repeatedly, he asserted, "we have to deal with the facts as they are." It was time to bring the "revolutionary

phase" of Reconstruction to a close, he declared, and to let lingering controversies connected with the war gradually "drift into the
background." That said, the "complete moral pacification" of the
South could not be achieved until the exclusion of large numbers
of people—that is, *white* people—from the ballot box had stopped.

(The *Washington Chronicle* noted with irony that when Schurz was
"ultra Radical," in 1865, Grant was urging kindness and forbearance toward the defeated South. Now it was Grant who was sternly
enforcing the law against the same men he was formerly inclined
to indulge, while Schurz, then "unforgiving, domineering, dicta-
torial in regard to the same class of men," had now become one of
their idols, apologizing for their crimes and assailing the laws which
should justly fall upon many of them.)

In Schurz's eyes, the very nature of the United States as a republic
hung in the balance. The war had centralized power in the national
government, as everyone knew. Now, he said, both the public and
its elected representatives had to be weaned away from their reflex-
ive habit of always looking to the government for redress whenever
anything went wrong. Deprive them of the "great lesson of failure
to be corrected by themselves," and they would all too soon lose
their ability to recognize political abuses or the remedies for them.
That in turn could lead only to military tyranny. The struggle to
reestablish the republic's true character had to begin in the South.
To legislate against the Klan now amounted to interference with
states' constitutional rights and thus fundamentally undermined
basic American liberties.

A year earlier, he had voted grudgingly for the First Enforcement
Act. Not this time. He would like to have been able to support the
current bill but he could not, Schurz said. "I consider the rights and
liberties of the whole American people of still higher importance
than the interests of those in the South whose dangers and sufferings appeal so strongly to our sympathy." He readily admitted that
the Klan systematically practiced murder, torture, and other acts
of terror. But look at such "distempers" in perspective, he urged.
Reconstruction had also delivered "bad government" to much of
the South. Bestowing the ballot on the freedmen had been a disap-
pointment: "An ignorant class of people became voters." The laws
that Congress had already passed in hope of ending the violence had

accomplished nothing, he asserted. "There are many social disorders which it is very difficult to cure by laws," all the more so when there was "a morbid public sentiment disabling the machinery of justice." Under such circumstances, the more severe the law, the less likely it was to be enforced.

The Republican Party in the South could never restore order "as long as ignorance there is led by unscrupulousness," he asserted. By "ignorance" he of course meant the freedmen, and by "unscrupulousness" their white Republican allies: accusations precisely congruent with the accusations of southern conservatives, and the Ku Klux Klan. There were many southern Democrats who wanted peace, he said, but they were overawed by the party's "lawless wing," to which they were unhappily bound as common victims of the federal discrimination against ex-Confederates. Honest southern Republicans also wanted better government. Decent citizens on both sides were thus ready to be drawn across party lines to form a new, enlightened majority committed to order and good government with sufficient "moral power" to suppress disorder. In practical terms, Schurz was calling for the creation of a new political party for which the Liberal Republican movement would serve as the armature.

First, the disabilities suffered by former Confederates must be eliminated, he said. This would generate a "healthy public sentiment" and reduce the cause of animosity between the races. Next, the Republicans must abandon the "schemers and tricksters" who were constantly begging for federal aid to preserve themselves in power in the South. Whatever "evils" still beset the South would then soon be remedied by the "soothing influence of time." In the meantime, courage was needed to ignore mere sentiment that blurred northern judgment. "When I hear of the dangers and sufferings of innocent and deserving people in the South the impulses of my heart are as warm and strong as yours to rush to the rescue," he said. "But our responsibilities as legislators, responsibilities involving the great future of this republic, will not always permit us to follow the voice of our emotions." In essence, he was saying that a higher duty, even a higher morality, commanded that the government cut loose southern Republicans, black and white, and let them either sink or swim on their own.

Fundamentally, Schurz's position was based on a pious assumption that southern moderates—a rather elusive chimera—were both willing and able to rein in their violent neighbors, if only they were shown sufficient tolerance. There was, he claimed, "a most beneficent and wonderful transformation" taking place in the South, a veritable revolution of public opinion led by enlightened men who were prepared to accept the new political reality. How much he may have been deluding himself is unclear. But he had to know that conciliation of the whites would do nothing to help the victims of terror. If he understood that he was betraying his oft-professed commitment to human equality, he could not admit it. What some might well see as a betrayal of the humanistic ideals that he had proclaimed for decades he regarded as a courageous willingness to abandon failed policies.

As Schurz's biographer Hans Trefousse observed, the real problem of stabilizing the former Confederate states was not a matter of establishing morally purified government of the sort that Schurz admired, but rather one of creating government that would include and benefit both the freed people and, eventually, the defeated whites. That required the indefinite disenfranchisement of men who still regarded Black Americans as unworthy of rights of any kind. It was hardly surprising that many newly enfranchised freedmen could not pass the kind of civil service tests that Schurz wanted to institutionalize; nor, probably, could most whites. But Schurz ignored the remarkable enthusiasm of freed people to gain education, learn the rules of citizenship, and exercise their rights. In addition, the corruption that disgusted him was hardly unique to the South. Nor were Blacks responsible for it, although they made tempting targets for unapologetic reactionaries, elitist reformers, and cynical journalists.

Southern conservatives loved what they heard from Schurz. Letters poured in praising his embrace of conciliation. The popular author Mary Howard Schoolcraft advised him that Ku-Klux violence was simply an understandable response to "odious taxes" and a government that was forcing "virtue and intelligence" to bow down beneath a "degraded race famed for ignorance and bestial vices." An Alabama lawyer praised Schurz for rising above partisanship in his effort to "drive back the vandals who seem bent on the destruction of the government." A Tennessean lauded him for challenging the "vindictiveness" of the North when all the South asked for were "kind words and generous feelings." Another correspondent helpfully suggested that Schurz could sharpen his arguments by studying the Confederate Constitution, with its staunch defense of states' rights.

Ben Butler would have none of it and launched an oratorical fusillade in response. In accordance with congressional manners, he declined to mention Schurz's name, but his target was unmistakable. If the Republican Party lacked the courage to stand up to protect its friends in the South then its usefulness as a party had ceased, he roared. And if there were any in the party who opposed decisive action against the Klan, they ought to get out. The bill's opponents, he charged, seemed to believe that the Constitution mainly existed to prevent the government from doing what it ought to do, "and to permit and allow everybody else untrammeled and untouched to do that which he ought not to do."

By mid-April, members of both houses were exhausted, having, as one congressman put it, traveled for long days "over a burnt district of debate." Butler derided members who mistook their "dyspepsia for conscience" and "their doubts and qualms for constitutional law." Thanks to his persistence and Grant's vigorous personal appeals, the administration's men were ultimately able to glean enough votes to pass the bill, now named "An Act to Enforce the Provisions of the Fourteenth Amendment." In its final form, it for the first time made federal courts responsible for protecting individual citizens in the exercise of their constitutional rights; punished conspiracies to deprive citizens of those rights; provided for the punishment of those who knew of imminent outrages but did not report them; empowered the president to use the army to suppress groups seeking to deny citizens equal protection of the law; and further allowed him to suspend habeas corpus as a tool in suppressing insurrection. (Butler's draconian proposal to make communities collectively and financially responsible for the suppression of the Klan in their area was dropped as too extreme.) Said the once skeptical James A. Garfield, "I believe that we have at last secured a bill, trenchant in its provisions, that reaches down into the very heart of the Ku Klux organization," and enables the federal courts "to strike these midnight assassins wherever they show themselves." The House voted to approve it by 93 to 74, along strict party lines, and the Senate by 36 to 13. Neither Schurz nor Trumbull showed up to vote.

On April 20, Grant once again entered the President's Room at the Capitol accompanied by a bevy of his aides. At 1 p.m., the bill was presented to him beneath a luminous ceiling decorated by groups representing Liberty, Legislation, and Executive Authority, and he signed it. He wasted little time acting on it. On May 3, he warned that he was prepared to use all the power at his command to see the new law enforced, declaring, "I will not hesitate to exhaust the powers thus vested in the Executive whenever and wherever it shall become necessary to do so for the purpose of securing to all citizens of the United States the peaceful enjoyment of the rights guaranteed to them by the Constitution and laws." He had already settled on South Carolina as the first target of the federal campaign.

12

AN OFFICER OF IMMENSE ENERGY AND ZEAL

It is utterly useless to attempt to do anything in
which the local civil authorities have a hand.

—Maj. Lewis Merrill

The few Reconstruction Era photographs of Maj. Lewis Merrill that
exist show a compact, slightly stocky man in his mid-thirties—he
was born in 1834—with a clear, round, deceptively inexpressive face
punctuated by a wispy Vandyke chin-beard, a popular military style
of the day. Merrill was a rare abolitionist in the antebellum officer
corps. Born into a locally prominent family in the mountains of
central Pennsylvania, he was drawn to both the law and soldiering,
and ultimately chose both, first studying for the bar and then going
to West Point, from which he graduated in 1855. As a lieutenant of
dragoons he served against the Kiowas and Comanches, and in Kansas Territory alongside J.E.B. Stuart, the future Confederate cavalry
commander, quelling the violence between pro- and anti-slavery
settlers. When war broke out in 1861, he recruited eight hundred
Unionist volunteers to form the Second Missouri Cavalry, often
called "Merrill's Horse," which he led through most of the war
against pro-Confederate irregulars in that divided state, where he
earned a sterling reputation as an exceptionally capable and aggressive officer. (A ballad dedicated to his regiment was titled "The
Guerrillas Conquered": "Wherever the 'Blue Caps' have been / All
glory and honor to Merrill shall be / He's the Champion and pride

of his men . . .") After the war, he served under Gen. George Armstrong Custer as a major in the newly formed Seventh Cavalry, once again fighting Indians on the frontier, until in March 1871 he was ordered to lead three companies from Fort Hays, Kansas, into the cauldron of Yorkville, South Carolina, where they would serve as the spearpoint for the coming assault against the Klan.

Merrill was an inspired choice for the task. His superior, Gen. Alfred H. Terry, wrote of him, "I know of few if any officers of the Army who are so well qualified for duty of the peculiar nature of that in which Major Merrill has been engaged as he. To a natural aptitude for and a considerable knowledge of the law he adds great general intelligence and sagacity." To these invaluable strengths, Terry wrote, he also brought immense energy and zeal that was limited only by his exceptional discretion. "All these qualities have been required & have been called into extreme activity by the circumstances in which he has been placed."

Merrill's troopers arrived in Yorkville at the end of March. Wrote a visiting reporter of the upstate village, "There was nothing about the appearance of this village to indicate that it was the center of what was probably the most powerful organization for the perpetuation of atrocious crimes that ever existed in any civilized country." Two- and three-story brick businesses flanked its main artery, tree-lined Congress Street, which was dominated by the imposing pillared portico of the county courthouse. In the surrounding blocks, the homes of the affluent stood in the midst of shrubbery clipped in stiff geometrical forms. With a flourishing economy based on cotton-growing, Yorkville's inhabitants saw themselves as enterprising and modern, taking pride in their churches and schools, and in the up-to-date gas lamps that lit Congress Street. Despite the carnage in the countryside, normal life went on. Families attended quilting bees and picnics, worried about catching "chollary" or "bilious fever," listened to their ministers preaching on sin and repentance, complained about drunken blacksmiths, broken wagon wheels, and uncooperative "servants." The local newspaper, the *Yorkville Enquirer,* alongside its daily, slanted accounts of the Klan's activities, published lively features on innovations in farming, the tribulations of Rep. C. C. Bowen who was on trial for bigamy, and the virtues of "civility." Ads for local stores announced the arrival of guano from the Pacific Ocean, Singer's "new family sewing machines," "nice merinos" and "black bombazines" at Dobson's—"Come with your pocket-books lined with Greenbacks, and you can buy more than you can carry away"—and solicited students for Yorkville Female College at $150 for the year with full room, board, and fuel, an extra $20 for classes in either French or German alone, and Latin a bargain at $16. Few saw a contradiction in the fact that their aspirationally cultivated community and the surrounding county of twenty thousand, equally divided between white and Black, was saturated with one of the most savage Ku Klux Klan cultures in the South. Caustically wrote the *New York Tribune*'s reporter, "a thin veneering" of manners, education, and Christianity covered "a depth of barbarism scarcely conceivable."

En route to Yorkville, Merrill had stopped in Louisville to be briefed by General Terry, the army's department commander for the South. "I fully believed that the stories in circulation were enormous exaggerations, and that the newspaper stories were incredible," Merrill later wrote. When he asked how much truth there was in them, Terry grimly cautioned, "When you get to South Carolina you will find that the half has not been told you." Despite this, Merrill was unprepared for what he found. He at first took the town's prominent citizens at their word when they assured him that although there had been a spate of barn-burnings, presumably by "unruly Negroes," the county was now entirely at peace. Capt. John Christopher of the 18th Infantry, who preceded Merrill, seconded the white leaders, sunnily averring that both races were determined to check anarchy and support the enforcement of law and order. "But very soon I had occasion to change my mind," Merrill reported.

As he probed beneath the bromides of Yorkville's white conservatives, he was appalled at the panorama of criminality that unfolded. Traumatized freed people turned up at his camp, many of them starving and suffering from exposure after weeks hiding in the woods. He initially supposed that their fears were exaggerated, but as the stories of murders, floggings, and assaults tumbled from their lips he began to appreciate the constant sense of danger with which they lived. The reports of family, friends, and neighbors tortured and killed by the Klan overwhelmed him: the killing of Alex Leech and Anderson Brown, whose body had been found in

the woods, "shot in two places once in the head & once in the bow-
els"; the two "colored" women savagely whipped by a party of nine
Klansmen; the beating of a woman and her child, who was said to
have divulged information about the Klan "and was impudent to
a white man who questioned her in regard to it." He determined
that as many as 80 percent of the Black men in the most disturbed
districts were afraid to sleep in their homes, and that out of some six
hundred white men in the county who had voted Republican with
the Black majority all but thirty or forty had openly renounced
their party under threats of violence. The situation in neighboring
Spartanburg was, if anything, even worse, but the military leadership there was weak and inadequate. "The illness and death of Capt.
Myers have left the sole responsibility of the military upon First
Lieutenant McDougall, who is too young and of too little experience to carry it." The pressing need of a judicious officer "of mature
judgment" at that station was desperately evident, Merrill reported.

The most notorious case Merrill encountered was the slaughter
just before his arrival of the captain of the local state militia, a former slave named Jim Williams. A large party of Klansmen wearing
false faces, hoods, and horns had swept through the county confiscating guns that the state had issued to Black militiamen. They
broke into Williams's home, pushed his wife aside, pulled up the
floorboards beneath which he was hiding, threw a rope around his
neck, and forced him onto the limb of a tree. Williams clung to the
branch until a Klansman climbed up and hacked his fingers with a
knife and forced him to drop. False rumors put about by the Klan,
mostly after the fact, claimed that Williams had threatened to burn
down Yorkville and "Ku-Klux the white ladies and children." In an
interview given many years later, a member of the gang that murdered Williams scoffed at such supposed threats, saying, "I cannot
say that we took them with especial seriousness." Whites had simply become "impatient" over the militia's drilling and parading, he
said. "We had stood as much as we could." Williams "died cursing,
pleading, and praying all in one breath. After the hanging we got
together again and proceeded over toward Brattonsville, where we
found an abundant lunch waiting."

Using skills of persuasion that he had learned during the internecine guerrilla war in Missouri, Merrill built a highly effective net-

work of secret informants. It included several disgruntled members of the Klan. But his most valuable sources were local freed people, many of whom worked as tenants on farms owned by Klansmen. "Any negro anywhere throughout the county would bring me information if he had reason to believe it would be valuable to me," he reported. Within two months of his arrival in Yorkville he was able to report that he felt thoroughly informed of the Klan's internal workings. One of his most productive Black informants was a man, his name unknown, who was sufficiently trusted by the Klan to have actually participated in its raids. He explained to Merrill that cooperating with them was the only way he would be allowed to live safely in his own home and tend his crops. Unlikely though it may seem, Blacks in South Carolina and elsewhere were sometimes compelled or frightened into serving the Klan as scouts and decoys, a role abetted by whites' deep-seated faith in the power of their racial superiority to win the allegiance of their cowed former slaves. (A self-employed Black seamstress, Christina Page, may also have been hired to make robes that were used by the Klan.) Merrill was well aware that Black informants divulged what they knew at the risk of their lives. "In almost every instance of outrage they have been threatened with death, in many instances if they simply told the fact that it had been done."

In addition to Merrill's network, and apparently unknown to him, at least one federal Secret Service agent was active in and around York County at the same time. (Professional detectives were not then the folk heroes romanticized by twentieth-century fiction and film; they were more typically likened to "sneak-thieves and spies" who plied a "crawling, dirty vocation until [they had] lost any spark of the human," as one newspaper put it.) This particular agent, German-born Michael G. Bauer, posed as the representative of a European agency exploring the area on behalf of prospective German emigrants. Although his findings were more limited than Merrill's, he learned from the contacts he made in the Klan—his primary technique seemed to be to lubricate them with alcohol—that the Klan's wiser leaders were urging their underlings to reduce the level of violence until the cavalry departed, as they assumed it would, before going back fully on the attack.

Merrill's more sustained investigation continued to expose the

Klan's internal operations. As in other parts of the South, its structure was military and hierarchical: each district was centralized under a "Grand Cyclops," who ruled over chiefs of "divisions," which in turn were subdivided into individual "klans," or "dens," generally consisting of about ten men. Merrill estimated that forty-five dens with between 1,800 and 2,300 members were active in York County alone, and that in the surrounding counties probably three-fourths of all white men were members. Yorkville itself, with a population of five hundred, hosted twelve dens with at least 120 members, including most of the business and professional men, and at least one trial justice. Den chiefs were responsible for furnishing weapons to men who couldn't afford them; otherwise, the individual members were required to supply disguises for themselves and their horses. New members were initiated in a ritual similar to the one invented in Tennessee, swearing to maintain obedience and secrecy on pain of death. Merrill reported, "The new brother is then tested in some minor acts of lawlessness until he is fully committed and is according to his zeal and unscrupulousness confided with graver and graver crimes to be committed." Raiding usually adhered to a standard pattern. "One klan would go and kick up their devilment for a day or two, and when it might reasonably be expected that they had gained my attention as military commander they would suddenly stop and at that time another klan in another part of the county would commence their operations," he told congressional investigators. Only those who were deemed to be "up to the mark of any sort of deviltry," were assigned the "more serious work of killing men or burning down buildings."

Merrill was deeply troubled both professionally and morally that the Klan's crimes could be repeated almost daily month after month with hardly even a pretense of official investigation, much less punishment. He was hampered partly by the Ku Klux Klan Act's stipulation that charges could be brought only for crimes that had been committed *after* the act's passage. He also faced a greater constraint. In mid-May, Grant had directed Merrill and other commanders to "arrest and break up disguised night marauders"—in collaboration with civil powers. That caveat presumed that the local authorities were willing to cooperate. This was far from the case. York County's entire political culture, including law enforcement, had been thoroughly infiltrated by the Klan. The local establishment reacted to such horrors with a collective shrug. "Whites may be compelled under the pressure of the federal bayonets and sabers, to live under negro rule," the *Yorkville Enquirer* editorialized, "but the natural feelings of the heart will rise to the surface and the white man will assert his supremacy." Merrill learned to his disgust that Yorkville's mayor had been among a gang that broke into the office of the probate judge, stole militia ammunition that was stored there, and distributed it to the Klan's terrorists. "It is utterly useless to attempt to do anything in which the local civil authorities have a hand," Merrill reported. The courts, he wrote, simply released Klansmen if they were arrested and shrugged at retaliation against witnesses. "They will not prosecute a case vigorously and I doubt much whether the plainest evidence would secure conviction."

As long as the local courts were in the Klan's grip it was difficult to induce freed people to give public testimony for fear of being murdered or sadistically degraded. Victims naturally resisted describing precisely what happened to them in detail: the point of torture, especially sexual abuse, was in part to humiliate the victim to the point where she, or he, felt so ashamed that she would keep her mouth shut. One Black witness called to give evidence at the inquest of a murder victim told Merrill that the coroner had simply laughed when he asked if he would be protected if he revealed what he knew. The victim's offense, Merrill noted, was that he had belonged to a Negro militia company, had been whipped for it, and knew who it was that had whipped him. Public sentiment among the whites, he reported, was that the execution had "served him right." The only time an alleged Klan member had actually been brought to court, a crowd of men armed with pistols appeared at the hearing, and cheered when the jury declined to lodge a charge against him. Thwarted by the institutions that supposedly existed to protect the public, Merrill could do little more than offer aid and legal advice to the victims, which he knew all too well was pathetically inadequate to meet the crisis.

Even as a newcomer to the area, Merrill had been able with the limited means at his command to track many of the Klan's crimes far enough to become convinced that vigorous action by civil officials would have fully exposed all the facts needed to bring offenses to trial. Had the obstacles of dishonest juries and perjured testimony been bravely confronted, it would have aroused the "better sentiment of the people" and broken the Klan's influence, he felt sure. But officials disingenuously claimed that they could do nothing if the victims didn't lodge formal complaints through the proper channels. That might be technically true, but he knew that it was really due to the calculated indifference with which complaints were met when they were made, and the fact that they never brought any kind of redress. "In all my conversations with people," he told the congressional investigators, "I have been met constantly with the palliative remark in regard to these outrages—conceding that they are wrong and all that—almost always the conversation has contained the substance of this remark, 'But you cannot but acknowledge that they have done some good,' as if lawless violence could ever do anything but harm. It is that point in the conversation of the best men of the community here which has so startled me as to the demoralization of public opinion."

Perhaps remarkably for a professional soldier, Merrill combined his natural aggressiveness with an acute and sensitive sociological eye. The "cowardice, ignorance, imbecility, and corruption of many of the officers of the law" had accelerated the Klan's spread, but there was, he felt, a more deep-seated and more poisonous illness that flowed through the veins of southern society. The root of "Ku-Kluxism" lay in the blind determination of white leaders to nullify the effects of the war; so much was obvious. But the human material that comprised the Klan had to be better understood if it was ever to be subdued. "Added to the ignorant classes from the lower orders was material ready to hand in a larger number of young men who by reason of superior influence and social standing were all the more dangerous when determined to conspire together to defy law," he reflected. "Then growing to manhood during the discordant social surroundings of the war, with scarcely even domestic control or discipline and in astonishing ignorance of the rights of free society, [they] are found now with no respect for law save what is bred of their fear of its penalties."

While Merrill worked surreptitiously to gather intelligence on the Klan, the order mounted its own counterintelligence operation to defeat him. He suspected, correctly enough, that the Klan's agents in telegraph offices in Yorkville and beyond, and on the railroad, were monitoring his dispatches; they always seemed to know well in advance when he had laid plans to ambush the night riders when they were out on a raid. Merrill also suspected that the town sheriff was rifling through the papers in his private office, which he confirmed by planting decoy messages that soon became common knowledge in the streets of Yorkville. From his own spies, Merrill also learned in June that the Klan was debating a massed attack on his camp in hope of driving him out of Yorkville, but ultimately decided that they were likely to lose a pitched battle. Instead, they began systematically trying to coax his soldiers into town, get enough of them drunk, and then dash on the camp in a hit-and-run raid. That attack never materialized either, "but the continued discussion of it is a good indication of the wish to do, while the pluck and will to carry it out are wanting," Merrill reported. The Klan achieved more success inducing desertions. Nearly all Merrill's troops were either working-class Yankees who were susceptible to racist insinuations that freed Blacks would compete with them for jobs, or southern men, some of them ex-Confederates, who had enlisted in the army because they couldn't find better work. Since their arrival in Yorkville, forty-two men had deserted from a single company of the 18th Infantry, and fourteen from K Troop of the Seventh Cavalry. Desertions were always a concern, wherever troops were posted. However, Merrill reported, evidence "points strongly to the belief that several deserters were taken in charge of by a party of Ku Klux in this place, and furnished with horses and escorted towards the Charlotte and Columbia R.R." While he was clearly incensed at these losses, Merrill reported them with military dispassion to Washington. Never did he betray even a hint of doubt that the Klan could and would be broken. Like the good lawyer that he was, he continued to build a case that could not be refuted by Klansmen's disingenuous lies and propaganda.

Merrill was also about to acquire powerful new allies with a political megaphone that would reach far beyond South Carolina. In March, Congress had formed the Joint Select Committee to Inquire into the Condition of Affairs in the Late Insurrectionary States, better known as the Ku Klux Klan Committee, to carry out an immensely ambitious investigation of terrorism across the entire

South. Chairing the committee was Republican senator John Scott, a forty-six-year-old, luxuriously bearded lawyer from Pennsylvania. Having been plucked from comparative obscurity primarily to represent the interests of the powerful Pennsylvania Railroad, Scott was something of a political innocent, who sometimes vexed his fellow party members with a streak of independence and moral rigidity. Like Scott, the committee's cochairman, Rep. Luke Poland, left only modest traces in the historical record. Fifty-six years old, beetle-browed and white-whiskered, he had worked his way upward from a farm in rural Vermont to become a successful lawyer and eventually chief justice of his state's Supreme Court before being named to the U.S. Senate in 1865. (Two years later, in a peculiar political pas de deux, he traded places with Rep. Justin Morrill and went on to serve for the next eight years in the House of Representatives.) The two men's virtues were not the obvious stuff of greatness, but they possessed an intense sense of justice coupled to a tireless work ethic, which propelled the committee to compile with remarkable speed a prodigious eight-thousand-page, thirteen-volume report that encompassed the two Carolinas, Georgia, Alabama, Mississippi, and Florida. (For reasons that are unclear, the committee interviewed no witnesses from Texas, Louisiana, or Virginia, and reported little from Arkansas and Tennessee.)

The committee's investigation concentrated on terrorism, but it also took abundant testimony on voter suppression, the vulnerability of Black citizens, the dysfunction of the courts, and—Democrats' preferred focus—the alleged corruption of Republican politicians. Hundreds of freed people testified, both male and female, victims of Klan terrorism, as well as army officers, federal attorneys, officials of every rank from local justices of the peace to sitting and ex officio governors, Republicans and Democrats, turncoat Klansmen, and several of the Klan's early leaders. Collectively, they presented a hellish panorama of great swaths of the nation under the sway of organized terror. The committee's report, much of it based on testimony collected in the field by traveling subcommittees and published in the spring of 1872, was damning. It demonstrated beyond any doubt that across the South law and order and the security of life and property had been fatally subverted by highly organized bands of "Ku-Klux," and that public sentiment in its favor widely paralyzed the will of the civil authorities. Officials who were willing to prosecute Klansmen at all clearly preferred to go after more obscure characters and to let the elite criminals go.

Witnesses who could afford the expense traveled to Washington to testify before Scott, who held hearings in the committee's august chamber at the Capitol from June into December. One of the first to testify was Essic Harris, a freedman who farmed in Chatham County, North Carolina. He told the committee that the Klan had come for him a few days before Christmas. He was half-asleep after an exhausting day cutting new ground. The dog barked, then barked again, then a third time. Harris leaped to the door and peered out to see a ghostly band coming toward him. Hurriedly, he barred the door, threw a bucket of water on the hearth, grabbed his gun from the head of the bed, and threw himself against the wall as the intruders knocked through the window and began shooting. The Klansmen broke in the door but couldn't push it all the way down because it tilted off its hinge against sacks of corn. Crouching beneath the window, Harris saw pistols firing over his head. The shooting was wild and random. Harris was hit nine times in all, in the hip, the scalp, in the muscled part of his arm, in the joint of his foot. He heard somebody saying that they ought to burn down the cabin with whoever was alive still in it.

In the gleam of the moonlight, Harris could see that some of the attackers had pulled off their masks. He recognized half a dozen of them as men he had grown up with in the neighborhood, and two men who owned a grocery a few miles away, where he had often bought a jar of whiskey. Harris figured that he was already a dead man, and that his wife and children, deep in the recesses of the cabin, must already be dead. He decided that he might as well fight. As the first Klansmen started to clamber over the half-fallen door, he fired, hitting the two men in front, Clark and Burgess, striking one in the chest and the other in an eye. As he reloaded, Harris began yelling for someone to hand him his pistol—which didn't exist—as if he had more armed men in the cabin with him. At the prospect of further losses, the Klansmen abruptly backed off, taking their wounded with them. Astonishingly, Harris's wife and children had all survived. The Klansmen's bullets had flown over their heads, though they had scarred the walls and shattered the bedsteads. Harris, to his amazement, had also survived, though badly wounded and still partially crippled by the ball lodged in his foot.

Asked why he thought he had been attacked, Harris said that only one thing singled him out for attention: he voted. He told the committee, "I do not expect to vote anymore. It is not worthwhile for a man to vote and run the risk of his life. The "colored people" throughout his neighborhood were all afraid to vote now, he said. "That is just the way it is."

Andrew J. Flowers, the only Black justice of the peace in Chattanooga, Tennessee, testified to the committee that he had been flogged by a gang of masked men because he had the "impudence" to run against a white man for office and beat him. Rev. Arad Lakin, a white Methodist missionary sent to northern Alabama to organize congregations among the freed people, described dodging Klansmen out to murder him, highlighted by a woodcut published in the *Tuskaloosa Monitor*—its editor was the city's Klan chief—showing his body hanging from a tree. Z. B. Hargrove, a Georgia lawyer, reported on the Klan's savage attack on a Black man named Joe Kenney: "The charge they had against [him] was that he had married this mulatto girl, and they did not intend he should marry so white a woman as she was; and they beat her also for marrying so black a man as he was." O. C. French, a Mississippi legislator, recounted the gory details of the Klan assault on Black Republicans at Meridian, Mississippi. A. P. Huggins, a former Union officer serving as a school superintendent in Mississippi, testified that the Klan had forced the closure of twenty-six freedmen's schools in his district, declaring that Negroes "did not need educating"; had "stove in" the head of a Black war veteran; and had stripped and beat the Black president of a local Republican club, and "cut him open from the throat to the straddle, took out all his insides." Then, on the night of March 8, Klansmen seized Huggins himself and, after promising not to harm him, savagely flogged him and ordered him to leave the state.

Several of the men instrumental to the Klan's early development testified at length, claiming in almost identical language that they knew of it only from hearsay, a pattern of implausible denial so consistent among Klan leaders that it seemed evidence, if not quite proof, of a coordinated policy. John B. Gordon, a former Confederate corps commander and presumed leader of the Klan in Georgia, testified that the group "of which I was a member," he carefully said, without naming it, "was purely a peace police," in which the "best men of the country" joined in self-defense. He declined to say what his position had been "in that particular organization," and insisted that he had never attended even one of its gatherings. He knew nothing about any "riding about at nights" or about the abuse of any Black men, or flogging of anyone, except perhaps as the expression of a community's disgust with some man who might have committed adultery. "Everything [in Georgia] now is as quiet and peaceable as it is anywhere in the world," he told the committee. Edmund W. Pettus, another former general, widely believed to be among the senior leaders of the Klan in Alabama, opined that no "white man would engage in that sort of business"—that is, the intimidation of Black voters, in Alabama—and asserted that the very term "Ku-Klux" had been invented by the Republicans as a smear to "cast odium on Democrats."

Nathan Bedford Forrest, who had once boasted to newspapers that the Klan could muster forty thousand men in Tennessee alone, now claimed that he had never even seen "the organization" together in any numbers and that as far as he knew it had no "political purpose" of any kind. Asked if the Klan's members went about in disguise, Forrest replied, "I suppose some of them did. . . . That was the rumor."

"Did they proceed to the extent of whipping or killing men?"

"I heard of men being killed, but I did not know who did it."

The Klan's only role, he said, was to "suppress the outrages, to keep peace." He supposed that whatever violence disguised men may have perpetrated had probably been committed either by "renegades" of some sort or by Negroes pretending to be Klansmen.

The members of the committee would hear much more obfuscation in this vein as its investigation ground on through the year. Since its hearings were not legal proceedings no one who testified could be charged with perjury. Moreover, at least with white witnesses, decorum prevailed. Rarely was a witness called to account for denying the reality of widespread violence that was obvious to every Black southerner and most whites no matter what their political affiliation. Even as the committee amassed its archive of victims' horrific accounts, countervailing testimony from partisan Democrats minimized the Klan's activities, lending political cover to those northerners, including disaffected Republicans such as Carl Schurz, who were eager to pretend that peace was descending on the benighted South.

In July, a five-man subcommittee led by the fierce Tennessee Radical Horace Maynard traveled to South Carolina, where they held hearings in Columbia, Spartanburg, Unionville, and Yorkville. The *Yorkville Enquirer* brushed these off as "a great cry but little wool," a political stunt designed to "manufacture political capital," but to those who had doubted the Klan's very existence the testimony was revelatory.

Scores of witnesses detailed the Klan's systematic campaign to interfere with voting and subvert elected Republican government. Governor Scott recited a litany of constables, census takers, poll workers, and trial justices who had been shot and whipped by disguised men. Samuel Poinier, a federal tax collector at Spartanburg, testified that two days before the last election disguised men flogged two white and three Negro poll workers, and warned them that they would be murdered if they dared to open the polls. Charles O'Keefe, an election official in Yorkville, described how frightened Republican voters hid their Republican ballots inside Democratic ones before they dropped them in the ballot box. John Neason, a businessman and Confederate veteran, testified that masked "Ku Klux" had ordered him to close his store because he had allowed Republicans to hold meetings on his property and had built a schoolhouse for "the colored children." Commodore Price, a fifty-three-year-old town constable, was offered a chance to save himself by joining the Klan, and when he declined was flogged until he was numb; Price's son-in-law was offered the same invitation and given a list of four Republicans he would have to "beat out" in order to prove himself, but he fled to the state capital instead. Jefferson Huskins, a Black Republican, said he was given more than one hundred lashes by horned Klansmen who then whipped his wife and three children, including his nine-year-old daughter. Francis Davie, a magistrate in Rock Hill, was dragged from his home and clubbed to the ground by a party of Klansmen that included the town marshal. John Genobles, a sixty-eight-year-old white native Carolinian who oversaw poll workers at the last election, testified that some ninety men disguised with "ears on their heads like mules," dragged him from his home with a rope, stripped him naked, flogged him while he crouched on all fours, and forced him to publicly declare his rejection of the Republican Party on the steps of the county courthouse: "I did it to save my life," he said. He added that he would never vote again.

The subcommittee also interviewed influential white men, some of them apologists for the Klan, and others active members of it. James Chesnut, a former U.S. senator who defected to the Confederacy in 1861 and served in its government, dismissively claimed that if any Blacks had been killed or whipped only "the lowest class of whites," ignorant men, who "were hardly better than Negroes themselves," could be blamed for it. Joseph Gist, a lawyer and leader of the attack on the Black militia at Chester, suggested that nothing the Klan did constituted a crime and that the murder of Black militiamen "did more for the peace and quiet of this country than anything that has ever transpired." Matthew Calbraith Butler, the former candidate for lieutenant governor under the banner of the short-lived anti-Reconstruction Reform Party, claimed absurdly that the Democrats had as much to do with emancipating the slaves as the Republicans had since "the authors of the rebellion were the active instruments of emancipation and therefore I think the negroes should be more thankful to us."

Merrill testified on July 26. He estimated that the Klan had perpetrated between three and four hundred whippings and beatings since the previous year. He named many of them: Creecy Adams, Phoebe Smith, Martha Woods, "greatly beaten and abused"; Charley Barron's wife, "knocked down and beaten because she would not tell where her husband was"; Sam Simmrell's wife, "whipped and ravished at the same time"; Abraham Webb's daughter, "whipped and made to dance"; Tony Wallace, "whipped and his watch stolen and his house ransacked"; Sylvester Barton, a boy, "beaten with clubs and pistols"; Addison Woods, "beaten with a gun"; Jesse McGill, "abused about the head and knocked with pistols"; Jerry Clowney, whipped and beaten because "he had a gun, was a preacher, and a sort of leader of the Negroes"; Elias Hill, a crippled preacher, dragged from his bed with a strap around his neck and "severely beaten with a pistol" and then horsewhipped. White Republicans, Merrill said, were also attacked, though in smaller numbers: Polly Weaver, "whipped near King's Mountain"; Dick Wilson, beaten for allowing his son to make Republican speeches; Abner Hambright, "whipped and partly hanged, but let down"; John Wallace, "a respectable man and a man of means," taken from his home and beaten for being a Republican; Dr. John Winsmith, a seventy-year-old former legislator who became a Republican after the war, shot down in a fusillade of bullets on the veranda of his home.

Rep. Philadelph Van Trump, a hostile congressional Democrat, tried to trap Merrill into confessing that he was nothing more than a partisan Republican with a Radical agenda, repeatedly pressing him about his personal politics. Merrill conceded only that his opinions "coincide more nearly with the Republican than with any other party," but asserted that he did not allow his politics, insofar as he had any, to affect his duty as a soldier. "I am an officer in the army," he said, "bred up in a school which taught me that officers of the army were not proper persons to mix in politics."

"Do you vote the Republican or Democratic ticket?" Van Trump demanded.

"I have never cast but one vote in my life," Merrill replied. "I have never had any connection or association with politics. I take a deep interest in the affairs of my country. But I do not take an active part in politics, and am not decided in expressing political opinions."

"You are a Pennsylvanian, are you not?"

"Yes, sir."

Then he could not know much about "the negro character," Van Trump sneered. Most of his so-called evidence came from Negroes, after all. Wouldn't "the Negro race" just make up stories that might win them some attention or reward?

Replied Merrill, "Their temper, I think, from the conversations I have had with the Negroes generally, is to ask that justice may be done them, and they may be secured in quiet lives."

In his testimony, Merrill reported at length on several of the murders that had been brought to his attention, including that of the militia captain Jim Williams. By now, his spies had unmasked the identities of several members of the gang that killed him, and

of its leader: James Rufus Bratton, a former Confederate army sur-
geon and a member of one of the county's most influential prewar
slaveowning families. At the war's end, Bratton had offered the
hospitality of his home to Jefferson Davis during his doomed flight
south. And just one day before Merrill, he had given testimony to
the subcommittee.

At forty-nine, Bratton presented himself well. He was tall and
slender, graying at the temples, with a patrician manner that some
found chilly but others said concealed a warm and generous heart.
Senator Scott, probably well briefed by Merrill, questioned Bratton
aggressively. He swore to tell the truth and then lied with breathtaking self-assurance. Asked what he could tell them about the Ku
Klux Klan, he replied, "I know nothing of their proceedings. I tell
you the feeling, the honest purpose of the people of this county and
state, so far as I know, are in favor of the negro, for his general good,
public and private. They do not wish to take away one particle of
the rights of the negro, civil, moral, religious, or political."

"Do you believe there is a Ku-Klux organization in this county?"
Scott asked.

Replied Bratton, "If there is, I do not know it."

"Have you any opinion as to whether we could rely on the testimony of men who were charged with being members of the Ku-
Klux organization?"

"I cannot say as to that. I do not know any who compose the
organization."

"Do you think they would be as likely to commit perjury, to get
clear of the imputation of those crimes, as the negroes who swear
that they suffer by them?"

"Not if they were white, honorable men."

Asked what he knew about extrajudicial punishments administered by the Ku Klux Klan, Bratton replied, "I merely hear rumors
and reports. Personally I know nothing about it." Was he aware of
the whipping of Blacks? Only vaguely: he supposed that he had
heard of perhaps fifteen or perhaps only a dozen such cases. But then
Negroes couldn't be trusted to report the truth. In most instances,
their claims ought to be ignored. "A great many of these people dislike to work, and if they can get the protection of the state or the
United States to relieve them from work they will do it, and I have

no faith in their testimony." Pressed harder, he supposed that he had heard vaguely about one Negro who "they say" was killed by some other Negroes in a robbery. And, yes, he had probably heard of a Jim Williams, perhaps sometime in February or March, killed "by some persons, who I cannot tell."

Did he know nothing about the men who participated in the hanging of Jim Williams?

"No, sir," Bratton politely but firmly responded. "No man has said, 'I did it,' or, 'he did.' I know nothing about it as to who hung him."

Major Merrill had been at work for some time gathering significant evidence concerning Williams's lynching. He had identified the owner of a mule that was present at the murder and the handwriting of the man who wrote the paper that had been pinned to Williams's chest, as well as a number of other details that he was sure would lead to the conviction of at least five of the murderers. Among them, he informed his superiors in Washington, was "one of the leading men of this county."

That man was Dr. James Rufus Bratton.

13

A MACHINERY FOR CRIMES

This disaffection is not a thing to be done by
wooing. Enough of that has already been done
in vain. Six years have not melted it.

—Attorney General Amos T. Akerman

Despite the stonewalling of Dr. Bratton and other accused Klansmen, the South Carolina hearings were a watershed. A remarkable
number of witnesses risked speaking publicly, and for the first time
detailed accounts of the Klan's terrorism entered the public record
under the aegis of the national government. There would be much
more to come as the subcommittees processed across the South. In
South Carolina, however, another legal debacle was in store, one
that anywhere outside the Klan-dominated South would have universally been recognized as a travesty of justice. In September, state
grand jury hearings were held ostensibly to examine the copious
evidence that Merrill had collected, along with revelations that
came to light in testimony delivered before the congressional subcommittee. In the event, reported Merrill, the hearings proved to be
"the most ghastly mocking of justice that it is possible to conceive"
by demonstrating how tightly the Klan held the local court system
in its grip. The grand jury's report simply ignored most of the material Merrill had provided about hundreds of crimes and concluded
astonishingly that "after careful examination of the facts" no "outrages" at all had occurred in York County. Merrill came to believe
that one-third of the members of both grand and petit juries were

Klan members, including high-ranking officers of the order, and that at least two of them had been accessories to murder; the few jurymen who wished to do their duty were browbeaten and over-ruled by the rest. "In view of this, it is small wonder that *eleven* murders and more than *six hundred* cases of whipping and other brutal outrages by the Ku Klux have to this day gone unnoticed" by the local courts, he fumed.

The grand jury fiasco provided yet more proof, if any was needed, that upcountry South Carolina was still reeling out of control. Merrill reported that the Klan, emboldened by its successful defiance of justice, was preparing for a renewed campaign of terror. His spies informed him that in an effort to thwart penetration by the government's agents, an even more secret Klan-within-the-Klan was forming. To President Grant, South Carolina governor Scott wrote, "The cruelties that have been inflicted in Spartanburg and York counties are shocking to humanity. Crime has run riot with impunity, all warnings have been disregarded and the efforts of the well-disposed citizens have proved unavailing." Another correspondent wrote to the president, "It is no uncommon thing for men to boast that when the 'Yankees' leave here then 'we'll have KuKluxing right.'"

The Klan believed that it would eventually prevail over Merrill, if not by force of arms then by thwarting the courts. However, it was not prepared to deal with the newest member of Ulysses Grant's cabinet, the underrated and unexpectedly bold Amos Akerman. The attorney general had spent most of the past year far from the battlefields of racial warfare, embroiled in a medley of pedestrian, if legally intricate, railroad cases. Now, at Grant's direction, he was turning his attention to the chaos in South Carolina. He would serve, at least for now, as the president's field commander for the first national antiterrorist campaign waged on American soil. "This disaffection is not thing to be won by wooing," he wrote to federal judge Robert A. Hill in Mississippi. "Enough of that has already been done in vain. Six years have not melted it. It will only disappear before an energetic exercise of power."

Akerman wielded a degree of power that no attorney general before him had enjoyed. Up to now, the administration of federal law was a rat's nest haphazardly managed by lawyers scattered among the various departments, often hired on an ad hoc basis and lacking clear lines of responsibility. Previous attorneys general had functioned mainly as the president's part-time counsel, providing legal advice and representing the government before the Supreme Court. (Attorneys general were not even required to live in Washington, and commonly maintained their own private legal practice on the side.) The new Justice Department was the brainchild of Republican civil service reformers, Lyman Trumbull and Carl Schurz among them, who hoped to shield the law from partisan politics; many Democrats supported it as well, because it seemed likely to diminish Republican patronage. The attorney general now centralized under his own authority the work of all federal attorneys and was responsible for setting rules and regulations for the government and, crucially, for the protection of civil rights under the Fourteenth Amendment, a job for which no man in federal service was better fitted than Akerman, with his roots in both New England and the South. With symbolic significance, he established his office in the new Freedman's Savings Bank building across the street from the White House.

Akerman differed from many other Radical Republicans in his affection for the South. Despite his Yankee upbringing, he felt an emotional attachment to the land, which he had worked with his hands as a farmer, as he still did whenever he visited his home in Georgia, where his wife continued to live while he was in Washington, braving the insults and threats of her neighbors, some of whom mobbed her home and threatened to burn it down around her. From long personal experience, he also understood the sometimes highly subjective working of the South's courts, believed with deep conviction in the rule of law, and felt that the national government had a moral duty to protect its most vulnerable citizens. He regarded the enforcement of the law as an opportunity not to punish the South, as some of his northern colleagues would, but to perfect it. To a friend in Georgia, he reflected with sadness,

> Our citizens, or those previously recognized as such had it in their power by the exercise of some patience and of some judgement, to settle forever the domestic question of the relations of the races, and the more general question of the relation of the

South to the general government and the North. There was a choice between acting in politics upon ideas which had prevailed in the war and upon the ideas which had been overcome. The former, I thought, was the part of wisdom and of honor, too: of wisdom, because it would soonest quiet the war, and whether we like it or not would bring us speedily to the shore on which we are bound ultimately to land; and of honor, because a surrender in good faith really signified a surrender of the substance as well as the form of the Confederate cause. But that portion of the people were not equal to the occasion. They consulted the past rather than the future, were moved in politics by resentment rather than by reason, and so got where they now are.

Grant asked Akerman to travel to South Carolina to personally oversee the army's work there. (They agreed that Akerman would communicate through the War Department only in code, since it had to be assumed that the Klan's agents regularly tapped the telegraph wires.) In Columbia, Akerman met with Governor Scott and U.S. Attorney David T. Corbin, both of them impatient to join in a coordinated campaign against the Klan. Also in Columbia, Akerman met Merrill for the first time, and was impressed. He wrote to General Terry, "He is just the man for the work—resolute, collected, bold and prudent, with a good legal head, very discriminating between truth and falsehood, very indignant at wrong, and yet master of his indignation; the safer, because incredulous at the outset, and therefore disposed to scrutinize reports the more keenly." Once settled in Yorkville, where he would remain for two weeks, Akerman quickly realized that reports he had read of the Klan's "infernal purpose" fell far short of the facts on the ground. "Your blood would be curdled if you knew one-tenth of what I know about the upper part of South Carolina, to say nothing of other states," he wrote to a friend in Georgia.

A deeply religious man, Akerman was appalled by what he called the Klan's "organized depravity" and its "perversion of moral sentiment," which infected even intelligent and otherwise respectable men. Unless harsh and unflinching treatment was applied, he feared that the disease would metastasize and poison every aspect of society far into the future in ways that could not yet be foreseen. "Without a thorough moral renovation, society there for many years will be—I can hardly bring myself to say savage, but certainly very far from Christian," he wrote to General Terry. And to E. P. Jacobson, the U.S. attorney in Jackson, Mississippi, he wrote, "Nothing is more idle than to attempt to conciliate by kindness that portion of the southern people who are still malcontent. They take all kindness on the part of the government as evidence of timidity, and hence are emboldened to lawlessness by it. It appears to be impossible for the government to win their affections. But it can command their respect by the exercise of its power. It is the business of a judge to terrify evildoers, not to coax them."

Akerman affirmed to Grant that in his official judgment a rebellion against the national government was under way in South Carolina. The locution was important. It provided the president with the explicit legal basis for the extreme measure that they both believed must now be taken, the suspension of habeas corpus, that is, the constitutional right to due process, which in turn would allow Klansmen to be quickly rounded up by the army and held for trial by federal judges. On October 12, in accordance with Akerman's ruling, Grant formally commanded "all persons composing the unlawful combinations and conspiracies" to turn over their weapons and disguises to federal officers. As expected, Klansmen ignored him. On October 16, Akerman wrote again to Grant, "Unless these combinations shall be thoroughly suppressed, no citizen who opposes their political objects will be permitted to live, and no freedman will enjoy essential liberty, in the territory now subject to their sway. Relief can only come from the power of the United States. They must now be taught that there is some force in the law which they have despised." The next day, Grant proclaimed the suspension of habeas corpus in nine counties of upcountry South Carolina where, he declared, conspiracies to hinder the execution of the law and deprive citizens of their rights had overwhelmed the power of the state government to protect its citizens. By Akerman's order, and to Merrill's rejoicing, army officers were authorized to act as federal marshals with the power to arrest, interrogate, and jail suspected Klan terrorists as well as reluctant witnesses. Two days after the suspension of habeas corpus, Merrill's troopers were in their saddles, carbines at the ready, and hunting the Klan.

Merrill's reports lie deep in the annals of the army's daily operations, in the Army Adjutant General's records at the National Archives, in Washington, D.C., among reports on the shipment of rifles to forts in the West, the punishment of soldiers arrested for gambling, news of Sioux raids in the Wyoming Territory, complaints about the variety of toothpaste, cigars, and shirt collars offered at a trading post in Nevada, approval for officers in Louisville to wear straw hats in summer, officers' applications for transfer, bookkeeping squabbles at posts in New Mexico. For a soldier in the midst of a guerrilla war, often sleepless, besieged by desperate Black people and frightened Republicans, living every day with the Ku Klux Klan's target on his back, Merrill's reports stand out for their calmness, clarity, intelligence, and remarkable sensitivity.

President Grant had already ordered six hundred more troops from the Seventh Cavalry and the 18th Infantry to upcountry South Carolina, raising the total in the state to more than one thousand, the most that had been posted to a single southern state in years. As soon as habeas corpus was suspended, Merrill and his counterparts in Spartanburg, Union, and other counties ordered their reinforced companies to begin simultaneously arresting Klansmen on the lists they had painstakingly compiled over months from the furtive testimony of the freed people. Ranging across countryside tufted with ripe cotton that resembled snowfall, Merrill's troopers apprehended some six hundred suspects in one month in York County alone. "Several citizens of the town were arrested while in the pursuit of their avocations, and many persons from the country, while in town on business, were also detained and lodged in prison," the *Yorkville Enquirer* reported with barely suppressed astonishment. Mary Davis Brown, several of whose menfolk were active members of the Klan, scrawled in her diary, "Great excitement today. It is reported that marshall law is declared and that the yankeys will commence arresting the men at eney time. Billy & Caty & John Lawson & Mag is here tonight afraid to lie down and go to sleep."

Merrill usually deployed his men in groups as small as ten or twenty, recording the accounts of terrorized freed people, protecting government witnesses, shielding threatened Republican officials, and chasing Klansmen. One of the few firsthand accounts of the tactics they employed was penned by Sgt. John Ryan of the Seventh Cavalry, a Massachusetts native of Irish extraction who had fought at Antietam and Gettysburg, and then in the West under Custer, before being posted to South Carolina. Ryan remembered how his company would sometimes surround an entire town before dawn with orders to allow no one to leave, and then ride in with a federal marshal carrying a wad of arrest warrants. More commonly, he said, they tried to take single Klansmen by surprise. "We would ride up to within a couple of hundred yards of the man's house that we were after, and dismount. Three or four privates would advance up to the house very quietly and a man would be posted at each corner of the house. The marshal and sergeant would knock at the door, and if the party we wanted was in the house and should attempt to make his escape, which was usually the case, and in making their escape jumped out of one of the windows, they would jump right into the arms of one of our men, or rather into the muzzle of one of their carbines." One night, Ryan's detachment searched a house but could not find their quarry anywhere, until Ryan opened the door to the bedroom of the man's daughters. "I advanced to the bed and pulled off the bed clothes and there I found the gentleman we were looking for secreted between his daughters." On another occasion, they found their man asleep in a hidden room above a barn. "I immediately whipped out my .44 caliber Colt's pistol and pointed it at his head. I very gently shook him in the bed. If you ever saw a surprised man, he was one, as his hair fairly stood up."

(Ryan also revealed a disheartening degree of casual racism. In a section recalling soldiers' "amusements," along with poker and monte, horse racing, and reading, he described playing "pranks" on the "colored" men and women who came to the camp to sell fresh fruit and vegetables. Sometimes the soldiers impulsively seized them and tossed them in blankets; when a prominent Black official drove up in a barouche to investigate such treatment, the troopers tossed him, too. Ryan wrote blithely, "This was quite a diversion for the enlisted men, and as there was nobody hurt it did not do any harm." On another occasion, an officer shot into the air to get the attention of a young Black man passing on the road and ordered him to swing him in his hammock, then gave him some money and sent him off with another shot in the air. At Spartanburg, men also crept off at night to "the Negro cabins" where they would "mingle in with the women . . . have a good time and sometimes get drunk, and in the morning before reveille roll call you could see them sneaking back to camp.")

The very nature of his troops posed a challenge for Merrill. Most soldiers disliked occupation duty, often intensely. They felt resented by most local whites and uneasy with Blacks. Few came from anti-slavery backgrounds. Most were likely to be Democrats. A study of the origins of hundreds of white enlisted men who served in the Eighth Infantry in North Carolina determined that more than half were foreign-born, the vast majority from Ireland and Germany, and that among the American-born, the largest category hailed from largely Democratic New York; 9 percent were born in the former Confederate states, some from as far away as Texas and Louisiana, some of whom were probably "galvanized Yankees"—that is, former Confederates. In Spartanburg, Merrill reported, his troops were less effective than they should be "arising greatly from the mistaken notions of duty of the officers who have been in command there, and I fear somewhat from lack of sympathy with the wish of the Executive to execute the law." In other words, they were hostile to Blacks and favored the same local whites they were policing. A Klan supporter in Union County, South Carolina, tellingly wrote, "we got on very pleasantly" with both officers and men. "They obeyed their orders but with few exceptions were all in sympathy with the white people." Soldiers detailed to guard jailed Klansmen at Spartanburg amiably allowed them to walk home to their families for meals, while deserters from Merrill's command apparently accepted the help of local Klansmen, to whom they sold or traded their horses and carbines when they left.

Southern sympathies were by no means confined to ordinary soldiers, or to Merrill's force in South Carolina. The Seventh Cavalry's flamboyant commanding officer, Lt. Col. George Armstrong Custer, embraced an attitude of deep-seated racism, contempt for the politics of Reconstruction, and resentment at being required to provide military assistance to civilian federal officials in their efforts to combat white terrorists. Fortunately for Merrill, who reported directly to General Terry, Custer was posted far way in Elizabethtown, Kentucky, where he expressed more enthusiasm for acquiring fast horses and hobnobbing with the local white elite than for chasing the Klan. Although a loyal state during the war, Kentucky remained infested with pro-Confederate and anti-Black sentiment that made fertile ground for Klan recruiters. Custer loathed Merrill and when later given the opportunity would work to undermine his career.

Merrill pushed his men hard, but he was scrupulous in avoiding unnecessary violence. Attorney General Akerman, still in Yorkville, made clear that the troops should carry out their mission sternly but without gratuitous aggression that could weaken the government's case against the men they arrested. The arrests spread panic through the upcountry. "Many of the KuKlux leaders suspected that means were being devised to bring them to justice, and with the cowardice which had characterized all their infamous crimes, fled, leaving their poorer followers and ignorant dupes to stand sponsors for the crimes of which they had been the chief authors and instigators." At first scores, then hundreds of Klansmen took to the mountains or fled to other states, some as far away as Texas and Canada. Wrote Mary Davis Brown in her diary: "Theire is a good many of the men left York. Marten Hall is now gone fore parts unknown. . . . Hiram & Lawson put on their hats this evening and stepped off. Butler & Willie left last week. . . . The yanks is going in every direction gathering up and putting in jail. . . . One by one oure friends are leeving, some to Tenesee some to Arcansis [Arkansas], some to Heaven, some to hell." By November, Akerman estimated that as many as two thousand South Carolinians had been arrested.

Among the fugitives was James W. Avery, the Klan chief in York County, who fled to Canada, forfeiting a $3,000 bond. Another was Dr. James Bratton, who led the lynching of the militia captain Jim Williams. According to private family papers, Bratton fled first to his sister's house in Barnwell, South Carolina, then via Augusta, Georgia, to a friend's home in Selma, Alabama, where he adopted the name "Simpson," and after that to Memphis, and finally to Canada, where he came to rest in London, Ontario, which hosted a number of fugitive Klansmen and their families, Avery included. Throughout his peregrinations, he received regular guidance from friends, family, and lawyers, often in code—"M" for Memphis, "A" for Augusta, the number "8" to mean "all well," and so on.

Soldiers and plainclothes federal detectives monitored the highways and railroads, on the lookout for fugitive Klansmen. Sergeant Ryan, disguised in civilian clothes, tracked one escaped prisoner to Augusta, Georgia, and then twenty miles beyond it into the country-side, having followed the man's wife and child, who changed trains several times. Others tracked their quarries as far west as Arkansas. Bratton's lawyer warned him to stay as far away from Yorkville as long as possible, since the courts could no longer be relied upon to let Klansmen go: "It seems about useless to attempt any defense in any case. The jurors are all negroes and are completely under the control and the influence of the prosecution. When this thing is to end, I know not."

By the end of the year, Merrill could report that some eight hundred York County men had been arrested, surrendered, or fled, many of them mere teenagers, including the thirteen-year-old son of a Klan chief who had sworn him in and taken him along on a raid the same night. (The boy was deemed not to be responsible for himself and released.) Most were released on bail. Nearly two hundred remained in jail. They included men of every social class, even ministers of the gospel who, Merrill remarked, "confessed every crime known to the law." Some of Merrill's prisoners were willing to turn state's evidence but had asked to be arrested to make it seem that they were being compelled to appear in court.

Merrill faced a growing problem of managing the tide of prison-ers. Hundreds of Klansmen begging to confess besieged his head-quarters at Rose's Hotel. Many claimed truthfully or not that they had never taken part in raids or that they were forced to join under threat of violence. Most of the Klan's rank and file were very poor men who could never shoulder the expense of hiring counsel and procuring witnesses. As discipline collapsed, internal dissension within the Klan also worked in Merrill's favor. In neighboring Union County, for instance, the chief of one den ordered his men to thrash a rival chief; the next night the whipped chief with his men retaliated in like manner on the first chief. "Looking about for their chiefs and councilors and finding that to get orders or advice they must go to them in jail or follow their flight, they rec-ognized the fact that the game was up," Merrill reported. "Conspir-ators of every grade of criminality have come in and surrendered by the score. Day after day for weeks men have come in in such numbers that the time to hear them confess and means to dispose of or take care of them both failed and I was powerless to do anything more than to secure the persons of those most deeply criminal and send the rest to their homes on their personal parole to be forthcoming when called for. In some instances, whole klans headed by their chief came in and surrendered together."

The jail's inmates enjoyed surprising privileges. Members of an Episcopal congregation brought the stove from their church and installed it in the jail's "sitting room" to keep the prisoners warm. Iredell Jones, a lawyer and Klan organizer, wrote cheerfully to his mother, "I have plenty of companions, books, papers, flowers and provisions, etc.," and to his wife, "ladies visit the prisoners every day," but, he assured her, "There is no impropriety whatever." Visitors were allowed to bring the prisoners packages of homecooked food, and in Spartanburg, and perhaps elsewhere, those who appeared to be "respectable men" were sometimes allowed simply to go home to their families for meals.

As the Klan began to crumble in York County, a new wave of violence erupted a day's ride to the north in Rutherford County, North Carolina, a rugged and comparatively isolated enclave forested with chestnut, hickory, and dogwood, maple, and sassafras where farmers' wives called their men in from the fields for dinner with an ox horn, and the sound of cow bells floated over the steep hills and deep glens that provided abundant hiding places for mustering Klansmen. Between mid-March and mid-April alone, at least fifty Republicans had been whipped and attacked by masked men; when U.S. marshals handed over fifteen suspected raiders to the local sheriff, himself a clandestine Klansman it was later learned, he freed them immediately. Governor Tod Caldwell—Holden's weak successor—wrote worriedly to Ulysses Grant, "If I were to call out the militia of the state it is likely that a large portion of the soldiers would be members of the organization that had perpetrated the outrages." J. B. Carpenter, the editor of the Republican *Rutherford Star,* wrote to Grant, "If we do not get help we are gone."

Then, in June, as many as a hundred emboldened Klansmen, many of them from across the state line in South Carolina, swarmed into Rutherfordton, the county seat, firing off pistols. They invaded the office of the *Rutherford Star,* destroying the presses, wrecking the office, and hurling the type and files into the street. Some of the band simultaneously attacked the home of James M. Justice, an outspoken white Republican member of the state legislature. They smashed his door down with an axe, pistol-whipped him, dragged him into the woods, and scourged him until he was nearly dead. Before he passed out, they warned him that the Democrats intended to restore the old prewar state constitution and "that the negroes should be put under the white men, and that every man that resisted would be killed."

The Klan's overly confident local chief, Randolph Abbott Shotwell, a Confederate veteran and editor of a violently anti-Reconstruction newspaper, had assured his followers that they could never be convicted for anything they did because every jury would be packed with Klansmen. But the Enforcement Acts had changed the legal battlefield. Just days after the attack on him, Justice was in Washington recounting his experience to the Ku Klux Klan Committee, on Capitol Hill, and detailing the months of Klan terrorism that had preceded it. Meanwhile, troops poured into Rutherford County. While wealthier Klansmen fled, federal marshals backed by soldiers from the Fourth Artillery and a company of the Seventh Cavalry, dispatched by Merrill from South Carolina, began arresting Klansmen wholesale. Scores more voluntarily surrendered. "Neighbor betrayed neighbor," Shotwell later wrote, "friend piloted the man-hunters to the home of his friend, and relatives persuaded each other with a fury born of mingled terror, shame and greed." By August, arrests were being made every day. The biggest prize was Shotwell, who failed to escape in time to save himself.

Comparatively few Klansmen of Shotwell's rank were ever captured, and even fewer revealed as much of themselves as he later did in a cloyingly self-serving memoir that was not published until the 1930s. Well educated, gifted as a writer, and a passionate defender of the Confederacy—he spent four years in its army and took part in Pickett's doomed charge at Gettysburg—he portrayed himself very much as the Klan's elite leaders typically wished to see themselves: proud, aggrieved, and aristocratic. (Shotwell was actually the son of a Pennsylvania-born Presbyterian minister and was an unstable, perhaps war-traumatized alcoholic.) Although he justified his Klan membership as a matter of honor, he never accepted any responsibility for its brutalities. Boastful and aggressive before his arrest, afterward he claimed that he had never gone on a raid or worn a disguise, and had always tried to keep the "wild, reckless young men under control." He self-pityingly blamed friends for betraying him and complained that "of all the 20,000 members of the Order in North Carolina only three dared to visit me" during his incarceration before trial; as he was "dragged" through the streets of Raleigh, he wrote, "not one dared say, 'Adieu, Brother, we will not forget you!'"

In September, fifty-six Klansmen went on trial in federal court before a racially mixed jury that also included Democrats and conservatives. Attorney General Akerman personally advised the prosecution, recognizing that the trials would likely set a precedent for the much more numerous prosecutions that he foresaw for South Carolina. Twenty-five of the defendants were convicted of conspiracy and acts of terror. Shotwell received the stiffest sentence of all: a $5,000 fine and five years at hard labor in the penitentiary at Albany, New York. Most of them received modest sentences: fines of $50 to $500, imprisonment for six months up to three years. There was some talk of eventual pardons if there was no resurgence of violence, but Akerman tamped it down. The Klan, he wrote to Benjamin Butler, "are well scared in certain parts of North Carolina. But in other States we have not yet made much impression; and the time for amnesty to the least guilty will come when the alarm spreads."

Nevertheless, the trials had demonstrated to frightened Republicans and to the terrorists alike that the Ku Klux Klan Act—the Third Enforcement Act—had teeth, and that political will and forceful prosecution could bring terrorism to heel. "The Ku Klux trials for the present are over," celebrated the *Weekly Carolina Era*, a Republican newspaper. "They will render the recent term of the Circuit Court forever memorable in the history of the state. Through it the first successful blow has been struck at a secret political organization which is the standing disgrace of the age." Radicals, Black and white, could finally feel a surge of optimism.

The convicted Shotwell bitterly characterized the government's campaign as a "reign of terror" in which "innocent men were dragged from their beds at midnight," and subjected to "every conceivable humiliation." (The worst of it, he groaned, was "a negro blacksmith hammering the rivets" of his chains.) The partisan Democratic press echoed such histrionics. The *Baltimore Sun* scoffed that the Klan was as harmless as the Masons or the Odd Fellows. The *New York Sun,* denouncing "Grant's Bayonet Law," imagined "decrepit old men, staggering under the weight of years, totter[ing] to the jail between the files of soldiery, there to be packed like herrings in the six-by-ten cells." (The vast majority of Klan prisoners were in fact only in their teens and twenties.) The *New York Herald,* one of the most widely read papers in the country, baselessly asserted that "more white men — Democrats, Rebels or whatever else they may be called—have been murdered by negroes since the war ended than negroes by white men," claiming that "they could murder white men with impunity, but a hair of their precious heads must not be touched. Is it at all a matter of surprise that [whites] finally took the law into their own hands?"

Lewis Merrill caustically brushed off such nonsense as "the chattering of such as sought to conceal crime by exciting public sympathy" on the part of men and women who had never expressed any concern for the victims of the Klan's crimes. As the hunt for fugitive Klansmen continued in South Carolina's upcountry, the first of Merrill's York County prisoners went on trial at Columbia at the beginning of November. The state capital's attention was divided between the arrival of the arrestees—"sallow, ragged-looking wretches," in the words of a Charleston journalist—and the exuberance of the state fair with its plowing matches, demonstrations of new-model steam engines, livestock exhibitions, hurdy-gurdies, hobby-horse rides for children, and a colorful midway where a "stump orator" held forth in praise of a Fat Lady, and a huckster in brown velveteen lured visitors to a "wild Indian" show where a number of "decidedly seedy" tribesmen (or white men impersonating them) performed a "kind of half-savage yell." The city was still recovering from the trauma of the war's end, when it fell to Sherman's troops and a third of its buildings were reduced to ash and ruins; visitors mordantly referred to it as "Chimneyville." Although new, humbler buildings were slowly filling the empty blocks, the once lordly but now gutted state capitol remained a worksite littered with blocks of stone strewn around a gloomy shell topped by a temporary roof—people called it a giant breadbox with windows—a vivid symbol of a government still barely stitched together after six years of Reconstruction. On the capital's streets, the ubiquitous sight of Black politicians and lawyers, businessmen, policemen, and soldiers rubbed raw the sensibilities of unchastened conservatives, reminding them constantly that they lived in a world turned upside down.

Hundreds of citizens, both Black and white, crowded into the courtroom to witness the trials. President Grant, in consultation with Amos Akerman, personally picked the lead judge, Hugh Lennox Bond of the Fourth Federal Circuit, a graduate of New York University and an antislavery founder of the Republican Party in Maryland. He was joined by George S. Bryan, a onetime anti-secessionist slaveowner who had been appointed to the federal court in South Carolina by Andrew Johnson. Because so few whites could swear that they had never been members of the Klan, as the Enforcement Act required, a majority of the jurors would be Black, a fact which, though unintended, fed whites' hostility to the whole judicial process. (The trial's chief stenographer was the later-to-be-famous Benjamin Pitman, the inventor of Pitman shorthand.)

The prosecution was led by flinty, thirty-eight-year-old, Vermont-born David Corbin, the highly capable Republican U.S. attorney for South Carolina, a Dartmouth graduate who had served in the Union Army and as a member of the postwar South Carolina state Senate. He was assisted by the state's attorney general, Daniel Chamberlain, a Union veteran from Massachusetts, and by the ubiquitous Lewis Merrill, who attended the trials at Corbin's side. The Klansmen selected for trial were essentially test cases. "It was not only the KKK that was on trial," historian Lou Falkner Williams has written. "The meaning and scope of the Reconstruction amendments and Enforcement Acts were also before the court. It was up to federal judges to breathe life and meaning into the ambiguous words and phrases of the Fourteenth Amendment and the laws of Congress." Essentially, the prosecutors sought to nationalize civil rights, a radical prospect in a country that had always left such matters to the vagaries of state enforcement. In particular, they hoped to enshrine for freed people the right to bear arms and to be safe from the invasion of their homes, both essential if they were to be able to make their new freedoms real. The Klan, Corbin declared, was "a machinery for crimes," whose goal was "no less vast and desperate than the destruction, the utter overthrow, nay the turning back of the entire tide of our history since the opening of the last great struggle on this continent between the spirit of slavery and the spirit of justice and liberty."

For the Klansmen's defense, wealthy conservatives hired two of the most eminent legal men in America: Henry Stanbery of Ohio and Sen. Reverdy Johnson of Maryland, both former attorneys general of the United States. Stanbery, a rigid states' rights Democrat from Ohio, had served in Andrew Johnson's cabinet and defended him in the president's impeachment trial. The elderly Reverdy Johnson, by now half-blind, was a morally complicated figure, a conservative who regarded slavery as un-Christian but had owned slaves though he later freed them; as a member of Franklin Pierce's cabinet, he had argued the government's side of the *Dred Scott* case in 1854, but a decade later delivered the single most eloquent speech in Congress on behalf of the Thirteenth Amendment. Both Stanbery and Johnson supported amnesty for former Confederates, the postponement of Black suffrage, and repeal of the Ku Klux Klan Act, which they regarded as flagrantly unconstitutional. Strategically, the defense hoped to stymie the court sufficiently that the judges would sidestep ruling on the constitutionality of the Enforcement Act and compel the cases to be elevated to the U.S. Supreme Court.

The prosecution presented a parade of witnesses, including both Black survivors of Klan attacks and turncoat Klansmen, who testified to the conspiratorial nature of the Klan and its willingness to resort to torture and murder. Kirkland Gunn, a professional photographer, one of the most forthcoming of the turncoat witnesses, said that the explicit purpose of the den he joined was "putting down Radical rule and negro suffrage by killing off the white Radicals, and by whipping and intimidating the Negroes, so as to keep them from voting." Others recounted how raiders invaded the home of Isaac Postle, a Black preacher, pinned his baby under their feet, stomped his pregnant wife, and tortured him by repeatedly hanging him from a tree . . . how Klansmen cut Tom Roundtree's neck from ear to ear with a bowie knife . . . how Henry Latham was flogged by robed men who told him they would "make me a good old Democrat."

The first case that Corbin brought was against a group of Klansmen who had invaded the home of Amzi Rainey, a Republican freedman, in March. Rainey testified that as his family was going to bed there was a pounding on the door of their cabin. Voices yelled, "God damn you, open the door!" They knocked it off its hinges, and pouring in they immediately began beating his wife, demanding to know where Rainey was. She claimed she didn't know, but they kept yelling, "Where is he, God damn him!" They forced her to climb ahead of them up into the loft where Rainey was hidden and dragged him down. "God damn him, I smell him, we'll kill him," their leader yelled, drawing his pistol, now saying, "I am going to blow your brains out." Another, turning to Rainey's wife, shouted, "God damn her, I will kill her now!" They commenced to beat her again. At this point, a small girl, one of Rainey's daughters, ran out from where she was crouching with the other children in a corner, crying, "Don't kill my pappy, please, don't kill my pappy." The man with the pistol shoved her back, and yelled, "You go back in the room, you God damned little bitch. I will blow your brains out," and he fired and shot her in the forehead.

A judge asked, "Did he hit her?"

"Yes, sir," Rainey testified. "He hit her, and after they had done that she went back into the room, and they commenced shooting over me—two shots over me and two shots over my wife. They shot almost fifteen shots. I had a sleeve-jacket on. It was woolen, and they set fire to it. Then they took me right out." They led Rainey about 150 yards up the road. The leader of the group asked him which way he had voted. "I told him I voted the Radical ticket. 'Well,' he says, 'now you raise your hand and swear that you will never vote another Radical ticket and I will not let them kill you.' And he made me stand and raise my hand before him and my God that I never would vote another Radical ticket." When Rainey returned to his cabin he learned that while he had been out the other Klansmen had gang-raped his elder daughter.

Corbin charged the defendants with a conspiracy to deprive Rainey of equal protection of the law, including his right to vote, as well as a conspiracy to deprive him of the Fourth Amendment's protection against illegal search and seizure. With this, Corbin was asserting that the federal government was constitutionally compelled to protect civil rights when a state failed to do so. Corbin was also testing the highly controversial section of the Enforcement Act that stated that if an ordinary crime such as assault was committed during the violation of the act the offender could be tried in federal court.

The prosecution further argued that the Fifteenth Amendment had made the right to vote "a great public fact throughout the length and breadth of the Union," and applied to every type of election. Corbin conceded that the original amendments to the Constitution were understood to restrain only the national government. But the country had grown far more complex since the 1780s; Civil War had also wrought a "revolution" that made new demands on the Constitution. Today, he said, the greatest threat to civil liberties lay in states' inability—or unwillingness—to protect vulnerable citizens from lawless individuals like those who had attacked Amzi Rainey, Isaac Postle, Tom Roundtree, and the others.

Stanbery, for the defense, insisted that the Fourteenth Amendment could only apply to the actions of states, not those of individuals, and that only the states were responsible for protecting individual rights, not the national government. The invasion of Rainey's home, he claimed, was no more than a domestic burglary, a mere common-law crime over which federal law had no authority whatever. "What surrounds me, when I am at home or here, but state law," he cried. "Great God! Have we forgotten altogether that we are citizens of states?" The Fifteenth Amendment, he argued, granted no universal right to vote, but only barred discrimination explicitly based on color or past servitude. Moreover, the states retained the power to enact any laws they chose for elections other than federal ones, he said. It was "ridiculous" to suggest that any man could be deprived of the right to vote "generally." And, in any case, he asserted, no conspiracy against voters could take place anytime except on Election Day itself.

To this, Reverdy Johnson added his claim that when the Thirteenth Amendment was passed in 1865, no member of Congress—he had been one of them—had dreamed that the right to vote would ever be extended "to a people so wholly uneducated and necessarily ignorant" as the former slaves. Nor was the Fifteenth Amendment ever intended to grant Congress the authority to regulate voting in the states, at the expense of the states' long-established rights. Had Congress meant to reinvent the whole character of government by seizing such new powers for itself? Hardly. Otherwise, he said, it could reinvent the requirements for voting in any way it wanted: arbitrarily shrinking the pool of those who could vote, for example, or enlarging it, or even giving the vote to women, who, "in my opinion, [were] not created for the purpose of joining in any of those questions which agitate men and excite their passions."

In another case, this one involving a rank-and-file Klansman named Robert Mitchell and thirty other men who had murdered the Black militia captain Jim Williams, Corbin sought to prove the power of the federal government to protect the right of freedmen to bear arms under the Second Amendment. Because much of the Klan's violence in York County centered on the confiscation of guns that had been issued to Black militia members, Corbin considered the Second Amendment vital to the prosecution. Without guns, the freedmen were effectively defenseless in rural areas where the law, such as it was, mostly likely was on the side of the Klan. Said Corbin, citing the Second Amendment, "If there is any right that is dear to the citizen, it is the right to keep and bear arms." Corbin also argued, first, that the Klan as a whole constituted a broad conspiracy to deter citizens from voting and, second, that its members had carried out a specific conspiracy to kill Williams for having exercised his right to vote. He recounted the details of the raid, led by the fugitive Dr. James Rufus Bratton, now in Canada, from the systematic seizure of guns from Williams's men through to the invasion of Williams's home, replete with open declarations in front of many of the participants that they were out to kill Williams and " 'all you damned niggers who vote the Radical ticket.' "

Several witnesses confessed to being on the raid, although they all insisted that they had been holding the murderers' horses in a thicket while Bratton led the group that attacked Williams. Klansman John Caldwell testified that afterward he had asked "the foremost man"—that is, Bratton—if he had "found the Negro." Bratton replied that he had. When Caldwell then asked, "Where is he?" Bratton answered, "He is in hell, I expect." Corbin argued that those who held the horses, as they claimed, or stood guard were no less guilty than Bratton. "If there are twelve men in the conspiracy when that conspiracy begins, they are in the eye of the law one man; they breathe one breath; they speak one voice; they wield one arm . . . the declarations of one of these twelve individuals, while in the pursuit of their unlawful purpose, is the act, the word, the declaration of all."

Corbin then offered a trenchant insight into how a terrorist group exploited mass psychology to control its own members. (That concept did not yet formally exist at the time, but Corbin understood the phenomenon clearly.) "Probably no one, no two, no three of that party could have been induced to commit murder; but under the cloak and sanction of that vast organization, the responsibility of crime was divided until it was not felt," said Corbin. "That is why these terrible combinations are made possible, because no man in that seventy felt that he, himself, had murdered Jim Williams." W. P. Burnett, a farmer, testified, "I was induced to join because they came to my house and told me if I didn't I'd have to pay five dollars and take fifty lashes. All the neighborhood were obliged to go." John Millar, a Republican, had initially resisted the Klan and even stored guns for members of the state militia, but had finally agreed to attend at least one Klan meeting. Daniel Carroll, another white Republican, testified that he had been obliged to join the Klan and take its oath in order "to protect myself and my colored hands." A store owner testified that he was told he would be shot if he didn't join the Klan. Twenty-three-year-old Andrew Cudd testified that "pretty much all" the members of his church had joined the Klan, and that his friends told him that he'd be flogged if he held back. Over and over, the turncoats told similar stories.

Mitchell's defense hinged almost entirely on the personality of the slain Williams and the question of what he intended to do with his militia. A white man named P. J. O'Connell described Williams as "a genuine, jovial, and good-hearted fellow" who had argued against retaliation for Klan persecutions. Even Williams's former owner, Julia Rainey, attested to Williams's good character; although his men were sometimes "boisterous," she said, she had never heard him make threats of any kind. Stanbery, however, portrayed Williams as a monster, "a dangerous character and a violent man" who was intimidating "an inoffensive community," and constantly drilling his men as if he were preparing them for war. He conjured up an imaginary alternative reality in which endangered whites were menaced by terrorist Blacks. "You cannot subject the white man to the absolute and uncontrolled dominion of an armed force of the colored race," he feverishly asserted. Speaking not of the Klan but of the militiamen, he posited, "A band of ruffians combine together to burn, pillage and murder all, from the cradle to the grave. Terror fills the whole region. It would be the worst sort of tyranny to prevent a freeman"—a white freeman, that is—"from defending himself against aggression" by a class whose interests, or supposed interests, it might be to wipe them off the face of the earth. Logically, Stanbery said, Williams could only have been killed in "self-defense" since whites feared being "Kukluxed" by the militia. Stanbery conceded that although the raid was "not absolutely legal," white men like Mitchell had felt a moral duty to take matters into their own hands. "It was such a duty as no man would shrink from." Following this, Stanbery turned to the ten Blacks on the jury and bluntly threatened them. He warned them not to "expect or desire to rule white men. If you go for anything like that your triumph will be short, and your doom inevitable."

The court's rulings were less decisive than either Corbin or Stanbery and Johnson had hoped for. Sustaining the defense's arguments, the judges ruled that the states, not the federal government, were responsible for protecting civil rights. They also ruled that the Fourteenth Amendment had not converted the original amendments into federal law, and that the Fifteenth Amendment had not, in fact, established a universal right to vote. The court declined to address the Second Amendment, or to rule on the constitutionality of the Enforcement Acts, leaving these questions to be considered by the U.S. Supreme Court, if they were willing to.

The court did uphold, however, Corbin's contention that the Klan could be prosecuted as a general conspiracy under the Enforcement Acts, and that a specific, prosecutable, conspiracy had existed to punish Amzi Rainey for voting. The court further ruled that to convict a Klansman it was enough to prove that the defendant belonged to a conspiratorial organization committed to preventing Blacks from voting. The judges also dismissed Stanbery's absurd proposition that voters could only be intimidated on Election Day. Finally, and significantly, they ruled that the Enforcement Acts applied to all elections, and that the federal government could take action if a state refused to protect a citizen's constitutional rights. These rulings at least provided the federal government with precedents that enabled its officers to successfully prosecute the Klan anywhere in the South. Coupled with Merrill's ongoing arrests, the trials crippled the Klan in upcountry South Carolina, and served notice that the Grant administration was both committed to a radically enlarged vision of civil rights and prepared to defend the freed people through the law and by force of arms if necessary.

The jurors convicted all of the Klansmen brought to trial. (Many defendants had by this time been severed and were carried over to the court's next term, however.) In its sentencing, the court's reasoning foreshadowed arguments that would be made in the war crimes trials of the twentieth century, essentially that "following orders" was no defense. Declared Bond, "It will not be taken as an excuse to hear it said: 'I slew this man because the chief ordered it, and I was afraid, and raped these others because I dreaded to be whipped if I did not.' You had no right, when you could escape, to make the price of your security the violation of your neighbor's."

Most of the men who had participated in only one or two raids and claimed to have committed no physical violence received light sentences. Robert Mitchell was sentenced to eighteen months in jail and a fine of $100, and John Millar, the reluctant Klansman, to three months in prison and a $20 fine. Klan leaders were treated more harshly. "Squire" Chambers Brown, a former magistrate, was sentenced to five years in federal prison and a $1,000 fine, a very hefty sum in 1871. "Those who were young and ignorant had a right to look to you for direction and advice," Bond told him. Bond particularly castigated John Mitchell, who received a similar sentence, because of his prominence in the community, yet "hearing of the ravishing, murders and whipping going on in York County, you never took any pains to inform anybody; you never went to the civil authorities, and you remained a chief until they elected somebody else."

In conclusion, Bond disgustedly declared, addressing the convicted Klansmen, and by extension the hundreds more who still faced trial, "What is quite as appalling to the court as the horrible nature of these offenses is the utter absence, on your part, and on the part of others who have made confession here, of any sense or feeling, that you have done anything very wrong. Some of your comrades recite the circumstances of a brutal, unprovoked murder, done by themselves, with as little apparent abhorrence as they would relate the incidents of a picnic, and you yourselves speak of the number of blows with a hickory, which you inflicted at midnight upon the lacerated, bleeding back of a defenseless woman, without so much as a blush of regret."

14

CONGRESS GOES SOUTH

I had to deny voting to save myself.

—LARRY WHITE, a freedman

Peering out from his photographs, Rep. Horace Maynard looks the part of a rough-hewn Tennessee mountaineer: lean and gimlet-eyed, gaunt, mustache drooping, thick, lank hair reaching almost to his shoulders. The impression is deceptive. Raised an abolitionist Yankee in Massachusetts, he was valedictorian of his class at Amherst College and moved to Knoxville to teach as a professor of mathematics and ancient languages until he was elected to Congress in 1856. Trained up in Tennessee's roughneck politics, he was famously caustic in debate and known to brawl with rivals on the campaign trail. He campaigned against secession in 1861 and when war broke out he left the state—along with Andrew Johnson and other prominent Tennessee Unionists—becoming one of the few southern members of Congress to remain in office. The price for his loyalty was the confiscation of his property and the harassment of his family, who fled north. He remained in exile until 1863, when federal troops liberated Knoxville.

Maynard dominated one of the two traveling subcommittees of the Joint Committee that Congress had formed to investigate the Klan. His fellow Republican members included Pennsylvania Rep. Glenni Scofield, a Radical and advocate for Black equality from rural Warren County, and Rep. William E. Lansing, a Republican attorney from central New York State. Both were backbenchers who had perhaps been appointed because more senior members resisted leaving Washington. The subcommittee's two Democrats had both been wartime Copperheads opposed to the Lincoln administration: Sen. Thomas F. Bayard of Delaware, the scion of a wealthy patrician family that had sent men to Congress since the 1790s, and Rep. Daniel W. Voorhees of Indiana, who was familiarly known by his supporters as "the tall sycamore of the Wabash" and stridently accused Republicans of ruining the states of the former Confederacy.

The subcommittee reached Atlanta on October 20 and took testimony until November 8, when they proceeded to Florida. Witnesses included public officials, military officers, professional men, white Republicans, and sixty-five freed people, both men and women—almost half the total number—surely the first time in history that Black Americans had ever testified in such numbers before a congressional committee. (Smaller numbers had testified before the committee in Washington and South Carolina.) The great majority of them had been enslaved less than a decade before. Some had been served with subpoenas to compel them to testify, but most came willingly, even eagerly, sometimes walking many miles from the hamlets where they lived, often at great risk, in order to tell their stories. They placed little confidence in local law enforcement, but these men from Washington had been sent, as they saw it, by President Grant in answer to their prayers. Their testimony was plain and direct. For the first time in their lives, they had the ear of powerful white men who wanted to hear what they had to say and would not harm them. They held little if anything back.

The presence of numbers of federal occupation troops ensured that the atmosphere around the hearings was safe and orderly. In an effort to protect those who testified, the hearings were closed to the public and the list of witnesses kept nominally secret, though many details seeped out. Partisan Democrats celebrated Bayard—"the best face we ever saw"—and Voorhees—"a noble-looking man"—with a "delightful entertainment" at the posh Kimball House, and cheered their "cordial speeches, full of good feeling to the South."

Whites hostile to the national government seethed: a local member of Congress, a Democrat, was heard to publicly curse the hearings and the witnesses alike, saying, "they ought to be driven away from here with a hickory, whipped off home, the whole damned kit and boodle of them."

Maynard was thorough. He usually led the interviews, except when a witness had been called by the Democratic minority, when he deferred to Bayard. After establishing the witness's background, questioning usually began with a standard script: What did witnesses know about the Ku Klux Klan? Had they suffered at the hands of men in disguise? How were they armed? Were they on horseback? What exactly had they done? How many participated? Could any of them be identified? (The terrorists were often their victims' nearest neighbors, employers, local farmers or storekeepers: witnesses recognized voices, horses, weapons, familiar articles of clothing. Often, in the throes of an attack, masks slipped off; trails were traced to local farms. In some cases, the attackers barely bothered to conceal their identity at all.) Witnesses of all types were also asked to assess the degree of fear that local freed people and Republicans felt, the safety of Black citizens when they tried to cast ballots, the reliability of law and order, whether the local authorities punished accused terrorists, the general attitudes of whites toward Blacks, and in the case of more conservative witnesses, their opinion of Republican Party government, taxation, and the truthfulness of Black witnesses.

M. V. Brand, the Republican-appointed sheriff of Gwinnett County, testified first. Maynard directed him to "state whether you know of any acts of lawlessness or violence attributed to organizations or bands of disguised men." Brand estimated that the Klan numbered between three and five hundred in the county, but "there is no chance to get at it exactly." He said, "We lost our courthouse on the night of the 10th of September last, and all our records were burned up," by "a party of men, shooting their pistols." Brand had tried to recruit a posse to pursue them, but he could find only one man willing to join him. All the rest were too frightened.

Maynard asked why the Ku-Klux would want to burn the courthouse. Because there were prosecutions of Klansmen pending,

Brand said. "They found they could not run off the witnesses for the state, and the only chance to keep off the prosecution was to burn the records."

Had people been injured by the Klan? "Yes, sir," said Brand, "a great many in our county, that is black people. The most of it has been done last year and this year; the worst part of it this year. They"—the Ku-Klux—"get worse all the time, get stronger. They get more of them, they ride more. About the time our courthouse was burned we heard of them riding almost every night in the week, going over the county and mistreating people."

Was there much support for the Klan among the county's whites? How could he tell? "Because they get so mad with everybody who has anything to do with trying to break it down. They are mad enough to cut my throat now because I am an officer trying to break down this thing. They say that they think it is a good thing," because, as one citizen told him, "the Ku-Klux were honester men than any men who passed the Ku-Klux law, or tried to carry out the law." The only local newspaper "come down pretty hard on us" when he tried to arrest anyone. "The civil authorities seem inclined not to touch them at all." Only one of Brand's deputies was able to serve warrants of any kind in the part of the county that was most infested with the Klan. But, he added, "The deputy does not do much arresting. He sort of leans to the other side."

Brand showed the subcommittee four statements from justices of the peace and notary publics declaring that they were too frightened to carry out their duties, having been threatened by the Klan and warned that they would be killed if they dared. "I hear flying reports every day that I shall be taken out and hung," he added.

Following Brand, Black witnesses from around the region described how they had been beaten or whipped because they were Republicans, belonged to the Union League, had urged men to vote, had "too much money," had outbid white men for property, had sued whites in court, or had simply "talked big." Mary Brown was attacked because Klansmen learned that she was prepared to testify in court against a member of the order who had murdered a federal revenue officer in her neighborhood. "They came up to the house with a dreadful noise. They just dragged me out in my night clothes. They threw me down on my face, stripped up my clothes over my head, and gave me about twenty-five licks." Joe Brown, her husband, testified, "They made all the women show their nakedness. They made them lie down, and they japed them with sticks and make them show their nakedness, and they made the little children show their nakedness, my mother-in-law and my sister-in-law, and my wife, and two little girls."

"Did they do any mischief to the children?" Maynard asked.

"They jabbed them with a stick, and went to playing with their backsides with a piece of fishing pole."

Caroline Smith, who fled her home in Walton County, said that men in false-faces "came to my house on Thursday night, and took us out and whipped us." One told me, " 'Take this off,' pointing to my dress. He whipped me some," then "gave me fifty more," and then said, "don't let's hear any big talk from you, and don't sass any white ladies." Maria Carter, from Haralson County, said that forty or fifty disguised men "came hollering and knocking at the door," then "busted both doors open" and ran in and whipped her husband, Jasper, "mightily." The next morning "his shoulder was almost like jelly." Sarah Ann Sturtevant said that five weeks earlier a mob of disguised men had kicked her in the head and given her "forty licks with a hickory: They said they had not heard I had done anything, but they wanted to give me a little 'shillala' for fear I would sauce white women." Letty Mills said that Klansmen had broken into her house in March, stripped her and her husband, Tobe, flogged them, hit them with pistols, and threatened to "mash" their four-year-old daughter unless she stopped crying. Sarah McCoy, a sixteen-year-old white girl, testified that white men with blackened faces broke into her home in Cherokee County, yelling that their father had no right to live there because he was "a Union man," stole the family's money, drove her and her sister into the yard during a sleet storm, set fire to their house, and shot their cow and mule. Jasper Carter, from Carroll County, said he'd been beaten because he had quit the white man he had worked for when he refused to pay him anything after a year and a half's labor. (Another witness said of Carter, "His head was beat all to pieces nearly.") A Black man with the surprising name of John C. Calhoun said that men who "had on white aprons, or sheets, or something with sleeves to it" was taken from his home, stripped naked, and flogged with "pine tops" for having talked casually to a white woman on the public road. Aury Jeter, a former slave who taught day classes for children and night classes for adult laborers, testified that masked men thrashed her and her husband in the middle of the night, and dragged their small daughter out of bed by the nape of the neck.

Henry Lowther, a Black farmer from Wilkinson County, described masked men breaking him out of jail, where he was being held on a trumped-up charge of organizing an armed company. They took him into a swamp, threw him on the ground, and castrated him, leaving him stark naked to hobble miles back to town, where he spent the night begging a doctor to treat him. Although Lowther maintained that he was punished for political activism, a Democratic witness—Rev. J. H. Caldwell, a district court judge—scoffed that Lowther was actually maimed for having sex with a white prostitute, a seemingly reasonable punishment in his eyes. In response to this, Maynard caustically asked the minister, "Have you ever heard of any white man being castrated for visiting low-down characters?" Admitted Caldwell, "No, sir."

G. B. Holcombe, a white man, said that disguised men came to his house and warned him that if he "wanted to live long and die happy" he had better not testify in court against one of their number. "I attended the court, and they waylaid me and killed a good horse from under me, and shot me through the leg as I returned from court." Solomon Woods, a Radical white farmer from Haralson County, said his neighbors Black and white were increasingly afraid to vote from fear of what might be done to them. "We are afraid that they will kill us. Because they know that we have come here" to testify. "The whole crowd that are with me are afraid they will be killed." J. R. Holliday, a white justice of the peace and until recently a lifelong Democrat, said the entire judicial system was riddled with Klansmen, including juries half comprised of Klansmen who were themselves nighttime raiders.

The subcommittee's Democrats made clear from the start that they had little interest in a probing investigation, and even less in listening to the complaints of Black men and women. Bayard, a large slaveowner before the war, disdainfully referred to them as "a very low class of Black people," pitifully dressed like "a set of scarecrows." He implied that people so hopelessly ignorant could hardly be trusted to give believable testimony, and repeatedly suggested that the alleged terrorists were probably just backcountry moonshiners settling scores with rivals or nosy neighbors. Voorhees further volunteered there was nothing unusual about the Klan's supposed "outrages." Rapes and lynchings could happen anywhere, even in his own state of Indiana. The *Atlanta Constitution* denounced the entire proceeding as a slanderous "inquisition" against "our people," and sneered venomously at the testimony of "dirty Negro girls" and others who had allegedly perjured themselves for pay.

The Democrats' witnesses consistently downplayed Klan violence. John D. Pope, the U.S. attorney for Georgia, although appointed by the federal government, seemed singularly passive when questioned about the prosecution of Klan crimes. Yet he gave away perhaps more than he intended. Questioned by Bayard, he said that he doubted anyone could be convicted for the attack on Henry Lowther, the castrated freedman, for example. Apart from the difficulty of identifying the perpetrators—the suspects all had alibis—"My experience is that upon the testimony of one man of his social position, in a case of that kind, a grand jury would hardly find a bill." It would require much stronger proof than it would if the position of the parties were reversed—that is, if the victim were white and the accused perpetrators Black, he said. "I suppose that would be true in any community. I think a great many men get off in this country that are guilty, but I suppose that is the case in all countries." Maynard seemed disgusted with Pope and asked if he could cite any case of violence perpetrated by the Klan that had resulted in conviction and punishment. Pope blandly replied, "I have heard that some were, but I do not know." Maynard then asked what information he could provide about the operations of the Klan. Pope added, astonishingly, using a formula typically employed by Klansmen and their enablers, "I know nothing except from hearsay" about such an organization, "if there is such a one."

Following Pope, Oliver Lyon, a former Union officer from Maryland and nominal Republican who was now a railroad contractor as well as an election supervisor, boasted that he was well informed about conditions everywhere in Georgia. He told the subcommittee with evident pride that far from suffering any kind of discrimination in Georgia, he had been introduced into the "best families" and had even married into one of them, proof to him that "northern men" were perfectly welcome in the state. Asked directly whether he believed there was any such organization as the Ku Klux Klan active in the state, he replied carefully, "That is rather a difficult question for me to answer. I have no knowledge of such an organization." Glenni Scofield, the Pennsylvania Radical, clearly exasperated with Lyon, exclaimed, "You have said that you have traveled everywhere over the state, that you have business connections with a great many men. Do you also give it as your opinion that there are no Ku-Klux in this state?"

"There are none to my knowledge, or that I have any idea of whatever," Lyon replied.

"Then," said Scofield, "you believe that the statements which have been made to us by witnesses here yesterday and this morning are fictions?"

Said Lyon, "I do not know anything about them at all."

While Maynard and his colleagues continued interviewing witnesses in Atlanta, the second subcommittee, headed by Sen. Daniel Pratt of Indiana, began taking testimony in Alabama, where they would interview forty-two freed people and a somewhat larger number of whites. They started in Huntsville, in the Tennessee River Valley, on October 6, followed by Montgomery, Demopolis, and Livingston, near the Mississippi state line. The fifty-eight-year-old Pratt, a lawyer with a reputation as a magnetic force in the courtroom, was rotund enough for it sometimes to be commented on by witnesses and clean-shaven in an era of notably hirsute politicos. His fellow Republican, Charles Buckley, was a thirty-six-year-old New York–born representative from Alabama, a graduate of Union Theological Seminary who had served as a chaplain for two Black regiments during the war. Of the subcommittee's two Democrats, Edward Rice, a first-term representative from Illinois, was far overshadowed by the combative Rep. Frank Blair of Missouri, the 1868 Democratic vice presidential candidate, who followed the same strategic playbook as Bayard did in Maynard's subcommittee, disparaging freed people as licentious and dishonest, belittling allegations of Klan terrorism, and complaining that the Democrats hadn't been allowed enough time to call as many witnesses as they wanted. (In fact, about half the witnesses were summoned by the

Democrats.) In the southern style, he often referred to Black witnesses, no matter what their age, as "boys," and at one point even defended a Democratic sheriff who tried to arrest a federal marshal and his troops for refusing to hand over a group of Klan prisoners. In a speech at Montgomery, he accused northerners of lacking sympathy for the South and compared "miserable carpetbaggers" to the hooligans who looted Chicago after the recent great fire that ravaged the city.

In striking contrast to the defeatist federal attorney in Georgia, John Pope, John A. Minnis, the U.S. attorney for northern Alabama, pulled no punches about the extent of Klan activity. "There is, no doubt, a very violent prejudice against Negroes with white men generally," he told the congressmen, "especially against their exercising any of the privileges that they consider belonging to white men, and among that class of men who never held any Negroes that prejudice is very violent." Minnis estimated that in one county at least forty and perhaps more than fifty Black men had been murdered over the previous two years. In another county, three-quarters of the Blacks had fled "to the Negro regions," where they felt marginally safer.

He went on to offer a list of representative outrages against the government's supporters, most of which had never been reported. "I think the laws themselves would be effectual if they were enforced, but I do not believe they can be enforced in many places, especially in cases of outrages against Negroes," he said. He cited a case in Jefferson County, where the county solicitor, a member of the Klan, had actually charged the Republican sheriff with "assault and battery" for arresting an alleged Klansman. Ku-Klux then forced the sheriff to move out of town for his own safety, ousted the deputy he left in charge, and refused to allow enforcement of any laws until a successor ceased serving warrants against the Klan.

Scores of Black witnesses trooped through the room in the county courthouse where the hearings were held. George Taylor, a Black preacher from Colbert County, said that although a Radical in sentiment he voted Democratic because "I thought [the Ku-Klux] wouldn't interfere with me," but they flogged him anyway and ordered him to abandon his home. When he asked what they were abusing him for, "They told me, 'It's none of your business.'"

William Henderson, a Black farmer, was beaten, pistol-whipped, tied up, and thrown out of a boat, to keep him from testifying in court against a white farmer and Klan leader who cheated him out of his share of a crop. George W. Houston, a Black former member of the state legislature, was assaulted in his home in Sumter County by Klansmen shouting, "God damn you, we are going to burn your God-damned house down on top of you, and your wife and children," because, he supposed, "They looked upon me as being the prominent Negro of the county." Henry Giles, a Black church deacon in Coosa County, told the subcommittee, "We run a mighty risk when we were going to the polls to vote" during the last election.

"What kind of risk?" asked Pratt.

"Why, we expected some of us to get killed on the way."

"Did anybody threaten you?"

"Yes, sir; all the time before the election and after the election," said Giles. "Because we voted the Republican ticket."

James Alston, the state representative from Macon County, said that he had fled for his life to Montgomery. "They told me that they were going to kill me, but if I would join the Ku-Klux they would spare my life." Otherwise, they said, he was going to be shot "to show me that a nigger couldn't hold no office in that county no longer, that a nigger wasn't fit for nothing else than to drive oxen, and the carriage of white folks." He would return to Macon County, he said, only when "I am protected by the thirteenth, fourteenth, and fifteenth amendments as a man amongst men."

Burton Long, who had been brought to Alabama before the war from Virginia by slave traders, said he had run for the legislature in Russell County but the white clerk closed the voting at midday and refused to open the polls again, claiming that he had run out of paper on which to register the Black voters who came in. "Judge Waddell, the leading man of the Democratic party," Long said, told him "that God Almighty never made a nigger to legislate for a white man, and he would be damned if I ever should do it." Shortly afterward, Long received a letter with two coffins drawn on it, and the words: "Ku-Klux, Ku-Klux: look out for death, hell, and judgment."

At Demopolis, Betsey Westbrook described Klansmen "busting open the back door" and shooting her husband, Robin, in the back with a double-barreled shotgun while he tried to fight them off with a fire-iron.

"What were they mad at your husband about?" Pratt asked.

Said Westbrook, "He would just hold up his head and say he was a strong Radical. He would hang on to that."

Eliza Lyon, from Choctaw County, testified that as many as seventy-five disguised men surrounded her home and carried off her husband, Abe, a blacksmith and outspoken Radical, into the nearby woods. "I believed there was colored people in it because they deliberately picked him up, and I thought no white man would pick up such a noble-looking man as he was—a large man, as large as that man sitting there," she said, pointing at the corpulent Senator Pratt. No white people, she said, would "lower themselves low enough to pick up a darkey." They shouted as they took him away, "We just want your damned heart." They shot him to death and then cut off his head. Asked if there had been a coroner's inquest, Lyon said that the doctor could not get anyone to attend. "Nobody put themselves to any trouble about it."

In Livingston, in Sumter County, Robert Fullerlove, a prosperous Black farmer, testified that he had been seized while on his way to meet the committee. "They punished me a great deal. They knocked me down with a gun, knocked me and took my stirrup leather, and broke off about half of the strap, the end that had the buckle to it, and they beat me scandalous." Fullerlove had been summoned to testify because disguised Klansmen had previously burned his house, shot his son, and tried to force him off the farm he owned. He had been living outdoors for the past six months for fear of being murdered. He was too frightened to return to his crops, farm, and herd of cattle, and now hoped only that he could raise the money to move to Kansas. "I love what I have worked and earned, but I declare I can't stay with no satisfaction."

John Childers said that a great many colored people now voted the Democratic ticket simply out of fear. "I voted it myself," he said. "When I was going to the polls there was a man standing in the door and says, 'Here comes you, God damn your soul, I have a coffin already made for you.' I had two tickets in my pocket then, a Democratic ticket and a Republican ticket. I pulled out the Democratic ticket and showed it to him, and he says, 'You are all right, go on.'"

Reuben Meredith, a white Republican, explained that he had been a candidate to the state legislature in the last election and tried to persuade Blacks in Gainesville to hand out tickets for him just before the election. "They told me they could not do it, for they were afraid." At several polling stations in Sumter County, he said, where at least two hundred Negroes had voted in previous elections, not a single Republican vote was tallied.

Wiley Hargrove, a one-legged freedman, testified that the previous winter disguised men had thrown him on the frozen ground, stripped him, and flogged him for voting Republican. "I voted it because I thought it was right," he told them. The leader of the attackers then said, "God damn you, we are going to let you know you were not right, and see we are going to give you hell to pay for it."

On November 6, Pratt's subcommittee traveled to Mississippi, beginning in the town of Macon. Witnesses, mainly from the northern part of the state, recounted the by now familiar but no less horrifying litany of floggings, shootings, hangings, rapes, church and school burnings, and violent evictions. Saunders Flint, a Black sharecropper, said that after he fell out with a white neighbor over the division of the season's crop, masked men took away his two sons, shot them in the face, and dumped their bodies in the Tombigbee River. Edward Carter, a Black teacher, testified that masked men had raided his home, raped his daughter, and driven him off his land. "Since I have left, they have taken everything I had and sold it, and I have nothing to go upon." Peter Cooper, another teacher, said that the Klan had raided his house, taken his money, destroyed his clothes, and burned all his books. Sarah Allen, a white schoolteacher from Illinois, said that men with horns affixed to their heads yelling "like Comanche Indians" swarmed into her room in the middle of the night and gave her two days to leave town, saying they wanted no northern people teaching in their county. Although she did not testify in person, several witnesses referred to the plight of Anna David, the extraordinarily brave white postmistress at Tupelo, the sister of the presiding elder of the Methodist Church and founder of a school for Black children, who repeatedly fended off at pistol-point Klansmen who tried to invade her home, and accused her of prostituting herself with Black men. William Coleman, a Black Radical, described how he was run off his land by men with "long, white cow-tails" hanging from their hoods who "busted the door open" and came in shooting. "Some had me by the legs and some by the arms and the neck and anywhere, just like hogs string out a coon, and they took me out to the big road before my gate and whipped me until I couldn't move." The man who flogged him kept telling him, "I'll learn you, God damn you, that you are a nigger, and not to be going about like you thought yourself a white man." They left him, he said, "as bloody as a hog that had been knocked down and stuck in a hog-pen and wallered in his own blood."

Joseph Davis, a Black farmhand in Monroe County, in northeastern Mississippi, where at least three to four hundred Klansmen were estimated to be active, admitted that he had been forced to "join" the Klan and to participate in its raids. "They asked me if I was in favor of Ku-Kluxing," Davis told the subcommittee. "I told them I was not; they said I was one of the strict Radicals, and for that reason they were going to force me to go with them." Davis was given a robe to put on, and along with two other similarly disguised Black men was carried along on a raid against a freedman name Henry Lewis, a local Republican leader and "a sort of teacher," dragged him from his wife's arms, and whipped him. White Klansmen then took him away. Davis said, "When they came back to where we were and the horses, they said they had cut his damned guts out." On the next raid, they ordered Davis to tie up a man named Aleck Page, "because he was a Republican man"; they "knocked him about right smart," then hanged him, and ordered Davis and the other Black men to dig a hole into which they dumped Page's body. On Davis's third raid, the Klansmen whipped several freedmen and told them to tell their friends that unless they voted the Democratic ticket in the next elections they would be "done" the same way.

Most of the witnesses called by the Democratic minority, as elsewhere, complained about having to pay taxes for free schools, particularly Black ones, dismissed Black witnesses as "trifling, unreliable, lazy," and praised accused Klansmen as law-abiding pillars of their communities. The most notorious minority witness was Samuel J. Gholson, the Democratic boss of Monroe County, who was widely assumed to also be the Klan's chief in the county and one of its state leaders. Few witnesses offered as clear a window into the thinking of those who led or defended the Klan. Gaunt, hollow-eyed, and long-bearded, Gholson, now sixty-three, served for more than twenty years as a federal judge before the war, when he resigned to join the Confederate army, eventually rising to become a major general. Despite losing a fortune in enslaved property with emancipation, he was still worth an astonishing $5 million in 1871. Gholson presented himself to the subcommittee as a reasonable, for-giving sort of man, telling them, "We came out of the war with great confidence in the Negro. We did not regard his emancipation as his fault or of his seeking." Until the Freedmen's Bureau came to Mississippi, "there never were two races of people agreeing better than we agreed with the Negro." They—"the Negroes I owned"—didn't want any laws "that did not give old master a fair chance."

He consistently blamed the murders of freed people on other Blacks: maybe they had accidentally shot themselves with their own guns, he suggested, or had been killed when they were masquer-ading as Ku-Klux in order to commit crimes. If anyone had been flogged it was probably because he was a "bad man." In any case, the violent "altercations" Republicans complained of were all purely personal matters that had nothing to do with elections or politics. One Black victim, he did concede, had been taken from a jail and lynched, but the man had stolen a hog and shot the white man it belonged to. The murder of Tobe Hutchinson, abducted by masked men on Election Day and never heard from again? "I have not heard of it," Gholson claimed. The persecuted postmistress, Miss Davis? Said Gholson, "She is universally understood to be one of easy vir-tue." If schools had closed, it was doubtless because the teachers hadn't been paid.

Gholson denied that he had ever talked to anyone he suspected of belonging to a secret organization. Nor had he ever heard anything more than rumors that such an organization existed. Although many of his clients were charged with Klan-related crimes, they had all "earnestly protested and sworn" that they were not guilty. It did appear, he allowed, that in 1867 or 1868 there had been some kind of organization that people called the Ku-Klux, but whatever it was, its members were "the best men in the country," and such men could never have engaged in whipping either Negroes or white men. Its only known purpose was "to promote the success of the white man."

Gholson tried, as all the Klan's mouthpieces did, to turn the charge of barbarism back against the federal government and its officers. In particular, he cited the actions of A. P. Huggins, who, acting in his capacity as a federal marshal, had led the search by a party of soldiers of the home of an accused Klan terrorist by the name of Bell. (The facts of the case were these: In the course of the search, a sergeant saw a human form hidden under bedclothes and ordered the person to show his face. When there was no reply, the sergeant peeled back the cover to find only the accused man's presumably frightened wife, Ada, and then left the room.) Said Gholson, Ada Bell's husband should have killed the sergeant who "insulted the ladies in their bedroom: in his place, I would hunt him up like a wolf."

Asked Pratt, with some surprise, "You [would] kill the man without hearing him?"

"Yes, sir, without hearing him," Gholson declared.

"That is the common law of Mississippi?"

"Yes, sir. That is the common law of the South." This, in Gholson's view, was evidently a moral clincher that brooked no further argument.

Under Pratt's persistent questioning, Gholson gradually revealed that he knew considerably more about the Klan than he had at first admitted. Although he continued to maintain that, in his opinion, there was no "united organization" active in Mississippi, he did finally admit that there were "neighborhood or spasmodic efforts of young men to do things they wanted to conceal that has brought about the outrages." He then allowed that there might be some coordination after all: that there might be, say, four "encampments" of supposed Ku-Klux in a county, and if one of them decreed that a certain person should be punished they could call on men from another county to carry it out. "That is the way I have heard it reported."

Pratt asked, would such men lie in court in order to protect their secrets? This was a freighted question, since Gholson was the most sought-after defender of accused Klan terrorists in court; he was lying through his own teeth to the committee.

Gholson finally said, as a matter of logic "that is a natural conclusion."

Pratt then went a step further. "Would there not be a double motive for them to prevaricate, first, to save themselves from the vengeance of associates, and next, to protect themselves from punishment for the outrages inflicted?"

"I think it might result in men's refusing to testify. When it came to such circumstances I should refuse to testify."

The Mississippi hearings concluded in the town of Columbus on November 17. Meanwhile, Horace Maynard's subcommittee had moved on to Florida, where it began taking testimony in Jacksonville on November 11. Demographically, Florida was the smallest and least settled of the former Confederate states, with only 187,000 residents, mostly scattered through the northern counties along the borders of Georgia and Alabama. (Georgia, by comparison, had 1,184,000 inhabitants, and Alabama nearly one million.) In much of this isolated and only lightly policed region, "Ku-Kluxing" took place openly, with no more than perfunctory disguises or rituals of membership, if any. But the patterns of violence were the same.

R. W. Cone, a white Republican carpenter, recounted being dragged from his home and flogged because he had served on a jury that took Black witnesses' evidence against a white defendant. Rebecca Kreminger described how on October 5 her husband, John, a Republican judge in Lafayette County, had been assassinated by a gunman just as he sat down on the veranda after his morning walk. B. F. Tidwell, a Republican judge who had served in the Confederate army, estimated that there had been at least twenty murders of Black men in thinly populated Madison County in the past two or three years by parties of "men not known." W. J. Purman, a white state senator from Jackson County, estimated that between twenty and twenty-five leading Republicans had been murdered, "all of our prominent political men—our best men." Richard Pousser, the Black constable in Jackson County, reported that a week earlier he had been beaten to the ground in broad daylight while attempting to arrest a white man, by local Democrats who damned him as a "Radical son of a bitch." J. C. Gibbs, a Pennsylvania-born and Dartmouth-educated Black man serving as Florida secretary of state, submitted a list of 153 homicides committed in Jackson County alone since the beginning of Reconstruction. E. G. Johnson, a white state senator from Columbia County, showed the committee a letter ordering him to resign his office, for "there is not a glimmer of hope left for you if you persist in your course of pretending to be elected."

The subcommittee's last witness before it returned to Washington was a forty-year-old blacksmith named Larry White, a former slave, who lived near the Klan-infested town of Marianna, in Jackson County. His testimony was a fitting capstone to the weeks of hearings across the South, delivered by hundreds of frightened but extraordinarily courageous voices. It grimly encapsulated what many thousands of others, both the heard and the unheard, the living and the now dead, had faced in their struggle to make real the rights they had been granted since the Civil War, and to simply stay alive in the face of the Klan's vengeful violence.

"I can see a heap of sign of people that they say the Ku-Klux have been afoul of," White said. "I have seen people killed, some run off, and some that were shot at. I have seen as many as three dead lying in one pile."

Maynard asked, "How do you stand on political questions?"

"I had to deny voting to save myself," White replied. "I said I would not do it anywhere, and after I said that they seemed to excuse me, and said, 'Old Larry is a good nigger, that old Larry took the right track.'"

"What induced you to do that?"

"When I went up to vote I saw so many stabbed and knocked down that day, and a great many shot at, that I thought I would take the easiest way I could."

What about legal protections, Maynard asked. "How is it when a man commits a crime there? Can he be punished?"

"It is according to who he is," said White. "I mean whether he be a white man or a black man. If he is a white man they don't punish him, but if he is a black man they punish him."

"Does not the sheriff try to arrest white men, too?"

"They will not let him. They tell him that he shall not arrest a white man for a damned nigger. If he is an honest man he will quit his office and go home, and some other man will take it."

"Do you think a colored man would be safe to vote the Radical ticket in that country now?"

"No, sir," said White. "It is against our interest to do it anymore, as long as a man wants his life, and I want to save myself as well as I can. He better have nothing to do with it, because if he does they will kill him certain."

"To whom do your people look to protect them?"

"We look to the government to protect us, but they are so slow to do it that we are all afraid to go back."

"What sort of men would you send, soldiers?"

"Yes, sir, and stop it, because we voted for them. I would not care who they were so they stopped them from killing. I have never offered to kill any man and I do not want any man to kill me."

15

THE KLAN AT BAY

This organization is now being broken up in every
part of the state and will soon be buried with the
institution of which it is but the offspring.

—G. C. WHARTON, U.S. Attorney

As the year neared its end, Ulysses Grant could take justified pride in the impending triumph of the campaign against the Klan. Judges and prosecutors in the South heaped praise on the forcefulness of his policy. From North Carolina, the crusading Judge Albion Tourgée reported to him that a grand jury had just indicted sixty-three Klansmen, including the murderers of the Black Republican leader Wyatt Outlaw, who had been lynched in front of the Alamance County courthouse in 1870. "Nothing, Mr. President but the prompt and unflinching firmness of your course in relation to this vexatious question could have rendered such a thing possible," Tourgée wrote. "To the state government, the KuKlux was an impregnable fortress. And so it would have remained until the end of time, had not your wise and patriotic course so frightened the adherents of the Invisible Empire that they began to desert in squads." And from Alabama, U.S. Attorney John Minnis reported that his grand jury had indicted sixty-seven men for "Ku Kluxing." He told Grant, "I think a vigorous prosecution in the courts can and will put them down. I am sure we have them now demoralized, and upon a routed retreat."

Heartening as such news was for the president, he was simultaneously beset by the Democrats, of course, who relentlessly attacked Reconstruction as unconstitutional and despotic, and also by vocal insurgents within his own party. Along with their attacks on Grant's war against the Klan, disaffected Republicans led by Carl Schurz claimed that pervasive official greed was fatally corrupting the party, and belittled Grant himself with scurrilous personal attacks; Senator Charles Sumner, second to none in his demonization, called Grant "an incubus and a mill-stone upon us." Schurz's Liberal Republicans fully expected either the mainstream Republicans or the Democrats to disintegrate like the bygone Whigs, and the even more short-lived Free-Soilers and Know-Nothings. As Schurz memorably put it, "Party! What more should it be than a mere engine to accomplish objects of public good?" If any of the Republicans' "vitality" could be salvaged, Grant must be defeated so that the party's "better element" could gain control. "Unless I greatly mistake the signs of the times, the superstition that Grant is the necessary man is rapidly giving way," Schurz wrote confidently to his ally Ohio governor Jacob Cox. "The spell is broken and we only have to push through the breach." Liberal organizations were springing up around the country, a happy sight for Democrats, out of power since 1860, who hoped to triumph in the 1872 elections. Since the previous spring, Schurz had begun meeting with prominent Democrats and building bridges to former Confederates in the South. Grant was also under siege from important segments of the press, most notably Horace Greeley's *New York Tribune,* which had once championed Blacks' rights but now echoed the most pernicious tropes of slavery's apologists, complaining that the administration had deprived of power the most intelligent men of the South and had systematically supplanted them with "ignorant, superstitious, semi-barbarians" who only yesterday had hoed the planters' fields and toiled in their kitchens. Greeley even endorsed the comments of a former Confederate secretary of state, Robert Toombs, who likened the freed people to the revolutionary Communards who had briefly seized power in Paris in 1871, an image that struck fear into the hearts of northern conservatives.

"These disaffections in our ranks of eminent men may work our ruin," one nervous Republican organizer in Massachusetts gloomily reflected. He was hardly alone. If Grant was worried, however, he never showed it, at least in public. In private, he could be blunt and brutal. "Mr. Sumner has been unreasonable, cowardly, slanderous, unblushing false," he wrote to Sen. Henry Wilson. "Schurz is an ungrateful man, a disorganize[r] by nature and one who can render much greater service to the party he does not belong to than the one he pretends to have an attachment for. The sooner he allies himself with our enemies openly, the better." Ignoring others' anxieties, Grant faced the coming year with the same cool stoicism with which he had waged war.

On December 4, Grant delivered his third State of the Union message to Congress. As was customary, it covered a range of issues. He announced a treaty between Britain and the United States to delineate the water boundary between the U.S. and Canada, reported that the nation continued to enjoy good relations with Japan ("the Mikado," as he referred to it), proposed reducing the size of the navy's officer corps while improving its ships and armament, announced that an expedition had been fitted out to explore "the unknown ocean of the North," reported that the national debt had been reduced to just over $86 million, promised improvements in the postal service, expressed hope that more Indians would soon settle down to farm, and called forcefully for legislation to punish Americans who owned or invested in slaves in Cuba. But the most significant part of his speech was devoted to the passage of the Ku Klux Klan Act, the suspension of habeas corpus in South Carolina, and the arrest of hundreds of members of the "combinations" that had been terrorizing American citizens. "The condition of the southern states is, unhappily, not such as all true patriotic citizens would like to see," he said. He condemned "social ostracism for opinion's sake" and urged the "old citizens" of the South to learn to "tolerate the same freedom of expression and ballot" for its new ones, the freedmen, that they themselves enjoyed. There would be, he promised, no slackening in the war against the Klan.

Then, eight days later, Grant fired the man who had so vigorously led that war, Attorney General Amos Akerman. The president cryptically informed him, "Circumstances convince me that a change in the office which you now hold is advisable, consulting the best interests of the government, and I therefore ask your resignation." Neither Grant nor Akerman ever explained just what those "circumstances" were. Grant praised Akerman's "zeal, integrity, and industry" in language that had the dull ring of administrative boilerplate. He also offered Akerman the choice of a federal judgeship in Florida or Texas, or a foreign diplomatic posting, none of which Akerman wanted, pleading his ignorance of foreign affairs, and a desire to return to Georgia.

After his weeks in South Carolina, Akerman had toiled through the daunting backlog of departmental business that had accumulated while he was away, not least a tide of prosecutions against the Tweed Ring's graft machine in New York. Akerman's preoccupation with the Klan had, if anything, only grown. Its atrocities caused him to reflect anew on the cruelties that had been perpetrated against starving Union prisoners at the Andersonville prison camp in his own state of Georgia. The same morally diseased mentality that had normalized those atrocities for southerners, he felt, now animated the Klan. Although he did not explicitly put it in such terms, he had briefly worn the Confederate uniform, and as a man of deep moral conviction he very likely felt a degree of personal guilt for the horrors that the Confederacy, and now its heirs, had wrought upon the helpless and defenseless.

His anguish irritated at least some other members of the cabinet. Secretary of State Hamilton Fish, a conservative Republican who had little patience with the plight of southern Republicans, Black or white, complained in his diary that Akerman "kept harping upon Democratic outrages in his section. He tells a number of stories, one of a fellow being castrated, with terribly minute and tedious details of each case. It has gotten to be a bore to listen twice a week to this sort of thing." Akerman could feel the chill. "I am chronically garrulous on the Ku-Klux, and therefore will force myself to stop," he wrote to a friend, a month before his dismissal.

To U.S. attorney Corbin, Akerman wrote on December 15, "you will by now have learned that I have resigned. The reasons for this step I could not detail fully without saying what perhaps ought not to be said." Akerman later diplomatically allowed that he did not wish to expose the president "to annoyance and perhaps censure and dislike of powerful interests," adding, "It is enough to contend against political opposition, but to be fighting for one's foothold against the machinations of professed friends is too hard a life." The historian Allan Nevins, who disliked Radical Reconstruction, blamed Akerman for annoying Grant by "always bringing up absurd questions," such as pressing him to interfere in Georgia state politics on behalf of his political friends there. It is also possible that Solicitor General Benjamin Bristow deliberately undermined Akerman in a vain hope of being appointed to replace him. Most historians hold that Akerman was actually forced out because he had run afoul of Jay Gould and other powerful moneymen by challenging vast land grants that Congress had made to the railroads they owned. Brief as his tenure was, as he prepared to return to Georgia, Akerman allowed himself a measure of optimism. To a friend in New York, he wrote, "I cannot but hope good results from the grapple which we are making with violent disloyalty in the South."

Grant, too, was optimistic. He encouragingly told a group of Black Baltimore churchmen that their people's civil rights were fast becoming recognized throughout the land: "It may be some little time before they enjoyed all the rights which belong to citizens," he said, "but that day is surely coming," and he hoped it would come soon. Almost daily, he received personal letters such as one from Georgia representative George Hooks, who wrote that "every few weeks these masked assassins ride as if your arms had never prevailed over this country." But he felt confident that the aggressive prosecutions that were under way across the South would soon break the back of the Klan.

Lewis Merrill, tough-minded as he was, felt a surge of hope, too. On January 30, the secretary of war directed Gen. Alfred Terry to put Merrill in command of all the troops in the Carolinas that had been committed to the campaign against the Klan. The exposure of the Klan's "revolting wickedness" and the imminent punishment of the worst perpetrators, Merrill felt, must give heart to "the better element" of the white community once they realized that they, too, had been freed from the Klan's domination. "Very many good men do exist here, who now for the first time are fully aware of the magnitude and number of the crimes, although they have long felt so strongly the social influence of the order"—that is, the Klan—"that few dared to speak of its crimes except in the most guarded tones." Yes, the motives that had ignited the Klan still existed. But with time, education, and effective government "the ignorance of the lower orders [of white men] and their servile obedience to the dictation of their social leaders" could be overcome. All the same, Merrill cautioned his superiors in Washington not to withdraw the occupation troops prematurely. "How long this must continue it is hard to say."

On February 19, John Scott of Pennsylvania rose from his desk in the Senate Chamber to formally deliver the mammoth report of the Joint Select Committee on Insurrectionary States—the Ku Klux Klan Committee—to the Senate. A bold-face headline on the front page of the *New York Times* blared:

THE KUKLUX KLAN HYENAS.

Report of the Select Committee
Of Congress.
When, How and Why the Secret
Order was Formed.
The Most Intelligent Negroes Selected
For Immolation.
Extension of the President's
Powers Recommended.
What the Minority of the Committee
Have to Say.

The report had been completed at breakneck speed, remarkable especially given that all the testimony it contained had been compiled in manuscript. (The typewriter would not be invented for another four years.) Forty-five thousand copies would be printed for distribution by members of Congress, very likely the largest single print run of a single investigation in history, to that point. Democratic senator Thomas Bayard sourly protested that the report was *too big,* that it had been dropped in the committee room "in proportions truly terrific to men who had something else to do than sit there probably for weeks or months before they could possibly read through that mass of manuscript. To point a man to a mountain of manuscript and say, 'Go through that by Saturday next,' would be as reasonable as to tell him to go to Europe and return in the course of three days." The Republicans, of course, wanted the report's conclusions disseminated well ahead of the November elections to galvanize the party's rank and file.

Democrats were desperate to discredit the report, or to at least diminish its importance. They leaked to the press an excerpt from a minority draft report, in which they wildly claimed that the committee's Republican majority had wrought "the grossest outrage, the foulest calumny, ever perpetrated upon or against a helpless people by their rulers." This was a peculiarly startling assertion since the committee's Democratic members, Bayard among them, had shown very little interest in the victims of the Klan's actual terrorism. They alleged that there had never even been any disguised bands in more than one-tenth of the South's counties, and that the Ku Klux Klan bill had been enacted only because Republican legislators feared to "disobey the orders of their imperious, not to say imperial president." During a stormy partisan debate in the House, sometimes as many as half the members were on their feet simultaneously shouting to be heard. Finally, Speaker James G. Blaine impatiently reminded the fulminating Democrats that the Republicans were under no obligation to indulge them: "Gentlemen seem to make the mistake of supposing that the minority and the majority have equal rights so far as making reports is concerned. Under the rules there is no such thing as a minority report." Chastened, the Democrats defensively agreed to temper their language.

Amos Akerman predicted that when the report was released it would horrify the entire North. Although the report's ultimate impact is hard to gauge, it landed upon the country like a cannonade. The *New York Herald,* the most widely read newspaper in the country and often unabashedly racist in its coverage of the South, declared unequivocally, "The existence of the Ku-Klux organization is no longer doubtful. It is the duty of the United States government to protect the colored race in those rights guaranteed to them by the Constitution." Less surprisingly, the pro-administration *New York Times* gave the report extensive positive coverage. An editorialist declared that if there was truth to white conservatives' accusations that southern legislatures suffered from rampant venality it was their own fault for shunning cooperation with "ignorant but honest" freedmen. Added the *Times,* the rights of a citizen could not be abrogated by whipping him, and "if he is ignorant he will not be educated by burning his schoolhouses." The *Times* particularly praised the effectiveness of the controversial suspension of habeas corpus in South Carolina, which had broken the Klan's wall of secrecy where nothing else could. To bring the Klan War to a successful conclusion, the *Times* made two recommendations: massively increase the staff of the federal judiciary to ensure that arrested Klansmen were promptly tried and properly punished, and offer amnesty to the rest of the Confederacy's former leaders. Of these, only the second would ever come fully to fruition.

This "removal of disabilities," as the common coinage of the time put it, was a knotty problem. The vast majority of former rebels had already been pardoned, but thousands of secessionist leaders, defecting onetime federal officeholders, Confederate politicians, and high-ranking military officers were still barred from holding state or national office. Restoring their full rights as U.S. citizens worked as a potent rallying cry for Democrats and increasingly for Liberal Republicans, who exploited the issue to leverage southern support. Just days before the release of the Joint Committee's report, Carl Schurz emotionally urged Republicans to stop blaming southerners for the past. The "late rebels," he pleaded, had suffered enough pain, degradation, and mortification—why continue to "torture their feelings"? The South's real problem now was no longer insurrection but the need for good government. It no longer made any sense to exclude the "more intelligent classes." In addition, he maintained, amnesty would benefit not just the abused whites, but the "colored people" too, by fostering warmer feelings between them and the former "master class." Indeed, he ventured, "Nothing better could happen to them." He tried, ultimately without success, to reassure his skeptical friend Sumner, "I know human nature and am not easily deceived. The great evil we have to overcome is that party spirit which has created a sort of terrorism to which but too many submit." The turn of phrase is startling. While Schurz dwelt on the metaphorical "terrorism" of the establishment Republicans toward rebellious members such as himself, he spared not a word for the actual, physical terrorism that was a daily fact of life for the freed people, which he had so presciently foretold in his report from the South six years earlier.

Schurz probably believed what he was saying. But he was also looking ahead with calculation to the presidential election. For months he had been trawling the South for allies. In Nashville, in September, speaking to an audience packed with former Confederates, he had praised the bravery of southern soldiers, called for an end to "carpetbagger rule," asserted that the protection of freedmen's rights was strictly a local responsibility, and claimed that central government was creeping toward "a monarchical police state." Southerners were of course thrilled to hear such language from the lips of one of the most influential Republicans in the country.

Sumner saw what Schurz chose not to: that once the Confederate chieftains were rehabilitated, they would soon regain office and purge Republicans from the southern state governments. To ensure that that would not happen, he set out single-handedly to destroy the amnesty bill with a poison pill: an amendment larded with civil rights measures that he knew the bill's Democratic sponsors could never swallow. The amendment stipulated that all citizens were entitled to the equal enjoyment of any accommodation, facility, or privilege upon common carriers—trains, omnibuses, ships—hotels, inns, theaters, and all other places of amusement, as well as schools, churches, cemeteries, and benevolent institutions. Violators would be subject to substantial fines and a minimum of thirty days in prison, for each offense. Moreover, every state and national law and regulation that discriminated by the use of the word "white" would be immediately repealed. "A measure that seeks to benefit only the former rebels and neglects the colored race does not deserve success," he argued. Although he supported amnesty in principle, Sumner was more doubtful than many other Republicans that it would win the loyalty of unreconstructed southern whites, much less ensure that the freed people—or northern Blacks, for that matter—were treated fairly and with dignity. He believed that society's compulsion to subjugate Blacks, even the most educated and urbane among them, was less a matter of economic policy than rooted in the deepest color prejudice, which would remain intractable until it was forced out by the arm of government.

During the "spicy debate" that followed, Democrats didn't bother to veil their Negrophobia behind high-minded platitudes. Senator Willard Saulsbury of Delaware charged that Sumner's amendment would break up his state's school system, invade the rights of white

citizens, and cripple their freedom to "regulate social intercourse."
He utterly refused, he declared, to "assist in striking down the race
to which I belong to a common level with the Negro population."
Reported the *New York Tribune,* "The Democrats ranged themselves
solidly on the side of proscription and caste, and refused to accept
the political rehabilitation of their Southern brethren if that measure of generosity must be bought at the price of equal rights."

The prospect of full civil rights made some Republicans nervous,
too. Joshua Hill, a Georgia Republican, who represented thousands
of Black voters, extolled segregation, saying, "When it pleased the
Creator of heaven and earth to make different races of men it was
His purpose to keep them distinct and separate. [I]n matters of pure
taste I cannot get away from the idea that I do them no injustice if
I separate them on some occasions." To this, Sumner retorted, the
question was not one of "taste or of social preferences: it is a stern,
austere, hard question of rights."

John Scott, who chaired the investigation into the Klan, weighed
in against amnesty, charging that it would, in effect, reward many
of the Klan's prominent enablers, such as former Confederate generals Wade Hampton and Matthew Calbraith Butler, who had raised
the money to defend the Klan's terrorists in South Carolina. Oliver Morton, an administration stalwart, caustically added that to
allow former Confederates to reenter high office would imply that
the war and its bloody aftermath was no more than "an honest difference of opinion."

When Sumner's amendment came up for a vote, the Liberal Republicans joined the Democrats in an effort to vote it down. In
February, they managed to muster twenty-eight votes, achieving
a tie, but it was broken in favor of the civil rights measure by Vice
President Colfax, certainly with the approval if not at the explicit
direction of President Grant. With the amendment attached, the
amnesty bill was now dead in the water, as Sumner had foreseen.
"Rather than accord the colored man equal rights, [the Democrats]
preferred to kill amnesty," reported the Republican *Columbia Union.*
Although the amnesty question would rise again and again, the vote
could be construed as a tactical victory for Grant, since it put most,
though not all, of the administration's supporters on record as supporting both civil rights and amnesty.

On April 19, Grant submitted to Congress his own eighty-three-page report on the crisis in the South, drawn from the Joint Committee's findings, his correspondence with Akerman, military officers—Lewis Merrill prominent among them—U.S. attorneys, state officials, detectives, and other sources. Couched though it was in the dry argot of officialdom, it was a document redolent of triumph and hope, rooted in Grant's confidence that if the Klan had not yet been wholly eradicated it was on the brink of decisive defeat. (Democrats, unsurprisingly, derided it as a demonstration of the president's "sleepless vindictiveness" and "an accumulation of deliberate exaggerations.") In its understatement and its reliance on simple facts rather than rhetoric, Grant's report was much like the man, methodically listing the victories achieved by federal attorneys and their mustered battalions of marshals, soldiers, detectives, and courageous freed people who risked their lives by the hundreds to testify against their tormentors in open court.

Although the Ku Klux Act had authorized the president to suspend habeas corpus anywhere, he had actually done so only in the nine counties of South Carolina. By throttling the Klan where it was most virulent, Grant hoped that Klansmen in other localities would be sufficiently frightened to disband or face similarly aggressive massive federal military retaliation. Elsewhere, responsibility fell to federal attorneys and marshals, who could, in principle, call on soldiers for help in making arrests, although the number of troops was small, sometimes vanishingly so, and their distribution uneven. Despite such limitations, the federal judiciary had been far more effective in the suppression and punishment of the Klan than the public generally realized. In 1871, the number of Enforcement Act prosecutions multiplied six times over the previous year. And in state after state, the Klan hemorrhaged members. Wrote a federal judge to his wife, "Everybody now wants to confess & we are picking out the top poppies only for trial."

D. H. Starbuck, the U.S. attorney for North Carolina, reported that 981 men had been indicted for violations of the Enforcement Acts, and another thirty-seven sentenced to punishments. G. Wiley Wells, the U.S. attorney for northern Mississippi, reported 488 indictments, and another two hundred arrested and bound over for trial. E. P. Jacobson, the U.S. attorney for Mississippi's Southern

District, listed 152 indictments, adding that the Enforcement Acts had for the first time made "evil-disposed persons sensible of a power capable of reaching them." G. C. Wharton, the U.S. attorney for Kentucky, reported that the Klan "is now being broken up in every part of the state, and will soon be buried with the institution of which it is but the offspring." U.S. attorney C. T. Garland, based in Austin, Texas, wrote optimistically, "It cannot be long before all lawlessness and violence growing out of political differences, radical antagonisms, and social distinctions will be a thing of the past."

The U.S. attorney for South Carolina, David Corbin, provided the most detailed report of all. He listed 220 men who had confessed in open court to Klan-related crimes, their names and violations filling three pages of small, closely spaced type. Five more pages listed 281 more who had been arrested but not yet indicted, many of them now in jail, others released on their own recognizance. He further identified ninety-two separate conspiracies, among them twelve men charged with participating in the raid against the militia captain Jim Williams and another fifteen for direct participation in his murder. Others, in groups of anywhere from three to forty-six, were charged with crimes ranging from intimidation of witnesses, to rape, shooting, and beating, to violation of Blacks' Second Amendment right to bear arms, to a raid on the York County treasury. It was clear, he said, that the prosecutions already completed and under way had wrought a demoralizing effect upon the Klan in the state's upcountry.

There was evidence to support him. Following the first Klan trials in South Carolina, the Republican *Columbia Union* struck a triumphalist note, urging South Carolina's reactionaries to face racial reality: "It is a fact that the blacks are here—nearly five millions of them—and are not going away. It is a fact that they are free and cannot be reenslaved. You might as well attempt to recover the dew of last Fourth of July morning as to reenslave these five millions." Even the conservative *Yorkville Enquirer* pleaded for peace. "That the prosperity of the country is injured by the late difficulties cannot be truthfully denied," it editorialized in January. "It is in the interest of every man, woman, and child to live orderly and subject to the laws and live an orderly and upright life. This God requires—nay commands it. By obeying the laws of the land we do not understand that an individual endorses or approves of all of them in all their bearings, any more than our Savior endorsed the government of Rome." But, under the circumstances, He regarded it "as his duty and the duty of his disciples."

The state's second set of Klan trials began on April 13. While bitter Democrats roared that the trials had been "engineered by paid pimps, spies, and informers," and denounced the humiliation of "respectable men" by a "mock jury" and a "corrupt judge," Black Charlestonians packed the federal courthouse on Meeting Street, marveling at the sight of shackled white men facing punishment for abusing Blacks, something that no one in South Carolina even remotely imagined only a few years before. A parade of Klansmen and witnesses testified about their roles in the murders of the Black Republican leaders Thomas Roundtree and Jim Williams. Gadsden Steele, a Black man, testified that the night riders had forced him to accompany them partway to Jim Williams's house; Rosa Williams, Jim's wife, that she had heard Jim choking as they dragged him from their home; Andy Timms, a Black man, that he had seen Williams's corpse hanging from a pine tree. Damon Mosley matter-of-factly described how he had climbed up a tree and secured the ropes where Black prisoners seized from the Unionville jail were hanged. The prisoners' attorney, who was known by his Confederate rank as "Colonel" Hamilton, denounced as sheer slander the suggestion that "intelligent, virtuous" white people of South Carolina approved of murder and whipping. He attempted to generate sympathy by describing the "desolate and ruined cabins" of the arrested men, and the melancholy home of the eminent Dr. James Bratton—the ringleader of Williams's killers, now fled to Canada—where his wife now wept alone, "as innocent as any member of the jury."

On May 3, the presiding judge, Hugh Lennox Bond, handed down sentences ranging from one month and a $10 fine for the smallest fry to ten years in the federal penitentiary at Albany, New York, and a $1,000 fine for the most prominent defendants. Barely a year earlier, the Klan in South Carolina had seemed beyond reach, impervious to prosecution, poised to overwhelm the state authorities. No longer. This was news to hearten Republicans, certainly, but also all Americans who feared that great swaths of the nation had fallen into the hands of vicious men who held the rules of democratic government in contempt and were bent on reversing the political verdict of the Civil War. Bond was disgusted: few of the prisoners had even expressed shame at what they had done. Slavery, he had come to feel, had infected all of southern society like a disease, breeding a morally corrosive tolerance for the most sadistic brutality and human degradation. To his wife, he wrote, "I do not believe that any province in China has less to do with Christian civilization than many parts of this state."

Outside South Carolina, news of the trials was overwhelmed, however, by the reports from Cincinnati, where the Liberal Republicans were meeting in convention to nominate a candidate to challenge Grant in November. The infant party had an abundance of eminent men to choose from. Illinois senator Lyman Trumbull, the author of the Thirteenth Amendment, had pursued an independent course since breaking with the Republicans in 1868 to vote against the impeachment of Andrew Johnson. The scholarly Charles Francis Adams Sr. was the son of John Quincy Adams, the grandson of John Adams, a founder of the Republican Party, the wartime ambassador to Britain, and a favorite of intellectuals, including Carl Schurz, the party's primary driving engine. Missouri governor B. Gratz Brown had an unimpeachable antislavery résumé and a significant following in the western states, although a testy relationship with Schurz. Some favored Supreme Court chief justice Salmon P. Chase, others Supreme Court associate justice David Davis, Ohio governor Jacob Cox, or former Pennsylvania governor John Curtin. The colorful Horace Greeley, though a dark horse, was one of the most famous men in America as the editor of the influential *New York Tribune*. Sumner would have been a major contender: he despised Grant and shared the Liberal Republicans' aspirations for government reform, but he was reluctant to commit himself to a movement that slighted the cause of civil rights, his chief concern. Schurz himself was of course ineligible, being foreign-born. But as chairman of the convention, he was well positioned to dominate the selection, if he chose to.

To wild cheers from more than a thousand delegates, rather heavily weighted with New Yorkers and Missourians, Schurz attacked the Grant administration's "tyrannical insolence," its "wanton disregard of the laws of the land," and its "reckless and greedy party spirit." The Liberal Republicans, the party of "superior intelligence, coupled with superior virtue," he soaringly declared, "defiantly set our sense of duty against the arrogance of power, like the bugle blast of doomsday. We can crush corruption in our public concerns; we can give the Republic a pure and honest government; we can revive the authority of the laws; we can restore to full value the Constitutional safeguard of our liberties; we can infuse a higher moral spirit into our political life; we can reanimate in the hearts of the whole people in every section of the land a fraternal and proud national feeling."

The party's strongest ticket, the one that most observers expected to be named, would pair Adams and Trumbull, both widely respected as serious men who had served prominently for decades in public life. So sure was Schurz of the outcome that, rather than advocate for them, he left the choice to the convention. This was in keeping with his faith in the goodwill of like-minded reformers, but it was strategically inept. Adams, wishing to remain above the "dirt of electioneering," waited in dignified silence at his home in Massachusetts with the expectation that he would be acclaimed by a swell of popular support. In the event, however, the convention slipped from Schurz's control. Behind the scenes, Horace Greeley's New York operatives had cut a deal with Gratz Brown, who unexpectedly endorsed the editor and agreed to accept the party's vice presidential slot. After five seesawing ballots, Greeley finally prevailed on the sixth as delegates whooped, swore, stamped their feet, tossed their hats in the air, and "hurled anathemas" at the architects of the bargain. Schurz was stunned. He complained that not only had the convention selected the weakest of all the candidates, but the whole Liberal Republican project had been "stripped of its higher moral character and dragged down to the level of an ordinary political operation."

Greeley was indeed a problematic choice. His political ambitions were no secret. A lifelong abolitionist and early advocate for a hard-war policy against the Confederacy, before the war's end he had embraced schemes for a negotiated peace, and now urged conciliation with the South at the expense of the freed people. He had contributed 25 percent of the bail bond that freed Jefferson Davis from prison, and he shrugged at Grant's effort to protect freed people, dismissing them as "an easy, worthless race." His opposition to free trade and support for protectionism cut against the grain of the great majority of Liberal Republicans, and he had little interest in civil service reform, which Schurz and others saw as the great emerging issue of the future. Democrats could not forget that Greeley had always been a foe of their party. Many others were put off by his "interminable political wobblings" and his enthusiasm for then-fringe movements such as vegetarianism, temperance, and women's rights. "There is no department of business which he would not disorganize and unsettle; there is no wild 'ism' which he would not endeavor to incorporate into the framework of our government," the *New York Times* warned. Grant remarked of him, "Mr. Greeley is simply a disappointed man at not being estimated by others at the same value he places upon himself. He is a genius without common sense."

Of arguably more consequence than Greeley's personality was the party's platform. It accused the administration of "wanton disregard" for the laws of the land, the advancement of notoriously "unworthy" men, and "tyrannically" interfering in the affairs of the states. It called, of course, for civil service reform—"a most pressing necessity," a return to hard money policy, maintenance of the public credit, tax reform, and an end to the giveaway of public lands in the West to railroads. Notably, however, it made no mention at all of the embattled southern Republicans or of the freed people and their rights. Instead, echoing the Democrats' party line, calling for universal amnesty, it blamed the administration for keeping "alive the passions and resentments of the late civil war" for partisan advantage rather than "appealing to the better instincts and latent patriotism of the southern people" by restoring *them* to their rights.

How the party would fare in the coming presidential election remained to be seen. Its leaders still hoped to craft an alliance with the Democrats, though Greeley's presence at the head of the ticket made that less likely. Many Democrats believed that the Republican Party had suffered a decisive split, ensuring the election of their candidate, whoever he might be. However, the chaos in Cincinnati and the mockery that dogged Greeley masked the significance of the transformation that the Liberal Republicans were fostering, if not entirely creating, in both the Republican Party and in the nation at large. They had set the terms of the campaign to come by weakening confidence in the president and giving impetus to already waning public support for the Klan War and the weak Republican governments in the South. The rhetoric of the Liberal Republicans was already the language of the party's intellectual elite: they were telling Americans that they could abandon Reconstruction and the freed people in good conscience.

RECESSIONAL

16

THE COURT WEIGHS IN

I am still a Radical in principle, but I have
tried to be a conservative in working.

—CHIEF JUSTICE SALMON P. CHASE

By the spring of 1872, Ulysses Grant's renomination for a second term was assured. His putative rivals within the mainstream Republican Party had faded, although his enemies continued to launch wounding Parthian shots even as their hope of stopping his renomination died. Sumner, for one, feverishly tried to implicate him in a corrupt international arms deal, then promptly sailed for Europe, where he sat out the rest of the campaign. The party's convention, the shortest in American history, belonged entirely to Grant. It lasted just six roaring, sweaty hours spread over two days, on June 5 and 6, beneath glaring gas lamps and plagued by terrible acoustics, packed into the Academy of Music in Philadelphia, its deliberations tapped out by telegraph operators to newspapers around the country in the first gavel-to-gavel convention coverage in American history.

It was also the first national party convention in which Black men participated as both speakers and leaders of state delegations. Delegates of both races rose en masse to sing "John Brown's Body" and "Marching Through Georgia," after which a white delegate from the Montana Territory called for three cheers "for those loyal Black men who stood by us during that march through Georgia to the sea." Rep. Robert Elliott of South Carolina grandly pledged to

Grant the "earnest cooperation of the nine hundred thousand voters of our race." James D. Lynch, Mississippi's secretary of state, proclaimed that Black southerners looked to the Republican Party "as our political parent—we are born of them." He went on to memorably mock the Democratic Party in an elaborately ghoulish metaphor as a corpse left to rot in the summer heat "with its great cloven feet stuck out in the waters of the Gulf . . . one of its cold, clammy, bony hands grasps the Pacific and the other the Atlantic, and the stinking carcass emits an odor that breeds disease." Grant, Lynch promised, would "dig a grave so wide and deep, and bury it so it will never more be resuscitated." (Lynch also voiced a striking confluence of Black aspirations and imperial ambition, proclaiming that the United States must absorb Mexico, Central America, and the West Indies, asserting that neither the "underdeveloped resources" of those regions nor "the purposes of American civilization" could be achieved "without the black man's muscle.")

Other speakers ran the gamut of the party's core supporters. Oliver P. Morton of Indiana, Grant's staunchest ally in the U.S. Senate, declared that it was the party's job to secure the rights of "the colored men" throughout the country—a mission that could not be accomplished as long as any trace of the Ku Klux Klan survived. The abolitionist Gerrit Smith, at seventy-five a hulking if controversial spirit of the party's heroic prewar era, when he helped finance the Underground Railroad and John Brown's Harpers Ferry raid, boomed that if given more time Grant would "crush out Ku-Kluxism and save the negro." To thunderous applause, he cried that "the antislavery battle will not be fought out so long as a single man in this land is deprived of one single solitary right on account of his color." Representing beleaguered southern Republicans, a Texan named George W. Carter—"not very handsome to look upon, being bleached as to hair and freckled as to skin," the *New York Herald* snidely grumbled—described himself to loud friendly laughter as "an old Confederate soldier" who had "been pretty thoroughly reconstructed," and predicted that even southern *Democrats* would vote for Grant over Greeley.

When the president's name was put in nomination an enormous drop curtain unfurled to reveal a painting of Grant in uniform, saber at his side, riding toward a fortress by the sea. The entire body of four thousand rose and roared as "deafening cheers shook the old walls of the Academy," the *Herald* reported. "A perfect wilderness of hats, caps, and handkerchiefs waved to and fro in the surging masses. The band waved their instruments as though they had been flags," and then struck up "Hail to the Chief." Grant, of course, was not there to hear it. In that era, custom decreed that a candidate never appear in person at his party's convention. When he learned the news in Washington, Grant climbed into his carriage and drove in solitude through the capital city's empty outskirts, perhaps reflecting on the extraordinary arc of a life that over a single decade had carried him from embarrassed obscurity to the highest office in the nation. When, a few days later, a Republican delegation met him in the President's Room at the Capitol to present the party's formal endorsement, he promised to bring "the same zeal and devotion" to his second term as he had to his first, and humbly expressed his hope that "past experience may guide me in avoiding mistakes inevitable with novices in all professions."

The convention's only suspense centered on the party's choice for vice president. The sitting VP, Schuyler Colfax, had run afoul of Grant loyalists for hinting that he might challenge Grant for the presidency, and of reformers for his alleged connection with shady financial deals. When it came to a vote, Colfax was overwhelmed by the Massachusetts Radical, Sen. Henry Wilson, chairman of the Armed Forces Committee and a hardliner on Reconstruction. Wilson would shore up support for Grant in New England as well as among southern Radicals of both races and with white laboring men, who admired Wilson as a self-made man who had begun his working life as a shoemaker. (Newspapers catchily dubbed the ticket a partnership of "the Galena Tanner" and "the Natick Cobbler.")

In their platform, the Republicans rightly pointed to a record of important accomplishments under Grant's leadership. The president could credibly claim that he had broken the back of the Ku Klux Klan. The army, the Enforcement Acts, and the suspension of habeas corpus in South Carolina had shown his commitment to furthering the political revolution that was taking place in the South. The Transcontinental Railroad had been completed, vast tracts of public lands provided free to western settlers, and taxes lowered. A policy of peacemaking had been launched with the Native tribes of the West. A uniform national currency had been established, public credit strengthened, and the national debt reduced at the rate of $100 million a year. Relations with foreign nations were stable. The platform also, notably if vaguely, praised the entry of women into "wider fields of usefulness," a verbal landmark for the aspirations of the feminist movement. Significantly, the platform also strategically co-opted key parts of the Liberal Republican agenda by embracing the principle of civil service reform and full amnesty for former Confederates.

While the convention's noisy celebration of Blacks' expanding political role seemed to herald a new era, the platform was surprisingly terse on what had to be done to prevent interference with the freed people's civil liberties. Certainly, to its credit, it called for "exact equality" in all political, civil, and public rights. But it referred to the Ku Klux Klan only obliquely, in the thirteenth of its nineteen planks, where it praised the administration for its "suppression of violent and treasonable organizations in certain lately rebellious regions, and for the protection of the ballot box." Concerned Blacks noted that no plank explicitly promised more troops to fight the Klan or the suspension of habeas corpus in any other states.

It was a moment of surging confidence for Republicans. Grant's hard-handed approach in South Carolina had paid off. Klan attacks had diminished in much of the South. Wrote Frederick Douglass, "Peace has come to many places as never before." Sen. Adelbert Ames of Mississippi, who before the passage of the Enforcement Act warned that the Klan had been found in every county of the state, now reported that the recent convictions of Klansmen in the Carolinas "has had a very subduing effect." True, soldiers hunting Klansmen continued to face sometimes tenacious resistance, and federal marshals continued to receive death threats. In Chickasaw County, Mississippi, a local sheriff had even attempted to arrest a marshal and the soldiers with him after they served warrants on several alleged Klansmen, charging that the "Yankees" were violating the Ku Klux Klan Act by illegally seizing *white* civilians. But for the first time in almost four years, there was reason to hope that the Klan would soon be gone for good.

Southern Republicans felt less sanguine about the future than northern colleagues further removed from the towns and hamlets of the Deep South. Joe Crews, for one, the Republican boss of Laurens County, South Carolina, wrote directly to Grant, asking for more federal troops, "so that I could return and conduct the present political canvass with safety for myself and my party." Before leaving office, Amos Akerman had warned his southern friends against complacency. He cautioned them that it was becoming harder to win public sympathy for racial issues, and that they should not always expect Washington to save them. "Very many of the Northern Republicans shrink from any further special legislation in regard to the South," he prophetically told Georgia's soon-to-be-unseated Republican governor Benjamin Conley. "Even such atrocities as KuKluxery do not hold their attention as long and as earnestly as we should expect. The northern mind being active and full of what is called progress runs away from the past."

To succeed Akerman, Grant named former senator George H. Williams of Oregon, an administration stalwart, the first cabinet appointee from the fast-developing West Coast, an asset that weighed strongly in his favor for political reasons. In contrast to the self-contained Akerman, Williams—a handsome man with classically symmetrical features framed by thickets of muttonchop whiskers—was a man about town, though less notoriously so than his louche young wife. (Williams's appointment, one gossipy administration man wrote to another, "sectionally may strengthen the administration, sexually also for all I know, & if half that has been said, is true.") With respect to the war against the Klan, Williams seemed a solid choice. Although a Democrat before the war, he had opposed slavery and after becoming a Republican had lent his ardent support to Reconstruction. He urged federal attorneys to act forcefully against the Klan, and promised to vigorously prosecute "every conspiracy against the peace of society and the safety of the unoffending citizens."

Williams overestimated the resources at his command, however. Not only the army was spread thin. So were the federal court officers who were responsible for processing and prosecuting the growing glut of Klan prisoners. While Congress had enacted a battery of strong anti-Klan laws, it failed to appropriate the money to fully enforce them. Apart from upcountry South Carolina where the temporary suspension of habeas corpus placed police power in the hands of Major Merrill and the Seventh Cavalry, federal law enforcement in the former Confederate states depended on an astonishingly small corps of overstretched and under-resourced Justice Department attorneys and their assistants.

The very success of the administration's campaign inexorably produced a new crisis, one which only Akerman seems to have clearly foreseen: the logistical challenge of trying the exploding number of prisoners. "Suppose that we have from five thousand to ten thousand cases (and I have no doubt that at least the former number and perhaps the latter could be brought to light) we have the judicial force to try only a small fraction of the number," the former attorney general had written in November. However, since its creation two years before, the Justice Department remained ill-equipped to prosecute the thousands of Klansmen already indicted, much less the even greater numbers that were turning themselves in and being rounded up. Just sixteen of the department's fifty-five U.S. attorneys were assigned to the former Confederacy. In South Carolina, it had taken more than a month to try just five men, at a cost to the federal government of $200 per hour. Even if more attorneys were available, the multiplied expense of processing hundreds or thousands more Klansmen would be astronomical. Williams, like Grant, was under heavy pressure to rein in expenditures. The department's appropriation of $2 million for fiscal 1872 had been increased by another $1.2 million just before the year ended, but it still fell short of what was needed by hundreds of thousands of dollars. Some officers were reportedly reduced to subsidizing court expenses out of their own pockets. Williams even told a Mississippi prosecutor who asked for money to retain a court stenographer that too many had already been hired in the Carolinas and the department couldn't afford any more.

Financial stress had been inadvertently baked into the department's basic structure. Traditionally, attorneys general had hired outside counsel as needed, a costly policy that ballooned out of control as the federal government expanded during the Civil War. When the department was formed, such ad hoc hiring was sharply curtailed as part of the broader, politically popular, effort to shrink government and reduce the federal budget. In a time of greater stability this might have made sense. But now it severely hobbled the attorney general's ability to take on new Klan-related work. The obvious solution was simply to increase the department's staff and budget. However, Grant was now campaigning for reelection on the Republican platform's promise to reduce the nation's war debt even more. There would be no budget increase.

The odor of retrenchment was in the political wind. Prosecutors were increasingly forced to choose between efficiency and convictions. G. Wiley Wells, the federal attorney for northern Mississippi, had, for instance, charged no fewer than twenty-eight Klansmen for invading the home of a Black Republican activist, Aleck Page, and cruelly killing him. In formal terms, the indictment alleged that the defendants had conspired to deny Page his constitutional guarantees of life and liberty, and his freedom from unreasonable search and seizure. The Klansmen's attorneys, predictably, argued that the Klansmen were in effect being unconstitutionally accused of murder, a state offense. (They also maintained, as the defendants' well-coached wives and sisters piously testified, that all the supposed perpetrators were quietly at home with their families when Page was killed.) Wells made a calculated decision. He had plenty of witnesses, but they were all poor and Black; the defendants' witnesses were all white and notables in the community. Winning convictions would mean a long and costly trial, with no certainty that he would prevail. With the agreement of Attorney General Williams, Wells plea-bargained the charges down to merely conspiring to deprive Page of his liberty. The defendants pled guilty, and the judge fined the Klansman $25 each and required them to post a $1,000 "peace bond" to ensure their good behavior for a period of two years. Statistically, the result counted as a conviction. But it was a poor substitute for a verdict of political murder. It would also serve as a template for leniency that would stand for decades to come in Mississippi trials of white men charged with crimes against Blacks, when they were tried at all.

The courts' worsening bottleneck may have seemed abstract to budget-conscious legislators in Washington. But to those on the front lines of the Klan War the long-term consequences were obvious. Pro-Klan newspapers predicted—accurately enough—that the federal courts would be overwhelmed, that prosecutions would have to be abandoned wholesale, and that few if any prisoners would ultimately be punished. Maj. Lewis Merrill also understood what was at stake. He warned Williams that unless punishment for terrorism was swift and severe the government would look weak, and Klansmen would "naturally construe their immunity from prosecution and punishment into license to do the like again."

Radicals who hoped for support from the Supreme Court hoped in vain. They had at one time looked to Chief Justice Salmon P. Chase as a critical ally: after all, he was one of them. A highly political abolitionist and lifelong advocate for Black Americans, he had once been known in Ohio politics as "the attorney general for fugitive slaves." To the chagrin of the Radicals, he now showed himself more committed to restoring the Court's oversight of the executive branch, which had largely lapsed during the war, than to validating the constitutionality of Reconstruction laws. In ill health, preoccupied with personal anxieties, and drifting toward the Democratic Party, he was a weakening hand on the judicial tiller. He was, he admitted, "still a Radical in principle, but I have tried to be a conservative in working." Although Republicans formed a majority on the Court, most members' commitment to Reconstruction was lukewarm at best.

Grant and Williams, like Akerman before him, based the legal framework of the Klan War on their conviction that the postwar constitutional amendments, the 1866 Civil Rights Act, and the Enforcement Acts firmly secured federal authority to supersede state courts in defense of civil rights. The Klan's defenders rooted their objections in the soil of states' rights ideology, insisting that Klan crimes—if they were crimes at all—fell under the purview of state law, and that federal attempts to prosecute them amounted to unconstitutional overreach. With Klansmen's lawyers challenging the authority of the federal government to prosecute their clients, and federal attorneys impatient for rulings that would sustain their prosecutions, it was inevitable that the colliding principles of constitutional law would sooner or later be tested. In the spring of 1872, that time had finally come, or so it initially seemed.

The first real test of Grant's policy had its roots in an event that had taken place almost four years before, in Kentucky. In the summer of 1868, two axe-wielding white men, John Blyew and George

Kennard, hacked to death a Black married couple, Jack and Sallie Foster, their sixteen-year-old son, Richard, and Jack's blind ninety-year-old grandmother. The Fosters' two young daughters were also cruelly injured but survived. Richard lived long enough to identify the murderers, who were not disguised. It is not known if the men were acting as members of the then still infant Ku Klux Klan.

Although a slave state that had provided thousands of men to the Confederate armies, Kentucky had officially remained loyal to the Union and was thus not subject to Reconstruction legislation. If anything, pro-southern sentiment increased *after* the Civil War, as the state's slaves were freed and enfranchised, and threatened white control of localities where Blacks were in the majority. The Ku Klux Klan spread early into the state, where, as it did elsewhere, it harassed vulnerable Blacks, isolated Republicans, and Union Army veterans. Troops under Col. George Armstrong Custer—a conservative Democrat—sometimes chased white terrorists, with comparatively little effect, even as the Klan devolved locally into what federal detectives determined was increasingly a criminal operation that specialized in moonshining, counterfeiting, and protection rackets.

Under Kentucky law, Blacks were still barred from testifying against whites in court, thus excluding Richard Foster's death-bed testimony and that of his maimed and traumatized daughters. Unpunished by the state courts, Blyew and Kennard were convicted by a federal grand jury in Louisville, under the Civil Rights Act, which explicitly empowered federal courts to try cases involving persons who had been denied their rights in state or local courts. There was no question that the white men were guilty. Shortly before the murders, Kennard had been heard to tell Blyew that "he thought there would soon be another war about the niggers; that when it did come, he intended to go to killing niggers, and that he was not sure that he would not begin his work of killing them before the war should actually commence." The all-white jury sentenced them to hang.

Conservative Kentuckians were so incensed at the verdict that a special session of the state legislature convened to appropriate public funds to hire a former U.S. attorney general, Jeremiah S. Black, a Pennsylvania Democrat who had helped defend Andrew Johnson against impeachment, to represent Kentucky's "sovereign rights" in a challenge to the Civil Rights Act. When the case reached the U.S. Supreme Court, Black argued that the trial had been an illegal assault on Kentucky's sovereignty because murder was not a crime under federal law. (The Democratic *Louisville Courier-Journal,* mincing no words, denounced the men's trial as "a bold, unmitigated and wanton usurpation.") To such critics, the hideous fate of the Fosters was irrelevant. Adding a more pointedly racial argument, Black further charged that upholding the lower court's verdict would swamp the federal courts with freed people seeking redress. Solicitor General Benjamin Bristow, representing the government, countered that under the Enforcement Acts federal jurisdiction was clear, and further pointed out that federal control of criminal justice was a necessity in lawless, Klan-infested areas of the South.

Whatever the Court decided, it was expected to set a precedent for enforcement of the administration's civil rights policy and for the future of the war against the Klan. The Court finally issued its ruling on Blyew on April 1, after more than a year of deliberation, reversing the lower court by a vote of five to two. Technically, the Court dismissed the case on procedural grounds. But no one could miss the Court's unstated but unmistakable rejection of the opportunity to affirm the expansion of national civil rights enforcement. In his dissent, Justice Joseph P. Bradley, a New Jersey Republican usually more focused on commercial law than on civil rights, charged the majority with leaving southern Blacks unprotected by laws and subjecting them to "wanton insults and fiendish assaults," virtually inviting "vindictive outlaws and felons to rush upon these helpless people and kill and slay them at will, as was done in this case." He was joined by just one other member of the Court, Noah Swayne, its only Quaker member.

The ruling marked the beginning of the Court's retreat from Reconstruction. Civil rights prosecutions in Kentucky immediately fell. Blyew and Kennard did not go entirely unpunished, however. Before the Supreme Court delivered its verdict, Kentucky repealed its discriminatory law banning Black testimony; in 1873, a county court convicted both men of murder. Kennard was sentenced to hard labor for life but would be pardoned twelve years later. Blyew fled the state. He was captured in 1890 and sentenced to life in prison. He, too, was later pardoned, in 1896.

The Court's evasiveness on civil rights was also underscored by another case that spring. Following South Carolina's Klan trials of the previous year, both the prosecution and the defense sought a clear ruling from the Supreme Court on the federal government's authority to prosecute crimes against freed people. The first clear-cut Klan case to reach the Court, *United States v. Avery*, centered on the prosecution of the York County Klan leaders James Avery and James Rufus Bratton. Avery was charged with the murder of a Black militiaman named Anderson Brown, while both Avery and Bratton were together accused of killing the Black militia captain Jim Williams and with seizing the weapons belonging to Williams's company. Avery, the county Klan chief, had ordered Williams's execution and Bratton had led the raid that carried the order out. Federal attorney David Corbin, a veteran of Klan trials, in particular sought a definitive ruling on two questions: whether protection of the Second Amendment right to bear arms fell under state law or federal law, and whether federal courts could impose the death penalty for a civil rights violation if that violation involved a murder. In a measure of the seriousness with which the administration regarded the case, Attorney General Williams personally presented the charges to the Court.

The Court's decision disappointed prosecutors and defense attorneys alike. By eight to one, it refused to rule and sent the case back to the lower court, where it eventually died. Attorney General Williams himself, somewhat perplexingly, had offered the Court an escape route. He asserted that he did not "perceive that the questions presented in [the case] are of such pressing public importance as to require immediate decision," a statement that the legal historian Robert J. Kaczorowski remarked seems to betray an "astounding indifference" to the importance of what was at stake. However, as Kaczorowski also observed, Williams—who doubtless had Grant's personal approval—may really have wanted to avoid a decisive ruling. He knew that the Court might rule against the government, thereby gutting the Enforcement Acts and crippling prosecutions of the Klan across the South. If that is true, then the Court's seeming dereliction of judiciary duty was actually a strategic maneuver which bought Grant more time to crush the Klan.

There was a dramatic coda to the Avery case. It took place far from the solemn chamber of the Supreme Court, some six hundred miles to the northwest, in Canada, in the streets of London, Ontario. On the evening of June 4, a bearded, slightly built man who called himself "James Simpson" was taking an afternoon stroll along a nearly empty stretch of Waterloo Street. He barely noticed two closed cabs approaching from opposite directions. When they came abreast of each other they stopped. Four men climbed out and spoke to each other briefly in the road. Three of them then got back into their cabs. The fourth, a large man, walked toward "Simpson," suddenly lunged at him, threw him to the ground, pressed a chloroform-soaked handkerchief over his face, clapped handcuffs onto his wrists, and threw him into one of the cabs.

"Simpson's" captor was a Canadian court officer named Isaac Cornwall. Cornwall told the cabman to drive them to the railway station. There he forced "Simpson" into a Pullman compartment on the next train bound for the city of Windsor. When "Simpson" came to, he demanded to know by what authority he had been arrested. "You'll find out soon enough," Cornwall told him, saying or at least implying that he would be brought before a magistrate in Windsor. Somewhere en route, Cornwall again sedated "Simpson" with another dose of chloroform. The next thing "Simpson" knew, the train was arriving in Detroit, the cars having been transferred by ferry across the Detroit River to the United States. When the compartment's door was opened, a tall, blue-eyed man appeared and identified himself as an American federal marshal named Joseph Hester, who showed him an arrest warrant signed by President Ulysses S. Grant. He told "Simpson," "You go with me now."

Hester had masterminded "Simpson's" arrest. He was something of a legend in the small universe of federal detectives. A North Carolina preacher's son, and a man of fungible loyalties, he had served variously as a rifleman in the Seminole War, a soldier of fortune in South America, a sailor aboard a Confederate raider, and a Union spy. He had joined the Secret Service and the Republican Party about a year earlier and quickly proved his value as a crack investigator in North Carolina, successfully arresting six white men in Moore County for whipping Black Republicans, another half-dozen in Caswell County for torturing the freedman Essic Harris, and thirty more for attacking a white Republican in Cleveland County. So impressed with him was Sen. John Scott that he sent him to meet President Grant at West Point, where the president was attending his son's graduation, to explain what he could do. Grant's chief of staff subsequently wrote to Amos Akerman on behalf of the president urging the recruitment of other agents as efficient as Hester. Hester's men had traced "Simpson" from York County, South Carolina, through Georgia, Alabama, Tennessee, and eventually to Ontario. There, under Hester's personal direction, they had closely observed him since his arrival, hired Cornwall, and on the basis of an open warrant issued by a magistrate at Windsor, had established themselves at the Post Office in London, where they were permitted to open "Simpson's" letters.

In Detroit, Hester showed "Simpson" a U.S. warrant for the arrest of James W. Avery, the fugitive Klan chief from York County, South Carolina. "Simpson" argued that they had the wrong man, that he was an innocent Alabamian. Hester ignored his protests and entrained with him for South Carolina, where U.S. attorney David Corbin expected to put him on trial. There was a problem, however: "Simpson" was right. He wasn't Avery. He *was,* however, James Rufus Bratton, the Yorkville doctor who had directed the lynching of Jim Williams.

On one hand, the Bratton affair demonstrated the lengths to which the Grant administration was prepared to go to bring terrorists to justice. On the other, it revealed the limitations of the government's primitive investigative apparatus in an era when criminal detection was in its infancy and depended largely on amateurs such as Hester. It wasn't difficult for wanted men to disappear in the vastness of America; detectives rarely recovered eastern fugitives from faraway Arkansas and Texas, or even Tennessee. What had at first seemed like brilliant detective work quickly turned into an international fiasco.

The government of Canada and the British crown were outraged that Bratton had been illegally kidnapped from a Canadian street. Relations were already sticky between the United States and Canada, which was still a British dependency. Canadians were deeply suspicious of their southern neighbor. For most of a century, dema-gogic American politicians had urged Canada's annexation. They had attempted to accomplish that by force during the American Revolution and the War of 1812. Then, in 1837, Canadian republicans had plotted to mount an invasion from American soil, and in 1867, armed Irish nationalists operating from the U.S. had staged incursions as part of their campaign against British rule. Although Canada had provided a safe haven for fugitive American slaves before the Civil War, it had also welcomed escaped Confederate prisoners, and after the war fugitive Klansmen such as Bratton and Avery, whom the Canadian authorities considered political refugees.

Bratton's arrest threatened to destabilize relations between Britain and the United States. The case was raised in the Canadian House of Commons and by the British ambassador in Washington. The *Toronto Globe* attacked the kidnapping as an "official outrage" that insulted the national honor. In the United States, the Democratic press stridently denounced Bratton's seizure as "revolting" proof of Grant's "odious despotism [which] he employs to grind out the spirit of the people." In South Carolina, Bratton was hailed as a hero. When he was jailed in Yorkville, the local cornet band stood outside and serenaded him with the strains of "Dixie." His friends claimed that he was merely an "honorable and upright" citizen who was innocent of any wrongdoing at all.

U.S. attorney Corbin was hamstrung. Proof that Bratton was a murderer was abundant. But it was maddeningly insufficient to ensure his prosecution. Although murder was unquestionably a legal basis for a fugitive's extradition from Canada, it was not yet a *federal* crime in the United States. So Corbin's grand jury could at best only indict Bratton for the *nonextraditable* federal crime of "interfering with the voting rights of a Negro citizen." Bratton easily found friends to post his $12,000 bail, with the open understanding that he would forfeit it and abscond again as soon as he could. The federal authorities, unwilling to further exacerbate international tensions, quietly allowed Bratton to slip away to Canada in July. The outcome was a less happy one for Hester's hapless Canadian accomplice, Isaac Cornwall, who was charged with kidnapping. His trial, in London, came to a stunning climax on July 17, when Bratton suddenly strode into the courtroom to tell his story. The highly sympathetic court sentenced Cornwall to three years in prison, while Bratton resumed his comfortable life in London and went on to profitably practice medicine there for the years afterward.

Exactly a week before the denouement in Canada, Democrats met at the Baltimore Opera House to anoint the Liberal Republican candidate Horace Greeley as their nominee to challenge Grant for the presidency. Although some predicted a mass refusal of southern conservatives to vote for an arch-abolitionist, others saw his nomination as the surest way to bring Reconstruction to an end. (At least some former slaveowners believed that when Greeley was elected he would ensure that the government paid them reparations for the loss—that is, the emancipation—of their slaves.) Although Greeley's nomination was deftly stage-managed by the party's northern leaders, the convention was packed with former Confederates and antiwar Copperheads. Delegates included, among others, Gen. Jubal Early, who had attempted to invade the city of Washington in 1864, while one of Greeley's floor managers was Rep. Fernando Wood, who as New York City's mayor in early 1861 had encouraged the city to secede from the Union along with the southern states of the Confederacy. Bands played "Yankee Doodle," "Dixie," and the secessionist anthem "Bonny Blue Flag" in 100-degree heat while boys with buckets passed out ice water to the withering delegates. Speaker after speaker called on the party to "come to the rescue of the downtrodden and afflicted South." Sen. Thomas F. Bayard of Delaware, who as a member of the Joint Committee on the Ku Klux Klan had done his utmost to thwart its investigation, declared that the election was "a plain, straightforward issue between tyranny and freedom, between limited government and unqualified despotism."

An attempt to replace Greeley with a more conventional Democrat quickly fizzled, and although some delegates grumbled that the convention adopted the Liberal Republican platform without changes, recognizing (at least in principle) the equality of all men before the law, accepting the three postwar amendments to the Constitution, demanding the removal of all former Confederates' "disabilities," calling for "local self-government" and supremacy of civilian rule in the South, as well as reformist principles on taxation, finance, and civil service reform. The *New York Herald,* which had battled Greeley for years but now endorsed him, trumpeted that the Liberal Republican agenda would reinvent the Democrats in "the most extraordinary party transformation in our political history." Greeley's own *New York Tribune* trilled that his nomination was "a day of miracles" as delegates from both North and South "clasp[ed] hands on the broad platform of reform and the reign of peace and good will."

Accepting his nomination in a public letter, Greeley attacked the "capricious tyranny" of federal policy in the South, and declared, "Having done what I could for the complete emancipation of blacks, I now insist on the full enfranchisement of all my white country-men." He promised a return to local self-government and an end to federal "interference" in the South. Black voters well knew what was at stake. They would contrast Greeley's words with those of Grant, who, in his own acceptance of the Republican nomination, had expressed his profound hope to see the day when "the title of citizen carried with it all the protection and privileges to the humblest that it does to the most exalted."

17

GRANT TRIUMPHANT

The scourging and slaughter of
our people have so far ceased.

—FREDERICK DOUGLASS

One of the least likely figures to thrust himself into the politics of
the Klan War was a shambling real estate investor from rural New
York, the old abolitionist Gerrit Smith. At seventy-five, Smith was
the country's best-known philanthropist, for decades a generous
supporter of reformist causes, and donor to many seminaries, librar-
ies, and racially integrated schools. Any hint of oppression filled
him with indignation. In past years, he had lived his principles by
harboring fugitive slaves in his home and providing land in New
York to former slaves and free Blacks. "Does not Christ pity the
sufferings of the vilest man on earth?" he had once demanded as
he single-handedly quelled a mob that was tormenting a man in
his hometown of Peterboro. "Then must not his disciples do like-
wise?" In 1867, to the astonishment of countless Radicals, with his
old friend Horace Greeley, he raised $100,000 as an act of "charity"
to bail out Jefferson Davis.

Smith now embraced with his usual moral intensity what Greeley persuaded him was the suffering of the Klansmen imprisoned
in the penitentiary at Albany. Smith's view of Reconstruction was
complex. He did not deny that the Klansmen were guilty of crimes,
but he favored a policy of Christian mercy toward the people of the

South. He also believed as did many other Republicans that with their enfranchisement the former slaves ought to be able to take care of themselves without constant federal assistance.

On July 8, having obtained permission from President Grant to visit the incarcerated Klansmen, Smith passed through the iron gates of the penitentiary, a turreted Gothic pile overlooking New York's state capital as it descended toward the Hudson River. (Primarily a state prison, since 1862 it had also served as the official penitentiary for the District of Columbia.) Although southern propagandists habitually harped on supposedly wretched conditions at the prison, it was a model institution by the standards of the time, boasting a philosophy of discipline that sought to balance control with benevolence for its seven hundred inmates, who mainly worked caning chairs and making shoes under a regime of near constant silence.

Smith interviewed almost forty of the seventy-five Klan prisoners then in the penitentiary. The only one to leave an account of Smith's visit was Randolph Shotwell, the burly twenty-seven-year-old Confederate veteran and former newspaper editor from Rutherfordton, North Carolina. Shotwell readily admitted to serving as the chief of the Klan in his county, but denied taking part in its raids and claimed that he had no authority over the "reckless young country boys" who were responsible for the "whipping, etc." Shotwell later described Smith as "an elderly gentleman, of portly bearing, having thick locks of long white hair hanging upon his shoulders, giving him rather a leonine aspect," who immediately offered to shake his hand and declared that he was in favor of clemency. Shotwell told his rather gullible interlocutor that the jailed Klansmen had been "grievously maligned" by perjurers and Radical journalists, and that most of the "disorders" blamed on the Klan were merely private feuds among families.

According to Shotwell, after a long discussion, Smith told him, "The worst thing I can find against you is your intelligence." This pleased the intensely class-conscious Shotwell, who complained with disgust of being "hectored and abused by [prison guards] whom I should not have thought of treating as my equals in any respect, morally, mentally, socially, or physically," and being made to share his workbench and, at mealtimes, a wash basin and cloth towel with "big, greasy, odorous" Black men. Despite his many grievances, Shotwell was in fact treated as something of a pet by the warden, a Democrat, who made him the prison librarian and a trustee at the hospital, and personally provided him with better underclothes than the general run of prisoners.

On July 9, Smith wrote to Grant petitioning for the release of the eighteen men he thought most worthy of pardon, specifically urging the release of three whom he described as simple, ignorant men who had been duped into joining the Klan: a "youth" who was in ill health, another "because of his weak intellect," and the third due to his advanced age of sixty-three. Shotwell was not among them: the North Carolinian rejected any pardon that required him to admit to a crime, and scorned those who "confessed" as men of no more value "than negroes."

Smith was not alone in his plea for clemency. Republicans both South and North joined in the chorus. The *New York Herald* advised the president to "throw open the prison doors to these Carolina Ku Klux," arguing that they would thereby be transformed from enemies into "emissaries" who would in return persuade their brethren and friends to vote for a president who showed such gentleness and mercy. In early December, South Carolina's Republican governor, Robert Scott, and other state officials, appealed to Grant to pardon all the imprisoned Klansmen. Jacob Davis, the president of a Republican organization in Georgia, begged Grant "on behalf of suffering innocent women and children, to pardon their husbands fathers and Sons who are known as Ku Klux. Could you not consistent with your kindness of heart—pardon the poor doops [*sic*]." H. K. Thurber, a New York businessman with investments in the South, similarly urged, "They are no longer dangerous, and we know from daily personal contact with the better class of Southern merchants that such actions would make many support your administration as the one most likely to give them in the end prosperity to all their main interests."

Grant was of two minds. In December, he had expressed his general support for granting amnesty to the remaining disenfranchised former Confederates, telling Congress that he saw no advantage in excluding men from office "merely because they were before the rebellion of standing and character sufficient to be elected." But he still hesitated to extend mercy to Klansmen who had been tried and convicted for vicious crimes against defenseless civilians. He worried that leniency would be misinterpreted as a confession of federal weakness rather than strength. At the same time, he wrote somewhat equivocally to Gerrit Smith, "If any innocent persons are being punished, I have no desire to keep them longer in confinement. My oft expressed desire is that all citizens, white or black, native or foreign, may be left free, in all parts of our common country, to vote, speak & act, in obedience to law, without intimidation or ostrasism [sic] on account of his views, color, or nativity." He promised Smith that he would have Attorney General Williams send a personal representative to Albany to report on the prisoners there.

For this politically fraught task, Williams tapped Secret Service chief Hiram Whitley. A forty-year-old native of Maine, a onetime cattle drover and grocer, Whitley had discovered in himself a talent for investigation as an agent for the military during the Union occupation of New Orleans. Like Smith, he interviewed nearly forty prisoners, mostly the same ones. Virtually all—with the notable exception of the defiant Randolph Shotwell—claimed that they had joined the Klan in ignorance and had been incited to violence by leaders who had fled, leaving them to bear the punishment. Several told Whitley that they had joined only to save themselves and their families from punishment by the Klan. Whitley wasn't fooled. His own agents had penetrated the Klan, knew its secrets, and had helped to gather the evidence that put men like these on trial. He told a reporter for the *New York Herald* that in his opinion "on the whole they have got off pretty lightly." A ten-year sentence for murder was "certainly not too heavy." He cited in particular sixty-three-year-old Samuel Brown, who because of his age and supposed infirmity had become a symbol for the advocates of conciliation. Brown, Whitley said, was a flat-out liar who was in fact a Klan leader and active raider, even as he had served as a local public official in South Carolina. Perhaps with a finger to the political winds, however, Whitley nevertheless reported to Grant that the majority of the men he interviewed were "frank and communicative," and contrite. Some of them were indeed "very poor and unlearned," suggesting that they may not have been able to fully understand what they were getting into, and had large families that wholly depended on them. He recommended twenty-four men as candidates for clemency, but urged a full pardon for just one, a South Carolinian named David Collins. Based on Whitley's report, Grant initially agreed to pardon four men, but quickly backtracked when North Carolina Republicans vigorously protested that at least two of them were "the most ferocious" Klan terrorists in their districts.

Grant was coming to believe that the Klan War had accomplished its purpose. Reports from diverse localities were encouraging. The Klan had clearly been shattered in its strongholds in the Carolinas and knocked back on its heels almost everywhere. There was widespread fear among demoralized members that the Klan had been thoroughly penetrated by government agents and informers. Organized raids had greatly diminished. Thousands of Klansmen had been arrested or voluntarily surrendered, and many of them had given sworn testimony against their onetime friends. In many areas, the mere threat of enforcement was enough to scare the Klan. In all, about five thousand men had been indicted. The Klan's once mysterious oaths, signs, and passwords were now public knowledge. Its spooky outfits had been exposed as little more than gaudy clownsuits. "The organization is broken up and scattered," a North Carolina prosecutor assured Grant, while Senator Robertson of South Carolina confidently told his colleagues that May that "the Ku Klux organizations are broken up forever in South Carolina." Alexander Stephens of Georgia, the Confederacy's former vice president, professed in a letter to the president that no one "has any serious apprehensions of any further disturbances of this sort." Even Frederick Douglass, the most prominent Black man in America, declared, "The scourging and slaughter of our people have so far ceased."

Not all Blacks were as sanguine as Douglass. Pleaded one anxious Louisiana freedman in a letter to Grant, "Bayonets is What we wish to See." Others feared that although the Klan appeared to be broken, it was only dormant. Declared Rep. Job Stevenson of Ohio, a member of the Ku Klux Klan Committee, in May, "The conspiracy is so organized that it may remain quiescent for a year or for two years ready to be called into the field by a blast of the bugle of Forrest, or by the click of the telegraph. Within one week, this organization could throw into action a quarter of a million men, armed for conflict with the revolver and the bowie knife and the knout."

Such voices were not to be ignored. But they were less politically potent than they had formerly been. If, as more and more Republicans maintained, the war against the Klan had essentially been won, how much longer could continued deployment of the army be justified? As the presidential elections neared, Grant's enemies assailed him as an aspiring dictator for stubbornly failing to offer mercy to harmless ex-Confederates. Such attacks were to be expected from Democrats. But those from the acid-tongued Carl Schurz and his fellow Liberal Republicans struck at the party's core of usually reliable Republicans who wanted to be assured that the South's problems were over. They were tired of the incessant stories about corruption in southern states, tired of plaintive pleas for more troops, tired of hearing about racial conflict, and, in truth, tired of the whole "Negro problem."

On June 1, Grant outfoxed his critics with a clever, if arguably shortsighted, tactical maneuver, doing what they said he would never do. He proclaimed a near complete amnesty for all the remaining former Confederates who lived under restriction, except for a few men who had been high-ranking members of the United States government, such as Jefferson Davis, its military, or the federal judiciary when they defected in 1861. He also directed federal attorneys to drop all charges against lower-ranking former Confederate officials who had been elected or appointed to office in southern states in violation of the provisions of the Enforcement Acts. While Grant's embrace of the measure was probably decisive, he was standing on the shoulders of the Republican majority in Congress, who a week earlier, after months of intermittent debate and years of hesitation, had at last agreed to remove the former Confederates' "disabilities," freeing them to hold public office.

Although the restrictions on many thousands had been removed by means of individual pardons, it was normally a slow process requiring either a presidential pardon or an act of Congress for each individual. Ben Butler, the chairman of the House Judiciary Committee, had a list of more than seventeen thousand such pending names in hand when the committee decided to bring the whole unwieldy process to an end with a single piece of legislation. Grant and the congressional Republicans knew they were taking a chance. The enfranchisement of the disaffected was more than likely to benefit the Democratic Party to the Republicans' disadvantage. But Grant felt that it was still worth the risk, concluding that the festering issue of "disabilities" made political martyrs of those they applied to, and that appeasing them would earn a political profit of gratitude for the administration, not just in the South.

There were votes enough in Congress to pass the amnesty bill. But it had been stalled for months by the infirm but insistent Sen. Charles Sumner, who held it as a parliamentary hostage to his radical civil rights amendment. (It would outlaw racial discrimination on all forms of public transport, inns and hotels, schools, churches, and jury selection, and severely fine violators.) Discrimination, Sumner declared, was but another form of slavery. "Again the barbarous tyranny stalks into this chamber, denying to a whole race the equal rights promised by a just citizenship. Some have thought slavery dead. This is a mistake. If not in body, at least in spirit or as a ghost making our country hideous, the ancient criminal yet lingers among us." Until Black Americans were ensured equality before the law, the promises of the Declaration of Independence would remain unfulfilled. It was a deeply shocking proposal to many members of Congress in a society where hardly anyone questioned racial segregation or either the morality or consequences of discrimination in any sphere.

Congress had repeatedly shunted aside Sumner's rider only to find him proposing it again with—to those who disliked him, and they were many— incorrigible and stentorian persistence. As long as the rider remained to impale the amnesty bill, Sumner and everyone else knew the bill would remain effectively paralyzed. The rider was twice rejected during a series of contentious sessions that were most notable for the appeals made by Black members of the House of Representatives, who promised their support to the amnesty bill with the hope that their white Republican colleagues would repay them with the passage of the Civil Rights bill. Even the passionate Robert Elliott of South Carolina, who the previous December had sneered at the removal of "disabilities" as "nothing but an attempt to pay a premium for disloyalty and treason at the expense of loyalty," now threw his support behind the bill as its House cosponsor.

Most moving of all was light-skinned, dramatically whiskered Joseph Rainey, also of South Carolina, a onetime barber at Charleston's posh Mills House hotel who during the war had been forced to serve first as a laborer on Confederate fortifications and then as a steward on a blockade runner before he managed to escape to freedom in British Bermuda. "There is no member on this floor who hails with greater satisfaction and gratification than myself a bill of this description, having for its avowed purpose the removal of those disabilities imposed by the Fourteenth Amendment," Rainey declared in what one imagines was a polished Carolina drawl. "We are desirous of being magnanimous; it may be that we are so to a fault. Nevertheless, we have open and frank hearts toward those who were our former oppressors and taskmasters. We foster no enmity now, and we desire to foster none for their acts in the past to us. But while we are willing to accord to them their enfranchisement, and here today give our votes that they may be amnestied, while we declare our hearts open and free from any vindictive feelings toward them." But there was another group of American citizens, he said, who had "certain dear rights" "which they would like you, sirs, to remember and respect." He was, of course, talking about himself and the basic civil rights of all freed people. "Now, in our country's comparative peace and tranquility, we are in earnest for our rights. We now invoke you, gentlemen, to show the same magnanimity and kindly feeling toward us—a race long oppressed. I implore you, give support to the Civil Rights bill which we have been asking at your hands, lo! these many days."

Initially, it appeared that the civil rights measure would pass with a slim but safe majority. The Republicans managed to push the amnesty bill through in a torturous all-night session that had senators nearly crying with exhaustion and didn't finally come to a vote until after dawn on May 14. But while Sumner was temporarily out of the chamber, his Civil Rights bill was once again sidelined. Returning to the floor, he cried, "I plead for the colored race. I cannot, I will not cease. I ask, sirs, that this great strife may be brought to an end, and the cause settled forever. It cannot be except by the establishment of equal rights absolutely and completely whenever the law can reach. Why will you not give to the colored race that same amnesty which you now offer to the former rebels?" But it was not to be. The senators listened, then voted down his amendment for the last time in the debate, and went on to pass the amnesty bill by a vote of 38 to 2, with only Sumner and his Nevada ally, James Nye, voting against it.

Ultimately, the fate of southern Blacks lay in the hands of the voters. Everyone regarded the November presidential election as a referendum on Grant and Reconstruction. The Liberal Republicans and their Democratic allies professed unbounded optimism. Sen. Lyman Trumbull predicted ebulliently that Greeley's odds of victory against Grant were twice as good as Lincoln's against Douglas in 1860. In the South, the Democratic press cheered on the ticket. "If the white vote will only go to the polls, the state is redeemed," declared the *Charleston Courier;* the *Atlanta Constitution* shrilled that any vote for Grant was an endorsement of tyranny while every one for Greeley was one for "southern equality." Greeley barnstormed and whistle-stopped across the North, delivering hundreds of speeches, an impressive performance for a man of sixty-one in less than perfect health. He harped relentlessly on racist themes, blaming the Republicans for thwarting the aspirations of southern whites and hectoring a mainly Black audience at one point that they should stop expecting help from whites "beyond what is reasonable and beyond what is wholesome." In a speech at Pleasantville, New York, he even denied that any "outrages" against Blacks were still taking place in the South and declared that all the national questions pertaining to race and rights were now dead and buried. Men might reasonably differ over banking, or tariffs, or railroads, he opined, "But the first of all questions is the emancipation of all the White men in the country, so that they shall enjoy equal rights with the Black men. That is the question on which I stand as a candidate."

In spite of Greeley's blatant racist appeals, Democrats hoped to pry Black voters away from the Republicans by claiming that Grant had never been a friend to their race. Few were fooled. "We have fet [*sic*] the lash and we have smell pow[d]er and we have tasted freedom and we have resolve to stand by the President of the United States And the Republica[n] Party," one Black Union veteran assured Grant. Frederick Douglass scathingly repudiated the Democrats' charges with characteristic passion. As president, Douglass reminded Blacks, Grant had advocated for the Fifteenth Amendment, triumphed over the Ku Klux Klan, and appointed Black men to thousands of federal jobs, nearly 250 in one department alone.

Moreover, Grant personally treated Blacks with dignity and respect. Douglass declared that apart from Lincoln and Sumner, no white man he knew was as free of personal prejudice as Grant. "The liberty which Mr. Lincoln declared with his pen General Grant made effectual with his sword—by his skill in leading the Union armies to final victory."

As the leading champion of the Liberal Democrats, Carl Schurz campaigned vigorously for Greeley across the Midwest and into the South. Speaking to a rally in St. Louis, he delivered a vicious personal assault on Grant and his administration, which, he said, was "absolutely barren of ideas and originality, bare of striking achievements, void of noble sentiments and inspiring example. It is simply dull and heavy, stupid and stubborn in its selfishness." The South—the *white* South, he of course meant—had been "most cruelly oppressed and plundered" by the rule of "unprincipled and rapacious leaders at the head of the colored population." In a similar vein, the *Springfield Republican,* once a staunch advocate for Black rights, sneered that " 'Sambo' is trumps in politics this year." Charles Sumner, in a quixotic effort to win Black votes for the fusion ticket, tried to smear Grant as an old "pro-slavery Democrat" backed only by grafters and crooks, who had made the presidency his personal "plaything"—"How [to] expect reform from a president who needs it so much himself?" he fairly spat. "Who shall purify the purifier?"

In keeping with custom, Grant did not campaign, instead spending much of the summer at his seaside favorite retreat at Long Branch, New Jersey. Visitors found him almost preternaturally calm, "just as easy as tho' he were driving horses on a smooth road with a good cigar in his mouth," as one put it. He was surely heartened by letters such as this from a schoolgirl from West Virginia, Jenny Richie, who wrote telling him, "My papa was killed in your army. . . . We love you and always will. Mr. President please don't let them kill you as they did President Lincoln. You must be awful careful." Nevertheless, although he rarely showed it, Grant in fact felt hurt by the cascade of cruel insults emanating from his enemies, complaining to a friend, "The severest test I have had to undergo has been slanderous and false abuse with hands and tongue tied." Concerned to deflate the Democrats' accusations of "Caesarism,"

Grant firmly refused to use federal troops to influence voters, reject-ing direct appeals from the Republican governors of Florida and Arkansas.

While Grant maintained his reserve, other Republicans fought back. One biting cartoon by Thomas Nast in *Harper's Weekly* showed Greeley handing over a terrified Black man to a ghoulish Klans-man with a skull and crossbones on the back of his outfit; another portrayed him as a grotesque Richard III plagued by the ghosts of murdered Black and white Republicans. An entire 150-page book-let, *The Nation's Peril,* sought to tie the Democrats directly to the Ku Klux Klan, declaring "that Democracy in the South meant rebel-lion, and . . . Ku Kluxism meant both." (Anonymously printed, it drew heavily on the files of federal detectives and was probably instigated by Secret Service chief Hiram Whitley.) It revealed the Klan's oaths and codes, and recounted in vivid prose the assassina-tion of Republican leaders and innocent Black farmers, midnight raids, floggings, torture, and the subjection of women to "revolt-ing indecencies." But thanks to the Republican Party, the booklet declared, "bands of deadly assassins, skulking at midnight behind hideous disguises, and warring upon innocent women and children have been suppressed and broken up. And by it they have been com-pelled to answer for their numerous crimes."

Grant's surrogates on the stump also reminded voters that apart from crushing the Klan, he had expanded the electorate to include Black Americans, cracked down on ballot fraud, dispatched soldiers to protect the polls, and reformed Indian policy; not least, he had also reduced the national debt by almost $100 million over the previous year alone, and by an astonishing $364 million since the beginning of his presidency in 1869. The *New York Times,* stead-fast for Grant, warned that Greeley's election would lead to "wild and chaotic experiments" in financial policy, economic instability, the appointment of wartime Copperheads to top government jobs, and "fresh disturbance" in the South. Some Republicans even rather wildly charged that Greeley's election would lead to a restoration of slavery.

As Election Day approached, Republicans worried that Greeley might sweep the South and the border states, along with New York and perhaps even the swing state of Pennsylvania. Many voters were torn. The Danish immigrant Jacob Riis, later to become famous as a social reformer, found himself in Pittsburgh during the campaign.

On my second night in town I went to hear Horace Greeley address an open-air meeting. I can see his noble old head yet above the crowd, and hear his opening appeal. Farther I never got. A marching band of uniformed shouters for Grant had cut right through the crowd. As it passed I felt myself suddenly seized; an oilcloth cape was thrown over my head, a campaign hat jammed after, and I found myself marching away with a torch on my shoulder to the tune of a brass band just ahead. How many others of Mr. Greeley's hearers fared as I did I do not know. The thing seemed so ludicrous (and if I must march I really care very little whether it was for Greeley or Grant) that I stuck it out, hoping as we went to come somewhere upon my hat, which had been lost in the sudden attack.

Grant's quiet confidence was vindicated on Election Day. When he awoke the next morning, November 6, he learned that he had won the largest majority in the nation's history with nearly 56 percent of the popular vote, and an overwhelming 286 electoral votes to Greeley's 66. He carried every northern and western state and eight southern ones. (Irregularities were so widespread in Arkansas and Louisiana that Congress declined even to count their electoral votes.) The Republicans also regained a two-thirds majority in both houses of Congress. "Victory! A Sweeping Republican Triumph," the *New York Times* trumpeted. Grant was doubtless charmed by the letter he received from eight-year-old Harry Atwater of Cranberry, New Jersey, who had met the president at Long Branch, and cheerfully informed him that on Election Day he had bedecked his ponies with flags and ribbons and driven twenty-three voters to the polls, "12 of them were black man." The ponies, he assured Grant, whom the boy perhaps knew to be a horse-lover, "have not got sick yet and they can trot auful fast."

Young Harry's twelve Black New Jerseyans were, at least symbolically, the key to Grant's victory. Hundreds of thousands of Black men voted in the election. Despite an ominous decline in the Black vote in some counties that had delivered solid majorities for Republicans in past elections, the freedmen's vote was massive, perhaps as high as 400,000 overall. It is impossible to say how much direct effect the widely publicized congressional Ku Klux Klan report had on voters, but it must have helped to counter southern apologetics for the Klan and anti-administration propaganda. Democrats themselves were also a factor in Greeley's defeat: many simply couldn't force themselves to vote for a notorious abolitionist. Others sank into vengeful despair. In his prison diary, Klansman Randolph Shotwell ranted, "All is over! It is absolutely amazing, the apathy, the blindness, the infatuation of the people!" Greeley himself fell into a funk from which he never recovered. "I was the worst beaten man that ever ran for high office," he lamented. "And I have been assailed so bitterly that I hardly know whether I was running for president or the penitentiary." His wife's death just before the election crushed him emotionally, and his defeat finished him off. Humiliated, drained, and awash in grief, he entered a sanitorium to recuperate, then died suddenly on November 29, before the electoral votes had even been officially counted. Grant, with characteristic magnanimity, led Greeley's mourners in a procession down Fifth Avenue, in New York.

A month after his reelection, Grant struck a justifiable note of optimism in his annual message to Congress. "I look with confidence to the time, not far distant, when the obvious advantages of good order and peace will induce an abandonment of all combinations"— that is, Klan organizations—prohibited by the Enforcement Acts "and when it will be unnecessary to carry on prosecutions or inflict punishment to protect citizens from the lawless doings of such combinations." He had, he said, received applications for pardons upon the ground that clemency in such cases would "tranquillize the public mind, and to test the virtue of that policy I am disposed, as far as my sense of justice will permit, to give these applications a favorable consideration." Such leniency, he cautioned, ought not to be construed to mean he was any less determined to "enforce with vigor" the law as it stood as long as conspiracies continued to disturb the country: he would continue to confront terrorism. But he was now prepared, he strongly implied, to temper stern justice with mercy and forgiveness.

Grant stood now at the high-water mark of his presidency. Despite his resounding victory, however, behind the triumphalism of the moment, he was emerging from the contest scarred and weakened. Shortly before the election, an exploding scandal seemed to suck into itself everything that disgusted Americans about money and politics. During the Johnson administration, the transcontinental Union Pacific Railroad had created the false facade of a construction company, known as Crédit Mobilier, which shared its directors with the railroad itself. Not only had they paid themselves exorbitant salaries covered by government subsidies, but they had bribed members of Congress, including major committee chairmen, House Speaker James G. Blaine, Rep. James A. Garfield, who had been regarded as a particularly trustworthy voice of probity, along with former vice president Schuyler Colfax and Grant's new vice president, Henry Wilson, with deeply discounted Crédit Mobilier stock. A congressional investigation revealed even more sordid details. On the heels of *that* scandal, with obtusely bad timing, Congress voted itself a 50 percent salary increase, from $5,000 to $7,500 annually, retroactive to 1871. Neither branch had received a raise since the era of George Washington, but it so incensed the public that Congress rescinded the raise. The fiasco left both the administration and the Republican Party seriously wounded.

The election had also left the Liberal Republicans a spent force. They had failed to unseat Grant, their southern strategy had won them few votes, and their hopes for a wave of support in New England had never panned out. "The men who called together the Cincinnati convention found themselves in the absurd position of being unable to control the machinery which they had framed," the *New York Times* editorialized. "All the wheels turned the wrong way." Lyman Trumbull would be defeated for reelection within the year, after more than two decades in Congress. Charles Sumner, already marginalized, would linger on in limbo for another year. The *Times* was particularly scathing toward Schurz, accusing him of having "done his best to sell out the Republican party to the Democrats."

Grant brusquely dismissed the Liberal Republicans as "soreheads & thieves" who had "only strengthened the Republican party by leaving it." In this, he was wrong. The Liberal Republicans had prevailed in other, if less obvious, ways. As the political historian Richard Hofstadter memorably wrote, "Third parties are like bees: once they have stung, they die." There was no compelling need for the Liberal Republicans to survive. Pressure from them had already forced Grant to adopt some of their positions: funding the Civil Service Commission, lowering tariffs, and passing the amnesty bill of 1872. They had significantly undermined the principle of strong central government that the Republicans attempted to enshrine during the Civil War. As the historian Eric Foner has pointed out, the fact that so many former Radicals supported Greeley sounded the death knell of Radicalism as both a political movement and a coherent ideology. By savaging Grant with relentless ad hominem attacks, they undermined trust in the president and contributed to the sense, even among Republicans, that his administration had become a sump of corruption and incompetence. With their full-throated demand to conciliate the South, they had also weakened Republican resolve and opened the door to the return to power of white supremacist conservatives and the ultimate subversion of equal rights.

For the time being, however, the Republicans could still savor their triumph. They had reason for hope. They had been vindicated by the voters. And peace in the South seemed to finally be at hand. At the end of the year, Secret Service chief Hiram Whitley reported to Attorney General Williams: "Judging from all the evidence that has thus far reached me, there remains but little of the Ku Klux Klan as a distinctive order." Deeming a revitalization of the Klan to be virtually impossible, Whitley wound up his investigations and dismissed most of the detectives who had been assigned to the Klan. Williams, with Grant's presumed approval, then advised federal attorneys to stop pursuing all but the most outrageous Klan-related crimes. To them, Williams wrote, "My desire is that the pending prosecutions be pushed only as far as may appear to be necessary to preserve the public peace and prevent further violations."

Grant's inauguration on March 4 was planned with all the formal panoply commensurate with the political triumph that his election represented. Unfortunately, nature failed to cooperate. Thermometers registered 16 degrees, but a merciless twenty-eight-mile-per-hour north wind hurled the real temperature far below zero, making it the coldest presidential inauguration in history. Fitful gusts tore at the flags and bunting that garnished every building along Pennsylvania Avenue and froze to the bone the hapless citizens who had packed into the city. The parade trudged along as best it could: regiments of militia—lancers from Boston, dragoons from Philadelphia, Black Zouaves in gay Algerian-style uniforms, New Yorkers, Pennsylvanians, Ohioans, even hardy souls from faraway California, their hats blowing off in the wind—bands with frozen instruments, cadets from West Point, and midshipmen from the Naval Academy gamely pressed on toward the Capitol, along with contingents of Civil War veterans clad in their ragged old uniforms marching beneath bullet-torn regimental flags inscribed "Fredericksburg," "East Tennessee," "Atlanta," and the names of a hundred other campaigns.

Speaking from the East Portico of the Capitol, Grant told a shivering, racially mixed crowd that the Klan War was at an end. (His words were lost in the hammering wind, but they would soon reach the nation via telegraph and newspapers.) "The states lately at war with the General Government are now happily rehabilitated, and no executive control is exercised in any one of them that would not be exercised in any other state under like circumstances." He boldly declared his support for the package of radical civil rights measures crafted by his nemesis Charles Sumner. "The effects of the late civil strife have been to free the slave and make him a citizen," said Grant. "Yet he is not possessed of the civil rights which citizenship should carry with it. This is wrong, and should be corrected. To this correction, I stand committed, as far as Executive influence can avail." At this point, Grant hedged a little. "Social equality is not a subject to be legislated upon, nor shall I ask that anything be done to advance the social status of the colored man, except to give him a fair chance to develop what there is good in him, give him access to the schools, and when he travels let him feel assured that his conduct will regulate the treatment and fare he will receive." Laws, Grant understood, could not immediately transform people's feelings. He knew how deep color prejudice ran in most Americans, in the North as well as South. But he believed that the law could point the way clearly toward the moral horizon that Americans must reach.

Grant knew that conditions in the South were less than serene.

In Arkansas, the day before the inauguration voters by a ten-to-one margin voted to fully restore the voting rights of former Confederates, ensuring that Democrats would regain political power, as they did before the year was out. Rival legislatures were at each others' throats in Alabama. The Republican Party was on the slide in North Carolina. From Savannah, Georgia, H. W. Marshall, a Black Republican, complained, "the democrats have ful persession of ballots to handle and count So they take most all of our tickets an disstroy them to let theirs count Ahead." Louisiana was on the brink of a fratricidal civil war within the Republican Party, between Radicals and a breakaway faction allied with white supremacist Democrats. From Vernon Parish, a merchant wrote that his store had been attacked by a mob who threatened to burn it down unless he left town: "And for what cause? Why I voted the Grant and Kellogg or Republican ticket."

Even so, Grant felt that most of the South had reached a degree of stability, or at least tolerable disorder. The nation's politics had always been strident, disorderly, and plagued by recurrent mob violence: it was all part of the rumbustious American way. Black Americans were now part of it, for better and worse. With organized terrorism reduced to a minimum, they now had if not an open-ended guarantee of political power then at least a fair chance to compete for it. Or so Grant believed. With hindsight, this seems naive, even culpably so. Grant was envisioning a more democratic South that he deeply wanted to believe was taking shape, and he tended to discount evidence that continuing racial violence was more than just an unfortunate iteration of the country's traditional politics.

To a degree, Grant was also conforming his hopes to political reality. Northerners simply would not pay for even the vestigial occupation of the South much longer, or for enough court personnel to try the Klansmen who had already been apprehended. Politically, the smart thing would seem to be to declare victory and withdraw, which was essentially what Grant was doing. Yet, in his address, he revealed a remarkably idealistic vision of America, indeed of the world, a kind of liberal universalism that rested on self-confident humanism and tolerance far more than they did on power and the self-interest of nations. "I believe that our Great

Maker is preparing the world, in His own good time, to become one nation, speaking one language, and when armies and navies will no longer be required," he declared into the wild icy wind of Inauguration Day.

He called not only for the full admittance of Black Americans into civic life, but also for a new "leniency" toward Native Americans built on empathy and respect. To at least some present-day Americans, his choice of language may have the unappealing ring of complacent colonialism. Grant certainly envisioned the assimilation of the Indians into the larger American society and the abandonment of their tribal traditions. But he also embodied the humanitarian aspirations of his day—views that were by no means shared by all Americans, many of whom eagerly embraced the most aggressive policies toward native peoples. "The wrong inflicted upon [the Indian] should be taken into account and the balance paid to his credit. The moral view of the question should be considered and the question asked, Cannot the Indian be made a useful and productive member of society by proper teaching and treatment? If the effort is made in good faith, we will stand better before the civilized nations of the earth and in our own consciences for having made it."

That evening, Pennsylvania Avenue was ablaze with lights. The Treasury Building glowed red so that the national flag that waved above it seemed to rise from a sea of fire, as rockets lit the sky far overhead. An immense wooden building had been built for the evening's gala ball. At 350 feet long, it was the largest single room ever constructed in the United States. Inside, a magnificent repast had been spread, including eighteen thousand oysters, three thousand pounds of boiled lobsters, four hundred partridges, twenty-five stuffed boars' heads, two hundred dozen quails, seventy-five twelve-pound roast turkeys, three hundred gallons of ice cream, oceans of champagne and claret punch, and much else. But one crucial thing had been forgotten: the cavernous room had been left unheated. The ball had been planned for six thousand guests. Only half that many showed up. Many fled almost as soon as they had arrived, driven away by the cold, which reached zero indoors. The drinks and food froze. The band couldn't keep its instruments tuned. Guests who attempted to dance did so clumsily, swaddled like mummies in furs, overcoats and top hats. (The sight of West

Point cadets dancing with elegantly turned-out Black women scandalized those who were repelled by the mingling of races.) A tour de force had been planned to charm the guests: hundreds of canaries had been brought in to serenade the dancers from perches overhead. But they were too cold to sing, and instead tucked their beaks into their feathers in a pathetic effort to keep warm. Then they began to die, falling like little lumps of frozen yellow fruit on the diners and dancers below.

18

COLFAX

The state has gone beyond redemption.
—Mississippi Gov. Adelbert Ames

In April of 1873, Colfax, Louisiana, was a scruffy, thrown-together sort of place, a scattering of barns and workshops that had belonged to a former cotton plantation before Grant Parish was formed to create a new Black-majority county on the Red River, north of New Orleans. (The county had been named for the president, and the town, such as it was, for Vice President Schuyler Colfax.) Beyond the hamlet lay open fields, and beyond them pine woods and the huddled cabins of onetime slaves. A pall of imminent violence had infected the parish for weeks as Democrats and Republicans jockeyed for political advantage.

Low-grade warfare had convulsed the entire state since the close, chaotic, and vastly corrupt autumn election. In New Orleans, then the state capital, two separate governors and state legislatures squared off against each other. Both appointed election boards that in turn appointed rival parish judges and sheriffs. Federal troops finally seized the statehouse, expelled the rebellious Democrats who occupied it, and seated the Republicans in their place, but it failed to palliate the widening climate of crisis. Grant Parish was one of the few rural districts where Black Republicans still managed to retain precarious political control, though it remained an isolated political island awash in a rising tide of militant white supremacist agitation.

Armed Democrats were mustering in the adjoining counties, led by a former deputy sheriff with the imposing name of Christopher Columbus Nash, who had participated in the earlier murder of two Black officeholders and now claimed the office of sheriff. Panicky freed people converged on Colfax, seeking safety in a former stable, a fortresslike structure of whitewashed brick, that had been converted into a courtroom with offices for the parish officials. Of the three hundred people there, half or more were women and children.

The whites later baselessly claimed that the freedmen were planning plunder and rapine, and demanded that they disarm and that the local Republican officials turn their offices over to Democrats. With their backs both figuratively and literally against the wall, the Blacks refused. On April 13, Easter Sunday, more than 150 whites took up positions in the pine forests. Half of them were veteran Confederate soldiers—three were demobilized *federal* soldiers—and most of the rest men and boys too young to have fought in the war. Some were former members of local Klan-like organizations. None wore masks or costumes. They bristled with new breechloading rifles, shotguns, cavalry pistols, and a four-pounder cannon borrowed from a riverboat. "Boys, this is a struggle for white supremacy," one of their leaders assured them.

When it became clear that the whites were about to attack, the Republicans sent their women and children to their cabins, leaving probably fewer than a hundred Black men to defend the courthouse. Those who were armed, an unknown number, carried shotguns and hunting rifles, and all were short of ammunition. The whites advanced behind pickets shooting repeaters, supported by terrifying blasts from the cannon. Driven from the shallow ditches where they had taken cover, the defenders fought back as best they could until most of them were forced back into the courthouse. The rest took flight across the fields, where mounted whites ran them down and shot them as they fled. The whites then forced a captive Black man to set fire to the building's shingle roof. Faced with roasting to death or surrender, and encouraged by promises of mercy, the Blacks decided to capitulate and poured out in a rush, waving scraps of white cloth. They were met with a fusillade of bullets. Many died on the spot. Others, wounded, were shot where they lay and cut up with swords and bayonets. Some died in the flames of the burning courthouse.

That night, the whites gathered up the thirty-five or forty survivors they had captured alive. There was some halfhearted discussion about what to do with them, but one of the whites was heard to say, "I didn't come four hundred miles to kill niggers for nothing." William Cruikshank, a middle-aged planter, ordered his friends to kill them to the last man. He personally made two Black men stand next to each other and he shot them through the head, to see if he could kill them with a single bullet. During the killing, a visitor from Texas, R. G. Hill, wandered around the site of the massacre when the steamboat on which he was traveling stopped to pick up the few wounded white men. Many of the murderers were still there. One of them announced to the passengers "that if we wanted to see dead niggers," this was their chance. Wrote Hill, in a letter to a New Orleans newspaper,

Almost as soon as we got to the top of the landing, sure enough, we began to stumble on them, most of them lying on their faces, and, I could see by the dim light of the lanterns, riddled with bullets. One poor wretch, a stalwart-looking fellow, had been in the burning courthouse, and as he ran out with his clothes on fire, had been shot. His clothes to his waist were all burnt off, and he was literally broiled. We came upon bodies every few steps. I counted eighteen of the misguided darkies, and was informed that they were one-fourth of the number killed. We came across one negro whose clothes were smoking, and who had probably been in the fire. Some of our party remarked that he was alive. Instantly one of our guides whipped out a six-shooter, saying, "I'll finish the black dog."

But the man was already dead.

Precisely how many Black men were killed at Colfax remains uncertain. Estimates have ranged into the hundreds. The toll most likely fell somewhere between sixty and seventy, the majority after they had surrendered or fled. Three white men died, two of them probably killed by wild shots from their own side in the chaos of slaughter. Well into the twentieth century, white Louisianians referred to what happened there as a "Negro riot." In 1921, a white marble obelisk was raised in a local cemetery to the memory of the white dead "who fell in the Colfax Riot fighting for White Supremacy." It still stands.

President Grant later declared, "A butchery of citizens was committed at Colfax, which in blood-thirstiness and barbarity is hardly surpassed by any acts of savage warfare." The Colfax massacre was hardly the first slaughter of freedmen by inflamed whites. But it set in train a legal battle that would help to determine the fate of Reconstruction. It also marked the end of the era of clandestine guerrilla warfare embodied by the Ku Klux Klan and previewed the development of coordinated Democratic campaigns that paired conventional political movements with open intimidation on a mass scale to recapture counties and states from what their leaders called "Black rule." The time of masks, grotesque get-ups, and performative spookiness was over. Such trappings did not totally disappear, nor did references to "the Ku Klux" as generic allusions to white terrorists, but they were rarely needed anymore as communities fell under the control of Democratic administrations that delivered what white supremacists wanted. Louisiana's White League, founded less than a year after the Colfax massacre, like the White Line in Mississippi, the Red Shirts in South Carolina, and similar movements, typified the new organizations that grew up after the demise of the Ku Klux Klan. Unlike the Klan, they were not secret societies and were for the most part open to any white man who wanted to join. Newspapers reported their activities and the names of their officers. They drilled on public roads and held mass meetings that included women and children, and had the lively atmosphere of a county fair. Their purpose was also unambiguous. As the *Alexandria Caucasian,* a Louisiana newspaper that served as a mouthpiece for the White League, put it, what the movement stood for was "a fair, square fight, Caucasian versus African."

It might have been supposed that the Colfax massacre would spur more federal support for endangered southern Republicans. News of the massacre inspired widespread public revulsion. Editorialized the *New York Times,* "The nation that supposed the rebellion had been suppressed and peace restored is suddenly startled by an outrage that has a parallel only in the dark scenes of that woeful strife," recalling the slaughter by Nathan Bedford Forrest's cavalry of almost two hundred disarmed Black federal soldiers at Fort Pillow, Tennessee, in 1864. And, indeed, over the ensuing weeks detectives, federal marshals, and troops descended on Colfax to collect evidence and hunt down the perpetrators. Several Black men, though badly wounded, had survived the massacre and more had witnessed it from hiding. Most of the murderers were well-known local men who had openly boasted about their "victory."

In June, the U.S. attorney in New Orleans, a New York–raised Radical named James Beckwith, indicted under the Enforcement Acts no fewer than ninety-seven white men who had participated in the massacre. In a thunderous prosecutorial broadside, he charged them with thirty-two counts of conspiring to prevent Black citizens from exercising their rights to assemble and to bear arms, depriving them of life and liberty without due process, interfering with their right to vote, and denying them equal protection of the law under the Constitution. Several counts charged them with murder, which, though not normally a federal crime, could be tried as one if it was committed in the process of denying civil and political rights to the victims.

If ever the federal courts had an unassailable case, it was this one, or so it seemed. Its ultimate outcome, however, hinged on a seemingly unrelated decision that the U.S. Supreme Court issued on April 14, even as the bodies of the Colfax dead still lay exposed and bloating.

By coincidence, this other case also originated in Louisiana. Although it addressed neither race nor Reconstruction in so many words, the Court's *Slaughterhouse* ruling set off a judicial earthquake beneath the Enforcement Acts and the established interpretation of the Thirteen and Fourteenth Amendments. In New Orleans, butchers had always dumped the offal of the animals they killed into the Mississippi River, where it polluted the drinking water of what was an already notoriously disease-ridden city. Republican reformers in the state legislature had chartered a corporation—the Crescent City Live-Stock Landing and Slaughter-House Company—to regulate the industry. Independent butchers feared it would put them out of business, and they went to court to fight it.

The defendants' lawyer, John Campbell, had been a member of the U.S. Supreme Court who resigned from it in 1861 to serve the Confederacy. Although he had vigorously condemned the postwar amendments, he now strategically distorted their intent, claiming that the legislature's plan reduced the butchers—all of whom were white—to "servitude" by interfering with their traditional way of doing business. Writing for the majority, Justice Samuel F. Miller, a Republican, brushed off Campbell's preposterous argument. But then, rather too cleverly, he tried to turn the tables on him by employing states' rights reasoning to sustain Louisiana's slaughter-house law. He first stated, as southern conservatives had asserted for years, that the Thirteenth Amendment had done no more than simply abolish the institution of slavery, and that the Fourteenth had only reversed the *Dred Scott* decision. Neither, he wrote, granted Congress the crucial constitutional authority to *protect* the rights of the freed people, a power that remained with the states alone.

The majority may have intended their ruling to strengthen the southern Republican state governments. But their inept reasoning was cataclysmic for the cause of civil rights. They failed to see that it would cripple the efforts of federal attorneys, such as Beckwith, who were trying to protect endangered Blacks when their states left them at the mercy of those who meant to destroy them. Public reaction was muted at best. The *New York Times* registered its approval, declaring in an editorial that had the Court ruled otherwise it would have made the federal courts "a perpetual censor upon all legislation of the states on the civil rights of its own citizens," while *The Nation* cited it as happy evidence that the Court was "recovering from the War fever, and is getting ready to abandon sentimental canons of constitutional interpretation."

That summer, Attorney General Williams directed federal attorneys to suspend prosecutions under the Enforcement Acts. "It is to be understood that the government does not intend to abandon said acts, but to induce, if possible, a willing obedience to their reasonable requirements," he disingenuously wrote. Although *Slaughter-house* was not the sole cause of the change in policy, it led directly to subsequent rulings that ate away at the constitutional girding that Grant and the Justice Department had relied on to prosecute civil rights abuses. In North Carolina, for instance, federal officers directed their deputies to issue no more subpoenas under the Enforcement Acts and excused those who had been indicted from appearing in court, along with all witnesses who had been summoned to testify in Klan trials. Williams ordered federal attorney Beckwith, in New Orleans, to pick a dozen or fewer of accused perpetrators of the Colfax massacre for trial, and let the others go. It was a dreadful precedent that would be replicated elsewhere, making clear that many men who committed murder and other terrorist crimes against Black citizens would never have to face trial.

Williams was at least to some degree taking his cue from the president, who had handed him the responsibility for carrying out enforcement policy. Grant knew perfectly well that intimidation of the freed people had not died with the Klan. He continued to receive a stream of letters from suffering freedmen like Isaac Bourne, from Mississippi, who wrote in September, "the White Peapel in Laurence County an in linclon County Miss thae tak up the Corlded Peapel an Haung thim. We are so Prass so We Cant Stand it." However, as the midterm elections approached, clemency was both politically expedient and, Grant hoped, a potent inducement to the still unreconstructed to finally acquiesce to the racial verdict of the war. Prisoners convicted under the Enforcement Acts "should be treated with as much leniency as possible," Williams declared, since the Ku Klux Klan had been "almost if not altogether broken up" and its sympathizers had come to see "the folly, wickedness, and danger of such organizations." Appeasement, Grant desperately hoped, would gradually encourage obedience to the law and quell resistance to the government. "At all events, it affords the government pleasure to make an experiment based upon these views," Williams wrote.

In the course of the spring and summer, Grant issued a spate of pardons, freeing imprisoned Klansmen from the penitentiary at Albany. On August 9, a pardon came for the defiant North Carolina Klan leader Randolph Shotwell, after three years behind bars, two in Albany preceded by one in his home state, "in durance vile, the vilest that ever man bore," as he grandiosely put it. Upon unrolling the bundle of civilian clothing he had deposited two years before, "it was found to consist of funky rags white with moths and mildew, and so in tatters," having been stored "with the filthy rags of all classes, Negroes, Chinese, Malays, Turks." Hooted at by boys shouting, "Here's yere con-wicks" and "bet you them fellers killed somebody," he found a "fifth-class hotel" for his first days of freedom, and then he made his way by stagecoach to New York City, then by train and steamboat to North Carolina. "So, I came home quietly, receiving many warm welcomes from friends; and even from the better class of Republicans." Bitter, unrepentant, devoid of empathy for the Klan's victims, he was even soured on the Klan itself. His friend Colin Leventhorpe advised him, "You must not be surprised to find that the Ku Klux excitement has died out and cannot be revived."

While Shotwell traveled slowly home to North Carolina, pitying "the mortification and misery" of his situation, the rest of America was riding the crest of a surging economy. Then, on September 18, 1873, the wave crashed. The financial empire of Jay Cooke imploded, brought down by overleveraged investment in railroads. Cooke was a prince among the era's moneymen, a national hero of sterling reputation whose brilliant bond-selling strategy had raised prodigious sums for the Union at the beginning of the Civil War. Since then, he had pioneered the fusion of government interests with those of Wall Street's speculators in a symbiotic marriage that defined the Gilded Age. His firm's collapse, the *Philadelphia Press* exclaimed, was "a thunderclap in a clear sky." Two days later, the stock exchange suspended trading for the first time in its history as wild crowds of desperate lenders and borrowers swirled around lower Manhattan. Brokerage houses collapsed, banks shut their doors, and businesses failed in a terrifying cascade, sparking the nation's worst financial panic in nearly forty years. In the months that followed, crop prices plummeted, half the nation's iron foundries shuttered, 25 percent of New York's workers lost their jobs, crime increased, and tramps became a bleakly familiar sight on the nation's roads. Crushed in the wreckage was a showpiece of Reconstruction, the Freedman's Bank. Since 1865, it had embodied the hopes of tens of thousands of frugal former slaves to achieve economic independence. When it crashed, more than seventy thousand depositors lost $57 million in savings, virtually all they had.

As the panic spread, public revenues continued to sink, states' debts swelled, and credit withered. In the South, costly plans for expanding public education, improving health, and spurring local economies faded as anticipated northern and foreign investment evaporated. Southern corruption, already scandalous in several states, became both financially and politically unsustainable. When exposed, it seemed only to justify conservatives' accusations against already vulnerable Republican, mixed-race legislatures, even when Democrats' hands were found just as deep in the public till. The Republicans faced violent headwinds not only in the South. Everywhere, as always in times of economic stress, the voters blamed the party in power, resentment that was further compounded when the administration declined to increase the money supply or address epidemic unemployment.

Economic crisis soon became political crisis. The Republicans had already been wounded by accusations of scandal, charges of "Caesarism," and the thousand cuts of the Liberal Republican defectors. Democrats now taunted the administration for its coziness with New York speculators and condemned it for supporting failing Republican regimes that the country could no longer afford. A cruelly racist book by a Republican writer and former abolitionist, James Pike, reinforced the growing sentiment that the freed people were worth neither the concern nor the money expended on them. Throughout the North, idealistic sympathy for the slave had curdled into resentment toward freed people who demanded political power, personal respect, and the right to sit alongside whites in trains, restaurants, and theaters. In *The Prostrate State,* Pike portrayed South Carolina as drowning beneath the "dusky tide" of "the most ignorant democracy that mankind ever saw. It is barbarism overwhelming civilization by physical force." The *New York Tribune,* now advocating a white supremacist line, told its wide national readership that outrages against southern Blacks were mere "myths . . . more and more microscopic the nearer you draw to its locale," and alleged that Black churches held "the poor, ignorant creatures" in "political slavery," threatening them with terrible reprisals if they dared to vote for their true allies, their former masters in the Democratic Party. Even the *New York Times,* the house organ of the Republican Party's establishment wing, argued that there was no longer any excuse for perpetuating "war measures" or "robber regimes" in the South, and called upon Grant to fire Attorney General Williams, who "has no sort of right to decide questions of local government in the southern or any other states."

Although the elections were peaceful compared to those of previous years, they were not free of intimidation. One white Democrat wrote blithely that in his town where Black voters outnumbered the whites by a factor of five, "by some manipulation which nobody ever clearly understood except those who performed it the precinct went Democratic. It was an object lesson in the possibilities of what white nerves and brains can accomplish when desperation and necessity prompt." In Eufaula, Alabama, gun-toting whites murdered at least seven Black voters on Election Day, and openly threatened to kill any Republican who had been elected, if he dared to take office. And when five Black men swore out a warrant against a white man for interfering with voting in Randolph County, Georgia, a grand jury charged the Blacks with perjury and ordered them arrested. President Grant hoped that these and similar reports could be dismissed as isolated cases, although it was apparent that the Republican vote in many counties was continuing to drop. In Grant Parish, Louisiana, for instance, the site of the Colfax massacre, where the number of registered Black voters collapsed from about seven hundred in previous years to 441, whites prevailed by a margin of thirty votes.

When the national results came in, the Republicans had suffered a calamitous defeat. Declared the conservative *Raleigh Sentinel,* "The news from Massachusetts to Louisiana strikes all white men of correct feeling with amazement. We have waited and watched and fought and prayed for nine years for the result of last Tuesday's battle, and it has come at last." Republicans were routed even in traditional bastions like Massachusetts, central New York State, and Ohio's Western Reserve. Zachariah Chandler of Michigan, one of Grant's most dependable allies in the Senate, lost his seat when the Democrats captured the state's legislature. Ben Butler, the most prominent Radical in Congress, had already been defeated in his primary, in Boston. Rep. Luke Poland, the cochair of the Ku Klux Klan Committee, went down in Vermont. Although the Republicans managed to retain the Senate, the Democratic juggernaut crushed them in the House of Representatives, which flipped from a 110-vote Republican majority to a 60-vote Democratic one. "The verdict against Grantism is delivered," pronounced the *New York Tribune*.

Another of the election's notable losers was Carl Schurz. His leadership of the Liberal Republican movement had alienated Missouri Radicals and party regulars alike, while his enthusiasm for conciliation with the former Confederates earned him few friends among the state's Democrats. He lost whatever Black support he had with his constant attacks on Grant's southern policy and his opposition to civil rights legislation. When his Senate term ended, Missouri's now Democratic legislature spurned him without a thought. They replaced him with a former Confederate general.

Eighty members of the new Congress were veterans of the Confederate army. Of the once promising Republican Party in the South, with few exceptions, only its Black loyalists remained "from necessity as well as choice," as one Mississippi Black leader sadly wrote. Blacks' influence inexorably shrank as that of conservative whites swelled in local and state governments, and now the federal. Typical of the oncoming political tide, newly elected Virginia governor James L. Kemper, a former Confederate general, declared, "Let it be understood by all that any organized attempt on the part of the weaker and relatively diminishing race to dominate the domestic governments is the wildest chimera of political insanity." Their prospects for the future were not lost on Black Americans. "We Casted our votes for you twice," a Tennessee minister wrote sadly to Grant, in September 1874. "We stood to you in the War and I beleave this our Colared race will stand to you until your eyes are chilled with death." The minister then added despairingly that his congregants "all wish to be Colonize in a territory or state to them Selves."

Grant's first major speech after the Republicans' shellacking at the polls came a month later, on December 7, in his annual address to Congress. As a matter of form, presidents were customarily upbeat and triumphal in these addresses, but Grant could hardly fail to acknowledge the nation's ruinous economic landscape, bleakly referring to "the prostration in business and industries" that was now in its second year. Powerless to turn things around, he blamed the country's economic ills on "a spirit of speculation involving an extravagance and luxury not required for the happiness or prosperity of a people." After outlining several measures to restore the country's credit, surveying the nation's foreign relations, and praising improvements in military armament, he spoke directly to the troubled South. Was it not time to bring an end to the "unhappy questions" of racial violence and political defiance by reflecting on where the responsibility for them lay? "Is there not a disposition on one side to magnify wrongs and outrages, and on the other to belittle them or justify them?" He wished to be fair to southerners, who had certain valid grievances, he said. Most, he felt sure, desired to quietly obey the law, not to break it. "But do they do right in ignoring the existence of violence and bloodshed in resistance to constituted authority? I sympathize with their prostrate condition, and would do all in my power to relieve them, acknowledging that in some instances they have had most trying governments to live under, and very oppressive ones in the way of taxation for nominal improvements. But can they proclaim themselves entirely irresponsible for their condition? They cannot. Violence has been rampant in some localities, and has either been justified or denied by those who could have prevented it." If all parties faced these "occurrences" fairly and honestly, "contemning the wrong and upholding the right," soon "all will be well. Treat the negro as a citizen and a voter, as he is and must remain, and soon parties will be divided, not on the color line but on principle." So far, rising to near eloquence, Grant had spoken from his heart, evoking his empathy with Black Americans as human beings and as citizens, appealing to a sense of common humanity and shared moral responsibility. But he also offered a warning. Without referring directly to the Supreme Court's *Slaughterhouse* decision, he said that a "theory" had been raised claiming that the federal government had no legal right to protect citizens within a state even when that state's government had failed to protect them. "This is a great mistake," Grant said. "While I remain Executive all the laws of Congress and the provisions of the Constitution, including the recent amendments added thereunto, will be enforced with rigor."

His words had an invigorating ring of steel. But they were a promise that he could not keep. Grant had little room for maneuver. The Republicans' power in Congress was wounded beyond immediate repair, and voters' support for a forceful policy in the South was at an end. Nor would the Supreme Court provide succor for the cause of civil rights. Despite its nominal Republican majority, it was rapidly evolving into an engine of revived states' rights jurisprudence, in which the hopes and safety of the freed people figured not at all. The Court's ruling in *Blyew,* in 1872, had barred the prosecution of white offenders under the Civil Rights Act of 1866 and allowed already convicted prisoners to sue federal officers for "false imprisonment." (In Louisiana, a Democratic sheriff, backed by a huge posse, had even arrested an entire detachment of federal cavalrymen for attempting to seize white terrorists.)

The Enforcement Acts hung in shreds. The rate of federal prosecutions rapidly shrank. From 1871 to 1872, the peak years of the Klan War, federal convictions under the Enforcement Acts had swelled from 108 to 448. In 1873, convictions rose to 466, but 683 cases were dismissed, more than four times the number the previous year. In 1874, however, following *Blyew* and *Slaughterhouse,* federal courts achieved only 97 convictions and registered 793 dismissals. After that, prosecutions continued rapidly to fade. In North Carolina, where the crusading state judge Albion Tourgée doggedly pursued the murderers of Wyatt Outlaw, the Democrat-dominated state Assembly repealed the law under which the charges had been brought, erasing the legal basis for the indictments. In South Carolina, more than a thousand cases were dropped before they even made it into a courtroom. In Mississippi, federal judge Robert Hill, a conservative Republican, typically imposed a mere $25 fine and the posting of a "peace bond" that was sometimes as low as one dollar.

Grant's conciliatory rhetoric had little impact on white conservatives in the South. Black Republicans still remained in many offices, including Congress and state legislatures, but their power was ebbing as states slipped from the Republicans' grasp. Five white-majority states were already governed or effectively dominated by the Democrats: Alabama, Georgia, North Carolina, Tennessee, and Virginia. In Florida, the governing Republicans shunned Black candidates in a hapless effort to win Democrats' support. Grant regarded as lost causes the Republican governors who clung precariously to power in Arkansas and Texas. Republicans were left depending on the three majority-Black states—Louisiana, Mississippi, and South Carolina—to preserve the party's narrowing foothold in the region.

Louisiana was in political chaos. Although the Republicans controlled the state administration, they were weak and factionalized. Meanwhile, the White League openly imported arms and ammunition. In at least fifteen parishes, Republican sheriffs, judges, tax collectors, and other officials were forced to flee. In Mansfield, White Leaguers confronted Black voters with warning blasts from cannon; and in the Republican bastion of Coushatta, up the Red River from Colfax, they murdered the parish's most prominent white and Black leaders, including its Vermont-born sheriff. In several parishes no Republicans at all were willing to risk voting. Maj. Lewis Merrill, redeployed to Louisiana with a contingent of the Seventh Cavalry, told visiting congressmen, "The state government has no power outside of the United States Army. The White League is the only power in the state."

Grant had explicitly referred to the disorder in Louisiana in his annual address, declaring that if the Fifteenth Amendment and the Enforcement Acts did not provide for "interference" against violence and intimidation, then "the whole scheme of colored enfranchisement is worse than mockery and little better than a crime." At the same time, he was painfully aware of the political price that Republicans were already paying for enforcing the law. Then, in January, the state Assembly's Democrats attempted a legislative coup, with support from the White League massed in the streets. They tried to seat members of their party who had been defeated in the November election in order to claim a majority and the power to impeach embattled Republican governor William Kellogg. Federal soldiers ousted the insurgents—New Orleans was one of the few places in the South where troops were plentiful—but it was no more than a stopgap solution. The northern public reacted with shock: reports of armed soldiers physically evicting (mostly) legally elected legislators smacked of precisely the "Caesarism" that Grant's enemies decried. Even in Boston, citizens rallied in *support* of the White League, comparing its defiance of the Republican state government to the patriots of Lexington and Concord. Politically splintered, overwhelmed by the Democratic tide, wracked by the national press, the Republicans surrendered control of the Assembly as part of a face-saving compromise, while in return the Democrats agreed not to impeach the now powerless Kellogg.

Mississippi Democrats pursued a similar strategy. In December 1874, armed whites belonging to what they euphemistically called the "Tax-Payers' League" seized control of the Republican-governed city of Vicksburg, forcing the resignation of its Black sheriff and the Board of Supervisors. They then proceeded to hunt down poorly armed Black militiamen, killing somewhere between fifty and a hundred people. On January 4, in a cri de coeur to the state legislature, former U.S. senator and now governor Adelbert Ames exclaimed, "It cannot be possible that the people of the state will permit a few lawless, violent men to inflame the mind of a community appealing to class or race prejudices, and then by force overthrow regularly constituted authorities." But it was only the beginning. In the following months, Democratic rifle clubs, now calling themselves "White Liners," sprang up around the state. In September, armed whites attacked Black Republicans gathered at a barbecue in the town of Clinton, to which they had been invited as a gesture of reconciliation, killing seven or eight men on the spot, and an estimated fifty in the chaotic aftermath.

Grant was torn. On September 13, he confessed to his new attorney general, Edwards Pierrepont, a conservative Republican from New York, "I am somewhat perplexed to know what directions to give in the matter. The whole public are tired out with these annual, autumnal outbreaks in the South, and there is so much unwholesome lying done by the press and people in regard to the cause & extent of these breaches of the peace that the great majority are now ready to condemn any interference on the part of the government." Grant wanted to respond forcefully, but he was dissuaded by members of his cabinet and by a panicky white Republican delegation from Ohio, who warned him that intervening on Ames's behalf would mean the party's defeat in *their* state elections in November. They argued that Mississippi was already lost but that Ohio could be saved if Grant acted with restraint. Mississippi's former Black congressman John Lynch wrote years later that Grant had confessed to him in a private White House meeting that he had given way against his best judgment. "I believed at the time I was making a grave mistake," Grant told him. "It was duty on one side and party obligation on the other. If a mistake was made, it was one of the head and not of the heart. If I had believed that any effort on my part would have saved Mississippi I would have made it." When Ames learned that Grant had cast him loose he wrote dejectedly to his wife, Blanche, "Why should I fight on a hopeless battle for two years more, when no possible good to the Negro or anyone else would be the result?"

The Republicans edged to victory in Ohio and were routed in Mississippi. Ames wrote gloomily on November 4, "So complete and thorough was the intimidation of Republican voters that we have yet to hear of a county which has gone Republican. The legislature will be nearly unanimous in both branches and will be able to do anything it may incline to do." Once seated, it prepared to impeach the impeccably honest Ames on charges of corruption and inciting a nonexistent Negro insurrection. Furious, isolated, and politically impotent, Ames knew he was licked. "The state has gone beyond redemption," he wrote to Blanche. In the spring of 1876, the Democrats withdrew their charges against Ames in return for his agreement to resign.

In early 1875, a deceptively hope-filled pause occurred in the collapse of Reconstruction when, with Grant's support, Congress once again took up the Radical Civil Rights bill that Sen. Charles Sumner had tirelessly championed until his death the previous year. Pushed forward by Ben Butler in the last weeks of the Forty-second Congress, it represented the final gasp of the once muscular idealism that had once driven the Republican Party. "We have been told we must respect the prejudices of the South," Butler told the House. "Pardon me, we must *lament* the prejudices of the South. Prejudice can never be the ground of legislation in regard to the rights of citizens." The debate inspired memorable eloquence from Black members of the House. "If I come [to Washington] by way of Louisville or Chattanooga, I am treated not as an American citizen, but as a brute," declared John Lynch. "Forced to occupy a filthy smoking car both day and night, with drunkards, gamblers, and criminals; and for what? Not that I am unable or unwilling to pay my way; not that I am obnoxious in my personal appearance or disrespectful in my conduct, but simply because I happen to be of a darker complexion."

Attacking the bill, the amnestied Confederate vice president Alexander Stephens, now a member of the House from Georgia, cited the Supreme Court's *Slaughterhouse* decision as a decisive constitutional repudiation of any federal attempt to insert itself into matters that only pertained to the states. To this, the impassioned Robert Elliott of South Carolina retorted, "The Slaughter-House Cases! The Slaughter-House Cases!" The enemies of civil rights were converting the postwar amendments into weapons to justify discrimination against precisely the people for whose benefit they had been crafted, he cried. He added, with a perspicacity that perhaps many of his colleagues failed to fully appreciate, "The passage of this bill will determine the civil status not only of the negro but of any other class of citizens who may feel themselves discriminated against. It will form the capstone of that temple of liberty begun on this continent." He was quite right, but it would take nearly a century to bring that truth to fruition. Just before the end of the session, the Civil Rights bill—the provision desegregating schools having been struck out—passed by a vote of 38 to 26 in the Senate, with Carl Schurz and his Liberal Republican friends aligned in opposition with the Democrats, and by 162 to 99 in the House. Grant quickly signed it into law. However, it was effectively a dead letter as soon as it was enacted, widely disregarded and difficult to enforce, where there was a will to enforce it at all. In truth it was a kind of legislative recessional, a stirring but ultimately empty dirge for the cause of civil rights. Three weeks after Grant signed the act, a federal judge in Memphis contemptuously declared that it embodied an "almost grotesque exercise of national authority," and ruled it unconstitutional. In 1883, the Supreme Court would agree.

In March of 1876, the Supreme Court finally issued its decision in *United States v. Cruikshank,* the climactic judicial act of the murderous tragedy that took place at Colfax, three years earlier. The Court voided all thirty-two counts of the indictment, reversing the convictions of Cruikshank and his two fellow defendants. It ruled that the Bill of Rights didn't apply within the states, and that the federal government had no constitutional authority to enforce it there. Chief Justice Morrison R. Waite, an undistinguished Ohio lawyer whom Grant had tapped to replace the deceased Salmon P. Chase, wrote—in a decision based, like *Slaughterhouse,* on the prewar principles of states' rights—that the government had no constitutional authority to enforce either the First Amendment right of assembly or the Second Amendment right to bear arms in any state. "The people, for their protection in the enjoyment of [their rights] must therefore look to the states, where the power for that purpose was originally placed," Waite wrote. In short, the survivors of the Colfax massacre had no alternative but to take their case to the state courts of Louisiana, which no longer even pretended to punish crimes against Blacks. The Court completely ignored both the facts of the massacre and the centrality of race. In an astonishingly obtuse parsing of the prosecution's charges, Waite wrote, "We may suspect that race was the cause of the hostility, but it is not so averred." The public was satisfied, however. The *New York Times* loftily praised Waite's "admirable clearness," while the Democratic *New York World* effusively compared him to the great leaders of the early Court John Jay and John Marshall. None of the perpetrators of the Colfax massacre ever stood trial again.

The last chapter in what conservatives called the "redemption" of the formerly Confederate South was played out where federal forces had scored their greatest triumph in the war against the Klan, South Carolina. On paper, Blacks had what ought to have been an insurmountable 35,000-vote majority. The state's white governor, Daniel Chamberlain, a former Union officer, had prosecuted the York County Klansmen. Two of the state's congressmen were Black. Hundreds of state officials identified as Radicals, many of them Black. Chamberlain had been elected by a majority of twelve thousand votes in 1874. For Republicans, for the freed people, all that translated into real power. By 1876, that power had turned to political dust.

Although the Klan had disappeared as a force in the state, much of the white population remained unreconciled to what they persisted in calling "Negro rule." The resurgent Democrats chose as their champion for governor in the 1876 elections the spectacularly whiskered, eminently respectable former Confederate general Wade Hampton, the state's largest prewar slaveowner and still one of its wealthiest men. Hampton campaigned on a platform of clean government, low taxes, and states' rights. On race issues; he counted as a moderate, at least sufficiently so to reassure voters still traumatized by the aftershocks of the Klan War. While the Democratic Party proclaimed a platform of undiluted white supremacy, Hampton assured Blacks that he would respect the postwar amendments. In soft words salted with a dash of menace, he told them, "We propose to protect you and give you all your rights, but while we do this you cannot expect that we should discriminate in your favor, and say that because you are a colored man, you have the right to rule in the state."

Officially, the Democrats forswore violence. At the core of Hampton's movement, however, like a Praetorian guard, stood some fifteen thousand men drawn from the "rifle clubs," who adopted red shirts as their quasi-uniform, marched armed in torchlight parades, shrieked rebel yells, and attacked Black Republicans in broad daylight. Their leaders, wrote Benjamin Tillman, an enthusiastic Red Shirt who later became both state governor and a U.S. senator, "had to my personal knowledge agreed on the policy of terrorizing the negroes at the first opportunity, by letting them provoke trouble and then having the whites demonstrate their superiority by killing as many of them as was justifiable." In the months before the election, the Red Shirts and their ostensibly less militarized allies in the Hampton campaign followed a systematic plan: boycotting Republicans' businesses, refusing to rent them land or lend them money, or even to treat them when they were sick. Each Democrat also committed to preventing at least one Black voter from casting his ballot, by persuasion if possible, otherwise by bribery, intimidation, or worse. "If he needs to be threatened," remarked one Hampton man, "a dead Radical is very harmless."

Wherever the Red Shirts and gun clubs were active, the atmosphere was explosive. On July 4, in the mostly Black town of Hamburg, a contingent of Black militiamen refused to give way to a swaggering white man who, in a possible act of deliberate provocation, demanded that they let him pass. Four days later, hundreds of armed whites descended on the town, where they bottled up the militiamen in a warehouse and began firing into it with long guns and a cannon lent to them by sympathizers in Georgia. Between thirty and forty men surrendered; six of them were shot dead on the spot. (Wrote Tillman, "We were all tired but more than satisfied with the result.") Some eighty whites were charged in the killings, but none were ever tried, much less jailed. In another confrontation, on September 19, near Ellenton, hundreds of whites trapped a body of Black militiamen and killed between thirty and fifty of them over two days, including a state senator, who was executed while praying on his knees. Neither incident could be traced to Hampton, who pleaded, perhaps sincerely, for calm. Nonetheless, also in September, he set out with three thousand of his red-shirted followers in a triumphal march across the state, to be greeted in town after town with cheers and celebratory cannonades.

On Election Day, enough federal troops were distributed around the state to ensure a semblance of order. But the Red Shirts had already achieved their purpose. Blacks kept away from the polls in droves. When they attempted to vote, whites physically blocked them, tampered with their ballots, and shipped in bogus conservative voters from the neighboring states. The Republicans eked out a majority, but one so slim that the Democrats aggressively contested it. The state's Republican-dominated elections board then threw out enough fraud-tainted ballots to both enlarge Chamberlain's margin and to prevent the legislature from flipping to the Democrats. When the Democrats still refused to concede, certification fell to the state legislature. There both parties claimed victory, and, for a time, rival bodies held forth simultaneously on the floor of the Assembly. Chamberlain begged the federal government for support but got no more than a detachment of soldiers to protect him from the red-shirted mob.

South Carolina's political drama was a more lurid version of what was taking place on the national plane in Washington. The election of 1876 has traditionally been treated as the de facto end of Reconstruction. In reality, it was an anticlimax. By the time the votes were counted, Reconstruction was hardly a ghost of itself. The Democrats already controlled the House of Representatives. Troop levels in the South stood close to rock bottom. The political steam had gone out of northern Radicalism. The Supreme Court had gutted the Enforcement Acts. And federal prosecutions in the South had petered out. For the presidency, the Democrats nominated Governor Samuel Tilden of New York, a plutocratic anti-Tammany reformer. The leading Republican candidate was Maine's popular, Radical but scandal-tarnished congressman James G. Blaine;

instead, the party nominated Rutherford B. Hayes, the colorless but respected governor of Ohio, a crucial toss-up state. Hayes promised "honest and local" government to the South, a formula that would appeal to whites; in a nod to the shrinking pool of Black voters, he also asserted that he would protect "all classes" of citizens. The Republicans presented the contest as a verdict on the war, asking in a campaign pamphlet, "Should the South be allowed to reverse the fruits of victory?" The Democrats railed tirelessly against the continuing presence of federal troops in the South, although by this time they numbered fewer than four thousand scattered from Virginia to Texas.

Tilden beat Hayes in the popular vote, with a landslide in the South and northern victories in New York, New Jersey, Indiana, and Connecticut. The ultimate outcome hinged on the contested results in Florida, Louisiana, and South Carolina, however. Florida turned in three separate sets of numbers, two for Hayes and one for Tilden. In Louisiana, the head of the election commission tried to sell the results to the highest bidder. And in South Carolina, more votes were cast than there were adult males. After much bitter wrangling behind closed doors on Capitol Hill, the three states were finally awarded to Hayes. Then the Democrats managed to invalidate one electoral vote in Oregon, leaving the candidates tied 184 to 184. An otherwise evenly divided ad hoc commission drawn from members of Congress and the Supreme Court left its deciding vote in the hands of Justice Joseph Bradley, the author of the Court's *Slaughterhouse* decision. Bradley cast it with the Republicans, finally delivering the election to Hayes. But this was not quite the end of the country's electoral agony. Rather than approve the commission's decision, the Democrats could easily have brought government to a halt. Given their control of the House, they could have forced a confrontation with the Senate, and then crippled that body with a filibuster. There were rumors that thousands of armed Democrats were marching on the Capitol under the leadership of former general George B. McClellan, who had lost the 1864 election to Lincoln. But the Democrats, like their fellow party members in South Carolina, decided to wait: it was obvious to everyone that Republican rule in the South was at its last gasp. A hard-nose deal was cut behind closed doors. The Democrats would allow Hayes to keep the three states' challenged votes, and the presidency. In exchange, the Republicans would agree to stop propping up the remaining tottering Reconstruction governments.

In his characteristically prolix and lawyerly inaugural address, on March 5, Hayes declared, "With respect to the two distinct races whose peculiar relations to each other have brought upon us the most deplorable complications and perplexities" the time for "peaceful self-government" had arrived. "It is a question in which every citizen of the nation is deeply interested." The national government, he said, had a moral obligation to "establish" the rights of the freed people and to protect their rights. (Blacks may have thought that their rights had *already* been established.) However, said Hayes, "The evils which afflict the southern states can only be removed or remedied by the united and harmonious efforts of both races, actuated by motives of mutual sympathy and regard."

Once in office, Hayes downplayed civil rights in the hope of fostering a southern Republican Party that no longer depended on Black votes. In an effort to win over Democrats, he appointed a cabinet friendly to the South, including a former Confederate general as postmaster general, Andrew Johnson's attorney general William Evarts as secretary of state, and as secretary of the interior Carl Schurz, who was, not surprisingly, an enthusiastic supporter of the president's conciliatory southern policy. Hayes was chasing a chimera. Republican votes in the South continued to evaporate. Two years later, the party lost control of the Senate for the first time since the 1850s.

On the same day that the Court handed down the *Cruikshank* decision, it also handed down a decision that hammered yet another legal nail in the coffin of Reconstruction. In *United States v. Reese,* it threw out the convictions of Kentucky officials who had conspired to prevent Blacks from voting in a local election. With this, the Court declared the few surviving clauses of the Enforcement Acts unconstitutional because they prohibited interference in voting per se when the Fifteenth Amendment had only barred voter suppression based explicitly on race. "The Fifteenth Amendment does not confer the right to vote upon anyone," Chief Justice Waite wrote.

The standoff in South Carolina dragged on into April. At last, the legislature declared Hampton the election's victor by a thousand votes. For months, the soldiers billeted in the statehouse had enabled Chamberlain to retain control of his physical office, if not its authority. On the 10th, on orders from President Hayes, the soldiers returned to their camps. The next day, Chamberlain handed over to Wade Hampton the keys to the governor's office. Although some Republican officials would remain in office for years to come in parts of the state where Blacks still enjoyed overwhelming majorities, the era of biracial government that the Klan had worked to destroy and Maj. Lewis Merrill had struggled so hard to protect was over.

In May 1877, accompanied by his wife, Julia, and son Jesse, Ulysses Grant set sail from Philadelphia to see the world. He was fifty-five years old and had not been out of the United States since the Mexican War. He traveled first to England, where he dined with Queen Victoria, then crossed the channel to make a circuit through Belgium, Germany, Switzerland, and Italy before returning to Britain. There, in a series of events attended by some eighty thousand workingmen he was hailed for his role in ending slavery and defending "the rights of man." He then returned to the continent and traveled through France and Italy, where he visited Pompeii and climbed Mount Vesuvius. From Palermo, he sailed to Egypt, toured Jerusalem and the biblical towns of Ottoman Palestine, then Constantinople, and from there, after visiting Greece, he returned once again to northern Europe, where he discussed the Civil War with the German chancellor, Otto von Bismarck, and later American Indian warfare with Tsar Alexander II in St. Petersburg. By 1879, he was in Asia, touring India, Burma, Malaya, French Indochina, China, and Japan. He and Julia returned to the United States via San Francisco only in September of that year, having circumnavigated the globe. At the Republican National Convention the following year, Grant was promoted by supporters as a contender for the nomination to what would have been his third term as president, leading for thirty-five ballots, until he was finally defeated by Ohio congressman James A. Garfield, who would go on to prevail in that November's elections. Weary of politics, scarred by the years of personal attacks he had endured, and at best ambivalent about embarking on another term, Grant was not sorry.

He wrote very little about his presidency, or for that matter the entire postwar period, in his 1885 memoirs, which dealt mainly and in great detail with his war years. In a brief passage about Andrew Johnson, Grant expressed the view that a president "ought to be a representative of the feeling, wishes and judgment of those over whom he presides." He was referring, critically, to Johnson's contempt for northern public opinion. But he was also implicitly describing the credo that he brought to his own presidency. As a man, Grant had evolved mightily from the midwestern farmer and clerk who thought little about race and had, if very briefly, owned an enslaved man in Missouri. It was an extraordinary journey, perhaps one of the most dramatic political evolutions in American history. Once the war was under way, when many of his military peers remained mired in racist contempt for freedom-seeking slaves, he welcomed them into the safety of his army's camps, advocated for the enlistment of Black men, and praised emancipation. He supported the Fourteenth Amendment, and as president he appealed personally to Congress to pass the Fifteenth. With the limited resources allowed him by Congress, he sent his troops and his Justice Department into the fight against the Ku Klux Klan, and prevailed over it until public opinion and much of the Republican political establishment abandoned him. In his stoical way he soldiered on as long as he politically could. Perhaps he remembered his terse declaration during the Overland Campaign of 1864 when, checked at the Wilderness, his generals expected him to retreat to Washington as previous Union commanders had before him. Instead, he telegraphed Abraham Lincoln, "I propose to fight it out on this line if it takes all summer." He was a stubborn soldier and he was an equally stubborn president. He hoped that victory over the Klan would purchase permanent peace in the South. In that, he was wrong.

Grant realized when he left office, and saw even more clearly by the time he wrote his memoir, that the racial chasm that replaced slavery was wider than he had imagined. "It is possible that the question of a conflict between races may come up in the future, as did that between freedom and slavery before," Grant wrote on nearly the last page of his memoir. What form that conflict might take he didn't speculate. But he had enough experience with the courage that Black Americans had demonstrated during the war and Reconstruction, and enough appreciation of their determination to force the nation to honor the rights that they had earned, to know that they would not acquiesce forever in the new serfdom that was replacing slavery. Grant knew that he had not prevailed over the demons of race, but he hoped, intensely, that Americans someday would.

EPILOGUE

Riverside Park, New York City

Just after 8 a.m. on July 23, 1885, Ulysses Grant died surrounded by his family, in a borrowed cottage in the Adirondack Mountains of New York, where he had retreated to finish his memoirs. The end was not a surprise. For many months, he had suffered from advancing cancer of the throat, which had left him unable to speak above a whisper. In the face of extreme pain, he had soldiered on, scribbling final additions to his manuscript on scraps of paper. The last photograph taken of him showed a man shrunken by illness—he weighed barely one hundred pounds at the end—swathed in an overcoat, top-hatted and bespectacled, and hunched over pages of his manuscript, stoic to the last. Grant was sixty-three years old.

On the morning of August 8, a sweltering day in Manhattan, an honor guard bore Grant's coffin from City Hall, where it had lain in state for three days. They placed it on a black-draped catafalque harnessed to eight jet-black horses, which then led a slow and solemn procession of sixty thousand marchers up Broadway past the great flag-draped emporiums of Ladies Mile, through Union Square and onto Fifth Avenue, past St. Patrick's Cathedral and the mansions of the city's elite to 57th Street, where the funeral column turned west to Broadway, and again north to 72nd Street, then west to Riverside Drive and finally north to the site that had been selected for Grant's tomb near 122nd Street, overlooking the Hudson River and the majestic Palisades.

From head to tail, the parade stretched for seven miles, in heat so withering that numbers of spectators and marchers alike passed out in the street. All America, it seemed, had come together to mourn. A million and a half people witnessed the parade, the largest gathering ever held in North America up to that time. Grant's wife, Julia, and their children rode in a closed carriage just behind the catafalque, followed by President Grover Cleveland, members of his cabinet, former presidents Chester A. Arthur and Rutherford B. Hayes, graying generals, regiments of regular infantry, artillery batteries, marines, sailors, veterans bearing tattered battle flags, members of Congress and the Supreme Court, the diplomatic corps, representatives from all the states and scores of cities, state militia units, and even contingents of former Confederate soldiers wearing civilian clothes. The great guns of warships anchored in the Hudson River boomed to announce the progress of the procession hour after hour. Balconies, windows, doors, and roofs were crowded with silent onlookers all along the line of march, standing ten and twenty deep along the avenues. Boys perched on trees, fences, and the crosspieces of telegraph poles. Black spectators wept openly.

At the gravesite, troops wheeled into line to fill the bluffs above the river. Drums rolled, bugles blared, musket fire snapped through the heavy air. Masons had worked all night and through the morning to build an asphalt-covered brick vault that would hold the former president's coffin until an appropriately magnificent memorial could be erected nearby. It stood open now, more like a bunker than a president's tomb, but in its way fitting for a soldier who had always shunned glamour and show. A white rose was laid atop the coffin, then a laurel wreath. "As the years roll on we, too, shall have fought our battles through and be laid to rest, our souls following the long column to the realms above," a minister intoned. "Let us live so that when that time shall come, those left behind may say above our graves, 'Here lies the body of a true-hearted, brave, and earnest defender of the republic.'" Finally, the soldiers of the Seventh Regiment fired three parting volleys of musketry. The 22nd Regiment then fired three volleys more, followed by three salvos from the unlimbered cannon, and a salute of twenty-one guns from the *Powhatan,* a warship anchored offshore, echoed by cannonades from more ships further down the river, then silence.

Grant's funeral was designed as a spectacle of national reconciliation, the symbolic coda to an era of sectional rancor that was now ending. Detachments of gray-clad militia from Virginia and Georgia marched alongside units from Massachusetts and New York. Winfield Scott Hancock, the hero of Gettysburg, rode alongside Robert E. Lee's nephew, former Confederate general Fitzhugh Lee; William Tecumseh Sherman rode alongside former Confederate general Joseph Johnson; and Philip Sheridan with former Confederate general Simon Buckner. Such tableaux were proof, enthused the *New York Times,* that "the war is over" and that "its bitterness has passed away."

Encomiums to Grant were lavish. The Democratic *New York Herald,* which had viciously attacked him when he was in office, declared that although Grant had his faults, "We cannot see them because the brilliancy of his deeds shines in our eyes." The Republican *New York Times* celebrated him as a transcendent American hero, a "man who by force of character and circumstance had come, more conspicuously than any other, to personify the victory of 'government of the people by the people and for the people.'" Frederick Douglass later summed him up more acutely as a man driven by moral purpose who had shown his "superiority to popular prejudice" first by employing Black troops during the war, when other generals recoiled at the prospect, and then by ordering white soldiers to treat them with respect. "In this way he proved himself to be not only a wise general, but a great man—one who could adjust himself to new conditions, and adopt the lessons taught by the events of the hour." But few obituaries even bothered to mention Grant's struggles on behalf of civil rights or his war against the Klan. By the end of the century, Grant had almost wholly become abstracted from his policies, a latter-day Washington, more a symbol than a man the modest soldier from Galena and the Reconstruction Era Radical would hardly have recognized. They were paying homage to the general who had led the North to victory, who had triumphed like an ancient hero in America's Iliad, not to the president who had championed Blacks' rights and waged war against the Ku Klux Klan. Even as tourists flocked to the imposing classical edifice that later became Grant's permanent tomb, which for twenty years or so drew more than half a million visitors annually, his presidential reputation sank, along with the legacy of Reconstruction.

The Supreme Court continued the systematic deconstruction of civil rights that it had begun during Grant's presidency, with its *Slaughterhouse* and *Cruishank* decisions. In 1896, the Court decisively ratified systemic racial discrimination in *Plessy v. Ferguson,* which upheld a Louisiana law that required railroads to maintain separate cars for whites and Blacks in order "to promote the comfort of passengers." The ruling's author, Justice Henry Brown, opined that skin color was a "distinction that must always exist," and declared of the Fourteenth Amendment—in blunt defiance of history—that "it could not have been intended to abolish distinctions based on color, or to enforce social, as distinguished from political equality, or a commingling of the two races." In effect, *Plessy* ordered Americans to discriminate or suffer punishment. Although Brown was a northern Republican, the bench included four Democrats, one of whom had loudly denounced the Emancipation Proclamation, another an ex-Confederate and reputed Klan member, and a third who had voted to strike down the Civil Rights Act. The case for the plaintiff, Homer Plessy, was argued before the Court by no less a champion of civil rights than Albion W. Tourgée, who had heroically defied the Klan as a judge in North Carolina during the 1870s. He now described the Fourteenth Amendment as the "*magna charta* of American citizens' rights" and attacked the whole concept of "race" as a meaningless human distinction. His arguments had no impact on a Court that had almost wholly reabsorbed the principles of states' rights and the "redeemed" South.

There was only a single dissent from *Plessy,* by Associate Justice John Marshall Harlan, a Kentuckian who had been raised in a slave-owning family but was radicalized by the *Dred Scott* decision and later led a Union regiment through the bloody battles of the Civil War. "The judgment this day rendered will, in time, prove to be quite as pernicious as the decision made by this tribunal in the Dred Scott case," Harlan predicted.

The white race deems itself to be the dominant race in this country. But in the view of the Constitution, in the eye of the law, there is in this country no superior, dominant, ruling class of citizens. Our Constitution is color-blind. The law regards man as man, and takes no account of his surroundings or of his color when his civil rights as guaranteed by the supreme law of the land are involved. We boast of the freedom enjoyed by our people above all other peoples. But it is difficult to reconcile that boast with a state of the law which, practically, puts the brand of servitude and degradation upon a large class of our fellow citizens, our equals before the law.

In 1954, the NAACP's lawyer Thurgood Marshall would quote Harlan's words in the watershed civil rights case *Brown v. Board of Education*.

Meanwhile, what remained of Black voting rights in the South was being systematically stripped away with twisted legality. The Fifteenth Amendment had left a gaping loophole: it banned explicitly *racial* tests intended to disenfranchise Black voters, but it failed to outlaw supposedly "race-neutral" measures that had the same effect. Soon every southern state had adopted poll taxes and literacy tests that required Black voters to interpret complicated texts, which joined more traditional forms of manipulation such as gerrymandering, the sudden shifting of poll locations, truncated poll hours in Black areas, and the physical muscling away of Black voters from ballot boxes. Whites were quite open about what they were doing. Governor William C. Oates of Alabama, a former Confederate colonel, bluntly told the graduating class of the Tuskegee Institute, "I want to give you niggers a few words of plain talk and advice. You might just as well understand that this is a white man's country as far as the South is concerned, and we are going to make you keep your place." And in a speech to the 1901 Alabama Constitutional Convention, its chairman, John Knox, declared, "The new constitution eliminates the ignorant Negro vote and places the control of our government where God Almighty intended it should be—with the Anglo-Saxon race." Likening Black voters to the anarchist who had recently assassinated President McKinley, he added, "We would take the right to vote from the ignorant and the vicious as we would take the torch from the hand of a child." Three years later, the Alabama Democratic Party adopted "White Supremacy" as its official motto. It appeared at the top of every ballot on Election Day until 1966. In the late nineteenth century, about one-third of southern congressional districts were majority Black by population; voter suppression may thus have cost the Republicans on average over at least twenty seats in the House of Representatives. Everywhere, the number of Black voters plummeted. There were 130,334 registered Black voters in Louisiana in 1896; by 1904, there were 1,342. Black voters in Alabama dropped from 180,000 to 3,000 during the same period. In Virginia, in 1904, no Blacks voted at all.

Black men continued to serve in Congress until the end of the century from a handful of districts where whites were so heavily outnumbered by Black voters that efforts to disenfranchise them were slow to take effect. Well into the 1880s, the former slave and war hero Robert Smalls continued to be elected from Beaufort on the South Carolina coast. And in 1888, the multitalented lawyer John Mercer Langston, the grand-uncle of the poet Langston Hughes, won a seat in Virginia, though he only managed to keep it for one term. Eight Black members served in the Forty-fourth Congress from 1875 to 1877, the largest representation of Blacks to sit in any Congress until the late twentieth century. Only three were left by the Fifty-first Congress of 1889 to 1891. After that, just one remained. George H. White of North Carolina, a talented young attorney from Tarboro, was the last. From the moment of his arrival he felt a responsibility to speak for the great mass of silenced Black Americans, denouncing lynching, demanding that white members of Congress speak respectfully of Blacks, and arguing that southern states ought to be deprived of congressional seats as the price for disenfranchising Black voters. In January 1901, as the end of his term approached, North Carolina having rigged its laws so that he could not be reelected, White decried the failure of Congress to advance his anti-lynching bill to the floor, then offered a valedictory for all the Black men who had struggled to defend their place in post–Civil War America: "This is perhaps the Negro's temporary farewell to the American Congress, but let me say, Phoenix-like he will rise up some day and come again. These parting words are in behalf of an outraged, heart-broken, bruised and bleeding, but God-fearing people; faithful, industrious, loyal, rising people—full of potential force."

In April of 1874, former attorney general Amos Akerman reflected, "To persons who had not the strongest evidence of the facts, a history of the Ku Klux would be incredible. That any large portion of our people should be so ensavaged as to perpetuate or excuse such actions is the darkest blot on Southern character in this age." The Klan's terrorism was no secret. Its murders, massacres, floggings, rapes, and castrations had been well publicized for years, while the report of the Ku Klux Klan Committee, in 1872, had delivered overwhelming proof that the Klan's terrorism was not random but deliberate and political. Many southerners celebrated the terrorists as heroes. When Nathan Bedford Forrest died in 1877, his pastor, Rev. George Stainback, warmly lauded his "noble spirit," declaring, "How well he did his part in that heroic struggle the historian, on his brightest page, will tell and the poet sing in his sweet strain his valor and his genius." In 1900, the *York Enquirer* praised Dr. James Bratton for "nobly" facing the trials of "the dark days of Reconstruction," commending him particularly for being the prime mover of the disarming of Jim Williams's militia company; it didn't mention that Bratton had led Williams's murderers, but that was public knowledge.

Northern Republicans were bored with the South's troubles and, in truth, bored with the fate of Blacks. The nation's greatest demographic growth was shifting westward. In the South, white supremacy was no mere slogan but an institutionalized way of life. For the vast majority of southern Blacks, voting was a dimming memory. In 1890, the citizens of Aberdeen, Mississippi, took up a collection to reward a white mason for both the cost of his whip and for the $30 fine he received for "disturbing the peace" after he gave a black man two hundred lashes for daring to speak up about politics. "Under their fear of the dreaded Ku-Klux, the negroes made more progress in a few months in the needed lessons of self-control, industry, and respect for the rights of property and general good behavior than they would have done in as many years but for this or some equally powerful impulse," one early-twentieth-century historian of the Klan smugly reflected. "It was a rough and a dangerous way to teach such lessons, but, under all the circumstances, it seemed the only possible way." Lynchings, which in the time of the Klan War mostly took place in the dark of night and were carried out by men afraid of being recognized, evolved into public spectacles, announced in advance by local newspapers, attended by huge crowds including children, and by photographers on hand to record the events for postcards and posterity. In the 1890s alone, between seventy-eight and 161 Black men were lynched every year, a barbaric drumbeat that continued without diminishing through the 1920s. (Recent research by the Equal Justice Initiative, based in Montgomery, Alabama, has documented nearly 6,500 racial terror lynchings between 1865 and 1950.)

Americans embraced a kind of vast willful forgetting, the mental erasure of an entire era, which in turn shaped the writing of a falsified history that influenced generations to follow. The replacement of fact with fiction was breathtaking. "The ultimate root of the trouble in the South had been, not the institution of slavery, but the coexistence in one society of two races so distinct in characteristics as to render coalescence impossible," the influential, New Jersey–born, Columbia University historian William Dunning wrote in 1901. Slavery, he said, had been merely a *"modus vivendi"*—a way of getting along—through which social life was possible. "It was logical that its place had now been taken by some set of conditions which, if more humane and beneficent in accidents, must in essence express the same fact of racial inequality." He approvingly asserted that by the end of the nineteenth century "Southern whites had made enormous positive advances in the suppression of the other race." A generation later, Illinois-born Allan Nevins, one of the mid-century's most widely read historians, and a political liberal, would describe Grant's southern policy as "reactionary" and the conservative reaction to Reconstruction's "intolerable yoke of Negroes, Scalawags, and Carpetbaggers" as "a great pacifying force" that produced "less oppression of the Negro than might have been expected [and] a fair degree of racial concord." It was a damning judgment that remained largely unchanged until the late twentieth century.

Into the blank space left by the collective erasure of Reconstruction history, Americans poured an amoral amalgam of myth and disingenuous apologetics, a dizzying inversion of truth in which mostly helpless victims were redefined as the perpetrators of monstrous crime and terrorists were celebrated as heroes. Klansmen soon percolated into local and national office, from sheriffs' departments to governors' mansions and the U.S. Congress. One of the Klan's original founders, John C. Lester, was elected to the Tennessee legislature. Rutherford County, North Carolina, Klan chief Randolph Shotwell was appointed to the position of state librarian. Georgia Klan leader John B. Gordon was elected governor of his state in 1886, and later served in the U.S. Senate. In 1888, Grover Cleveland named to the U.S. Supreme Court the fiery Klan lawyer, and likely member, L. Q. C. Lamar, who had knocked a federal marshal to the ground with a club in a courtroom during a Mississippi terrorism trial. In 1910, when the white residents of Graham, North Carolina, gathered in the town square to dedicate a Confederate monument where Wyatt Outlaw was lynched in 1870, the master of ceremonies was Jacob Long, who had led the murderers: he declared that the monument would "recall the achievements of the great and good of our own race and blood." In 1900, E. A. Crawford, a member of the gang that lynched Jim Williams, was named sergeant-at-arms of the South Carolina state Senate; the leader of the gang, Dr. Bratton, was appointed the chairman of South Carolina's state Board of Health. Of Bratton, the *Charleston Sunday News* later declared, "there was no Klansman more active and none more zealous in the work of maintaining the supremacy of the Southern white man," at a time when "the Ku Klux Klans were spread over the South like the dew." Noting his stonewalling testimony before the congressional Joint Committee in 1871, the newspaper approvingly asserted that he did not "divulge the slightest scintilla of evidence. Men of his caliber didn't tell."

The Klan also became the stuff of poetry. In 1913, the Tennessee poet Elizabeth Wilkes Romine, the poet laureate of the state's chapters of the Daughters of the American Revolution and the United Daughters of the Confederacy, penned a fulsome ode to the Klan's birthplace.

> Pulaski: Rich in song and story.
> Pulaski: Hallowed on the page of glory.
> Pulaski: God's blessings rest on thee.
> Pulaski: The garden spot of Tennessee.

Pulaski: The gift of a princely hand.
Pulaski: Who gave the flower of her land.
Pulaski: Sent them forth man after man.
Pulaski: Mother of the Ku Klux Klan.

Already the rehabilitated property of the South, the Klan's legend was about to become the nation's. The transformative moment took place at Clune's Auditorium in Los Angeles, in February 1915, with the premiere of an epic film like none that had ever been seen before on the screen: D. W. Griffith's *The Birth of a Nation*. It was based on one of the best-selling novels of the day, *The Clansman,* by Thomas Dixon Jr., the son of a North Carolina slaveowner, who felt inspired to warn America of what he called "creeping negroism." Audiences cheered as robed Klansmen galloped "hell-for-leather on an errand of stern justice," as one rapt viewer put it, to save a virginal white girl from a "forced marriage" to a lascivious Black politician. The film unfurled virtually every racist cliché bequeathed by the South's revisionist version of Reconstruction: Black predators, bloodthirsty Black soldiers, drunken Black politicians, vicious abolitionists, genteel Confederates—and heroic Klansmen. After a private screening at the White House—the first film to be so privileged—President Woodrow Wilson, who was raised in Georgia during the Civil War and educated in South Carolina during Reconstruction, reportedly declared, "It is like writing history with lightning. And my only regret is that it is all so terribly true." Black Americans protested the film's virulent racism and called for boycotts, but audiences loved it. One contemporary hailed it as the "greatest picture yet produced," and as late as 1948 the preeminent film critic James Agee declared it "the one great epic tragic film," and praised Griffith, the son of a Confederate officer, for "degrees of understanding, honesty, and compassion far beyond the capacity of his accusers."

Although the film's immense popularity brought a few old Klansmen out of the woodwork to testify to its "authenticity," the original Klan was long defunct. However, in the highly racialized America of the Jim Crow era, *Birth of a Nation* ignited the formation of a new Klan retooled for the twentieth century. After seeing the film in Atlanta, an alcoholic promoter and onetime garter salesman named William Simmons hit on the idea of reviving the Klan as a sort of fraternal order devoted to bigotry and "patriotic" nativism in general, limiting membership to native-born white Protestants, and targeting Catholics, Jews, immigrants, alleged Communists, labor organizers, supposed gangsters and bootleggers, and of course Blacks. Simmons acquired a copy of the original Klan's "Prescript," its catechism, copied imagery from *Birth of a Nation,* invented cross-burning, and sent a group of his friends dressed in bedsheets riding through Atlanta, shooting off their guns in front of theaters where the film was being shown. From its hucksterish beginning, Simmons's creature swelled with remarkable speed into a behemoth national organization with as many as four million members and "Klaverns" as far north as New England and as far west as Oregon. In 1921, the Klan even acquired a short-lived college near Atlanta to inculcate "pure, 100 percent Americanism," and hired Nathan Bedford Forrest's grandson and namesake, the Grand Dragon of Georgia, as its business manager. Throwing itself into politics, the Klan backed candidates for state government across the South and beyond. Unlike the original Klan, Simmons's Klan was also a profit-making enterprise that sold memberships for up to $40 apiece, along with robes and other paraphernalia, without paying taxes on its income. Simmons and his associates kept 80 percent of the proceeds and became very rich. The Klan's fall was as sudden as its dizzying rise. Awash in scandal, it collapsed by the end of the decade, disappearing almost everywhere even faster than it had appeared.

The reinvented Klan never quite ceased to exist in the South, where it lingered in reduced form through the Depression and World War II. From those roots it rose for the third time during the civil rights era, in reaction to the desegregation of schools and public facilities, boycotts, and demands for the restoration of voting rights to Black citizens under the Kennedy and Johnson administrations. Klan membership rebounded to more than fifty thousand across the South, spread among at least twenty-seven often fractious and competitive groups, the largest of which counted perhaps fifteen thousand members, many of them claiming to be the only "true" Klan. Most abandoned the anti-Semitic and anti-Catholic polemics of the 1920s to "patriotically" focus on an imaginary Communist conspiracy they claimed was behind the civil rights movement. Although individual groups varied in their willingness to break the law, the period was characterized by pervasive intimidation, church bombings, the assassination of civil rights organizers, and the vicious suppression of peaceful demonstrations. In contrast to Grant's determined but ultimately crippled campaign against the original Klan, the federal government this time did not stint in its support for law, order, and justice.

In the darkest days of the Jim Crow era, in 1901, the former Radical congressman George Boutwell predicted that although the Fifteenth Amendment had been defeated, "Nevertheless the influence of the amendment is felt by all, and the time is not distant when it will be accepted by all." He wasn't wrong, but it would take generations. Backed by a Supreme Court committed to revitalizing the Fourteenth Amendment, Amos Akerman's heirs put the might of the Justice Department behind the restoration of Black Americans' voting rights and ultimately the social rights that the Civil Rights Act of 1875 hoped, but failed, to secure. The spirit of Reconstruction would be dramatically renewed when President Dwight Eisenhower deployed the 101st Airborne Division—the symbolic heirs of Maj. Lewis Merrill's Seventh Cavalry—to enforce the federally mandated desegregation of Central High School in Little Rock, Arkansas, in 1957, setting in motion a new era of civil rights enforcement.

Armed with the long-moribund provision of the 1871 Ku Klux Klan Act that permitted the national government to suppress criminal conspiracies intended to deny persons equal protection under the law, federal agents infiltrated the Klan wholesale and by the 1970s had broken it as a force to be politically reckoned with. Iterations of the Ku Klux Klan still linger within the cosmos of today's radical right, as evidenced by their presence in the agitation that took place in Charlottesville, Virginia, in 2017, over the proposed removal of a statue of Robert E. Lee. It would be naive to suggest that it could never rise again, given its stunning and unexpected revival in the twentieth century. But for the present at least its remnants are mere ghosts of its savage Reconstruction Era ancestors. Since then, the Fourteenth Amendment's insistence on equal protection under the law for all citizens has become the transformative engine of legislation ensuring the rights of minorities of every kind, as well as women, in employment, voting, education, public facilities, housing, transportation, and other spheres of American life.

In March of 1896, Lewis Merrill died in Philadelphia from kidney disease complicated by nephritis, at the age of sixty-one. When his service in the South finally came to an end in early 1876, after a tour in Louisiana, he might have expected to join the rest of the Seventh Cavalry on the Great Plains. But he was instead detailed to serve temporarily as chief of staff to the president of the Centennial International Exhibition in Philadelphia, America's first World's Fair, which celebrated the nation's first hundred years. The posting probably saved his life. That June, the Seventh Cavalry's impulsive commander, George Armstrong Custer, misguidedly attacked a huge army of Sioux and Cheyenne at the battle of the Little Big Horn, taking the lives of nearly his entire command. Many of the men who had served under Merrill in South Carolina thus died on the arid hills of Montana, overwhelmed by Sitting Bull's warriors. Merrill afterward returned to the frontier, to various posts mostly in the Dakota Territory, guarding railroad lines as his health steadily deteriorated. He remained a major until just before his retirement in 1886, when he received a pro forma elevation to lieutenant colonel, having been deliberately held back for years by southern influence in Washington, his career a casualty of his unbending commitment to civil rights.

In South Carolina, Merrill had demonstrated that even with the limited resources he was given the law could be enforced, terrorism suppressed, and Black Americans sufficiently protected that they could advance in political and public life. Where men of his caliber had a free hand, the defenders of civil rights prevailed in the war against the Klan. Temporary though that victory was, it demonstrated for the first time in American history that the national government could enforce legal principles of civil rights. That bought precious time for significant numbers of Blacks to gain an education, establish themselves in professions, practice politics, and to begin to make their way in the South's segregated commercial economy, from which they had been universally barred before the Civil War. Had Grant's campaign been properly financed, sustained over time, and supported by consistent punishment by the courts it could have not only destroyed the Klan but ensured the survival of a two-party system and civil rights in the South. In the end, lasting change required more than white America was prepared to give.

It is difficult to know precisely how many Black men and women—or whites either, for that matter—were murdered, tortured, and flogged by the Ku Klux Klan. The Equal Justice Initiative of Montgomery, Alabama, has determined that a minimum of two thousand freed people were murdered just between 1865 and 1876, including those killed before the Klan's rise in 1868. The actual number is undoubtedly higher. The murders of the Klan's white victims like John Stephens of Caswell County, North Carolina, and George Ashburn of Columbus, Georgia, were recorded at length in the newspapers and court records. Comparatively few Black victims, such as Wyatt Outlaw and Jim Williams, left the same kind of personal mark in history, although the congressional investigation of 1871 attempted to record many in at least some detail. The vast majority remain merely names, or not even that, unidentified as nothing more than simply "a negro," condemned to the further indignity of historical oblivion, their deaths hardly noted. In any event, bare numbers cannot convey the havoc wrought upon Black families and communities by the Klan. For every father, brother, son, or husband slain or flogged, for every girl or woman raped and beaten, there were also children, grandparents, brothers and sisters, who suffered shattering terror, sudden impoverishment, lasting physical damage and psychological trauma, along with the never-ending terror of what might come again in the night with six-shooters, bullwhips, and ropes.

Ingrained racism was one reason for Americans' fading commitment to civil rights. It infected the actions of military commanders and ordinary soldiers charged with protecting the freed people, as well as juries and judges who sat in judgment on terrorists, and the decision-making of national politicians. Punishment for the majority of terrorist crimes was too often merely symbolic, fostering a sense that crimes against Blacks ought to be forgiven with a warning and a $10 fine. The shortcomings of Reconstruction were less the fault of Republican state governments in the South, as Lost Cause propaganda claimed, than of the weakening of political will in the North. Ultimately, the freed people were betrayed by elements of the North's political class, Carl Schurz, Lyman Trumbull, Horace Greeley, and their Liberal Republican friends, who were seduced by the illusory vision of conciliation with the unrepentant white South. At best, they allowed themselves to believe that if federal pressure was removed the former Confederates would graciously accept Blacks as political equals; at worst, they callously abandoned the freed people to men who regarded them as subhuman and considered violence against them no crime at all.

Of Schurz's abandonment of the freed people, his biographer Hans Trefousse wrote, "Thus the politics of virtue ended in disaster for the freedmen and the nation." As secretary of the interior under Rutherford Hays, he instituted civil service examinations, reformed the Bureau of Indian Affairs, and initiated the country's first land conservation measures. In 1872, Schurz had succinctly encapsulated his philosophy in a memorable phrase that continues to resonate in American politics: "My country right or wrong; if right to be kept right; and if wrong to be set right." He was supremely self-confident in his principles. But nothing was more important either politically or morally than the full assimilation of the freed people into American life. Schurz had once understood this. But by failing to fight for their civil rights he contributed to the defeat of the very principles that he had once cherished. In his last years, Schurz was much admired in certain quarters as the liberal conscience of America, notably as an outspoken critic of imperialism in general and the Philippine-American War in particular. In 1904, two years before his death, he published his final thoughts on race, writing in *McClure's Magazine* that he regretted that the Negro had been reduced "to a permanent condition of serfdom—, 'alongside the mule,' practically without any rights of citizenship." He never acknowledged his own role in the destruction of Blacks' civil rights.

W. E. B. Du Bois wrote in 1935, in his seminal study of the postwar years, *Black Reconstruction in America,* "One is astonished in the study of history at the recurrence of the idea that evil must be forgotten, distorted, skimmed over. The difficulty, of course, with this philosophy is that history loses its value as an incentive, an example; it paints perfect men and noble nations, but it does not tell the truth." If, Du Bois suggests, "we are going to use history for our pleasure and amusement, for inflating our national ego, and giving us a false but pleasurable sense of accomplishment, then we must give up the idea of history either as a science or an art." The story of the war against the Klan, and more broadly of the entire Reconstruction Era, requires Americans to face some harsh truths. It offers a warning that rights that have been gained can also be taken away. It also shows all too vividly that racial terrorism is as inescapable a part of the nation's heritage as the more familiar themes of the steady enlargement of democracy, the rise of capitalism, and the westward march of settlement across the continent. More darkly still, it is a reminder that in the United States as elsewhere in the world barbarism may lie only a small distance beneath the skin of civilization.

Graham, North Carolina, today has the frayed look of many Piedmont towns whose vitality has been sapped by the automobile, suburbanization, and the vanquishing of local stores by shopping malls. Its small downtown is still dominated by its yellow-brick, antebellum Italianate courthouse. Fronting the square are a movie theater, two craft brewery taprooms, a vintage clothing shop, and a soda fountain that sells banana splits and cheese dogs. Across the square from the courthouse lies a scrap of a park with a few benches. It was there, in 1870, that the cabinetmaker, Union veteran, and conciliator Wyatt Outlaw was lynched in his nightclothes by the Ku Klux Klan and left to dangle as a graphic threat to the town's Republicans.

In recent years, the square has been the scene of numerous civil rights protests that were sometimes harshly dealt with by the local police. In 2020, a man was seized for "impeding traffic" because he was standing on a curb holding a placard protesting the death of George Floyd; the same year, a Black woman awoke one night to see a man disguised in a white hood pounding on her garage door. Marchers would gather at Wayman Chapel, the church that Wyatt Outlaw helped to organize. The chapel is a plain, single-story brick building on North Main Street, not far from the square. It is a lively presence in Graham, with a welcoming and politically active congregation. Its website, along with profiles of deceased congregants and holiday announcements, invites members to attend "Gun Violence Prevention Weekend," and posts a remembrance adorned with doves of peace for the nine Black men and women who were murdered in their Charleston church by a young white supremacist. At election time every year, the chapel promotes a program it calls "Souls to the Polls" to assist voters: "Make your mark on history by voting with your friends and community."

Wyatt Outlaw's murder went unavenged and unpunished. Graham's Blacks were all too soon forced back into the semi-slavery of Jim Crow. But his death was not in vain. His aspirations remain alive in Wayman Chapel's commitment to public service, democracy, forgiveness, and nonviolence, a remarkable testimony to the persistence of the values that he stood for and tried to advance in a community, indeed a country, that was not yet ready to listen.

ACKNOWLEDGMENTS

Many people and institutions have helped to make this book possible, among them the exceptionally helpful staffs of the Manuscript Room of the Library of Congress; the Southern Historical Collection at the University of North Carolina, at Chapel Hill; the South Caroliniana Collection at the University of South Carolina, at Columbia; and LancasterHistory (formerly the Lancaster County Historical Society), in Pennsylvania. Anne Causey of the Alderman Library, at the University of Virginia, in Charlottesville; Wanda Fowler of the Historical Center of York County, in Yorkville, South Carolina; and archivist Gwen Gosney Erickson, curator of the Quaker Archives at Guilford College, in Greensboro, North Carolina, were of exceptional help, as was United States Senate Historian Betty Koed and her generous staff whose resources once again were invaluable for my exploration of the Senate's workings and the thinking of its leading members in the late 1860s and early 1870s.

Friends and colleagues provided many insights that illuminated the southern context in which the Klan thrived and aspects of the larger American political scene during the era of the Klan War: among others, Karen Branan, Orville Vernon Burton, Norman Dann, Chuck Fager, Wilson Golden, Ross Hetrick, Mark Pinsky, and David Wright. Charles Lane bestowed upon me a wealth of primary source material bearing on Hiram Whitley and the federal agents who infiltrated the Ku Klux Klan. T. J. Styles provided me with illuminating material on Gen. George Custer's Reconstruction Era activities in Kentucky.

My agent Adam Eaglin of the Elyse Cheney Literary Agency was an always supportive presence throughout the writing of this book, as were my editors at Knopf, Andrew Miller and Todd Portnowitz. No one, however, has contributed more than my wife, Jean Parvin Bordewich, who has once again served as my most provocative and clarifying interlocutor, as well as a source of patient tolerance for a spouse who has a penchant for repeatedly slipping away into another century.

NOTES

ABBREVIATIONS

AA: Amos T. Akerman
AJ: Andrew Johnson
AWT: Albion W. Tourgée
CG: *Congressional Globe* (sessions are indicated with a slash, e.g.,
        42/1 indicates the Forty-second Congress, First Session, and
        so on)
CS: Carl Schurz
JC: Joint Select Committee to Inquire into the Condition of
        Affairs in the Late Insurrectionary States, aka Ku Klux Klan
        Committee
JCCW: Joint Committee on the Conduct of the War
LC: Library of Congress
NARA: National Archives and Records Administration
NYH: *New York Herald*
NYT: *New York Times*
TS: Thaddeus Stevens
UNC: University of North Carolina
USC: University of South Carolina
USG: Ulysses S. Grant
UVA: University of Virginia
WWH: William W. Holden
WTS: William Tecumseh Sherman

PREFACE

xiii   About 11 p.m.: *The Trial of William W. Holden, Governor of North Carolina Before
        the Senate of North Carolina,* Vol. 2 (Raleigh: Sentinel Printing Office, 1871),
        1244ff, 1363–66, 1931.
xiii   Wyatt Outlaw was: Ibid., 1194ff, 1916–18.

xiv Outlaw's captors dragged: Carole Watterson Troxler, *Shuttle and Plow: A History of Alamance County, North Carolina* (Burlington, NC: Alamance County Historical Association, 1999), 329ff; Mark L. Bradley, *Blue Coats and Tar Heels: Soldiers and Civilians in Reconstruction North Carolina* (Lexington: University Press of Kentucky, 2009), 217–18.

xv "chained themselves": *Columbia Daily Union,* February 7, 1872.

xv "The negroes are": Steve Humphrey, *"That D---d Brownlow"* (Boone, NC: Appalachian Consortium Press, 1978), 327.

xv "We have nothing": *NYT,* May 27, 1866.

xv "Neither [race] knows": JC, Vol. 6, 522–23.

xvi "What does it": Louise Sinclair to "Mr. Douglass," November 1871, Douglass/Thorn Papers, South Caroliniana Collection, USC.

xvi "They go to": J. F. Files to USG, June 16, 1871, John Y. Simon, ed., USG *Papers,* Vol. 22 (Carbondale: Southern Illinois University Press, 1995–2000), 14.

xvii "One would wake": Gordon McKinney, "The Klan in the Southern Mountains," *Appalachian Journal,* Vol. 8 (Winter 1981).

1: AN EXPERIMENT IN GOOD FAITH

3 Grant's brief report: USG to AJ, December 18, 1865, John Y. Simon, ed., USG *Papers,* Vol. 15 (Carbondale: Southern Illinois University Press, 1995–2000), 462–65; *NYT,* May 26, 1866.

4 "an institution abhorrent": USG, *Memoirs and Selected Letters* (New York: Library of America, 1990), 419.

4 "I have no hobby": USG to Jesse Root Grant, August 3, 1862, USG *Papers,* Vol. 5, 263–64.

5 "By arming the negro": USG to AL, August 23, 1863, *Memoirs and Selected Letters,* 1031.

5 "As anxious as": USG to Elihu B. Washburne, August 30, 1863, *Memoirs and Selected Letters,* 1033–34.

6 "one of the ablest": Ron Chernow, *Grant* (New York: Penguin, 2017), 549.

6 "I will be": Paul H. Bergeron, ed., *The Papers of Andrew Johnson,* (Knoxville: University of Tennessee Press, 1999), 251–53.

7 "In the question": David Herbert Donald, *Charles Sumner,* Vol. 2 (New York: Da Capo, 1996), 222.

7 "He's just like": Hans L. Trefousse, *Andrew Johnson* (New York: Norton, 1989), 242.

8 "I despair of": Charles Sumner to the Duchess of Argyll, April 3, 1866, Beverly W. Palmer, ed., *The Selected Papers of Charles Sumner,* Vol. 2, 1859–1874. (Boston: Northeastern University Press, 1990), 358–59.

8 "meetings of negroes": CG 42/1, 426; JC, Vol. 4, 968–69.

8 "They have the idea": JC, Vol. 7, 829.

8 "They must then": *Edgefield (SC) Advertiser,* November, 8, 1865.

8   "he was seized": Jack Hurst, *Nathan Bedford Forrest: A Biography* (New York: Vintage, 1994), 264.

9   "The President was": Oliver Otis Howard, *Autobiography*, Vol. 2 (New York: Baker & Taylor Co., 1908), 283.

9   In his first: AJ *Papers*, Vol. 9, 466ff.

10 Schurz described with: Carl Schurz, *Report on the Condition of the South 1865* (Washington: Government Printing Office, 1865), 4ff.

10 "The loyalty of": Ibid., 62–69.

11 "When I tell them": Ibid., 57–58.

11 "ignorance, carelessness, improvidence": *Mobile (AL) Register,* January 29, 1869.

11 "The prevailing sentiment": CS to Margarethe Schurz, July 25, 1865, Joseph Schafer, ed., *Intimate Letters of Carl Schurz, 1841–1869* (New York: Da Capo, 1970), 344–45.

11 At Selma alone: CS, *Report,* 27–39.

12 "The distrust between": July 25, 1865, CS Papers, LC.

12 The "whole organism": CS, *Report,* 65.

12 "violent reaction": Ibid., 57–58.

12 The many embittered: Joseph H. Mahaffey, ed., "Carl Schurz's Letters from the South," *The Georgia Historical Quarterly* 35 (September 1951).

12 a "featherweight" who: *NYT,* May 26, 1866.

12 In December, Schurz: Carl Schurz to Margarethe Schurz, December 20, 1866, Schafer, ed., *Intimate Letters of Carl Schurz, 1841–1869*, 457.

13 "There is a fairy-tale": Frank G. Carpenter, *Carp's Washington* (New York: McGraw-Hill, 1960), 2–6.

14 "Our worthy president": Beverly W. Palmer, ed., TS *Selected Papers,* Vol. 2 (Pittsburgh: University of Pittsburgh Press, 1998), 157ff.

14 "torn their constitutional": Ibid., 44–55.

14 "We have conquered": Ibid., 12–24.

15 The legislation that: CG 39/1, 322, 298; Howard, *Autobiography*, Vol. 2, 286–88.

15 More far-reaching was: *Statutes-at-Large,* Thirty-ninth Congress, First Session, 27.

16 "all our experience": Eric Foner, *Reconstruction: America's Unfinished Revolution, 1863–1877* (New York: Harper & Row, 1988), 249–51.

16 "The president has": Mark Washburne, *Elihu Benjamin Washburne: Congressman, Secretary of State, Envoy Extraordinary,* Vol. 3 (Xlibris, 2005), 109.

16 Standing in front: Palmer, ed., TS *Selected Papers,* Vol. 2, 94, 88, notes.

16 On the last day: *American Citizen,* May 23, 1866; George Stoneman to USG, 16 12, 1866, *Grant Papers*, Vol. 16, 235 note; Washburne, *Elihu Benjamin Washburne,* 110–11, 118–21; Elihu B. Washburne to Thaddeus Stevens, May 24, 1866, Palmer, ed., TS *Selected Papers,* Vol. 2, 151.

17 "A year ago": *NYT,* May 26, 1866.

17 "I think it": USG to Edwin M. Stanton, July 7, 1866, also August 16, 1866, Simon, ed., USG *Papers,* Vol. 16, 233, 232 note.

17   His decisiveness was: James Speed to AJ, July 13, 1866, Simon, ed., USG *Papers,* Vol. 16, 234 note.

17   "failed to take": George H. Thomas to USG, August 15, 1866, Simon, ed., USG *Papers,* Vol. 16, 232 note.

17   In Texas: Foner, *Reconstruction,* 119.

17   "The next morning": William Mallet to TS, May 28, 1866, Palmer, ed., TS *Selected Papers,* Vol. 2, 152.

18   Then, in July: Justin A. Nystrom, *New Orleans After the Civil War: Race, Politics and a New Birth of Freedom* (Baltimore: Johns Hopkins University Press, 2010), 66–68.

18   "It was an": James K. Hogue, *Uncivil War: Five New Orleans Street Battles and the Rise and Fall of Radical Reconstruction* (Baton Rouge: University of Louisiana Press, 2006), 44.

18   "Too strong?": Palmer, ed., TS *Selected Papers,* Vol. 2, 137–41.

19   But as Stevens: Ibid., 131–33.

19   "Otherwise, you furnish": George S. Boutwell, *Reminiscences of Sixty Years in Public Affairs,* Vol. 2 (New York: McClure, Phillips & Co., 1902), 22.

19   "In your resolutions": *Chicago Tribune,* September 7, 1866.

20   "It falls far": Palmer, ed., TS *Selected Papers,* Vol. 2, 131–33.

20   "a body called": Ibid., 194 note.

20   "negro governors": Heather Cox Richardson, *West from Appomattox: The Reconstruction of America After the Civil War* (New Haven: Yale University Press, 2007), 69.

21   "I have never": USG to Julia Dent Grant, September 9, 1866, Simon, ed., USG *Papers,* Vol. 16, 336.

21   "The army will": Brooks D. Simpson, *Let Us Have Peace: Ulysses S. Grant and the Politics of War and Reconstruction, 1861–1868* (Chapel Hill: University of North Carolina Press, 1991), 153.

21   "if a crisis": USG to Philip Sheridan, October 12, 1866, Simon, ed., USG *Papers,* Vol. 16, 7–8.

2: APPARITIONS IN TENNESSEE

23   "The Kuklux Klan": *Pulaski Citizen,* March 27, 1867.

23   One reported that: *Pulaski Citizen,* April 26, 1867.

23   Another story reported: *Pulaski Citizen,* July 26, 1867.

24   Pulaski, prosperous as: J. C. Lester and D. L. Wilson. Introduction by Walter L. Fleming, *Ku Klux Klan: Its Origin, Growth and Disbandment* (New York and Washington: Neale Publishing Company, 1905), 15–19; William T. Richardson, *Historic Pulaski: Birthplace of the Ku Klux Klan* (Privately published, 1913), 7–80; *Pulaski Citizen,* March 29, 1867.

24   In its early days: Lester and Wilson, *Ku Klux Klan,* 15–18; Mark C. Carnes, *Secret Ritual and Manhood in Victorian America* (New Haven: Yale University Press, 1989), 6–20; Wyn Craig Wade, *The Fiery Cross: The Ku Klux Klan in*

America (New York: Oxford University Press, 1987), 34–35; Richardson, *Historic Pulaski,* 15–19.

25   In its original: Elaine Franz Parsons, *Ku Klux: The Birth of the Klan During Reconstruction* (Chapel Hill: University of North Carolina Press, 2015), 47.

25   "the colored population": *Pulaski Citizen,* April 26, 1867.

26   Gradually, wrote an early member: Lester and Wilson, *Ku Klux Klan,* 25, 83.

26   Then something changed: Ibid., 44–59; Wade, *The Fiery Cross,* 38; Parsons, *Ku Klux,* 51.

26   The Prescript created: Lester and Wilson, *Ku Klux Klan,* 11, 27, 117; Richardson, *Historic Pulaski,* 88ff.

27   "take a dose": *Pulaski Citizen,* August 23, 1867.

27   Before the year: Parsons, *Ku Klux,* 60, 55, 322 note.

27   Now seventy-five: Beverly W. Palmer, ed., TS *Selected Papers,* Vol. 2 (Pittsburgh: University of Pittsburgh Press, 1998), 323.

28   The Freedmen's Bureau: Gregory P. Downs, *After Appomattox: Military Occupation and the Ends of War* (Cambridge: Harvard University Press, 2015), 145, 152–54.

28   By failing to: Palmer, ed., TS *Selected Papers,* Vol. 2, 212.

28   Rep. James G. Blaine: James G. Blaine, *Twenty Years in Congress, from Lincoln to Garfield,* Vol. 2 (Norwich: Henry Bill Publishing Company, 1886), 262.

29   "We must compel": CG 39/2, 1103–4.

29   Subsequent legislation: 14 Stat 428430, c.153; 15 Stat 2–5, c.6; 15 Stat 14–16, c.30; 15 Stat 41, c. 25; 14 Stat 385, c.27 and 28.

30   Johnson denounced: CG 39/2, 1729–30.

30   Still another measure: 14 Stat 430–431, c.154.

30   "The ballot is": Eric Foner, *Reconstruction: America's Unfinished Revolution, 1863–1877* (New York: Harper & Row 1988), 278.

31   Nor did Congress: Downs, *After Appomattox,* 257–65, 142, 153.

31   "A patchwork occupation": Ibid., 138.

31   Grant was determined. *NYT,* May 20, 1867.

32   "It is just the thing": Joseph Wheelan, *Terrible Swift Sword: The Life of General Philip H. Sheridan* (New York: Da Capo, 2012), 222.

32   "He shows himself": USG to Elihu B. Washburne, April 5, 1867, John Y. Simon, ed., USG *Papers,* Vol. 17 (Carbondale: Southern Illinois University Press, 1995–2000), 98.

33   "The best of us": JC, Vol. 7, 615.

33   Remarked one disconcerted white: Michael F. Fitzgerald, *The Union League Movement in the Deep South: Politics and Agricultural Change During Reconstruction* (Baton Rouge: Louisiana State University Press, 1989), 34.

33   Most dramatic was: Downs, *After Appomattox,* 193; Peggy Lamson, *The Glorious Failure: Black Congressman Robert Brown Elliott and the Reconstruction in South Carolina* (New York: Norton, 1973), 44; Michael F. Fitzgerald, *Reconstruction in Alabama: From Civil War to Redemption in the Cotton South* (Baton Rouge: Louisiana State University Press, 2017), 149; Fitzgerald, *The Union League Movement in the Deep South,* 43.

34   The pro-Klan *Atlanta Constitution: Atlanta Constitution,* July 28, 1868.

34   "worth a thousand": Hyman Rubin III, *South Carolina Scalawags* (Columbia: University of South Carolina Press, 2006), 18–19.

34   to Jefferson Allgood: JC, Vol. 11, 508.

35   "I am glad": Mrs. William F. McLean to Julia Dent Grant, March 7, 1869, Simon, ed., USG *Papers,* Vol. 19, 365.

35   "The slaves, since": *Knoxville Whig,* reprinted in *Raleigh Sentinel,* April 1, 1868.

35   "I shall be happy": *New Orleans Times,* June 8, 1867.

35   "Being elevated as": William Strather to TS, April 28, 1866, Palmer, ed., TS *Selected Papers,* Vol. 2, 121–22.

35   "If dere skins IS": Rupert Sargent Holland, ed., *Letters and Diary of Laura M. Towne* (San Bernardino: Big Byte Books, 2020), 140.

36   *"I am a carpet-bagger":* Ted Tunnell, *Edge of the Sword: The Ordeal of Carpetbagger Marshall H. Twitchell in the Civil War and Reconstruction* (Baton Rouge: Louisiana State University Press, 2001), 127.

37   By July 1867: Fitzgerald, *The Union League Movement,* 14.

37   One Alabama organizer: Fitzgerald, *Reconstruction in Alabama,* 124–25.

37   As J. C. Lester: Lester and Wilson, *Ku Klux Klan,* 25.

38   Grant, for his part: USG to AJ, August 1, 1867, Simon, ed., USG *Papers,* Vol. 17, 250–52.

38   "I feel the same": USG to Elihu B. Washburne, April 5, 1867, Simon, ed., USG *Papers,* Vol. 17, 98.

38   Grant protested that: USG to AJ, August 1, 1867, Simon, ed., USG *Papers,* Vol. 17, 250–52, also 277–78.

38   "I would not": USG to AJ, August 26, 1867, Simon, ed., *USG Papers,* Vol. 17, 301–3.

38   "All the romance": USG to WTS, September 18, 1867, Simon, ed., USG *Papers,* Vol. 17, 343.

39   "Congo convention": Chernow, *Grant* (New York: Penguin, 2017), 600.

40   "Shall the new state": Mark Elliott and John David Smith, eds., *Undaunted Radical: The Selected Writings and Speeches of Albion W. Tourgée* (New York: Oxford University Press, 2006), 26.

40   In an extraordinarily: Paul H. Bergeron, ed., *The Papers of Andrew Johnson,* Vol. 13 (Knoxville: University of Tennessee Press, 1999), 280–306.

41   "The people want": Henry J. Raymond to USG, October 13, 1867, Simon, ed., USG *Papers,* Vol. 18, 331.

3: A MONSTER TERRIBLE BEYOND QUESTION

42   On April 12, 1864: *Report of the Joint Committee on the Conduct of the War, 1864, Part 1,* 5, 14, 21, 31–39, 91, 105–10, 121–23; *NYT,* April 16, 1864; *NYH,* April 16, 1864; M. Brayman to Benjamin F. Wade, June 19, 1864, Wade Papers, LC.

42   A Confederate trooper: Achilles Clark to "Judith and Henrietta," Aaron

Sheehan-Dean, ed., *The Civil War: The Final Year Told by Those Who Lived It* (New York: Library of America, 2014), 42–44.

43 "It is hoped": Bruce Tap, *The Fort Pillow Massacre: North, South, and the Status of African Americans in the Civil War* (New York: Routledge, 2014), 62.

43 Forrest was a: John W. Morton, *The Artillery of Nathan Bedford Forrest's Cavalry* (Nashville: M. E. Church, 1909), 12–13, 16–17, 49, 64–65.

43 Lee Meriwether, the son: Lee Meriwether, *My Yesteryears* (St. Louis: Mound City Press, 1942), 59ff.

43 "never content unless": Morton, *The Artillery of Nathan Bedford Forrest's Cavalry*, 12–14.

43 In the late: Jack Hurst, *Nathan Bedford Forrest: A Biography* (New York: Vintage, 1994), 58, 65.

44 After the war: Ibid., 269–75, 280–82, 292–93.

44 Sometime toward the end: Ibid., 284–87.

44 "John, I hear": Morton, *The Artillery of Nathan Bedford Forrest's Cavalry*, 344–45.

44 An eyewitness to: Lee Meriwether, *My Yesteryears*, 66–67.

45 "Law was not enforced": Gordon McKinney, "The Klan in the Southern Mountains: The Lusk-Shotwell Controversy," *Appalachian Journal*, Vol. 8 (Winter 1981).

45 Yet, as late as: *New York Tribune*, April 1, 1868, April 6, 1868.

46 When he visited: *Atlanta Intelligencer*, March 14, 1868, in Hurst, *Nathan Bedford Forrest*, 295.

46 An editorial in: JC, Vol. 6, 452.

46 "Let him who": Beverly W. Palmer, TS *Selected Papers*, Vol. 2 (Pittsburgh: University of Pittsburgh Press, 1998), 425.

46 "It is too late": *New York Tribune*, January 18, 1868.

46 "In defiance of": Eric Foner, *Reconstruction: America's Unfinished Revolution, 1863–1867* (New York: Harper & Row, 1988), 291.

47 In Montgomery, Alabama: *New York Tribune*, January 17, 1868.

47 On March 5: Thomas B. Alexander, "KuKluxism in Tennessee, 1865–1869," *Tennessee Historical Quarterly*, Vol. 8 (September 1949).

47 The pro-Klan: *Nashville Union*, March 31, 1868.

47 A Union veteran: *New York Tribune*, January 20, 1868, April 6, 1868; Alexander, "Kukluxism in Tennessee"; Steve Humphrey, *"That D---d Brownlow"* (Boone, NC: Appalachian Consortium Press, 1978), 333.

48 "three notably offensive": J. C. Lester and D. L. Wilson. Introduction by Walter L. Fleming, *Ku Klux Klan: Its Origin, Growth and Disbandment* (New York and Washington: Neale Publishing Company, 1905), 42.

48 "The news of": Morton, *The Artillery of Nathan Bedford Forrest's Cavalry*, 339.

48 Morton viewed Klansmen: Ibid., 342.

48 "Those who advocated": Ibid., 341–42.

48 "They told me": CG 42/1, 320.

48 Sometime in 1868: Lester and Wilson, *Ku Klux Klan*, 75–79.

49 When James Boyd: *Proclamations by the Governor of North Carolina* (Raleigh: Standard Steam Book and Job Print, 1872), 206ff.

49   "Didn't I tell you": Hans L. Trefousse, *Thaddeus Stevens: Nineteenth-Century Egalitarian* (Chapel Hill: University of North Carolina Press), 1997), 224.

50   Grant's anger fairly: USG to AJ, January 28, 1868, John Y. Simon, ed., *USG Papers,* Vol. 18 (Carbondale: Southern Illinois University Press, 1995–2000), 116–18.

50   Stevens was impressed: Ronald C. White, *American Ulysses: A Life of Ulysses S. Grant* (New York: Random House, 2016), 455.

50   "Andrew Johnson has": *New York Tribune,* January 18, 1868.

50   "Who will be so good.": John W. Forney, *Anecdotes of Public Men* (New York: Harper and Brothers, 1873), 37.

50   On February 24: Palmer, ed., TS *Selected Papers,* Vol. 2, 352–58.

50   "We are not": Ibid., 377–81.

51   "To the Veiled": Ibid., 371–73.

51   "Thou hast eaten": Ibid., 397.

52   To an admiring: Brenda Wineapple, *The Impeachers: The Trial of Andrew Johnson and the Dream of a Just Nation* (New York: Random House, 2019), 286.

52   "impossible to embarrass": George Clemenceau, *American Reconstruction, 1865–1870* (New York: Da Capo, 1969), 172.

52   "We spurn the": Richard S. West Jr., *Lincoln's Scapegoat General: A Life of Benjamin F. Butler, 1818–1893* (Boston: Houghton Mifflin, 1965), 321–22.

53   On March 30: *New York Tribune,* March 31, 1868; Wineapple, *The Impeachers,* 294ff.

53   "By murder most": Hens L. Trefousse, *Andrew Johnson* (New York: Norton, 1989), 319.

54   "I have seen": JC, Vol. 6, 1036.

54   A minister who: Ibid., 434.

54   A soldier friend: *Raleigh Daily Standard,* April, 10, 1868.

55   "There's the damned": James Alex Baggett, *The Scalawags: Southern Dissenters in the Civil War and Reconstruction* (Baton Rouge: Louisiana State University Press, 2002), 79.

55   From the doorway: JC, Vol. 6, 59, 452; *New York Tribune,* April 7, 1868.

55   Four policemen were: George G. Meade, *Major General George G. Meade's Report on the Ashburn Murder* (Atlanta: U.S. Army, Department of the South, 1868), 12ff, 91–94.

55   Conservatives suggested that: *New York Tribune,* April 6 and 7, 1868; Meade, *Major General George G. Meade's Report on the Ashburn Murder,* 20; Elizabeth Otto Daniell, "The Ashburn Murder Case in Reconstruction Georgia," *The Georgia Historical Quarterly,* Vol. 59 (Fall 1975).

55   The *Louisville Courier: Louisville Courier Journal,* April 4, 1868.

56   The pro-Klan: Cited in *Nashville Union,* April 1, 1868.

56   "Andrew Johnson is": *New York Tribune,* April 9, 1868.

56   When he managed: Trefousse, *Thaddeus Stevens,* 229–30.

56   One memorably embarrassing: Thomas Domer, "The Role of George S. Boutwell in the Impeachment and Trial of Andrew Johnson," *New England Quarterly,* Vol. 49 (December 1976).

57 "stopped its ears": Ibid.

57 The president, "this": Palmer, ed., TS *Selected Papers,* Vol. 2, 414–17.

57 The visitors' galleries: *NYH,* May 17, 1868.

57 "Conviction had him": *NYT,* May 17, 1868.

58 His fellow Ohio: Michael Les Benedict, *The Impeachment of Andrew Johnson* (New York: Norton, 1973), 134.

58 "He preferred the": Robert J. Cook, *Civil War Senator: William Pitt Fessenden and the Fight to Save the American Republic* (Baton Rouge: Louisiana State University Press, 2011), 232–34.

58 "The country is": Trefousse, *Carl Schurz: A Biography* (Knoxville: University of Tennessee Press, 1982), 230.

58 "It is the meanest": Alexander K. McClure, *Abraham Lincoln and Men of War Times* (Lincoln: University of Nebraska Press, 1996), 285.

58 "The great Radical": *NYH,* May 17, 1868.

58 a "harlequinade": *Memphis Appeal,* June 2, 1868.

58 "Mr. Johnson, like": Clemenceau, *American Reconstruction,* 169.

59 "Grant's chance for": Allan Nevins and Thomas M. Halsey, eds., *The Diary of George Templeton Strong,* Vol. 4 (New York: Macmillan, 1952), 171–72.

59 "Let us have peace": USG to Joseph R. Hawley, May 29, 1868, USG *Papers,* Vol. 18, 263–64.

4: AN ALARM BELL IN THE NIGHT

61 On April 2: USG to George G. Meade, *Major General George G. Meade's Report on the Ashburn Murder* (Atlanta: U.S. Army, Department of the South, 1868), 8, 11–12.

61 Meade thereupon suddenly: Elizabeth Otto Daniell, "The Ashburn Murder Case in Reconstruction Georgia," *The Georgia Historical Quarterly,* Vol. 59 (Fall 1975); Meade, *Major General George G. Meade's Report on the Ashburn Murder,* 9–10, 100; JC, Vol. 6, 184, 782–84.

62 "Save your neck": Charles Lane, *Freedom's Detective: The Secret Service, the Ku Klux Klan, and the Man Who Masterminded America's First War on Terror* (Toronto: Hanover Square Press, 2019), 87–88.

62 "I know the negro": Meade, *Major General George G. Meade's Report on the Ashburn Murder,* 34.

63 As the trial unfolded: Ibid., 25–26, 52, 60, 65, 78, 89.

63 Marshall seemed nervous: Ibid., 57–58.

63 The prosecution's second: Ibid., 80–84.

63 The next witness: Ibid., 107, 95.

64 "I need not": Ibid., 102.

64 "Because you turned": Ibid., 107.

65 Patterson herself was: Ibid., 108–12.

65 "Dr. Kirkscey is": Ibid., 119.

65 Another witness, Sally: Ibid., 121–29.

66   Witnesses for the: Daniell, "The Ashburn Murder Case in Reconstruction Georgia"; *Atlanta Constitution,* July 22, 1868.

66   But evidence for: Daniell, "The Ashburn Murder Case in Reconstruction Georgia"; *Atlanta Constitution,* July 22, July 26, and July 29, 1868.

67   "there is solid reality": *New York Tribune,* April 6, 1868.

67   "It proposes to": *Richmond Examiner,* reprinted in the *New York Tribune,* April 6, 1868.

67   Although Ashburn's murder: JC, Vol. 6, 532–35; *Knoxville Whig,* June 17, 1868; Jack Hurst, *Nathan Bedford Forrest: A Biography* (New York: Vintage, 1994), 297–300.

68   profoundly "patriotic feeling": *Memphis Appeal,* June 2, 1868.

68   "We intend to": *"Stella Mortem"* to William G. Brownlow, April 1868, Tennessee Virtual Archive, Tennessee Historical Society website.

68   "If a war of races": Steve Humphrey, *"That D---d Brownlow"* (Boone, NC: Appalachian Consortium Press, 1978), 332.

68   Indeed, the convention's tone: *Official Proceedings of the National Democratic Convention Held at New York, July 4–9, 1868* (Boston: Rockwell & Rollins Printers, 1868).

69   Struggling to satisfy: Ibid.

69   "By the enfranchisement": *Atlanta Constitution,* July 22, 1868.

70   His advocates argued: *New York Tribune,* January 8, 1868.

70   "How can Reconstruction": Francis P. Blair Jr. to James O. Brodhead, June 30, 1868, Brooks D. Simpson, ed., *Reconstruction: Voices from America's First Great Struggle for Racial Equality* (New York: Library of America, 2018), 350–51.

70   On his return: *Memphis Appeal,* July 17, 1868; Lee Meriwether, *My Yesteryears* (St. Louis: Mound City Press, 1942), 66; Thomas B. Alexander, "Kukluxism in Tennessee, 1865–1869," *Tennessee Historical Quarterly,* Vol. 8 (September 1949).

70   "We are not": Hurst, *Nathan Bedford Forrest,* 307.

70   In an effort: Alexander, "Kukluxism in Tennessee"; Humphrey, *"That D---d Brownlow,"* 333; Hurst, *Nathan Bedford Forrest,* 309.

71   Both Black and white witnesses: *Report of the Evidence Taken Before the Military Commission in Relation to the Outrages Committed by the Ku Klux Klan in Middle and West Tennessee* (Nashville: S. C. Mercer, 1868), 15–36.

72   In response, Forrest: *Nashville Tennessean,* August 12, 1868.

72   He didn't want: *Memphis Bulletin,* August 12, 1868, in Hurst, *Nathan Bedford Forrest,* 310.

72   The Klan now: Reprinted in *Yorkville (SC) Enquirer,* February 1, 1921.

73   "They perpetuate the": Hiram C. Whitley to George H. Williams, March 27, 1872, Justice Department Records, NARA.

73   "A stranger from": J. C. Lester and D. L. Wilson. Introduction by Walter L. Fleming, *Ku Klux Klan* (New York and Washington: Neale Publishing Company, 1905), 23ff.

73   Another early member: William T. Richardson, *Historic Pulaski: Birthplace of the Ku Klux Klan* (Privately published, 1913), 7.

73   One tantalizing anecdotal: Gordon McKinney, "The Klan in the Southern

Mountains: The Lusk-Shotwell Controversy," *Appalachian Journal,* Vol. 8 (Winter 1981).

74 A rare Klan charter: Iredell Jones Papers, South Caroliniana Collection, USC.

75 "everything was done": *Mississippi Sentinel,* reprinted in *Nashville Tennessean,* August 12, 1868.

75 "the den of": *Tuskaloosa Monitor,* April 1, 1868.

75 "I have always": JC, Vol. 5, 1457–58.

76 "If any man": JC, Vol. 12, 929.

76 The Klan's defenders: *Nashville Tennessean,* July 21, 1868; John W. Morton, *The Artillery of Nathan Beford Forrest's Cavalry* (Nashville: M. E. Church, 1909), 341; *Proclamations by the Governor of North Carolina Together with the Opinion of Chief Justice Pearson* (Raleigh: Standard Steam Book and Job Print, 1870), 86–89.

77 At the end: *Cincinnati Commercial,* August 28, 1868.

78 Pressed to discuss: Ibid.

78 He quickly backpedaled: JC, Vol. 1, 8–11.

5: FIELD OF BLOOD

79 "Military rule has": *Charleston Mercury,* July 8, 1868.

79 "No true South": *Charleston Daily Courier,* July 8, 1868.

80 "Let us recognize": *Charleston Daily Courier,* July 10, 1868.

80 "This harangue": *Charleston Mercury,* July 8, 1868.

81 "My sands are": Beverly W. Palmer, ed., TS *Selected Papers,* Vol. 2 (Pittsburgh: University of Pittsburgh Press, 1998), 462.

81 "If it were not": Georges Clemenceau, *American Reconstruction, 1865–1870* (New York: Da Capo, 1969), 226.

81 "There was in him": Philip S. Foner, ed., *Life and Writings of Frederick Douglass,* Vol. 5 (New York: International Publishers, 1955), 217–18.

82 "Speech with him": CG 40/3, 150.

82 The urgency: *Tuskaloosa Monitor,* September 1, 1868.

82 The Democrats were: *Official Proceedings of the National Democratic Convention Held at New York, July 4–9, 1868* (Boston: Rockwell & Rollins Printers, 1868).

83 His running mate: *NYT,* November 1, 1868.

83 alleged "African supremacy": *New York World,* December 17, 1867.

83 "A soldier has": Julia Dent Grant, *The Personal Memoirs of Julia Dent Grant,* John Y. Simon, ed. (New York: Putnam, 1975), 171.

83 "I could not": *NYH,* June 6, 1871.

84 "Everybody seems to": "T.J." to "Billy," April 11, 1868, Douglass, Thorne, and Moores Papers, South Caroliniana Collection, USC.

84 Walt Whitman, a former: Walt Whitman to Louisa Van Velsor Whitman, July 10, 1868, The Walt Whitman Archive: Life & Letters, Correspondence, walt whitmanarchive.com.

84 "The Democrats simply": Clemenceau, *American Reconstruction,* 230–31.

85 as one editorialist: *Atlanta Constitution,* July 22, 1868.

85   The *Macon Telegraph:* Ibid.

85   In a typical: *Tuskaloosa Monitor,* September 1, 1868.

85   In the North: Clemenceau, *American Reconstruction,* 241, 249–51.

86   "Political murders seem": *NYT,* October 20, 1868.

86   "In all events": Clemenceau, *American Reconstruction,* 229.

86   A deputy sheriff: *NYT,* October 20 and November 2, 1868; *New Orleans Republican,* October 5, 1868; *Sunbury (PA) Gazette,* October 24, 1868.

86   In Abbeville County: *New York Tribune,* October 20, 1868; Peggy Lamson, *The Glorious Failure: Black Congressman Robert Brown Elliott and the Reconstruction in South Carolina* (New York: Norton, 1973), 82–83; JC, Vol. 3, 1258.

87   "I did not see": *New York Tribune,* October 31, 1868.

87   "Am I a man?": Stephen Ward Angell, *Bishop Henry McNeal Turner and African American Religion in the South* (Knoxville: University of Tennessee Press, 1992), 87.

87   Shortly before the massacre: *NYT,* September 26 and October 6, 1868; Lee W. Formwalt, "The Camilla Massacre of 1868: Racial Violence as Political Propaganda," *The Georgia Historical Quarterly,* Vol. 71 (Fall 1987).

88   Meade, once again: *New York Tribune,* December 1, 1868.

88   The bloodiest episode: *New Orleans Republican,* October 1, 3, 5, 12, and 20, 1868; *New Orleans Advocate,* October 10, 1868; *St. Landry Progress,* September 25, 1868; Carolyn E. DeLatte, "The St. Landry Riot: A Forgotten Incident of Reconstruction Violence," *Louisiana History,* Vol. 17 (Winter 1976).

88   "The plantations were": *New Orleans Advocate,* October 10, 1868.

89   Federal officials reported: *National Standard,* October 17, 1868; *New York Tribune,* October 20, 1868; *NYT,* November 2, 1868; Clemenceau, *American Reconstruction,* 259; Lovell H. Rousseau to USG, October 1, 24, and 26, 1868, John Y. Simon, ed., USG *Papers,* Vol. 19 (Carbondale: Southern Illinois University Press, 1995–2000), 301 note.

90   "I do not think": Lovell H. Rousseau to USG, October 24, 1868, Simon, ed., USG *Papers,* Vol. 19, 301 note.

90   When not fawning: *New York Tribune,* October 20, 1868; Horace Porter to USG, December 26, 1868, Simon, ed., USG *Papers,* Vol. 19, 112–13 note; Jack Hurst, *Nathan Bedford Forrest: A Biography* (New York: Vintage, 1994), 319–20.

90   Although he tried: *NYT,* September 13 and 14, 1868.

91   Benjamin Perry had heard: *New York Tribune,* October 20, 1868.

91   Despite Forrest's transparent: J. C. Lester and D. L. Wilson. Introduction by Walter L. Fleming, *Ku Klux Klan: Its Origin, Growth and Disbandment* (New York and Washington: Neale Publishing Company, 1905), 35ff; William Edward Hardy, "Farewell to All Radicals: Redeeming Tennessee, 1869–1870," PhD diss., University of Tennessee at Knoxville, 2013; Hurst, *Nathan Bedford Forrest,* 312.

92   "*Untrammeled freedom of*": Clemenceau, *American Reconstruction,* 241–43.

92   American newspapers, Clemenceau: Ibid.

93   "I have no": George G. Meade to John A. Rawlins, October 17, 1868, Simon, ed., USG *Papers,* Vol. 19, 299 note.

93 "We Republicans in": Thomas P. Robb to USG, November 3, 1868, Simon, ed., USG *Papers*, Vol. 19, 309.

93 By the last days: *NYT*, July 6, 1868; October 20, 1868; Charles F. Peck to John A. Rawlins, October 20, 1868, Simon, ed., USG *Papers*, Vol. 19, 304 note; Clemenceau, *American Reconstruction*, 252–53; Ron Chernow, *Grant* (New York: Penguin, 2017), 618–20.

94 On Election Day: Thomas B. Alexander, "KuKluxism in Tennessee, 1865–1869," *Tennessee Historical Quarterly*, Vol. 8 (September 1949); *Report of the Evidence Taken Before the Military Commission in Relation to the Outrages Committed by the Ku Klux Klan in Middle and West Tennessee* (Nashville: S. C. Mercer, 1868), 15–16; Joel Williamson, *After Slavery: The Negro in South Carolina During Reconstruction, 1861–1877* (New York: Norton, 1965), 351; Formwalt, "The Camilla Massacre of 1868"; Richard Zuczak, *State of Rebellion: Reconstruction in South Carolina* (Columbia: University of South Carolina Press, 1996), 52, 62; John H. Everitt to William W. Holden, August 24, 1868, Horace W. Raper, ed., *The Papers of William W. Holden*, Vol. 1 (Raleigh: Department of Archives and History, 2000), 361.

94 In Newberry County: JC, Vol. 4, 1256–57.

96 "No man on": DeLatte, "The St. Landry Riot."

96 "We intend to": Orville Vernon Burton, "Race and Reconstruction: Edgefield County, South Carolina," *Journal of Social History*, Vol. 12 (October 1978).

96 "We's a poor": Leon F. Litwack, *Been in the Storm So Long: The Aftermath of Slavery* (New York: Vintage, 1980), 548.

97 "A revolution gave": Clemenceau, *American Reconstruction*, 279.

6: THE SPHINX

101 Later, Johnson called it: *Knoxville Press*, March 21, 1869.

101 A seventy-man cavalry: *NYT*, March 5, 1869; Ben Perley Poore, *Perley's Reminiscences of Sixty Years in the National Metropolis*, Vol. 2 (Philadelphia: Hubbard Brothers, 1886), 249–53.

102 At 11:55, Grant's: *NYT*, March 7, 1869.

102 "The office has": John Y. Simon, ed., USG *Papers*, Vol. 19 (Carbondale: Southern Illinois University Press, 1995–2000), 137.

103 Enfranchising the freedman: *New York Tribune*, December 1, 1868.

104 "We beleav here": Stephen Walker to USG, Simon, ed., USG *Papers*, Vol. 19, 381 note.

104 "We desire that": George T. Downing to USG, Simon, ed., USG *Papers*, Vol. 19, 108.

104 The most politically: John M. Langston, speech, January 20, 1869, Simon, ed., USG *Papers*, Vol. 19, 107 note.

104 "On the whole": *New York Tribune*, January 23, 1869.

104 "There has been": *Washington Chronicle*, April 2, 1870.

105 Republicans had argued: CG 40/3 560–61.

105   Early in the debate: Ibid., 672.

105   Boutwell estimated: Ibid., 560–61.

106   "The learned and": Ibid., 861–62.

106   In reply, Rep.: Ibid., Appendix 97–98.

107   Sen. Charles Sumner's: Ibid., 1041.

108   "I am sorry": Ibid., 1291.

108   "They say he": Georges Clemenceau, *American Reconstruction, 1865–1870* (New York: Da Capo, 1969), 286.

108   "twenty years of": Allan Nevins, ed., *Hamilton Fish: The Inner History of the Grant Administration* (New York: Dodd, Mead, 1936), 139.

109   In keeping with: Ronald C. White, *American Ulysses: A Life of Ulysses S. Grant* (New York: Random House, 2016), 486–87.

109   "I hope sincerely": Simon, ed, USG *Papers,* Vol. 19, 107.

109   He appointed so many: *NYH,* April 9, 1869.

109   He tapped the: Ron Chernow, *Grant* (New York: Penguin, 2017), 656, 628.

111   "The authority of": James D. Richardson, ed., *A Compilation of the Messages and Papers of the Presidents, 1789–1897,* Vol. 7 (Washington: Government Printing Office, 1898), 11.

111   "a practical statesman": *NYH,* April 9, 1869.

112   As federal troops: Michael W. Fitzgerald, *Reconstruction in Alabama: From Civil War to Redemption in the Cotton South* (Baton Rouge: Louisiana State University Press, 2017), 186.

112   Meanwhile, the Klan: Mark L. Bradley, *Blue Coats and Tar Heels: Soldiers and Civilians in Reconstruction North Carolina* (Lexington: University Press of Kentucky, 2009), 207; James E. Sefton, *The United States Army and Reconstruction, 1865–1877* (Baton Rouge: Louisiana State University Press, 1967), 200.

112   "How long, O": Edward Hulbert to USG, April 19, 1869, Simon, ed., USG *Papers,* Vol. 19, 451 note; G. W. Barber to USG, June 7, 1869, USG *Papers,* Vol. 19, 493; D. Woodruff to USG, July 20, 1869, USG *Papers,* Vol. 19, 528 note; A. Bridgewater to USG, May 24, 1869, USG *Papers,* Vol. 19, 477; Charles Arnold to USG, May 18, 1869, USG *Papers,* Vol. 19, 117 note.

113   Another distraught Georgian: Sallie Adkins to USG, May 20, 1869, Simon, ed., USG *Papers,* Vol. 19, 475–77.

114   Whites felt that: *Edgefield Advertiser,* August 26, 1869.

115   "The great difficulty": CG 40/3, 81.

115   However, many northerners: Clemenceau, *American Reconstruction,* 265.

115   "We are not": CG 40/3, 83.

116   Typically, the *Charleston Mercury:* Lou Falkner Williams, *The Great South Carolina Ku Klux Klan Trials, 1871–1872* (Athens: University of Georgia Press, 1996), 24.

116   "In case of difficulty": Ibid., 23.

116   Governor Brownlow hired: *Union Flag* (Jonesboro, TN), March 5, 1869; Steve Humphrey, *"That D---d Brownlow"* (Boone, NC: Appalachian Consortium Press, 1978), 336–37; William Edward Hardy, "'Farewell to All Radicals':

Redeeming Tennessee, 1869–1870," PhD diss., University of Tennessee at Knoxville, 2015, 12–16.

117 In March, the "Grand Wizard": J. C. Lester and D. L. Wilson. Introduction by Walter L. Fleming, *Ku Klux Klan: Its Origin, Growth and Disbandment* (New York and Washington: Neale Publishing Company, 1905), 42ff.

117 When Forrest was: JC, Vol. 13, 15–17.

117 By this time: Ibid., 18–20.

7: THE FACE OF REVOLUTION

119 "The Ku Klux—nobody": *Raleigh (NC) Standard,* November 9, 1868.

120 "Lieut Daws thinks": John W. Stephens to WWH, August 29, 1868, Horace W. Raper, ed., *The Papers of William W. Holden,* Vol. 1 (Raleigh: Division of Archives and History, 2000), 364–65.

120 "we elected": Unidentified newspaper, October 2, 1935, Caswell County, NC, Historical Society files.

121 "The two races": *Raleigh (NC) Standard,* December 4, 1867.

121 in his inaugural: William C. Harris, *William Woods Holden: Firebrand of North Carolina Politics* (Baton Rouge: Louisiana State University Press, 1987), 245.

121 Reported one Gates County: John W. Hofler to WWH, August 22, 1868, Raper, ed., *The Papers of William W. Holden,* Vol. 1, 357.

121 "Its movements and": Diary, *David Schenck Papers,* Wilson Special Collections Library, UNC.

122 By that summer: Henry W. Paschall to WWH, August 18, 1868, Raper, ed., *The Papers of William W. Holden,* Vol. 1, 354; J. E. Cook to WWH, August 22, 1868, Raper, ed., *The Papers of William W. Holden,* Vol. 1, 358; F. W. Liedke to WWH, September 22, 1868, Raper, ed., *The Papers of William W. Holden,* Vol. 1, 374; Silas L. Curtis to WWH, October 11, 1868, Raper, ed., *The Papers of William W. Holden,* Vol. 1, 385.

122 The true size: *Proclamations by the Governor of North Carolina* (Raleigh: Standard Steam Book and Job Print, 1870), 139–63, 181, 206, 245; Otto H. Olsen, "The Ku Klux Klan: A Study in Reconstruction Politics and Propaganda," *North Carolina Historical Review,* Vol. 39 (July 1962).

123 James Boyd, a candidate: *Proclamations by the Governor of North Carolina,* 206–19.

124 David Schenck: JC, Vol. 2, 400.

124 Observed another: Ibid., 115.

124 John W. Long: *Proclamations by the Governor of North Carolina,* 181ff.

125 "Your strongest friends": JC, Vol. 2, 62.

125 From his own doorway: *Proclamations by the Governor of North Carolina,* 161ff.

126 The Klan's depredations: Jim D. Brisson, "Civil Government Was Crumbling Around Me," *North Carolina Historical Review,* Vol. 88 (April 2011); Stephen E. Massengill, "The Detectives of William W. Holden, 1869–1870," *North Carolina Historical Review,* Vol. 62 (October 1985); Harris, *William Woods Holden,*

279–80; Mark L. Bradley, *Blue Coats and Tar Heels: Soldiers and Civilians in Reconstruction North Carolina* (Lexington: University Press of Kentucky, 2009), 207, 211–12; Allen W. Trelease, *White Terror: The Ku Klux Klan Conspiracy and Southern Reconstruction* (Baton Rouge: Louisiana State University Press, 1971), 190–91.

126 One of the participants: *Proclamations by the Governor of North Carolina,* 224.

126 James Boyd, a lawyer: Ibid., 214.

126 In a shocking number: *Hillsboro (NC) Recorder,* November 2, 1869; *Proclamations by the Governor of North Carolina,* 198ff; Trelease, *White Terror,* 195; JC, Vol. 2, 36–37, 74–75, 84, 99.

126 Such behavior: Kidada E. Williams, *They Left Great Marks on Me: African American Testimonies of Racial Violence from Emancipation to World War I* (New York: New York University Press, 2012), 47, 32; Hannah Rosen, *Terror in the Heart of Freedom: Citizenship, Sexual Violence, and the Meaning of Race in the Post-emancipation South* (Chapel Hill: University of North Carolina Press, 2009), 343 note; JC, Vol. 4, 1182–84; JC, Vol. 3, 366.

128 In December 1869: James D. Richardson, *A Compilation of the Messages and Papers of the Presidents,* Vol. 7 (Washington: Government Printing Office, 1898), 27–42.

129 "If any proof": John Y. Simon, ed., *USG Papers,* Vol. 20 (Carbondale: Southern Illinois University Press, 1995–2000), 8–10.

129 In the words of: Ron Chernow, *Grant* (New York: Penguin, 2017), 648.

129 "Having acquired a": Allan Nevins, ed., *Hamilton Fish: The Inner History of the Grant Administration* (New York: Dodd, Mead, 1936), 132.

130 Admirers of Grant: Ibid., 131; Mark Washburne, *Elihu Benjamin Washburne: Congressman, Secretary of State, Envoy Extraordinary,* Vol. 3 (Xlibris, 2005), 262.

130 "For stretches of": Henry Adams, *The Education of Henry Adams* (New York: Modern Library, 1931), 264.

130 By now, North Carolina: *Proclamations by the Governor of North Carolina,* 5–6; Harris, *William Woods Holden,* 282.

131 In a somewhat: Massengill, "The Detectives of William W. Holden."

131 "The humblest and": *Proclamations by the Governor of North Carolina,* 8.

131 Further afield: Horace Porter to USG, December 26, 1868, Simon, ed., *USG Papers,* Vol. 19, 112–13 note; Powell Clayton, *The Aftermath of the Civil War in Arkansas* (New York: Neale Publishing Co., 1915), 63–69, 110, 134.

131 The crusading anti-Klan: Carole Watterson Troxler, *Shuttle and Plow: A History of Alamance County, North Carolina* (Burlington, NC: Alamance County Historical Association, 1999), 328.

132 Defectors from the: Olsen, "The Ku Klux Klan"; *Proclamations by the Governor of North Carolina,* 139–63, 192–95, 230ff; Trelease, *White Terror,* 194, 200–201; Damon Douglas Hickey, *Sojourners No More: The Quakers in the New South, 1865–1920* (Greensboro: North Carolina Friends Historical Society, 1997), 16–19, 24–25.

132 The Shoffner Act: *Proclamations by the Governor of North Carolina,* 161ff, 238ff; Massengill, "The Detectives of William W. Holden."

133 In court, Moore: *Proclamations by the Governor of North Carolina,* 161ff.

133 "There exists in": WWH to USG, March 10, 1870, *Proclamations by the Governor of North Carolina,* 47–48.

134 "Mr. [Hiram Rhodes] Revels, the colored": *NYT,* February 25, 1870.

134 Revels's admittance to: CG 41/2, 1543, 1566–68, Appendix 125–29; *Philadelphia Inquirer,* February 28, 1870, in Billy W. Libby, "Senator Hiram Revels of Mississippi Takes His Seat," *Journal of Mississippi History,* Vol. 37 (November 1975).

134 So little known: Libby, "Senator Hiram Revels of Mississippi Takes His Seat"; *Washington Evening Star,* January 31, 1870; *The Sun* (Pittsfield, MA), March 31, 1870.

135 To Radicals, Revels: George C. McKee to John A. Rawlins, April 15, 1869, Simon, ed., USG *Papers,* Vol. 19, 207.

135 Sen. Simon Cameron: CG 41/2, 1542–44.

8: A MEPHISTOPHELES IN GLASSES

136 The veteran Washington: Ben Perley Poore, *Perley's Reminiscences of Sixty Years in the National Metropolis,* Vol. 2 (Philadelphia: Hubbard Brothers, 1886), 343.

136 "between advancing civilization": Hans L. Trefousse, *Carl Schurz: A Biography* (Knoxville: University of Tennessee Press, 1982), 81.

136 Schurz campaigned: Tyler Dennett, ed., *Lincoln and the Civil War Diaries and Letters of John Hay* (New York: Dodd, Mead, 1939), 12–15, 23.

137 Schurz didn't hesitate: CG 41/2, 3607–10.

138 "They do not want": Frederic Bancroft, ed., *Speeches, Correspondence and Political Papers of Carl Schurz,* Vol. 2 (New York: G. P. Putnam's Sons, 1913), 55–64.

138 "I have tried": Louis Foy to USG, October 29, 1870, John Y. Simon, ed., USG *Papers,* Vol. 20 (Carbondale: Southern Illinois University Press, 1995), 475.

139 As Sen. Jacob Howard: CG 41/2, 473.

139 In his first: Ibid., 473ff.

140 On March 18: Ibid., 2061–63.

140 Then, shifting to: Ibid., 2064.

141 On April 19: Ibid., 2816.

141 Schurz was echoed: Ibid., 423–24, Appendix, 288–94; Mark M. Krug, *Lyman Trumbull: Conservative Radical* (New York: A. S. Barnes, 1965), 280–85.

142 "if I had not": Stephen Ward Angell, *Bishop Henry McNeal Turner and African American Religion in the South* (Knoxville: University of Tennessee Press, 1992), 90.

142 "Whose fault is it": CG 41/2, Appendix, 290–94.

142 "When is this": Ibid., 418–19.

142 "The people here": J. R. Warner to AWT, June 20, 1870, AWT Papers, Chautauqua County Historical Society, online at McClurgmuseum.org.

142 "The South ought": Krug, *Lyman Trumbull,* 287.

142 "I will die": CG 41/2, 2065–66.

143 And Sen. Oliver P. Morton: Cited by Trumbull, CG 41/2, Appendix 289.

143 "Not since the": CG 41/2, 1986–88.

143 The most passionate: Ibid., 2018–20; Michael F. Fitzgerald, *Reconstruction in Alabama: From Civil War to Redemption in the Cotton South* (Baton Rouge: Louisiana State University Press, 2017), 236–37, 144, 169.

144 By the spring: T. A. Donoho to WWH, May 16, 1870, *Proclamations by the Governor of North Carolina* (Raleigh: Standard Steam Book and Job Print, 1870), 54.

145 On May 16: Stephen E. Massengill, "The Detectives of William W. Holden, 1869–1870," *North Carolina Historical Review*, Vol. 62 (October 1985).

145 On May 21, Stephens: *Proclamations by the Governor of North Carolina*, 95–96, 101–2, 114–17; *Raleigh (NC) Standard*, August 31, 1870; *Raleigh (NC) Signal*, March 24, 1892; John Lea letter to North Carolina Historical Commission, July 2, 1919, and "65-Year-Old Homicide Is Solved," unidentified newspaper, October 2, 1935, both in John W. Stephens file at Caswell County Historical Society, Yanceyville, NC.

146 A little after dawn: *Proclamations by the Governor of North Carolina*, 92–94.

146 Republicans theorized: *Raleigh (NC) Standard*, June 8, 1870; AWT to Joseph C. Abbott, May 23, 1870, AWT Papers, Chautauqua County Historical Society.

147 "Another brave, honest": AWT to Joseph C. Abbott, May 23, 1870, AWT Papers.

148 "To the majority": WWH to Richmond M. Pearson, July 19, 1870, *Proclamations by the Governor of North Carolina*, 61–62.

148 He appointed two: WWH to USG, July 20, 1870, *Proclamations by the Governor of North Carolina*, 75–76; CG 42/1, 604ff; John Lea letter to North Carolina Historical Commission, July 2, 1919, Stephens file, Caswell County Historical Society; Mark L. Bradley, *Blue Coats and Tar Heels: Soldiers and Civilians in Reconstruction North Carolina* (Lexington: University of Kentucky Press, 2009), 223–26.

148 They also arrested: *Raleigh (NC) Sentinel*, July 25, August 1, and August 3, 1870; Josiah Turner to wife, July 8, 1870, Turner Papers, UNC; *Proclamations by the Governor of North Carolina*, 86–89.

149 In all, about: William C. Harris, *William Woods Holden: Firebrand of North Carolina Politics* (Baton Rouge: Louisiana State University Press, 1987), 290–93; *NYT*, August 2, 1870; *Raleigh (NC) Standard*, June 8, 1870.

149 Others fled: *Proclamations by the Governor of North Carolina*, 139–63.

149 In Caswell County: John Lea letter to North Carolina Historical Commission, July 2, 1919, Stephens file, Caswell County Historical Society.

149 Judge James Boyd: Ibid.

150 "All prisoners": WWH to George W. Kirk, August 3, 1870, *Proclamations by the Governor of North Carolina*, 79.

150 He also reiterated: WWH to USG, and USG to WWH, both July 20, 1870, *Proclamations by the Governor of North Carolina*, 75–78.

150 Holden's most controversial: WWH to USG, August 7, 1870, *Proclamations by the Governor of North Carolina*, 80; *Raleigh (NC) Standard*, August 31, 1870; Harris, *William Woods Holden*, 294–95.

151 Holden was confident: WWH to George W. Kirk, August 11, 1870, and August 15, 1870, *Proclamations by the Governor of North Carolina*, 82–83.

151 "My steps have": Mark Elliott, *Color-Blind Justice: Albion Tourgée and the Quest for Racial Equality* (New York: Oxford University Press, 2006), 157.

152 Tourgée's frightened wife: J. Gunnison to AWT, May 30, 1870, and J. R. Warner to AWT, June 20, 1870, AWT Papers, Chautauqua County Historical Society.

152 "And yet the government": AWT to Joseph C. Abbott, May 24, 1870, AWT Papers, Chautauqua County Historical Society.

9: THE FIRST ENFORCEMENT ACT

155 In a proclamation: James D. Richardson, ed. *A Compilation of the Messages and Papers of the Presidents, 1789–1897*, Vol. 7. (Washington: Government Printing Office), 55–56.

155 Black communities erupted: *NYH,* April 14, 1870.

156 "There has been": *New York Tribune,* April 16, 1870.

156 There was an unstated: *NYH,* April 14, 1870; John G. Stokes to USG, December 12, 1869, John Y. Simon, ed., USG *Papers,* Vol. 20 (Carbondale: Southern Illinois University Press, 1995), 340 note; W. B. Figures to USG, December 3, 1869, USG *Papers,* Vol. 20, 339–40; George W. Daniel to USG, undated, January 1870, USG *Papers,* Vol. 20, 380; CG 41/2, 3615.

157 Sen. George Spencer: CG 41/2, 3668–69.

158 The Democrats knew: Ibid., 3657, 3662, Appendix 360.

158 Carl Schurz, who: Ibid., 3607ff.

159 The pro-Klan *Weekly:* Cited in *New York Tribune,* August 3, 1870.

159 A Black farmhand: *Proclamations by the Governor of North Carolina* (Raleigh: Standard Steam Book and Job Print, 1870), 94–100, 125–30, 133–34.

160 Wiley's testimony: Ibid., 101–2.

160 A parade of: Ibid., 103–4, 106–13.

161 The court's ruling: Ibid., 137–38.

161 The governor's Conservative: *Yorkville Enquirer,* September 9, 1870.

162 Recalled John Lea: John Lea letter to North Carolina Historical Commission, July 2, 1919, Stephens file, Caswell County Historical Society, NC.

162 Sixty-five years later: Unidentified newspaper, October 2, 1935, Stephens file, Caswell County Historical Society.

163 In his last: Mark L. Bradley, *Blue Coats and Tar Heels: Soldiers and Civilians in Reconstruction North Carolina* (Lexington: University Press of Kentucky, 2009), 233.

164 Whatever "technical names": Orville Vernon Burton, "Race and Reconstruction: Edgefield County, South Carolina," *Journal of Social History,* Vol. 12 (October 1978).

165 In contrast to Holden's: Franklin Moses to A. P. Turner et al., Adjutant and Inspector General Letterbooks, South Carolina State Archives.

165 Whites almost universally: Robert B. Elliott to Robert Scott, April 1, 1870; Elliott to J. A. Green, March 25, 1870; Elliott to Prince Rivers, July 22, 1869; Franklin Moses to O. F. Winchester, June 26, 1869, Adjutant and Inspector General Letterbooks, South Carolina State Archives; Peggy Lamson, *The Glorious Failure: Black Congressman Robert Brown Elliott and the Reconstruction in South Carolina* (New York: Norton, 1973), 89, 94–95.

166 "We must by": Richard Zuczak, *State of Rebellion: Reconstruction in South Carolina* (Columbia: University of South Carolina Press, 1996), 77.

166 Scoffed Robert Elliott: Ibid., 78.

166 "With their present": *Yorkville Enquirer,* September 15, 1870.

167 "The unarmed race": *Yorkville Enquirer,* September 22, 1870.

167 The *Enquirer* also: *Yorkville Enquirer,* October 6, 1870.

167 The Carolina Rifle: Lamson, *Glorious Failure,* 86.

167 At Edgefield, whites: Burton, "Race and Reconstruction."

168 John Crews: JC, Vol. 4, 1144–48.

168 Governor Scott wrote: Robert K. Scott to USG, October 22, 1870, Simon, ed., USG *Papers,* Vol. 20, 249–51.

169 "We understand and": *Charleston Daily News,* November 7, 1870.

169 "Four peaceable and": Scott to USG, October 22, 1870, Simon, ed., USG *Papers,* Vol. 20, 249–51.

169 As the outrages: Ibid.

10: SOUTH CAROLINA IN THE BALANCE

173 "I recoiled from": J. Morgan Kousser and James M. McPherson, eds., *Region, Race and Reconstruction: Essays in Honor of C. Vann Woodward* (New York: Oxford University Press, 1982), 400.

174 "The extension of": Ibid., 403.

174 The *New York Tribune: New York Tribune,* June 17, 1870.

174 Grant reflected in: Memo dated 1869/1870, John Y. Simon, ed., USG *Papers,* Vol. 20 (Carbondale: Southern Illinois University Press, 1995), 74–75.

175 "Unless the people": AA to CS, April 2, 1869, in Eric Foner, *Reconstruction: America's Unfinished Revolution, 1863–1877* (New York: Harper & Row, 1988), 454.

175 On March 9, 1871: Message to Congress, Simon, ed., USG *Papers,* Vol. 21, 246.

175 "Grant appointed and": Allan Nevins, *Hamilton Fish: The Inner History of the Grant Administration* (New York: Dodd, Mead, 1936), 130ff.

176 Henry Adams: Henry Adams, *The Education of Henry Adams* (New York: Modern Library, 1931), 262–65.

176 Carl Schurz: CG 42/1, Appendix, 60–62.

176 He impressed George Boutwell: George S. Boutwell, *Reminiscences of Sixty Years in Public Affairs,* Vol. 1 (New York: McClure, Phillips & Co., 1902), 116.

176 The journalist Ben Perley Poore: Ben Perley Poore, *Perley's Reminiscences*

of Sixty Years in the National Metropolis, Vol. 2 (Philadelphia: Hubbard Bros., 1886), 260.

177   Although Grant was not: Orville E. Babcock to George T. Downing, January 1870, Simon, ed., USG *Papers,* Vol. 19, 109 note.

177   The crisis in: Bowden to USG, December 20, 1870, Simon, ed., USG *Papers,* Vol. 21, 402; William H. Irwin to USG, April 12, 1871, USG *Papers,* Vol. 21, 253 note; J. Aaron Moore to USG, January 6, 1871, USG *Papers,* Vol. 21, 407.

178   On February 8: Resolution sponsored by Alonzo Ransier et al., February 2, 1871, Adjutant General's Reports, NARA.

178   "There is neither": (Mrs.) S. E. Lane to USG, April 19, 1871, Simon, ed., USG *Papers,* Vol. 21, 263.

178   "The only plan": John C. Reister to John K. Scott, March 1, 1871, Scott Papers, South Carolina State Archives, Columbia.

178   When Klansmen couldn't: JC, Vol. 5, 1744–46, 1860–65.

178   Republican officials were: H. K. Roberts to Robert K. Scott, March 6 and March 8, 1871, Scott Papers, South Carolina State Archives; JC, Vol. 3, 27–28, 41–42, 274–75, 365–67; *Yorkville Enquirer,* January 12 and February 23, 1871; Robert K. Scott to Alfred H. Terry, January 17, 1871, Simon., ed, USG *Papers,* Vol. 21, 259 note; Lou Falkner Williams, *The Great South Carolina Ku Klux Klan Trials, 1871–1872* (Athens: University of Georgia Press, 1996), 30.

179   Robert Shand, a conservative: *Robert W. Shand Papers,* South Caroliniana Collection, USC; Warren D. Wilkes to USG, March 2, 1871, Simon, ed., USG *Papers,* Vol. 21, 261–62.

180   Essentially, the Klan: JC, Vol. 4, 1086–90.

180   The bootlegger's death: *Yorkville Enquirer,* February 2, February 16, February 23, March 16, and March 23, 1871.

181   At the beginning: *Yorkville Enquirer,* March 9, 1871.

181   When militia units: *Yorkville Enquirer,* March 16, 1871; JC, Vol. 4, 1058–63.

182   As armed parties: *Yorkville Enquirer,* March 23, March 30, April 6, and May 25, 1871.

182   "They are men": JC, Vol. 4, 1008.

182   And the *Yorkville Enquirer: Yorkville Enquirer,* February 17, 1871.

182   Robert Elliott, now: *Yorkville Enquirer,* January 19, 1871.

182   Scott didn't dispute: Robert K. Scott to USG, February 14, 1871, *Adjutant General's Reports,* NARA.

183   Grant also decided: Hamilton Fish diary, February 24, 1871, in Simon, ed., USG *Papers,* Vol. 21, 260 note.

183   In a last-ditch: William C. Harris, *William Woods Holden: Firebrand of North Carolina Politics* (Baton Rouge: Louisiana State University Press, 1987), 300–303.

185   "The Republican Party is": CS to E. L. Godkin, March 31, 1871, CS *Papers,* LC.

186   "There is a *dementia*": Charles Sumner to CS, August 1, 1871, CS *Papers,* LC.

186   "No, I suppose": Boutwell, *Reminiscences of Sixty Years in Public Affairs,* 140.

186   But he felt: Frederic Bancroft, ed., *Speeches, Correspondence and Political Papers of Carl Schurz,* Vol. 2 (New York: G. P. Putnam's Sons, 1913), 2–7.

187   "The growing political power": Ibid., 175.

187   Ambitious for personal: CS to Jacob D. Cox, April 4, 1871, CS Papers, LC; CG 41/3, 779–80, Appendix, 68–77; CG 42/1, 686–93; Bancroft, *Speeches, Correspondence and Political Papers of Carl Schurz,* Vol. 2, 126–74, esp. 152.

188   During the campaign: Bancroft, *Speeches, Correspondence and Political Papers of Carl Schurz,* Vol. 2, 8ff.

188   Accused of splitting: Ibid., 52.

189   The mission's leader: Simon, ed., USG *Papers,* Vol. 21, 291 note; David Blight, *Frederick Douglass: Prophet of Freedom* (New York: Simon & Schuster, 2018), 543.

189   Sumner accused the president: CG 42/1, 295, 304–5.

189   After he had: Bancroft, *Speeches, Correspondence and Political Papers of Carl Schurz,* Vol. 2, 246.

189   "Do you intend": CS to Charles Sumner, January 1, 1871, CS Papers, LC.

190   Schurz trashed Grant's: Bancroft, *Speeches, Correspondence and Political Papers of Carl Schurz,* Vol. 2, 77–90.

190   Resorting to specious: Ibid.

190   Schurz's disgust was: CG 42/1, 524ff.

191   "The present difficulty": Ron Chernow, *Grant* (New York: Penguin, 2017), 662.

191   "No man could": Charles W. Calhoun, *The Presidency of Ulysses S. Grant* (Lawrence: University Press of Kansas, 2017), 310.

11: BEN BUTLER'S APOTHEOSIS

193   He had held: Charles W. Calhoun, *The Presidency of Ulysses S. Grant* (Lawrence: University Press of Kansas, 2017), 29.

194   "Without the power": CG 42/1, 443ff.

194   "All the inhabitants": Ibid., 792.

195   Rep. James A. Garfield: James A. Garfield to Jacob D. Cox, March 23, 1871, John Y. Simon, ed., USG *Papers,* Vol. 21 (Carbondale: Southern Illinois University Pres, 1998), 247–48.

196   On the morning of: George S. Boutwell, *Reminiscences of Sixty Years in Public Affairs,* Vol. 1 (New York: McClure, Phillips & Co., 1902), 141.

196   "A condition of": CG 42/1, 244.

196   Therefore, "I Ulysses S. Grant": *NYH,* March 25, 1871.

197   "Democratic clamor": *NYT,* March 25, 1871.

197   Robert Elliott: CG 42/1, 103.

197   "Those men," he: Ibid., 519.

197   "save by its hates": CG 42/1, 443–44.

197   In the Senate: Ibid., 650–51.

198   Handsome and compact: Blanche Butler Ames, *Adelbert Ames, 1835—1933* (New York: Columbia University Press, 1964), 188.

198   "In public matters": USG to Lewis Dent, August 1, 1869, Simon, ed., USG

Papers, Vol. 21, 221–22; *New York Tribune*, August 14, 1869; William C. Harris, *The Day of the Carpetbagger: Republican Reconstruction in Mississippi* (Baton Rouge: Louisiana State University Press, 1979), 228–29, 237–46.

199 "That I should": Ames, *Adelbert Ames*, 285.

199 Now, in this: CG 42/1, 196–97.

200 Ames then told: *New York Tribune*, March 24, 1871; JC, Vol. 11, 6–29, 97–100, 173–76, 426; James Wilford Garner, *Reconstruction in Mississippi* (New York: Macmillan, 1902), 349–51.

201 As the courthouse: *New York Tribune*, March 24, 1871.

201 Ames went on to: CG 42/1, 194–98.

202 Congressional Democrats universally: Ibid., 377–78, 645–49, 600–603.

202 Rep. Samuel S. Cox: Ibid., 630, 245, 451ff.

203 Rep. Boyd Winchester: Ibid., 423.

203 The oddest Democratic: Ibid., 398–99.

204 Writing privately to: CS to E. L. Godkin, March 31, 1871, Schurz Papers, LC.

204 Godkin cavalierly editorialized: CG 42/1, 398–99.

204 "I am not willing": Ibid., Appendix, 288–94.

204 He was convinced: Frederic Bancroft, ed., *Speeches, Correspondence and Political Papers of Carl Schurz*, Vol. 2 (New York: G. P. Putnam's Sons, 1913), 2–7.

205 In Schurz's eyes: Bancroft, *Speeches, Correspondence and Political Papers of Carl Schurz*, 8ff.

205 "I consider the": CG 42/1, 686–87.

206 The Republican Party: Ibid., 688–90.

207 Fundamentally, Schurz's position: Bancroft, *Speeches, Correspondence and Political Papers of Carl Schurz*, 8ff; CS to Jacob D. Cox, February 3, 1871, Schurz Papers, LC; Hans L. Trefousse, *Carl Schurz: A Biography* (Knoxville: University of Tennessee Press, 1982), 196.

207 As Schurz's biographer: Abraham S. Eisenstadt, Ari Hoogenbaum, and Hans L. Trefousse, eds., *Before Watergate: Problems of Corruption in American Society* (New York: Brooklyn College Press, 1978), 107.

207 Southern conservatives loved: Mary Howard Schoolcraft to CS, March 1871; D. M. Seals to CS, April 8, 1871; Thomas P. Lilly to CS, October 7, 1872; G. G. Pope to CS, February 17, 1871, all in Schurz Papers, LC.

208 Ben Butler would have: CG 42/1, 793.

208 By mid-April: Ibid., 418.

208 Butler derided members: *NYT*, April 21, 1871.

208 Thanks to his persistence: CG 42/1, 806–7.

208 "I believe that": Ibid., 808.

209 "I will not hesitate": James D. Richardson, ed., *A Compilation of the Messages and Papers of the Presidents, 1789–1897*, Vol. 7 (Washington: Government Printing Office, 1898) (New York: Bureau of National Literature, 1909), 134–35.

12: AN OFFICER OF IMMENSE ENERGY AND ZEAL

210   A ballad dedicated: Bruce Nichols, *Guerrilla Warfare in Civil War Missouri,* Vol. 1 (Jefferson, NC: McFarland, 2004), 187ff.

211   "I know of few": Alfred H. Terry to Edward D. Townsend, February 21, 1872, Adjutant General's Reports, NARA.

211   Merrill's troopers arrived: *Yorkville Enquirer,* February 23 and March 30, 1981; *New York Tribune,* November 14, 1871.

212   "I fully believed": JC, Vol. 5, 1482; John Christopher to Robert K. Scott, March 17, 1871, Scott Papers, South Carolina State Archives.

212   As he probed: Lewis Merrill to Edward D. Townsend, May 17, June 9, June 10, and July 17, 1871, Adjutant General's Reports, NARA.

213   The most notorious: JC, Vol. 5, 1725–28, 1732–34, 1738–40; *Proceedings in the Ku Klux Klan Trials at Columbia, S.C., in the United States Circuit Court, November Term, 1871* (Columbia: Republican Printing Company, 1872), 397; C. D. Melton to John Rufus Bratton, December 14, 1871, Bratton Family Papers, South Caroliniana Library, USC; *Yorkville Enquirer,* February 18, 1921; Journal of Milus Carroll, York County Historical Society; Jerry L. West, *The Reconstruction Ku Klux Klan in York County, South Carolina, 1865–1877* (Jefferson, NC: McFarland, 2002), 123.

213   Using skills of persuasion: JC, Vol. 4, 1142–43; JC, Vol. 5, 1486; Merrill to Townsend, June 9 and June 10, 1871, Adjutant General's Reports, NARA.

214   Professional detectives were: *Wilmington (NC) Morning Star,* June 20, 1872.

214   This particular agent: Charles Lane: *Freedom's Detective: The Secret Service, the Ku Klux Klan, and the Man Who Masterminded America's First War on Terror* (Toronto: Hanover Square Press, 2019), 181.

214   Merrill's more sustained: Merrill to Townsend, June 9, 1871, Adjutant General's Reports, NARA.

215   In mid-May, Grant: John Y. Simon, ed., USG *Papers,* Vol. 21 (Carbondale: Southern Illinois University Press, 1998), 337, 355.

216   "Whites may be": *Yorkville Enquirer,* March 30, 1871.

216   "It is utterly": Merrill to Townsend, June 9, 1871, Adjutant General's Reports, NARA.

216   As long as: Merrill to Townsend, June 10, 1871, Adjutant General's Reports, NARA; JC, Vol. 3, 25–28, 33–34.

216   Even as a: Merrill to Townsend, September 14, 1872, Adjutant General's Reports, NARA.

217   "In all my": JC, Vol. 5, 1481–82.

217   Perhaps remarkably for: Merrill to Townsend, January 14, 1872, Adjutant General's Reports, NARA.

217   While Merrill worked: Merrill to Townsend, June 9, June 10, June 11, 1871; Alfred H. Terry to Townsend, July 23, 1871, Adjutant General's Reports, NARA.

220   One of the first: JC, Vol. 2, 86–103.

221 Andrew J. Flowers, the: JC, Vol. 13, 42; JC, Vol. 8, 111ff; JC, Vol. 6, 75; JC, Vol. 11, 6ff; JC, Vol. 11, 265ff.

221 Several of the men: JC, Vol. 6, 308ff, 320–21; JC, Vol. 8, 375–94.

222 Nathan Bedford Forrest: JC, Vol. 13, 3–41.

223 In July, a: *Yorkville Enquirer,* August 3, 1871.

223 Scores of witnesses: JC, Vol. 3, 25–42, 185–86, 274, 289, 296–99, 306–8, 349–53, 580–81; JC, Vol. 5, 1481ff.

224 The subcommittee also: JC, Vol. 3, 446ff; JC, Vol. 4, 1062ff, 1201, 1216.

224 Merrill testified on: JC., Vol. 5, 1474–78ff.

225 Rep. Philadelph Van Trump: Ibid., 1470, 1486.

226 At forty-nine, Bratton: Ibid., 1340–62.

227 Among them, he informed: Merrill to Townsend, June 9, 1871, Adjutant General's Reports, NARA.

13: A MACHINERY FOR CRIMES

228 In the event: Lewis Merrill to Edward D. Townsend, September 17, and July 17, 1871, NARA; JC, Vol. 6, 1599–1606, 1611–12.

229 The grand jury fiasco: Merrill to Townsend, September 17, 1871, Adjutant General's Reports, NARA; John K. Scott to USG, John Y. Simon, ed., USG *Papers,* Vol. 22 (Carbondale: Southern Illinois University Press, 1998), 163–65; Javan Bryant to USG, September 8, 1871, USG *Papers,* Vol. 22, 167.

229 "This disaffection is": AA to Robert A. Hill, September 12, 1871, Akerman Letterbooks, Alderman Library, UVA.

230 To a friend: AA to James Jackson, November 20, 1871, Akerman Letterbooks, Alderman Library, UVA.

231 He wrote to General Terry: AA to Alfred H. Terry, November 18, 1871, Akerman Letterbooks.

231 Once settled in: AA to James Jackson, November 20, 1871, Akerman Letterbooks.

231 A deeply religious man: AA to William M. Thomas, November 22, 1871; AA to Alfred H. Terry, November 18, 1871; AA to E. P. Jacobson, August 18, 1871, Akerman Letterbooks.

232 On October 12: Proclamation, Simon, ed., USG *Papers,* Vol. 22, 161.

232 "Unless these combinations": AA to USG, October 16, 1871, Simon, ed., USG *Papers,* Vol. 22, 179–80.

233 "Several citizens of ": *Yorkville Enquirer,* October 26, 1871.

233 "Great excitement today": Mary Davis Brown diary, *Oil in Our Lamps* (Published by Brown's descendants, York, SC, County Historical Society).

233 Merrill usually deployed: Sandy Barnard, *Custer's First Sergeant John Ryan* (Terre Haute: AST Press, 1996), 154–57, 163.

234 Ryan also revealed: Ibid., 137–38, 152, 159.

235 The very nature: Mark L. Bradley: *Blue Coats and Tar Heels: Soldiers and Civilians in Reconstruction North Carolina* (Lexington: University of Kentucky Press, 2009), 271–73.

235 In Spartanburg, Merrill: Merrill to Townsend, May 28, 1872, Adjutant General's Reports, NARA.

235 A Klan supporter: Robert W. Shand, "Incidents in the Life of a Private Soldier in the War Waged by the United States Against the Confederate States, 1861–1865," 1907, unpublished memoir, South Caroliniana Collection, USC.

235 Southern sympathies were: T. J. Stiles, *Custer's Trials: A Life on the Frontier of a New America* (New York: Vintage, 2015), 356–68.

236 "Many of the Kuklux": Merrill to Townsend, January 17, 1872, Adjutant General's Reports, NARA; Simon, ed., USG *Papers,* Vol. 22, 361ff; Mary Davis Brown diary, *Oil in Our Lamps;* AA to B. D. Silliman, November 9, 1871, Akerman Letterbooks.

236 Among the fugitives: C. D. Melton to John R. Bratton, December 13, 1871; unsigned to John R. Bratton, March 28, 1872; unsigned to John R. Bratton, December 1871 or January 1872, Bratton Family Papers, South Caroliniana Library, USC.

237 Bratton's lawyer warned: C. D. Melton to John R. Bratton, December 25, 1871, Bratton Family Papers.

237 By the end: Merrill to Townsend, January 14, 1872, Adjutant General's Reports, NARA.

237 "Looking about for": Ibid.

238 The jail's inmates: Iredell Jones to "Dear Mother," November 1, 1871, and Jones to "Dearest Wife," November 3, 1871, Iredell Jones Papers, South Caroliniana Library, USC.

238 As the Klan began: Robin Spencer Lattimore, *Old Rutherfordton: A Hometown History* (Rutherfordton, NC: Hilltop Publications, 2006), 57–61; Tod R. Caldwell to USG, April 20, 1871, and J. B. Carpenter to USG, May 10, 1871, Simon., ed., USG *Papers,* Vol. 22, 362–63 note.

238 Then, in June: *Rutherford Star,* June 28, 1871; JC, Vol. 2, 117ff; John Pool to USG, June 16, 1871, Simon, ed., USG *Papers,* Vol. 22, 365; *Farmer and Mechanic (Raleigh, NC),* April 17, 1878.

239 The Klan's overly confident: *Rutherford Star,* June 28 and June 29, 1871; Nathan Scoggin to Charles H. Morgan, August 7, 1871, Simon, ed., USG *Papers,* Vol. 22, 369 note.

239 "Neighbor betrayed neighbor": Randolph Shotwell scrapbooks, Shotwell Family Papers, North Carolina Collection, UNC.

240 Boastful and aggressive: *Farmer and Mechanic (Raleigh, NC),* April 15 and April 17, 1878; Shotwell scrapbooks.

240 There was some talk: AA to Benjamin F. Butler, August 9, 1871, Akerman Letterbooks.

240 "The Ku Klux trials": *Weekly Carolina Era,* October 12, 1871.

240 The convicted Shotwell: *Farmer and Mechanic (Raleigh, NC),* April 15, 1878; Shotwell scrapbooks; *Baltimore Sun,* November 26, 1871; *New York Sun,* reprinted in *Daily Charleston Courier,* November 4, 1871; *NYH,* reprinted in *Daily Charleston Courier,* November 3, 1871.

241 Lewis Merrill caustically: Merrill to Townsend, January 14, 1872, Adjutant General's Reports, NARA.

241 The state capital's attention: *Daily Charleston Courier,* November 8 and November 10, 1871.

241 The city was still: *Daily Charleston Courier,* November 6, 1871; John M. Sherrer III, *Remembering Columbia* (Charleston: Arcadia Publishing, 2015), 15–27, 32–34; Tom Elmore, *Columbia Civil War Landmarks* (Charleston: History Press, 2011), 22–24, 47–50.

242 "It was not only": Lou Falkner Williams, *The Great South Carolina Ku Klux Klan Trials, 1871–1872* (Athens: University of Georgia Press, 1996), 59; David T. Corbin to AA, November 20, 1871, Adjutant General's Reports, NARA.

242 The Klan, Corbin declared: *Proceedings in the Ku Klux Klan Trials at Columbia, S.C., in the United States Circuit Court, November Term, 1871* (Columbia: Republican Printing Company, 1872), 381.

243 The prosecution presented: Ibid., 174, 178, 185, 490, 496, 502, 508; JC, Vol. 5, 1746–48; Williams, *The Great South Carolina Ku Klux Klan Trials,* 96–99.

244 The first case: *Proceedings in the Ku Klux Klan Trials,* 15ff, 55–66, 278–81; JC, Vol. 5, 1744–46.

245 Stanbery, for the defense: *Proceedings in the Ku Klux Klan Trials,* 17–22, 27–28, 31.

245 To this, Reverdy Johnson: Ibid., 77.

246 In another case: Ibid., 147ff, 163ff, 389ff.

246 Several witnesses confessed: Ibid., 243–48, 376.

247 Corbin then offered: Ibid., 391, 643–53, 779–81.

247 Mitchell's defense hinged: Ibid., 149–51, 288–89, 405, 413–15; JC, Vol. 5, 1757ff, 1778–79, 1781–84.

248 The court did uphold: *Proceedings in the Ku Klux Klan Trials,* 89–91; Williams, *The Great South Carolina Ku Klux Klan Trials,* 71–72.

249 Declared Bond: *Proceedings in the Ku Klux Klan Trials,* 790–91.

249 "Those who were": Ibid., 768.

249 Bond particularly castigated: Ibid., 605.

249 "What is quite": Ibid., 789.

14: CONGRESS GOES SOUTH

252 Partisan Democrats celebrated: *Atlanta Constitution,* October 21, 1871.

253 Whites hostile to: JC, Vol. 7, 1212–13.

253 M. V. Brand: JC, Vol. 6, 350–56.

254 Mary Brown was: Ibid., 375–78.

255 Joe Brown, her husband: Ibid., 502–3.

255 Caroline Smith, who: Ibid., 400–402, 412, 463–65, 390–91, 474, 478, 565–66.

256 Henry Lowther: Ibid., 431.

256 G. B. Holcombe: Ibid., 497, 544, 422–23.

256   The subcommittee's Democrats: JC, Vol. 7, 1213; JC, Vol. 6, 518, 541, 443; *Atlanta Constitution,* November 9, 1871.

257   The Democrats' witnesses: JC, Vol. 6, 368–72.

257   Following Pope: Ibid., 379–84.

259   In the southern style: JC, Vol. 12, 653, 825–27; *Atlanta Constitution,* October 22, 1871.

259   In striking contrast: JC, Vol. 8, 546–52, 568.

259   Scores of Black: Ibid., 572ff; JC, Vol. 9, 997–1010.

260   James Alston: JC, Vol. 9, 1016–21.

260   Burton Long: Ibid., 1149–51.

260   At Demopolis, Betsey: Ibid., 1243–44.

261   Eliza Lyon: Ibid., 1262–66.

261   In Livingston: JC, Vol. 10, 1650–56.

261   John Childers said: Ibid., 1719–26.

262   Reuben Meredith: Ibid., 1775.

262   Wiley Hargrove: Ibid., 1993ff.

262   On November 6: JC, Vol. 12, 803–4, 718, 1084, 777–78, 889, 823; JC, Vol. 11, 493, 483–88.

263   Joseph Davis: JC, Vol. 12, 809–11; Allen P. Huggins to USG, May 10, 1871, John Y. Simon, ed., USG *Papers,* Vol. 21 (Carbondale: Southern Illinois University Press, 1998), 342, 343.

263   Most of the witnesses: JC, Vol. 12, 829ff, 839–55, 859–60, 876, 1023–27.

266   R. W. Cone: JC, Vol. 13, 65ff, 177, 113–14, 147, 273, 239, 261.

267   "I can see": Ibid., 309–10.

15: THE KLAN AT BAY

269   "Nothing, Mr. President": AWT to USG, December 28, 1871, John Y. Simon, ed., USG *Papers,* Vol. 22 (Carbondale: Southern Illinois University Press, 1998), 370.

269   And from Alabama: John A. Minnis to USG, December 12, 1871, Simon, ed., USG *Papers,* Vol. 22, 18–19.

270   "an incubus and a mill-stone": David Herbert Donald, *Charles Sumner,* Vol. 2 (New York: Da Capo, 1996), 526.

270   "Party! What more": Frederic Bancroft, ed., *Speeches, Correspondence and Political Papers of Carl Schurz,* Vol. 2 (New York: G. P. Putnam's Sons, 1913), 305.

270   "Unless I greatly": CS to Jacob D. Cox, April 4, 1871, Simon, ed., USG *Papers,* Vol. 21, 370.

270   Grant was also under: Heather Cox Richardson, *To Make Men Free: A History of the Republican Party* (New York: Basic Books, 2015), 94–95.

270   "These disaffections in": John B. Alley to Henry Wilson, November 30, 1871, Simon, ed., USG *Papers,* Vol. 22, 233–34.

271   "Mr. Sumner has": USG to Henry Wilson, November 15, 1871, Simon, ed., USG *Papers,* Vol. 22, 233–34.

271 On December 4: Simon, ed., USG *Papers,* Vol. 22, 268ff.

271 Then, eight days: USG to AA, December 12, 1871, Simon, ed., USG *Papers,* Vol. 22, 288.

272 Its atrocities caused: AA to unknown addressee, January 1, 1872, Akerman Letterbooks, Alderman Library, UVA.

272 His anguish irritated: J. Morgan Kousser and James M. McPherson, eds., *Region, Race and Reconstruction: Essays in Honor of C. Vann Woodward* (New York: Oxford University Press, 1982), 410; Allan Nevins, *Hamilton Fish: The Inner History of the Grant Administration* (New York: Dodd, Mead, 1936), 591; AA to B. D. Silliman, November 9, 1871, Akerman Letterbooks.

273 To a friend: AA to David Corbin, December 15, 1871, Akerman Letterbooks; Nevins, *Hamilton Fish,* 591; Kousser and McPherson, eds., *Region, Race and Reconstruction,* 405, 410; AA to B. D. Silliman, November 9, 1871, Akerman Letterbooks.

273 Grant, too, was: *Washington Evening Star,* April 17, 1872, in Simon, ed., USG *Papers,* Vol. 23, 100.

273 Almost daily, he: Charles Hooks to USG, November 20, 1871, Simon, ed., USG *Papers,* Vol. 22, 183.

273 Lewis Merrill, tough-minded: Lewis Merrill to Edward D. Townsend, January 14, 1872, Adjutant General's Reports, NARA.

274 Democratic senator Thomas Bayard: CG 42/2, 1111.

275 Democrats were desperate: CG 42/2, 1119–22; *NYH,* February 19, 1872; *NYT,* February 20, 1872.

275 Amos Akerman predicted: AA to Foster Blodgett, November 8, 1871, Akerman Letterbooks; *NYH,* February 19, 1872, *NYT,* February 19, 1872.

276 Just days before: CG 42/2, 698–703.

276 He tried, ultimately: CS to Charles Sumner, September 30, 1871, Schurz Papers, LC.

277 In Nashville, in September: Bancroft, ed., *Speeches, Correspondence and Political Papers of Carl Schurz,* 257ff.

277 "A measure that": CG 42/2, 278.

277 During the "spicy debate": Ibid., 928.

278 "The Democrats ranged": Reprinted in *Columbia Union,* February 16, 1872.

278 The prospect of: CG 42/2 242–43.

278 John Scott, who: Ibid., 920–21.

278 "Rather than accord": *Columbia Union,* February 14, 1872.

279 Democrats, unsurprisingly: *Daily Charleston Courier,* April 26, 1872.

279 "Everybody now wants": Robert J. Kaczorowski, *The Politics of Judicial Interpretation: The Federal Courts, Department of Justice, and Civil Rights, 1866–1876* (New York: Fordham University Press, 2005), 70.

279 D. H. Starbuck: House of Representatives, Executive Document No. 268, "Conditions of Affairs in the Southern States," 20ff, 30–42, 49.

280 The U.S. attorney: Ibid., 5–19.

280 "It is a fact": *Columbia Union,* February 15, 1872.

280 Even the conservative: *Yorkville Enquirer,* January 11, 1872.

281 The state's second set: *Wilmington (NC) Morning Star*, June 20, 1872; *Daily Charleston Courier*, April 13, 1872; *Columbia Union*, May 4, 1872; *Yorkville Enquirer*, April 30, 1872.

281 The prisoners' attorney: *Daily Charleston Courier*, May 2, 1872; *Columbia Union*, April 29, 1872.

282 Bond was disgusted: Kaczorowski, *The Politics of Judicial Interpretation*, 43.

282 To wild cheers: Bancroft, ed., *Speeches, Correspondence and Political Papers of Carl Schurz*, 354ff.

283 "dirt of electioneering": Andrew W. Slap, *The Doom of Reconstruction: The Liberal Republicans in the Civil War Era* (New York: Fordham University Press, 2006), 140.

283 After five seesawing: *NYT*, May 4, 1872.

283 Schurz was stunned: Hans L. Trefousse, *Carl Schurz: A Biography* (Knoxville: University of Tennessee Press, 1982), 206.

284 "an easy, worthless race"; Ronald C. White, *American Ulysses: A Life of Ulysses S. Grant* (New York: Random House, 2016), 533.

284 "interminable political wobblings": *Philadelphia Bulletin*, reprinted in *Columbia Union*, May 6, 1872.

284 "There is no": *NYT*, May 4, 1872.

284 "Mr. Greeley is": USG to Henry Wilson, November 15, 1871, Simon, ed., USG *Papers*, Vol. 22, 231–32.

284 Of arguably more: *NYT*, May 4, 1872; *Columbia Union*, May 8, 1872.

16: THE COURT WEIGHS IN

289 It was also: *Proceedings of the National Union Republican Convention Held at Philadelphia, June 5 and 6, 1872* (Washington: Gibson Brothers, Printers, 1872), 44, 21, 33–34, 11–12.

290 When the president's: *NYH*, June 7, 1872.

291 When, a few days later: *NYT, June* 11, 1872.

291 Newspapers catchily dubbed: *NYH,* June 7, 1872.

292 The platform also: *Proceedings of the National Union Republican Convention*, 61.

292 But it referred: Ibid., 51–52.

292 Concerned Blacks noted: *NYH,* June 7, 1872.

292 Wrote Frederick Douglass: Douglas R. Egerton, *The Wars of Reconstruction: The Brief, Violent History of America's Most Progressive Era* (New York: Bloomsbury, 2013), 301.

292 Sen. Adelbert Ames: Adelbert Ames to Blanche Ames, October 26, 1871, Blanche Butler Ames, *Chronicles from the Nineteenth Century: Family Letters of Blanche Butler and Adelbert Ames,* Vol. 1 (Privately printed, Clinton, MA: Colonial Press, 1957), 344.

292 In Chickasaw County: JC, Vol. 12, 825–27.

293 Joe Crews, for one: Joseph Crews to Lewis Merrill, July 24, 1872, Adjutant General's Reports, NARA.

293 "Very many of ": AA to Benjamin Conley, December 28, 1871, Akerman Letterbooks, Alderman Library, UVA.

293 Williams's appointment, one: Charles W. Calhoun, *The Presidency of Ulysses S. Grant* (Lawrence: University Press of Kansas, 2017), 327.

293 He urged federal: Ibid.

294 The very success: AA to B. D. Silliman, November 9, 1871, Akerman Letterbooks; Scott Farris, *Freedom on Trial: The First Post–Civil War Battle over Civil Rights and Voter Suppression* (Lanham, MD: Rowman & Littlefield, 2020), 258; Robert J. Kaczorowski, *The Politics of Judicial Interpretation: The Federal Courts, Department of Justice, and Civil Rights, 1866–1876* (New York: Fordham University Press, 2005), 80–81; Stephen Cresswell, "Enforcing the Enforcement Acts: The Department of Justice in Northern Mississippi, 1870–1890," *Journal of Southern History*, Vol. 53 (August 1987).

295 The odor of retrenchment: Stephen Cresswell, *Mormons & Cowboys, Moonshiners and Klansmen* (Tuscaloosa: University of Alabama Press, 1991), 27.

296 Maj. Lewis Merrill also: Lou Falkner Williams, *The Great South Carolina Ku Klux Klan Trials, 1871–1872* (Athens: University of Georgia Press, 1996), 104.

296 He was, he admitted: Allen C. Guelzo, *Reconstruction: A Concise History* (New York: Oxford University Press, 2018), 88.

297 Shortly before the: *Blyew v. U.S.*, 80 U.S. 13 Wall. 581 (1871) at https://supreme .justia.com/cases/federal/us/80/581/.

298 "a bold, unmitigated": Kaczorowski, *The Politics of Judicial Interpretation*, 109.

298 Whatever the Court: Frank J. Scaturro, *The Supreme Court's Retreat from Reconstruction: A Distortion of Constitutional Jurisprudence* (Westport, CT: Greenwood Press, 2000), 20–22; A. Leon Higginbotham Jr., *Shades of Freedom: Racial Politics and Presumptions of the American Legal Process* (New York: Oxford University Press, 1996), 78–90; Kaczorowski, *The Politics of Judicial Interpretation*, 109, 113–15.

299 The Court's decision: *United States v. Avery* at www.law.cornell.edu/supreme court/text/80/251; Kaczorowski, *The Politics of Judicial Interpretation*, 106.

300 There was a dramatic coda: *Yorkville Enquirer*, June 20, June 27, July 7, July 14, July 25, August 1, and November 14, 1872; *Wilmington (NC) Morning Star*, June 20, 1872; *Charleston Democrat*, July 30, 1872; Charles Lane, *Freedom's Detective: The Secret Service, the Ku Klux Klan and the Man Who Masterminded America's First War on Terror* (Toronto: Hanover Square Press, 2019), 219ff.

300 Hester had masterminded: Lane, *Freedom's Detective*, 153–55, 161ff; John Scott to USG, June 8, 1871, John Y. Simon, ed., *USG Papers*, Vol. 22 (Carbondale: Southern Illinois University Press, 1995–2000), 11 note; Orville E. Babcock to AA, June 15, 1871, *USG Papers*, Vol. 22, 13 note.

302 Bratton's arrest threatened: *Wilmington (NC) Morning Star*, June 20, 1872; *New York Sun*, June 12, 1872; *Charleston Daily News*, June 15, 1872; *Charleston Democrat*, July 30, 1872; *Yorkville Enquirer*, September 4, 1897; Orlo Miller, "The Bratton Kidnapping," *The Canadian Science Digest*, Vol. 1 (April 1938).

302 In South Carolina: *Yorkville Enquirer*, February 1, 1921.

303 Exactly a week: *NYT*, July 9, 1872; *New York Tribune*, July 11, 1872.

303 An attempt to replace: *New York Tribune,* July 11, 1872 (all quotes).

304 Accepting his nomination: *Sacramento Daily Union,* July 25, 1872.

304 Black voters well: *NYT,* June 11, 1872.

17: GRANT TRIUMPHANT

305 "Does not Christ": Octavius Frothingham, *Gerrit Smith* (New York: G. P. Putnam's Sons, 1880), 130–31.

305 In 1867, to: *Baltimore Sun,* May 16, 1867.

306 Shotwell readily admitted: J. G. De Roulhac Hamilton, ed., *The Papers of Randolph Abbott Shotwell,* Vol. 3 (Raleigh: North Carolina Historical Commission, 1936), 46.

306 Shotwell later described: Ibid., 234–37.

306 According to Shotwell: Ibid., 269, 231, 165, 138, 149, 154–59, 171, 200.

307 On July 9, Smith: *NYT,* August 24, 1872.

307 Shotwell was not: Hamilton, ed., *The Papers of Randolph Abbott Shotwell,* Vol. 3, 253.

307 Smith was not alone: *NYH,* August 14, 1872; Hamilton, ed., *The Papers of Randolph Abbott Shotwell,* Vol. 3, 287; Jacob R. Davis to USG, May 29, 1872, John Y. Simon, ed., USG *Papers,* Vol. 23 (Carbondale: Southern Illinois University Press, 1998), 212; H. K. Thurber to USG, October 9, 1872, Simon, ed., USG *Papers,* Vol. 23, 213.

307 Grant was of: James D. Richardson, ed., *A Compilation of the Messages and Papers of the Presidents, 1789–1897,* Vol. 7 (Washington: Government Printing Office, 1898), 153.

307 But he still: USG to Gerrit Smith, July 28, 1872, Simon, ed., USG *Papers,* Vol. 23, 210–11.

308 For this politically: Charles Lane, *Freedom's Detective: The Secret Service, the Ku Klux Klan and the Man Who Masterminded America's First War on Terror* (Toronto: Hanover Square Press, 2019), 43ff.

308 He told a reporter: *NYH,* August 14, 1872.

309 He recommended: Simon, ed., USG *Papers,* Vol. 23, 228–29.

309 "The organization is": Gordon McKinney, "The Klan in the Southern Mountains: The Lusk-Shotwell Controversy," *Appalachian Journal,* Vol. 8 (Winter 1981).

309 while Senator Robertson: CG 42/2, 3713.

309 Alexander Stephens: Alexander H. Stephens to USG, August 6, 1872, Simon, ed., USG *Papers,* Vol. 23, 213.

309 "The scourging and": Frederick Douglass, *U.S. Grant and the Colored People,* pamphlet, 1872.

309 "Bayonets is What": Edwin Prucha to USG, September 22, 1872, Simon, ed., USG *Papers,* Vol. 23, 102.

309 Declared Rep. Job Stevenson: CG 42/2, 4028.

311 Again the barbarous: Ibid., 381.

311 Even the passionate: CG 42/1, 102–3.

312 "There is no member": CG 42/2, 3382.

312 "I plead for": Ibid., 3737.

313 Sen. Lyman Trumbull predicted: *NYH,* June 21, 1872.

313 In the South: *Daily Charleston Courier,* November 5, 1872; *Atlanta Constitution,* November 5, 1872.

313 He harped relentlessly: Charles W. Calhoun, *The Presidency of Ulysses S. Grant* (Lawrence: University Press of Kansas, 2017), 391.

313 "But the first": *New York Tribune,* October 14, 1872.

313 "We have fet": C. T. Brown to USG, November 8, 1872, Simon, ed., USG *Papers,* Vol. 23, 290.

314 "The liberty which": Douglass, *U.S. Grant and the Colored People.*

314 Speaking to a rally: Frederic Bancroft, ed., *Speeches, Correspondence and Political Papers of Carl Schurz,* Vol. 2 (New York: G. P. Putnam's Sons, 1913), 394, 422–25.

314 The South—the *white:* Ibid., 438–41.

314 In a similar: Andrew W. Slap, *The Doom of Reconstruction: The Liberal Republicans in the Civil War Era* (New York: Fordham University Press, 2006), 208–9.

314 Charles Sumner, in: Charles Sumner, *Letter to Colored Citizens,* pamphlet (Washington: F. & J. Rives and Geo. A. Bailey, 1872); CG 42/2, 4110ff.

314 In keeping with: Ron Chernow, *Grant* (New York: Penguin, 2017), 747; Jenny Richie to USG, November 6, 1872, Simon, ed., USG *Papers,* Vol. 23, 286; USG to George H. Stuart, September 11, 1872, USG *Papers,* Vol. 23, 247.

315 While Grant maintained: *Harper's Weekly,* August 24 and September 7, 1872; *The Nation's Peril: Twelve Years' Experience in the South; Then and Now; The Ku Klux Klan,* anonymous pamphlet (New York: Friends of the Compiler, 1872), 118–20, 141.

315 The *New York Times: NYT,* November 4, 1872.

316 The Danish immigrant: Jacob A. Riis, *The Making of an American* (New York: Macmillan, 1901), 109–10.

316 "Victory! A Sweeping": *NYT,* November 6, 1872.

316 Grant was doubtless: Harry Atwater to USG, November 6, 1872, Simon, ed., USG *Papers,* Vol. 23, 285.

317 "All is over!": Hamilton, ed., *The Papers of Randolph Abbott Shotwell,* Vol. 3, 276.

317 Greeley himself fell: Richard White, *The Republic for Which It Stands: The United States During Reconstruction and the Gilded Age, 1865–1896* (New York: Oxford University Press, 2017), 211.

317 A month after: Richardson, ed., *A Compilation of the Messages and Papers of the Presidents,* 199.

318 "The men who": *NYT,* November 6, 1872.

318 Grant brusquely dismissed: USG to J. R. Jones, September 5, 1872, Simon, ed., USG *Papers,* Vol. 23, 242.

319 "Third parties are": Richard Hofstadter, *The Age of Reform* (New York: Vintage, 1955), 97.

319   As the historian Eric Foner has: Eric Foner, *Reconstruction: America's Unfinished Revolution, 1863–1877* (New York: Harper & Row, 1988), 510.

319   "Judging from all": Lane, *Freedom's Detective,* 207.

319   "My desire is": Lou Falkner Williams, *The Great South Carolina Ku Klux Klan Trials, 1871–1872* (Athens: University of Georgia Press, 1996), 123.

319   Grant's inauguration: *NYT,* March 5, 1873; *NYH,* March 5, 1873.

320   "The states lately": *NYT,* March 5, 1873.

321   "the democrats have ful": H. W. Marshall to USG, February 3, 1873, Simon, ed., USG *Papers,* Vol. 24, 332.

321   "And for what": Joseph T. Hatch to USG, January 21, 1873, Simon, ed., USG *Papers,* Vol. 24, 53.

321   "I believe that": Richardson, ed., *A Compilation of the Messages and Papers of the Presidents,* 222.

322   "The wrong inflicted": Ibid., 222.

322   That evening, Pennsylvania Avenue: *NYT,* March 5, 1873; *NYH,* March 5, 1873; *Evening Star* (Washington, DC), March 5, 1873; *Chicago Evening Post,* March 5, 1873; Chernow, *Grant,* 755–56.

18: COLFAX

325   On April 13, Easter: *NYT,* April 16 and April 20, 1873.

325   "Boys, this is": Charles Lane, *The Day Freedom Died: The Colfax Massacre, the Supreme Court, and the Betrayal of Reconstruction* (New York: Henry Holt, 2008), 91.

326   "I didn't come": Ibid., 102.

326   During the killing: *New Orleans Times,* April 16, 1873.

327   "A butchery of": USG, "Message Regarding Intervention in Louisiana," January 13, 1875, online at millercenter.org/thepresidency/presidentialspeeches.

327   As the *Alexandria Caucasian:* Ted Tunnell, *Edge of the Sword: The Ordeal of Carpetbagger Marshall H. Twitchell in the Civil War and Reconstruction* (Baton Rouge: Louisiana State University Press, 2001), 188.

327   "The nation that": *NYT,* April 16, 1873.

328   By coincidence, this other case: Robert J. Kaczorowski, *The Politics of Judicial Interpretation: The Federal Courts, Department of Justice, and Civil Rights, 1866–1876* (New York: Fordham University Press, 2005), 123ff; *NYT,* April 16, 1873.

329   Public reaction was: *NYT,* April 16, 1873; Kaczorowski, *The Politics of Judicial Interpretation,* 135.

329   "It is to be understood": *Yorkville Enquirer,* August 7, 1873.

329   Although *Slaughterhouse* was: Kaczorowski, *The Politics of Judicial Interpretation,* 138–43.

330   Williams was at least: USG to William W. Belknap, September 2, 1874, John Y. Simon, ed., USG *Papers,* Vol. 25 (Carbondale: Southern Illinois University Press, 2003), 187.

330 "the White Peapel": Isaac Bourne to USG, September 1, 1874, Simon, ed., USG *Papers,* Vol. 25, 188.

330 Prisoners convicted under: *Yorkville Enquirer,* August 7, 1873.

330 "At all events": Lou Falkner Williams, *The Great South Carolina Ku Klux Klan Trials, 1871–1872* (Athens: University of Georgia Press, 1996), 124.

330 On August 9, a pardon: J. G. De Roulhac Hamilton, ed., *The Papers of Randolph Abbott Shotwell,* Vol. 3 (Raleigh: North Carolina Historical Commission, 1936), 430ff, 451, 352–53; Shotwell scrapbooks, North Carolina Collection, UNC; *Farmer & Mechanic* (Raleigh, NC), April 15, 1878.

331 "the mortification": Hamilton, ed., *The Papers of Randolph Abbott Shotwell,* Vol. 3, 434.

331 "a thunderclap in": H. W. Brands, *The Money Men: Capitalism, Democracy, and the Hundred Years' War over the American Dollar* (New York: Norton, 2006), 162.

331 Two days later: *NYT,* September 19 and 21, 1873; David W. Blight, *Frederick Douglass: Prophet of Freedom* (New York: Simon & Schuster, 2018), 545–46; Richard White, *The Republic for Which It Stands: The United States During Reconstruction and the Gilded Age, 1865–1896* (New York: Oxford University Press, 2017), 265–72.

332 A cruelly racist book: James S. Pike, *The Prostrate State: South Carolina Under Negro Rule* (New York: D. Appleton and Co., 1874), 12, 20, 29.

332 The *New York Tribune: New York Tribune,* October 21, 1874.

332 Even the *New York Times: NYT,* November 25, 1874.

333 Although the elections: Williams, *The Great South Carolina Ku Klux Klan Trials,* 128; Elias M. Keils to USG, November 17, 1874, Simon, ed., USG *Papers,* Vol. 25, 197; *Atlanta Constitution,* November 6, 1874; Charles O. Fisher to USG, December 1864, USG *Papers,* Vol. 25, 194; Kyle Whitmire, "Ambushed in Eufaula: Alabama's Forgotten Race Massacre," *Birmingham News,* January 16, 2022.

333 "The news from": *Raleigh (NC) Sentinel,* November 5, 1874.

334 "The verdict against": *New York Tribune,* November 4, 1874.

334 Of the once promising: John R. Lynch, *The Facts of Reconstruction* (New York: Neale Publishing Co., 1913), 55.

334 "Let it be understood": "Reconstruction in America: Racial Violence After the Civil War," Report by the Equal Justice Initiative, Montgomery, AL, 2020, online at eji.org.

334 "We Casted our": H. W. Harris to USG, September 25, 1874, Simon, ed., USG *Papers,* Vol. 25, 230.

334 Grant's first major speech: James D. Richardson, ed., *A Compilation of the Messages and Papers of the Presidents* (New York: Bureau of National Literature, 1909), 284ff.

336 The Enforcement Acts hung: William Gillette, *Retreat from Reconstruction, 1869–1879* (Baton Rouge: Louisiana State University Press, 1979), 43–44; Carole Watterson Troxler, " 'To look more closely at the man': Wyatt Outlaw, a Nexus of National, Local, and Personal History," *North Carolina Historical Review,* Vol. 77 (October 2000); Troxler, *Shuttle and Plow: A History of Alamance*

County, North Carolina (Burlington, NC: Alamance County Historical Association, 1999), 308–12; Richard Zuczec, "The Federal Government's Attack on the Ku Klux Klan: A Reassessment," *South Carolina Historical Magazine,* Vol. 97 (January 1996); Stephen Cresswell, "Enforcing the Enforcement Acts: The Department of Justice in Northern Mississippi, 1870–1890," *Journal of Southern History,* Vol. 53 (August 1987).

337 In Mansfield, White Leaguers: Tunnell, *Edge of the Sword,* 193–94, 200–202.

337 Maj. Lewis Merrill, redeployed: Lewis Merrill to Edward D. Townsend, August 24, 1875, Adjutant General's Reports, NARA.

337 Grant had explicitly: Richardson, ed., *A Compilation of the Messages and Papers of the Presidents,* 296ff; USG, "Proclamation," September 15, 1874, Simon, ed., *USG Papers,* Vol. 25, 213–14, and notes 215–27; Justin A. Nystrom, *New Orleans After the Civil War: Race, Politics, and a New Birth of Freedom* (Baltimore: Johns Hopkins University Press, 2010), 171–85; James K. Hogue, *Uncivil War: Five New Orleans Street Battles and the Rise and Fall of Radical Reconstruction* (Baton Rouge: Louisiana State University Press, 2011), 116ff.

338 "It cannot be": Blanche Butler Ames and Adelbert Ames, *Chronicles from the Nineteenth Century: Family Letters of Blanche Butler and Adelbert Ames,* Vol. 2 (Privately printed, Clinton, MA: Colonial Press, 1957), 92.

338 "I am somewhat": USG to Edwards Pierrepont, Simon, ed., *USG Papers,* Vol. 25, 312.

338 Mississippi's former Black: Lynch, *The Facts of Reconstruction,* 67–70.

339 "Why should I": Adelbert Ames to Blanche Butler Ames, October 12, 1875, Ames and Ames, *Chronicles from the Nineteenth Century,* 216.

339 "So complete and": Adelbert Ames to Blanche Butler Ames, November 4, 1875, Ames, *Chronicles from the Nineteenth Century,* 249.

339 "We have been told": Richard S. West, *Lincoln's Scapegoat General: A Life of Benjamin F. Butler, 1818–1893* (Boston: Houghton Mifflin, 1965), 356.

339 "If I come": Ibid., 360.

340 Attacking the bill: Thomas E. Schott, *Alexander H. Stephens of Georgia* (Baton Rouge: Louisiana State University Press, 1988), 499–500.

340 "The Slaughter-House Cases!": Peggy Lamson, *Glorious Failure: Black Congressman Robert Brown Elliott and the Reconstruction in South Carolina* (New York: Norton, 1973), 175–82.

340 "almost grotesque exercise": Charles W. Calhoun, *The Presidency of Ulysses S. Grant* (Lawrence: University Press of Kansas, 2017), 479.

340 In March of 1876: *United States v. Cruikshank,* 92 U.S. 542 (1875); James Gray Pope, "Snubbed Landmark: Why *United States v. Cruikshank* (1876) Belongs at the Heart of the American Judicial Canon," *Harvard Civil Rights and Civil Liberties Law Review,* Vol. 49 (2014); Kaczorowski, *The Politics of Judicial Interpretation,* 150; Jack Beatty, *Age of Betrayal: The Triumph of Money in America, 1865–1900* (New York: Vintage, 2007), 142–43.

342 "We propose to": Williams, *The Great South Carolina Ku Klux Klan Trials,* 127.

342 Their leaders, wrote: Benjamin R. Tillman, "The Struggles of 76," unpub-

lished autobiographical essay, Benjamin R. Tillman Papers, South Caroliniana Library, USC.

342 "If he needs to": Rod Andrew Jr., *Wade Hampton: Confederate Warrior to Southern Redeemer* (Chapel Hill: University of North Carolina Press, 2008), 377.

342 "We were all tired": Tillman, "The Struggles of 76."

343 In another confrontation: Richard Zuczec, *State of Rebellion: Reconstruction in South Carolina* (Columbia: University of South Carolina Press, 1996), 171ff.

344 The Republicans presented: White, *The Republic for Which It Stands,* 327.

345 In his characteristically: Richardson, ed., *A Compilation of the Messages and Papers of the Presidents,* 442–44.

345 On the same day: Scott Farris, *Freedom on Trial: The First Post–Civil War Battle over Civil Rights and Voter Suppression* (Lanham, MD: Rowman & Littlefield, 2020), 271.

345 "The Fifteenth Amendment": Beatty, *Age of Betrayal,* 142.

347 In a brief passage: USG, *Memoirs and Selected Letters* (New York: Library of America, 1990), 751.

347 "I propose to fight": USG to Henry W. Halleck, May 11, 1864, Simon, ed., USG *Papers,* Vol. 10, 422.

347 "It is possible": USG, *Memoirs and Selected Letters,* 777.

EPILOGUE

349 On the morning: *NYT* August 9, 1885.

351 Encomiums to Grant: www.nps.gov/funeral-of-ulysses-s-grant; *NYT,* August 9, 1885; Frederick Douglass, *Autobiographies* (New York: Library of America, 1994), 795.

352 The Supreme Court: Orville Vernon Burton and Armand Derfner, *Justice Deferred: Race and the Supreme Court* (Cambridge: Belknap Press, 2012), 89–92; Carolyn L. Karcher, *A Refugee from His Race: Albion W. Tourgée and His Fight Against White Supremacy* (Chapel Hill: University of North Carolina Press, 2016), 253, 272–76.

352 "The judgment this day": "John Marshall Harlan, Dissent from *Plessy v. Ferguson* 1896," online at www.BillofRightsInstitute.org.

353 "I want to give you": "Reconstruction in America: Racial Violence After the Civil War," Report by the Equal Justice Initiative, Montgomery, AL, 2020, online at eji.org.

353 "The new constitution": online at thereconstructionera.com.

354 Everywhere, the number: David Blight, "150 Years of Suppression," *NYT,* April 12, 2020.

354 "This is perhaps": Documenting the South Archive, UNC, online at http://docsouth.unc.edu/nc/whitegh/menu.html.

355 "To persons who": J. Morgan Kousser and James M. McPherson, eds., *Region, Race, and Reconstruction: Essays in Honor of C. Vann Woodward* (New York: Oxford University Press, 1982), 411.

355   When Nathan Bedford Forrest: *Memphis Avalanche,* November 1, 1877.

355   In 1900, the: *Yorkville Enquirer,* September 26, 1900.

355   In 1890, the citizens: Stephen Cresswell, "Enforcing the Enforcement Acts: The Department of Justice in Northern Mississippi, 1870–1890," *Journal of Southern History,* Vol. 53 (August 1987).

355   "Under their fear": William T. Richardson, *Historic Pulaski: Birthplace of the Ku Klux Klan* (Privately published, 1913), 35.

356   Recent research by: "Reconstruction in America: Racial Violence After the Civil War."

356   "The ultimate root": William A. Dunning, "The Undoing of Reconstruction," *Atlantic Monthly,* October 1901.

356   A generation later: Allan Nevins, *Hamilton Fish: The Inner History of the Grant Administration* (New York: Dodd, Mead, 1936), 601, 740.

357   In 1910, when: "In a Small Town, a Battle for Racial Justice Confronts a Bloody Past and an Uncertain Future," *Raleigh (NC) News & Observer,* May 19, 2021.

357   Of Bratton, the: Reprinted in *Yorkville Enquirer,* September 4, 1897.

357   The Klan also: Richardson, *Historic Pulaski.*

358   "creeping negroism": Wyn Craig Wade, *The Fiery Cross: The Ku Klux Klan in America* (New York: Oxford University Press, 1987), 122.

358   Audiences cheered as: Melvyn Stokes, *D. W. Griffith's The Birth of a Nation* (New York: Oxford University Press, 2007), 5, 22–25, 111; Wade, *The Fiery Cross,* 119–22.

358   Although the film's: Generally, *The Ku Klux Klan: Hearings Before the Committee on Rules, House of Representatives* (Washington: Government Printing Office, 1921); Wade, *The Fiery Cross,* 143ff, 253ff; *NYT,* September 12, 1921; *Americus (GA) Times-Recorder,* August 22, 1921.

360   "Nevertheless the influence": George S. Boutwell, *Reminiscences of Sixty Years in Public Affairs,* Vol. 1 (New York: McClure, Phillips & Co., 1902), 26.

361   In March of 1896: J. Michael Martinez, *Carpetbaggers, Cavalry, and the Ku Klux Klan: Exposing the Invisible Empire During Reconstruction* (Lanham, MD: Rowman and Littlefield, 2007), 226ff.

363   "Thus the politics": Abraham S. Eisenstadt, Ari Hoogenboom, and Hans L. Trefousse, eds., *Before Watergate: Problems of Corruption in American Society* (New York: Brooklyn College Press, 1978), 112–13.

363   "My country right": CG 42/2, 1286.

363   In 1904, two years: L. Moody Simms Jr., "Carl Schurz and the Negro," *Bulletin of the Missouri Historical Society,* Vol. 25 (April 1969).

363   "One is astonished": W. E. B. Du Bois, *Black Reconstruction in America, 1860–1880* (New York: Free Press, 1998), 722.

363   If, Du Bois suggests: Ibid., 714.

BIBLIOGRAPHY

BOOKS

Abbott, Richard H. *Cobbler in Congress: The Life of Henry Wilson, 1812–1875*. Lexington: University Press of Kentucky, 1972.

Adams, Henry. *The Education of Henry Adams*. New York: Modern Library, 1931.

Ames, Blanche Butler. *Adelbert Ames, 1835–1933*. New York: Columbia University Press, 1964.

Ames, Blanche Butler, and Adelbert Ames. *Chronicles from the Nineteenth Century: Family Letters of Blanche Butler and Adelbert Ames*, Vols. 1 and 2. Privately printed, Clinton, MA: Colonial Press, 1957.

Andrew, Rod Jr. *Wade Hampton: Confederate Warrior to Southern Redeemer*. Chapel Hill: University of North Carolina Press, 2008.

Angell, Stephen Ward. *Bishop Henry McNeal Turner and African American Religion in the South*. Knoxville: University of Tennessee Press, 1992.

Ash, Stephen V. *A Massacre in Memphis: The Race Riot That Shook the Nation One Year After the Civil War*. New York: Hill & Wang, 2013.

Auman, William T. *Civil War in the North Carolina Quaker Belt*. Jefferson, NC: McFarland, 2014.

Avary, Myrta Lockett. *Dixie After the War*. New York: Doubleday, Page & Co., 1906.

Baggett, James Alex. *The Scalawags: Southern Dissenters in the Civil War and Reconstruction*. Baton Rouge: Louisiana State University Press, 2002.

Ball, Edward. *Life of a Klansman: A Family History in White Supremacy*. New York: Farrar, Straus & Giroux, 2020.

Bancroft, Frederic, ed. *Speeches, Correspondence and Political Papers of Carl Schurz*, Vol. 2. New York: G. P. Putnam's Sons, 1913.

Barnard, Sandy. *Custer's First Sergeant John Ryan*. Terre Haute: AST Press, 1996.

Beatty, Jack. *Age of Betrayal: The Triumph of Money in America, 1865–1900*. New York: Vintage, 2007.

Benedict, Michael Les. *A Compromise of Principle: Congressional Republicans and Reconstruction, 1863–1869*. New York: Norton, 1974.

———. *The Fruits of Victory: Alternatives in Restoring the Union, 1865–1877*. Lanham, MD: University Press of America, 1986.

————. *The Impeachment of Andrew Johnson*. New York: Norton, 1973.

Bergeron, Paul H., ed. *The Papers of Andrew Johnson*. Knoxville: University of Tennessee Press, 1999.

Blaine, James G. *Twenty Years in Congress, from Lincoln to Garfield,* Vol. 2. Norwich, CT: Henry Bill Publishing Company, 1886.

Blair, William A. *The Record of Murders and Outrages: Racial Violence and the Fight over Truth at the Dawn of Reconstruction*. Chapel Hill: University of North Carolina Press, 2021.

Blight, David W. *Frederick Douglass: Prophet of Freedom*. New York: Simon & Schuster, 2018.

Blue, Frederick L. *Salmon P. Chase: A Life in Politics*. Kent, OH: Kent State University Press, 1987.

Bonner, Michael B., and Fritz Hamer. *South Carolina in the Civil War and Reconstruction Eras*. Columbia: University of South Carolina Press, 2016.

Boutwell, George S. *Reminiscences of Sixty Years in Public Affairs,* Vols. 1 and 2. New York: McClure, Phillips & Co., 1902.

Bradley, Mark L. *Blue Coats and Tar Heels: Soldiers and Civilians in Reconstruction North Carolina*. Lexington: University Press of Kentucky, 2009.

Brands, H. W. *The Money Men: Capitalism, Democracy, and the Hundred Years' War over the American Dollar*. New York: Norton, 2006.

Brooks, Noah. *Washington in Lincoln's Time*. New York: Century Company, 1895.

Brown, Glenn. *Glenn Brown's History of the United States Capitol*. Washington: Government Printing Office, 1998.

Burton, Orville Vernon, and Armand Derfner. *In My Father's House Are Many Mansions: Family & Community in Edgefield, South Carolina*. Chapel Hill: University of North Carolina Press, 1985.

————. *Justice Deferred: Race and the Supreme Court*. Cambridge: Belknap Press, 2021.

Bynum, Victoria E. *The Long Shadow of the Civil War: Southern Dissent and Its Legacies*. Chapel Hill: University of North Carolina Press, 2010.

Calhoun, Charles W. *The Presidency of Ulysses S. Grant*. Lawrence: University Press of Kansas, 2017.

Campbell, Sir George. *White and Black: The Outcome of a Visit to the United States*. New York: R. Worthington, 1879.

Carnes, Mark C. *Secret Ritual and Manhood in Victorian America*. New Haven: Yale University Press, 1989.

Carpenter, Frank G. *Carp's Washington*. New York: McGraw-Hill, 1960.

Chernow, Ron. *Grant*. New York: Penguin, 2017.

Cherry, Kevin M. Sr. *Virtue of Cain: From Slave to Senator*. Takoma Park, MD: Rocky Pond Press, 2019.

Cimbala, Paul A., and Randall M. Miller, eds. *The Freedmen's Bureau and Reconstruction: Reconsiderations*. New York: Fordham University Press, 1999.

Clayton, Powell. *The Aftermath of the Civil War in Arkansas*. New York: Neale Publishing Co., 1915.

Clemenceau, Georges. *American Reconstruction, 1865–1870*. New York: Da Capo, 1969.

Cook, Robert J. *Civil War Senator: William Pitt Fessenden and the Fight to Save the American Republic*. Baton Rouge: Louisiana State University Press, 2011.

Coulter, E. Merton. *William G. Brownlow: Fighting Parson of the Southern Highlands*. Knoxville: University of Tennessee Press, 1971.

Cresswell, Stephen. *Mormons & Cowboys, Moonshiners & Klansmen*. Tuscaloosa: University of Alabama Press, 1991.

Current, Richard Nelson. *Those Terrible Carpetbaggers: A Reinterpretation*. New York: Oxford University Press, 1988.

Damer, Eyre. *When the Ku Klux Rode*. New York: Neale Publishing Co., 1912.

DeForest, John William. *A Union Officer in the Reconstruction*. Baton Rouge: Louisiana State University Press, 1997.

Dennett, Tyler, ed. *Lincoln and the Civil War Diaries and Letters of John Hay*. New York: Dodd, Mead, 1939.

Donald, David Herbert. *Charles Sumner*, Vol. 2. New York: Da Capo, 1996.

Douglass, Frederick. *Autobiographies*. New York: Library of America, 1994.

Downs, Gregory P. *After Appomattox: Military Occupation and the Ends of War*. Cambridge: Harvard University Press, 2015.

Dray, Philip. *Capitol Men: The Epic Story of Reconstruction Through the Lives of the First Black Congressmen*. New York: Mariner Books, 2010.

Du Bois, W. E. B. *Black Reconstruction in America, 1860–1880*. New York: Free Press, 1998.

Egerton, Douglas R. *The Wars of Reconstruction: The Brief, Violent History of America's Most Progressive Era*. New York: Bloomsbury, 2013.

Eisenstadt, Abraham S., Ari Hoogenboom, and Hans L. Trefousse, eds. *Before Watergate: Problems of Corruption in American Society*. Brooklyn: Brooklyn College Press, 1978.

Elliott, Mark. *Color-Blind Justice: Albion Tourgée and the Quest for Racial Equality*. New York: Oxford University Press, 2006.

Elliott, Mark, and John David Smith, eds. *Undaunted Radical: The Selected Writings and Speeches of Albion W. Tourgée*. Baton Rouge: Louisiana State University Press, 2010.

Elmore, Tom. *Columbia Civil War Landmarks*. Charleston: History Press, 2011.

Farris, Scott. *Freedom on Trial: The First Post–Civil War Battle over Civil Rights and Voter Suppression*. Lanham, MD: Rowman & Littlefield, 2020.

Fitzgerald, Michael F. *Reconstruction in Alabama: From Civil War to Redemption in the Cotton South*. Baton Rouge: Louisiana State University Press, 2017.

———. *The Union League Movement in the Deep South: Politics and Agricultural Change During Reconstruction*. Baton Rouge: Louisiana State University Press, 1989.

Foner, Eric. *Reconstruction: America's Unfinished Revolution, 1863–1877*. New York: Harper & Row, 1988.

Foner, Philip S., ed. *The Life and Writings of Frederick Douglass*, Vol. 5. New York: International Publishers, 1955.

Forney, John W. *Anecdotes of Public Men*. New York: Harper and Brothers, 1873.

Frothingham, Octavius. *Gerrit Smith*. New York: G. P. Putnam's Sons, 1880.

Garner, James Wilford. *Reconstruction in Mississippi*. New York: Macmillan, 1902.

Gillette, William. *Retreat from Reconstruction, 1869–1879*. Baton Rouge: Louisiana State University Press, 1979.

Grant, Julia Dent. *The Personal Memoirs of Julia Dent Grant*. John Y. Simon, ed. New York: Putnam, 1975.

Grant, Ulysses S. *Memoirs and Selected Letters*. New York: Library of America, 1990.

Guelzo, Allen C. *Reconstruction: A Concise History*. New York: Oxford University Press, 2018.

Hahn, Steven. *A Nation Under Our Feet: Black Political Struggles in the Rural South from Slavery to the Great Migration*. Cambridge: Harvard University Press, 2003.

Hamilton, J. G. De Roulhac, ed. *The Papers of Randolph Abbott Shotwell*, Vol. 3. Raleigh: North Carolina Historical Commission, 1936.

Hargrove, David M. *Mississippi's Federal Courts: A History*. Jackson: University of Mississippi Press, 2019.

Harris, William C. *The Day of the Carpetbagger: Republican Reconstruction in Mississippi*. Baton Rouge: Louisiana State University Press, 1979.

———. *William Woods Holden: Firebrand of North Carolina Politics*. Baton Rouge: Louisiana State University Press, 1987.

Hickey, Damon Douglas. *Sojourners No More: The Quakers in the New South, 1865–1920*. Greensboro: North Carolina Friends Historical Society, 1997.

Higginbotham, A. Leon Jr. *Shades of Freedom: Racial Politics and Presumptions of the American Legal Process*. New York: Oxford University Press, 1996.

Hofstadter, Richard. *The Age of Reform*. New York: Vintage, 1955.

Hogue, James K. *Uncivil War: Five New Orleans Street Battles and the Rise and Fall of Radical Reconstruction*. Baton Rouge: University of Louisiana Press, 2006.

Holland, Rupert Sargent, ed. *Letters and Diary of Laura M. Towne*. San Bernardino: Big Byte Books, 2020.

Holt, Thomas. *Black Over White: Negro Political Leadership in South Carolina During Reconstruction*. Urbana: University of Illinois Press, 1979.

Howard, Gene L. *Death at Cross Plains: An Alabama Reconstruction Tragedy*. Tuscaloosa: University of Alabama Press, 1984.

Howard, Oliver Otis. *Autobiography of Oliver Otis Howard*, Vol. 2. New York: Baker & Taylor Co., 1908.

Howell, Kenneth W., ed. *Still the Arena of Civil War: Violence and Turmoil in Reconstruction Texas, 1865–1874*. Denton: University of North Texas Press, 2012.

Hubbs, G. Ward. *Searching for Freedom after the Civil War: Klansman, Carpetbagger, Scalawag, and Freedman*. Tuscaloosa: University of Alabama Press, 2015.

Humphrey, Steve. *"That D---d Brownlow": Being a Saucy and Malicious Description of Fighting Parson William Gannaway Brownlow*. Boone, NC: Appalachian Consortium Press, 1978.

Hurst, Jack. *Nathan Bedford Forrest: A Biography*. New York: Vintage, 1994.

Kaczorowski, Robert J. *The Politics of Judicial Interpretation: The Federal Courts, Department of Justice, and Civil Rights, 1866–1876*. New York: Fordham University Press, 2005.

Karcher, Carolyn L. *A Refugee from His Race: Albion W. Tourgée and His Fight Against White Supremacy.* Chapel Hill: University of North Carolina Press, 2016.

Kousser, J. Morgan, and James M. McPherson, eds. *Region, Race, and Reconstruction: Essays in Honor of C. Vann Woodward.* New York: Oxford University Press, 1982.

Krug, Mark M. *Lyman Trumbull: Conservative Radical.* New York: A. S. Barnes, 1965.

Lamson, Peggy. *The Glorious Failure: Black Congressman Robert Brown Elliott and the Reconstruction in South Carolina.* New York: Norton, 1973.

Lane, Charles. *The Day Freedom Died: The Colfax Massacre, the Supreme Court, and the Betrayal of Reconstruction.* New York: Henry Holt, 2008.

———. *Freedom's Detective: The Secret Service, the Ku Klux Klan, and the Man Who Masterminded America's First War on Terror.* Toronto: Hanover Square Press, 2019.

Lang, Andrew F. *In the Wake of War: Military Occupation, Emancipation, and Civil War America.* Baton Rouge: Louisiana State University Press, 2017.

Lattimore, Robin Spencer. *Old Rutherfordton: A Hometown History.* Rutherfordton, NC: Hilltop Publications, 2006.

Lee, Edward, ed. *Yorkville to York.* Dallas: Taylor Publishing, 1998.

Leland, John A. *A Voice from South Carolina: Twelve Chapters Before Hampton, Two Chapters After Hampton, with a Journal of a Reputed Ku-Klux.* Charleston: Walker, Evans & Cogswell, 1879.

Lemann, Nicholas. *Redemption: The Last Battle of the Civil War.* New York: Farrar, Straus & Giroux, 2006.

Lester, J. C., and D. L. Wilson. Introduction by Walter L. Fleming. *Ku Klux Klan: Its Origin, Growth and Disbandment.* New York and Washington: Neale Publishing Company, 1905.

Lindsey, David. *"Sunset" Cox: Irrepressible Democrat.* Detroit: Wayne State University Press, 1959.

Link, William A. *Atlanta Cradle of the New South: Race and Remembering in the Civil War's Aftermath.* Chapel Hill: University of North Carolina Press, 2013.

Litwack, Leon F. *Been in the Storm So Long: The Aftermath of Slavery.* New York: Vintage, 1980.

Lynch, John R. *The Facts of Reconstruction.* New York: Neale Publishing Co., 1913.

Martinez, J. Michael. *Carpetbaggers, Cavalry, and the Ku Klux Klan: Exposing the Invisible Empire During Reconstruction.* Lanham, MD: Rowman & Littlefield, 2007.

McClure, Alexander K. *Abraham Lincoln and Men of War Times.* Lincoln: University of Nebraska Press, 1996.

McFeely, William S. *Yankee Stepfather: General O.O. Howard and the Freedmen.* New York: Norton, 1994.

McKay, Ernest A. *Henry Wilson: Practical Radical.* Port Washington, NY: Kennikat Press, 1971.

McPherson, James. *Ordeal by Fire: The Civil War and Reconstruction.* New York: Knopf, 1982.

Meriwether, Elizabeth A. *Recollections of 92 Years, 1824–1916.* Nashville: Tennessee Historical Commission, 1958.

Meriwether, Lee. *My Yesteryears.* St. Louis: Mound City Press, 1942.

Miller, Edward A. Jr. *Gullah Statesman: Robert Smalls from Slavery to Congress, 1839–1915*. Columbia: University of South Carolina Press, 1995.

Moneyhon, Carl H. *The Impact of the Civil War and Reconstruction in Arkansas*. Fayetteville: University of Arkansas Press, 2002.

Moore, John Hammond, ed. *The Juhl Letters to the Charleston Courier: A View of the South, 1865–1871*. Athens: University of Georgia Press, 1974.

Morris, Roy Jr. *Sheridan: The Life and Wars of General Phil Sheridan*. New York: Crown, 1992.

Morton, John W. *The Artillery of Nathan Bedford Forrest's Cavalry*. Nashville: M. E. Church, 1909.

Myers, John. L. *Senator Henry Wilson and the Civil War*. Lanham, MD: University Press of America, 2008.

Nathans, Elizabeth Studley. *Losing the Peace: Georgia Republicans and Reconstruction, 1865–1871*. Baton Rouge: Louisiana State University Press, 1968.

Nevins, Allan, ed. *Hamilton Fish: The Inner History of the Grant Administration*. New York: Dodd, Mead, 1936.

Nevins, Allan, and Thomas M. Halsey, eds. *The Diary of George Templeton Strong,* Vol. 4. New York: Macmillan, 1952.

Newton, Michael. *The Invisible Empire: The Ku Klux Klan in Florida*. Gainesville: University Press of Florida, 2001.

———. *The Ku Klux Klan in Mississippi*. Jefferson, NC: McFarland, 2010.

Nichols, Bruce. *Guerrilla Warfare in Civil War Missouri,* Vol. 1. Jefferson, NC: McFarland, 2004.

Nystrom, Justin A. *New Orleans After the Civil War: Race, Politics and a New Birth of Freedom*. Baltimore: Johns Hopkins University Press, 2010.

Palmer, Beverly W., ed. *The Selected Papers of Thaddeus Stevens, Vol. 2: April 1865–August 1868*. Pittsburgh: University of Pittsburgh Press, 1998.

———, ed. *The Selected Letters of Charles Sumner, Vol. 2, 1859–1874*. Boston: Northeastern University Press, 1990.

Parrish, William E. *Frank Blair: Lincoln's Conservative*. Columbia: University of Missouri Press, 1998.

Parsons, Elaine Franz. *Ku Klux: The Birth of the Klan During Reconstruction*. Chapel Hill: University of North Carolina Press, 2015.

Pike, James S. *The Prostrate State: South Carolina Under Negro Government*. New York: D. Appleton and Co., 1874.

Poore, Ben Perley. *Perley's Reminiscences of Sixty Years in the National Metropolis,* Vols. 1 and 2. Philadelphia: Hubbard Brothers, 1886.

Proceedings in the Ku Klux Trials at Columbia, S.C., in the United States Circuit Court, November Term, 1871. Columbia: Republican Printing Company, 1872.

Proclamations by the Governor of North Carolina Together with the Opinion of Chief Justice Pearson. Raleigh: Standard Steam Book and Job Print, 1870.

Raper, Horace W., ed. *The Papers of William W. Holden,* Vol. 1. Raleigh: Division of Archives and History, 2000.

Reid, Brian H. *The Scourge of War: The Life of William Tecumseh Sherman*. New York: Oxford University Press, 2020.

Reynolds, John S. *Reconstruction in South Carolina, 1865–1877*. Columbia, SC: The State Co., 1905.

Richardson, Heather Cox. *To Make Men Free: A History of the Republican Party*. New York: Basic Books, 2015.

———. *West from Appomattox: The Reconstruction of America After the Civil War*. New Haven: Yale University Press, 2007.

Richardson, James D., ed. *A Compilation of the Messages and Papers of the Presidents, 1789–1897*, Vol. 7. Washington: Government Printing Office, 1898.

Richardson, William T. *Historic Pulaski: Birthplace of the Ku Klux Klan*. Privately published, 1913.

Riddle, Albert Gallatin. *Recollections of War Times: Reminiscences of Men and Events in Washington, 1860–1865*. New York: G. P. Putnam's Sons, 1895.

Riis, Jacob A. *The Making of an American*. New York: Macmillan, 1901.

Rosen, Hannah. *Terror in the Heart of Freedom: Citizenship, Sexual Violence, and the Meaning of Race in the Postemancipation South*. Chapel Hill: University of North Carolina Press, 2009.

Roske, Ralph J. *His Own Counsel: The Life and Times of Lyman Trumbull*. Reno: University of Nevada Press, 1979.

Rubin, Hyman III. *South Carolina Scalawags*. Columbia: University of South Carolina Press, 2006.

Scaturro, Frank. J. *The Supreme Court's Retreat from Reconstruction: A Distortion of Constitutional Jurisprudence*. Westport, CT: Greenwood Press, 2000.

Schafer, Joseph, ed. *Intimate Letters of Carl Schurz, 1841–1869*. New York: Da Capo, 1970.

Schott, Thomas E. *Alexander H. Stephens of Georgia*. Baton Rouge: Louisiana State University Press, 1988.

Schurz, Carl. *Report on the Condition of the South 1865*. Washington: Government Printing Office, 1865.

Sefton, James E. *The United States Army and Reconstruction, 1865–1877*. Baton Rouge: Louisiana State University Press, 1967.

Shankman, Arnold, Thomas E. Crowson, Jack C. Tucker, and Joel Nichols. *York County, South Carolina: Its People and Its Heritage*. Virginia Beach: Donning Company, 1993.

Sheehan-Dean, Aaron, ed. *The Civil War: The Final Year Told by Those Who Lived It*. New York: Library of America, 2014.

Sherrer, John M. III. *Remembering Columbia*. Charleston: Arcadia Publishing, 2015.

Simon, John Y., ed. *The Papers of Ulysses S. Grant,* Vols. 19–25. Carbondale: Southern Illinois University Press, 1995–2003.

Simpson, Brooks D. *Let Us Have Peace: Ulysses S. Grant and the Politics of War and Reconstruction, 1861–1868*. Chapel Hill: University of North Carolina Press, 1991.

Simpson, Brooks D., ed. *Reconstruction: Voices from America's First Great Struggle for Racial Equality*. New York: Library of America, 2018.

Singletary, Otis A. *Negro Militia and Reconstruction*. New York: McGraw-Hill, 1963.

Slap, Andrew L. *The Doom of Reconstruction: The Liberal Republicans in the Civil War Era*. New York: Fordham University Press, 2006.

Smallwood, James M., Barry A. Crouch, and Larry Peacock. *Murder and Mayhem: The War of Reconstruction in Texas*. College Station: Texas A&M Press, 2003.

Smith, Jean Edward. *Grant*. New York: Simon & Schuster, 2001

Smith, John David. *A Just and Lasting Peace: A Documentary History of Reconstruction*. New York: Signet, 2013.

———. *We Ask Only for Even-Handed Justice: Black Voices from Reconstruction, 1865–1877*. Amherst: University of Massachusetts Press, 2014.

Stiles, T. J. *Custer's Trials: A Life on the Frontier of a New America*. New York: Vintage, 2015.

Stokes, Melvyn. *D. W. Griffith's The Birth of a Nation*. New York: Oxford University Press, 2007.

Tap, Bruce. *The Fort Pillow Massacre: North, South, and the Status of African Americans in the Civil War*. New York: Routledge, 2014.

Taylor, Alrutheus A. *The Negro in Tennessee, 1865–1880*. Washington: Associated Publishers, 1941.

Testimony Taken by the Joint Select Committee to Inquire into the Condition of Affairs in the Late Insurrectionary States, 13 vols. Washington: Government Printing Office, 1872.

Tourgée, Albion W. *A Fool's Errand*. New York: Fords, Howard & Hulbert, 1879.

Trefousse, Hans L. *Andrew Johnson*. New York: Norton, 1989.

———. *Carl Schurz: A Biography*. Knoxville: University of Tennessee Press, 1982.

———. *Thaddeus Stevens: Nineteenth-Century Egalitarian*. Chapel Hill: University of North Carolina Press, 1997.

Trelease, Allen W. *White Terror: The Ku Klux Klan Conspiracy and Southern Reconstruction*. Baton Rouge: Louisiana State University Press, 1971.

The Trial of William W. Holden, Governor of North Carolina Before the Senate of North Carolina, Vol. 2. Raleigh: Sentinel Printing Office, 1871.

Troxler, Carole Watterson. *Shuttle and Plow: A History of Alamance County, North Carolina*. Burlington, NC: Alamance County Historical Association, 1999.

Tunnell, Ted. *Crucible of Reconstruction: War, Radicalism and Race in Louisiana, 1862–1877*. Baton Rouge: Louisiana State University Press, 1984.

———. *Edge of the Sword: The Ordeal of Carpetbagger Marshall H. Twitchell in the Civil War and Reconstruction*. Baton Rouge: Louisiana State University Press, 2001.

Uya, Okon Edet. *From Slavery to Public Service: Robert Smalls, 1839–1915*. New York: Oxford University Press, 1971.

Wade, Wyn Craig. *The Fiery Cross: The Ku Klux Klan in America*. New York: Oxford University Press, 1987.

Washburne, Mark. *Elihu Benjamin Washburne: Congressman, Secretary of State, Envoy Extraordinary*, Vol. 3. Xlibris, 2005.

West, Jerry L. *The Reconstruction Ku Klux Klan in York County, South Carolina, 1865–1877*. Jefferson, NC: McFarland, 2002.

West, Richard S. *Lincoln's Scapegoat General: A Life of Benjamin F. Butler, 1818–1893*. Boston: Houghton Mifflin, 1965.

Wheelan, Joseph. *Terrible Swift Sword: The Life of General Philip H. Sheridan*. New York: Da Capo, 2012.

White, Horace. *The Life of Lyman Trumbull*. Boston: Houghton Mifflin Co., 1913.

White, Richard. *The Republic for Which It Stands: The United States During Reconstruction and the Gilded Age, 1865–1896*. New York: Oxford University Press, 2017.

White, Ronald C. *American Ulysses: A Life of Ulysses S. Grant*. New York: Random House, 2016.

Williams, Kidada E. *They Left Great Marks on Me: African American Testimonies of Racial Violence from Emancipation to World War I*. New York: New York University Press, 2012.

Williams, Lou Falkner. *The Great South Carolina Ku Klux Klan Trials, 1871–1872*. Athens: University of Georgia Press, 1996.

Williamson, Joel. *After Slavery: The Negro in South Carolina During Reconstruction, 1861–1877*. New York: Norton, 1965.

Willis, Brian Steel. *The Confederacy's Greatest Cavalryman Nathan Bedford Forrest*. Lawrence: University Press of Kansas, 1992.

Wilson, Henry. *History of the Reconstruction Measures of the Thirty-ninth and Fortieth Congresses, 1865–1868*. Hartford, CT: Hartford Publishing Company, 1868.

Wineapple, Brenda. *The Impeachers: The Trial of Andrew Johnson and the Dream of a Just Nation*. New York: Random House, 2019.

Wise, Jim. *Murder in the Courthouse: Reconstruction and Redemption in the North Carolina Piedmont*. Charleston: The History Press, 2010.

Wise, Stephen R., and Lawrence S. Rowland. *Rebellion, Reconstruction, and Redemption, 1861–1893: History of Beaufort County, South Carolina*, Vol. 2. Columbia: University of South Carolina Press, 2015.

Wish, Harvey, ed. *Reconstruction in the South*. New York: Farrar, Straus & Giroux, 1965.

Wynne, Ben. *The Man Who Punched Jefferson Davis: The Political Life of Henry S. Foote, Southern Unionist*. Baton Rouge: Louisiana State University Press, 2018.

Zuczak, Richard. *State of Rebellion: Reconstruction in South Carolina*. Columbia: University of South Carolina Press, 1996.

ARTICLES, PAMPHLETS, THESES, AND OTHER SOURCES

Alexander, Thomas B. "KuKluxism in Tennessee, 1865–1869." *Tennessee Historical Quarterly*, Vol. 8 (September 1949).

Anonymous. *Statement of Dr. Brannan's Case, Being Explanatory of the Ku-Klux Prosecutions in the Southern States*. London, ON: Free Press Steam Book and Job Printing Co., 1872.

Blight, David. "150 Years of Suppression." *New York Times*, April 12, 2020.

Bradley, Mark L. *The Army and Reconstruction*. Washington: Center of Military History, 2015.

Brisson, Jim D. "Civil Government Was Crumbling Around Me." *North Carolina Historical Review*, Vol. 88 (April 2011).

Brosseau, Carli. "In a Small Town, a Battle for Racial Justice Confronts a Bloody Past and an Uncertain Future." Raleigh (NC) *News & Observer*, May 19, 2021.

Brown, Mary Davis. *Oil in Our Lamps.* Published by Brown's descendants, York, SC: County Historical Society.

Brums, J. Dickson. *Address to the White League of New Orleans, September 14, 1875.* Pamphlet. New Orleans: W. Hyatt, 1875.

Burton, Orville Vernon. "Race and Reconstruction: Edgefield County, South Carolina." *Journal of Social History,* Vol. 12 (October 1978).

"Condition of Affairs in the Southern States." House of Representatives Ex. Doc. No. 268.

Constitution, Ordinances and Resolutions of the Georgia Convention. Atlanta: New Era Job Office, 1868.

Cresswell, Stephen. "Enforcing the Enforcement Acts: The Department of Justice in Northern Mississippi, 1870–1890." *Journal of Southern History,* Vol. 53 (August 1987).

Daniell, Elizabeth Otto. "The Ashburn Murder Case in Reconstruction Georgia." *The Georgia Historical Quarterly,* Vol. 59 (Fall 1975).

DeLatte, Carolyn E. "The St. Landry Riot: A Forgotten Incident of Reconstruction Violence." *Louisiana History,* Vol. 17 (Winter 1976).

Domer, Thomas. "The Role of George S. Boutwell in the Impeachment and Trial of Andrew Johnson." *The New England Quarterly,* Vol. 49 (December 1976).

Douglass, Frederick. *U.S. Grant and the Colored People.* Pamphlet. 1872.

Downs, Gregory P., and Scott Nesbit. "Mapping Occupation: Force, Freedom, and the Army in Reconstruction." Online at http://mappingoccupation.org.

Dunning, William A. "The Undoing of Reconstruction." *Atlantic Monthly,* October 1901.

Formwalt, Lee W. "The Camilla Massacre of 1868: Racial Violence as Political Propaganda." *The Georgia Historical Quarterly,* Vol. 71 (Fall 1987).

Hardy, William Edward. "'Farewell to All Radicals': Redeeming Tennessee, 1869–1870." PhD diss., University of Tennessee at Knoxville, 2013.

Hickey, Damon Douglas. "The Quakers in the New South, 1865–1920." PhD diss., University of South Carolina, 1989.

House, Albert V. Jr. "Northern Congressional Democrats as Defenders of the South During Reconstruction." *The Journal of Southern History,* Vol. 6 (February 1940).

"In a Small Town, a Battle for Racial Justice Confronts a Bloody Past and an Uncertain Future." *Raleigh (NC) News & Observer,* May 19, 2021.

Jenkins, Jeffery A., and Justin Peck. "The Erosion of the First Civil Rights Era: Congress and the Redemption of the White South, 1877–1891." Paper prepared for the 2015 Annual Congress & History Conference, Vanderbilt University.

Kinnison, William A. *Samuel Shellabarger (1817–1896).* Monograph. Springfield, OH: Clark County Historical Society, 1966.

The Ku Klux Klan: Hearings Before the Committee on Rules, House of Representatives. Washington: Government Printing Office, 1921.

Lang, Andrew F. "Union Demobilization and the Boundaries of War and Peace." *Journal of the Civil War Era,* Vol. 9 (June 2019).

Libby, Billy W. "Senator Hiram Revels of Mississippi Takes His Seat." *Journal of Mississippi History,* Vol. 37 (November 1975).

Magliocca, Gerald N. "Amnesty and Section Three of the Fourteenth Amendment."
    https://ssrn.com/abstract=3748639.

Mahaffey, Joseph H., ed. "Carl Schurz's Letters from the South." *The Georgia Histori-cal Quarterly*, Vol. 35 (September 1951).

Massengill, Stephen E. "The Detectives of William W. Holden, 1869–1870." *North Carolina Historical Review*, Vol. 62 (October 1985).

McKinney, Gordon. "The Klan in the Southern Mountains: The Lusk-Shotwell Controversy." *Appalachian Journal*, Vol. 8 (Winter 1981).

Meade, George G. *Major General George G. Meade's Report on the Ashburn Murder.* Atlanta: United States Army, Department of the South, 1868.

Miller, Orlo. "The Bratton Kidnapping." *The Canadian Science Digest*, Vol. 1 (April 1938).

The Nation's Peril: Twelve Years' Experience in the South; Then and Now; The Ku Klux Klan. Anonymous Pamphlet. New York: Friends of the Compiler, 1872.

Nineteenth Annual Report of the State Board of Health of South Carolina for the Fiscal Year 1898. Obituary of Dr. J. Rufus Bratton (YorkHist).

Official Proceedings of the National Democratic Convention Held at New York, July 4–9, 1868. Boston: Rockwell & Rollins Printers, 1868.

Olsen, Otto H. "The Ku Klux Klan: A Study in Reconstruction Politics and Propaganda." *North Carolina Historical Review*, Vol. 39 (July 1962).

Pierson, H. W. *A Letter to Hon. Charles Sumner, with Statements of Outrages Upon Freedmen in Georgia, and An Account of My Expulsion from Andersonville.* Pamphlet. Washington: Chronicle Printing, 1870.

Pope, James Gray. "Snubbed Landmark: Why *United States v. Cruikshank* (1876) Belongs at the Heart of the American Judicial Cannon." *Harvard Civil Rights and Civil Liberties Law Review*, Vol. 49 (2014).

Proceedings of the Colored People's Convention of the State of South Carolina Held in Zion Church, Charleston, November 1865. Pamphlet. Charleston: South Carolina Leader, 1865.

Proceedings of the National Union Republican Convention Held at Philadelphia, June 5 and 6, 1872. Washington: Gibson Brothers, Printers, 1872.

Proctor, Bradley David. "The Reconstruction of White Supremacy: The Ku Klux Klan in Piedmont, North Carolina." Master's thesis, University of North Carolina, Chapel Hill, 2009.

"Reconstruction in America: Racial Violence after the Civil War." Report by the Equal Justice Initiative, 2020, Montgomery, AL, online at eji.org.

Report of the Evidence Taken Before the Military Commission in Relation to the Outrages Committed by the Ku Klux Klan in Middle and West Tennessee. Nashville: S. C. Mercer, 1868.

Rogers, Abby. "Confederates and Quakers: The Shared Wartime Experience: *Quaker History*, Vol. 99 (Fall 2010).

Sacco, Nicholas W. "'I Never Was an Abolitionist': Ulysses S. Grant and Slavery, 1854–1863." *Journal of the Civil War Era*, Vol. 9 (September 2019).

Sawyer, Frederick A. *Removal of Disabilities—Outrages of the Ku Klux Klan.* Pamphlet. Washington: F&J Rives, 1871.

Schurz, Carl. "The Surrender of Rastatt." *The Wisconsin Magazine of History,* Vol. 12 (March 1929).

Shand, Robert W. "Incidents in the Life of a Private Soldier in the War Waged by the United States Against the Confederate States, 1861–1865." Unpublished memoir, 1907. South Caroliniana Collection, University of South Carolina.

Sheppard, William Arthur. *Some Reasons Why: Red Shirts Remembered.* Pamphlet. Greer, SC: Chas. P. Smith Co., 1940.

Shugerman, Jed Handelsman. "The Creation of the Department of Justice: Professionalization Without Civil Rights or Civil Service." *Stanford Law Review,* Vol. 66 (January 2014).

Simms, L. Moody Jr. "Carl Schurz and the Negro." *Bulletin of the Missouri Historical Society,* Vol. 25 (April 1969).

Singer, Donald L. "For Whites Only: The Seating of Hiram Revels in the United States Senate." *Negro History Bulletin,* Vol. 35 (March 1972).

Stowell, Daniel W. "'We Have Sinned, and God Has Smitten Us!' John H. Caldwell and the Religious Meaning of Confederate Defeat." *The Georgia Historical Quarterly,* Vol. 78 (Spring 1994).

Sumner, Charles. *Letter to Colored Citizens.* Pamphlet. Washington: F.&J. Rives & Geo. A. Bailey, 1872.

Teiser, Sidney. "Life of George H. Williams: Almost Chief-Justice," Parts 1 and 2. *Oregon Historical Quarterly,* Vol. 47 (September and December 1946).

Townsend, Belton O'Neal. "The Political Condition of South Carolina." *The Atlantic,* Vol. 39 (February 1877).

Troxler, Carole Watterson. "'To look more closely at the man': Wyatt Outlaw, a Nexus of National, Local, and Personal History." *North Carolina Historical Review,* Vol. 77 (October 2000).

United States v. Cruikshank, 92 U.S. 542 (1875).

Ward, Gladys. "Life of Ryland Randolph." Master's thesis, University of Alabama, 1932.

Whitley, Horace C. "Special Report of Ku Klux Outrages in Kentucky." September 24, 1873. Department of Justice reports, National Archives.

Whitmire, Kyle. "Ambushed in Eufaula: Alabama's Forgotten Race Massacre." *Birmingham News,* January 16, 2022.

Wiggins, Sarah Woolfolk. "The Life of Ryland Randolph as Seen Through His Letters to John W. DuBose." *Alabama Historical Quarterly,* Vol. 30 (Fall/Winter 1968).

Wittke, Carl. "Carl Schurz and Rutherford B. Hayes." *Ohio Historical Quarterly,* Vol. 65 (October 1956).

Zuczec, Richard. "The Federal Government's Attack on the Ku Klux Klan: A Reassessment." *South Carolina Historical Magazine,* Vol. 97 (January 1996).

INDEX

CONGRESS AT WAR

*How Republican Reformers Fought the Civil War,
Defied Lincoln, Ended Slavery, and Remade America*

This brilliantly argued new perspective on the Civil War overturns the popular conception that Abraham Lincoln single-handedly led the Union to victory and gives us a vivid account of the essential role Congress played in winning the war. Building a riveting narrative around four influential members of Congress—Thaddeus Stevens, Pitt Fessenden, Ben Wade, and the proslavery Clement Vallandigham—Fergus Bordewich shows us how a newly empowered Republican party shaped one of the most dynamic and consequential periods in American history. Brimming with drama and outsize characters, *Congress at War* is one of the most original books about the Civil War to appear in years and will change the way we understand the conflict.

History

MY MOTHER'S GHOST

A Courageous Woman, a Son's Love, and the Power of Memory

LaVerne Madigan led an extraordinary life. In an era when few women even worked outside the home, LaVerne was the executive director of the only major national rights advocacy group for American Indians. Brilliant, beautiful, and independent, she worked tirelessly for what she believed in and inspired those who knew her—perhaps no one as much as her young son, Fergus Bordewich. One morning when Fergus was fourteen, he and his mother went riding. Attempting to jump from her runaway horse, LaVerne fell under the hooves of her son's mount and was killed. More than thirty years later and after a lifetime of guilt and self-punishment, the son returned to his mother's life.

Memoir

KILLING THE WHITE MAN'S INDIAN
Reinventing Native Americans at the End of the Twentieth Century

Following two centuries of broken treaties and virtual government extermination of the "savage redmen," Americans today have recast Native Americans into another equally stereotyped role, that of eternal victims, politically powerless and weakened by poverty and alcoholism, yet whose spiritual ties with the natural world form our last, best hope of salvaging our natural environment and ennobling our souls. The truth, however, is neither as grim nor as blindly idealistic as many would expect. The fact is that a virtual revolution is underway. For the first time in generations, Native Americans are shaping their own destinies, largely beyond the control of whites, reinventing Native education and justice, exploiting the principle of tribal sovereignty in ways that empower tribal governments far beyond most American's imaginations. While newfound power has enriched tribal life and prospects, and has made Native Americans fuller participants in the American dream, it has brought tribal governments into direct conflict with local economics and the federal government. Based on three years of research on Native American reservations, *Killing the White Man's Indian* takes on Native American politics and policies today in all their contradictory guises.

History